Collins
POCKET ATLAS
LONDON

Contents

Collins

Published by Collins
An imprint of HarperCollins Publishers
Westerhill Road, Bishopbriggs, Glasgow G64 2QT

www.harpercollins.co.uk

New edition 2015

Mapping generated from Collins Bartholomew digital databases

London Underground Map by permission of Transport Trading Limited
Registered User No. 14/2635/P

Printed in China by South China Printing Co. Ltd

ISBN   978 0 00 810457 3   Imp 001

e-mail: roadcheck@harpercollins.co.uk
 facebook.com/collinsmaps   @collinsmaps

For more information about London please visit www.visitlondon.com

Key to map symbols

3

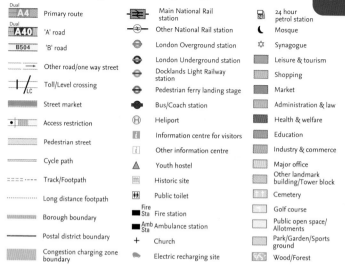

A4 Dual	Primary route	Main National Rail station
A40 Dual	'A' road	Other National Rail station
B504	'B' road	London Overground station

Other road/one way street

Toll/Level crossing LC

Street market

Access restriction

Pedestrian street

Cycle path

Track/Footpath

Long distance footpath

Borough boundary

Postal district boundary

Congestion charging zone boundary

Main National Rail station

Other National Rail station

London Overground station

London Underground station

Docklands Light Railway station

Pedestrian ferry landing stage

Bus/Coach station

(H) Heliport

i Information centre for visitors

i Other information centre

△ Youth hostel

Historic site

Public toilet

Fire Sta Fire station

Amb Sta Ambulance station

+ Church

Electric recharging site

24 hour petrol station

Mosque

☼ Synagogue

Leisure & tourism

Shopping

Market

Administration & law

Health & welfare

Education

Industry & commerce

Major office

Other landmark building/Tower block

Cemetery

Golf course

Public open space/Allotments

Park/Garden/Sports ground

Wood/Forest

The following symbols are unique to either the main maps or the central London maps.

Central maps pages 6-23 1:12,500

0   1/4 mile

0   0.25   0.5 kilometre

5.1 inches (13 cm) to 1 mile/8 cm to 1 km

Main maps pages 24-93 1:20,000

0   1/4 mile

0   0.25   0.5 kilometres

3.2 inches (8 cm) to 1 mile/5 cm to 1 km

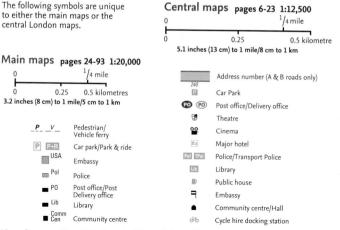

_P_ _V_	Pedestrian/Vehicle ferry	
P P+R	Car park/Park & ride	
USA	Embassy	
Pol	Police	
PO	Post office/Post Delivery office	
Lib	Library	
Comm Cen	Community centre	

240   Address number (A & B roads only)

P Car Park

PO PO Post office/Delivery office

🎭 Theatre

🎬 Cinema

Major hotel

Pol TPol Police/Transport Police

Lib Library

Public house

Embassy

Community centre/Hall

Cycle hire docking station

The reference grid on this atlas coincides with the Ordnance Survey National Grid System

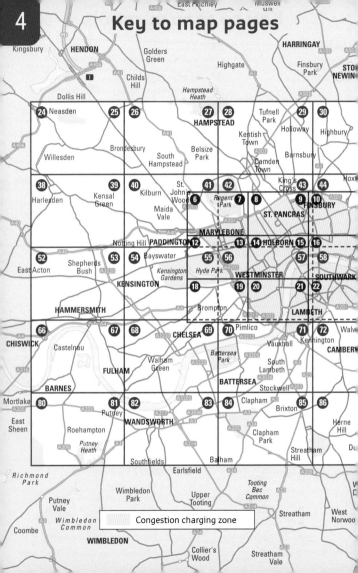

Key to map pages

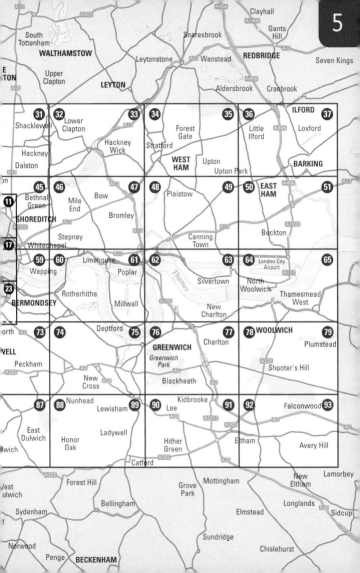

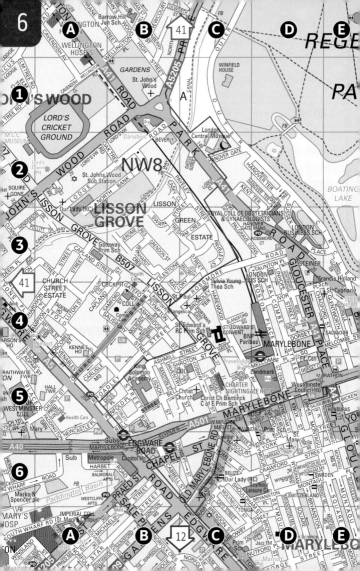

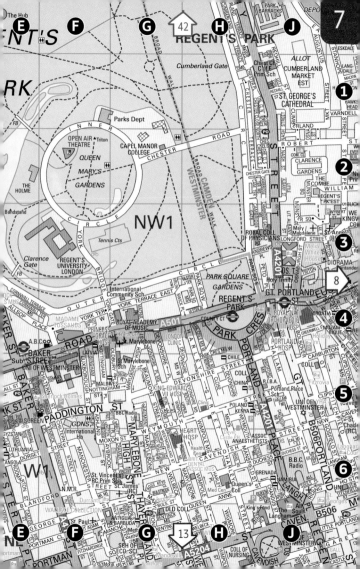

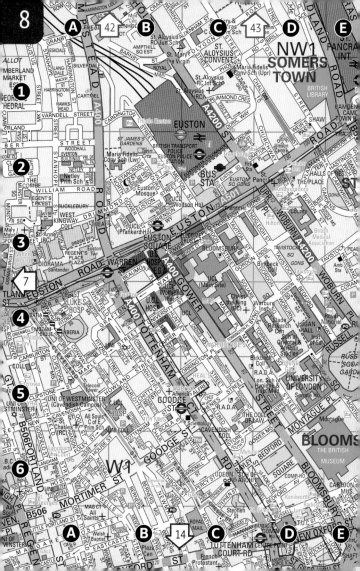

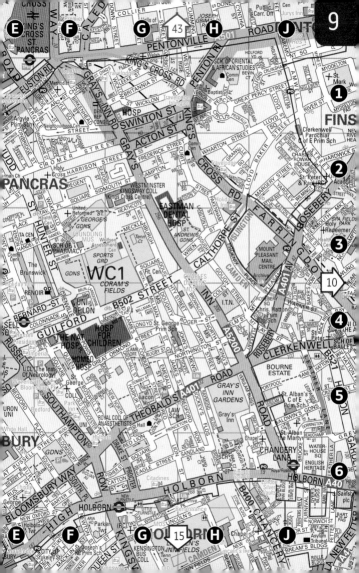

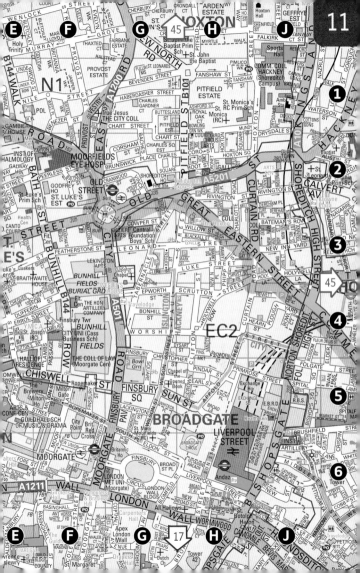

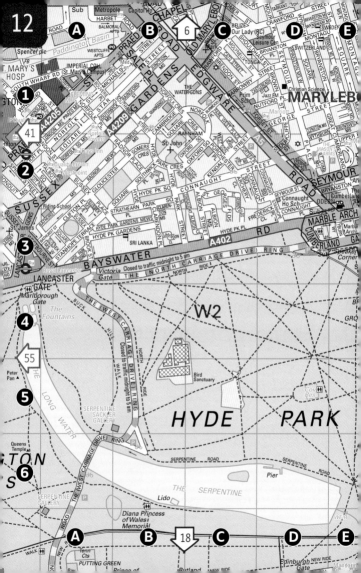

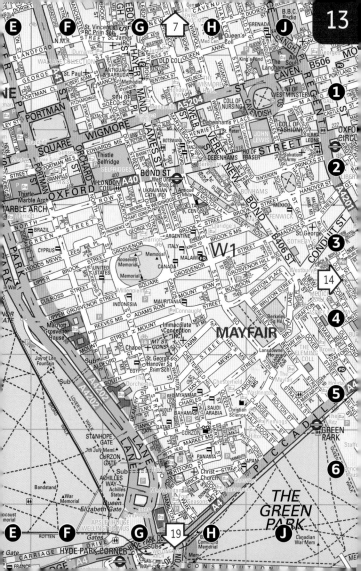

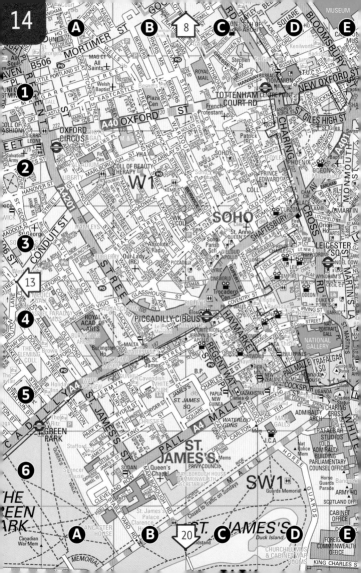

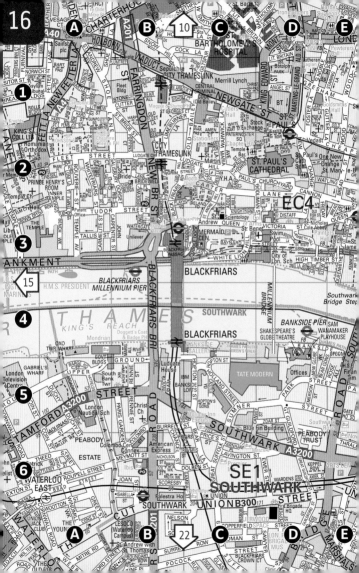

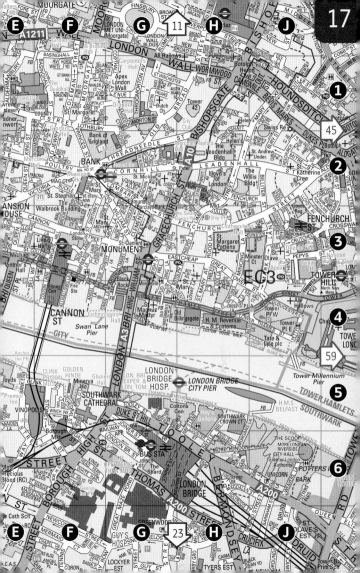

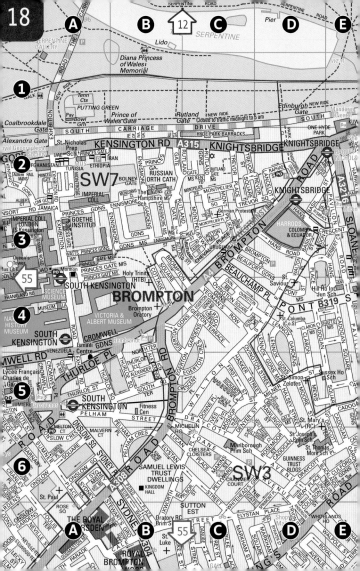

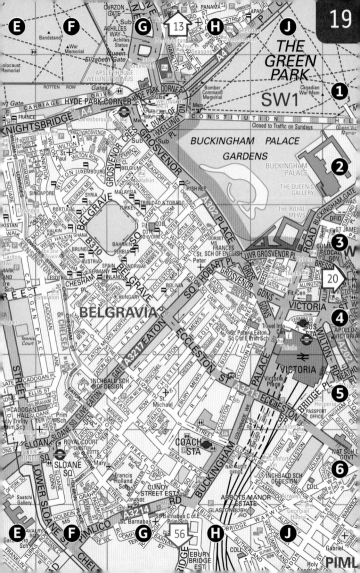

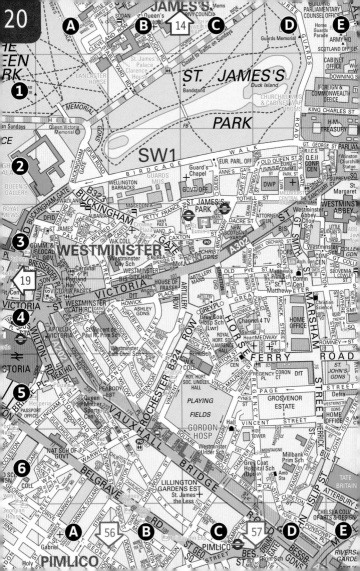

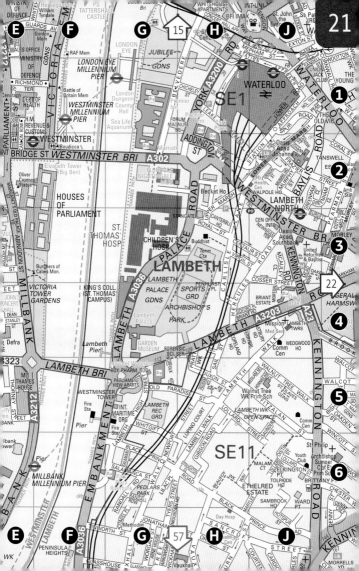

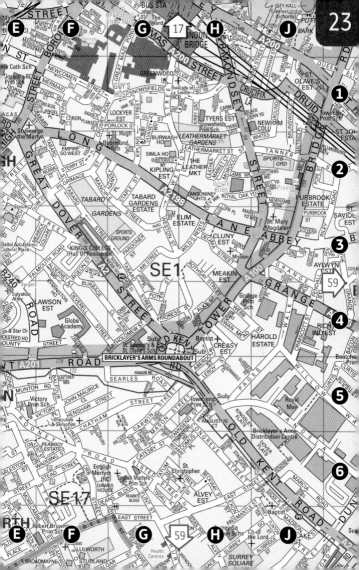

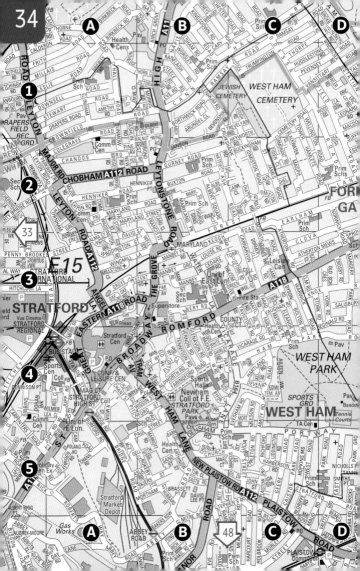

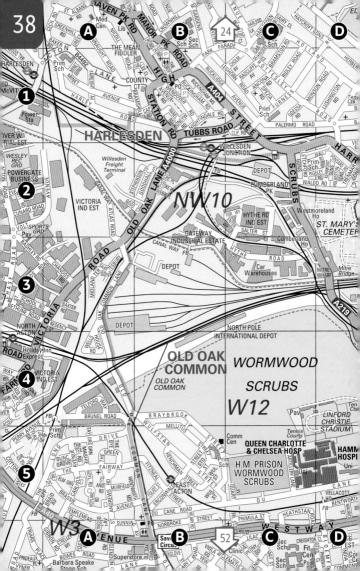

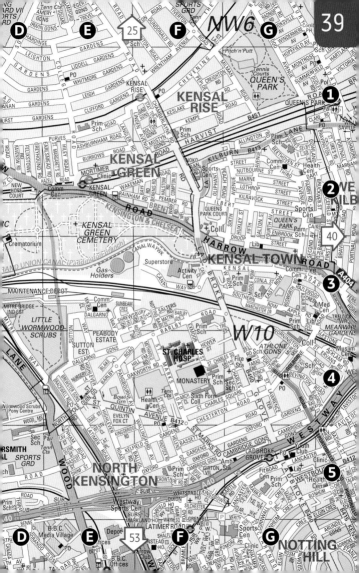

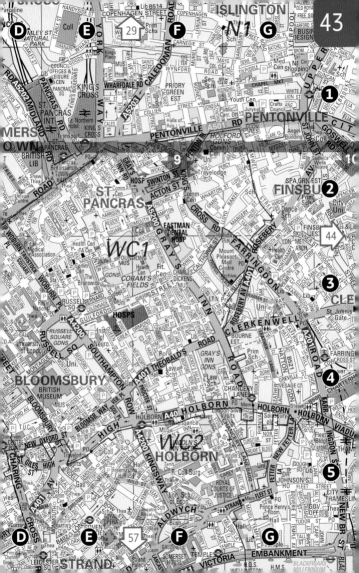

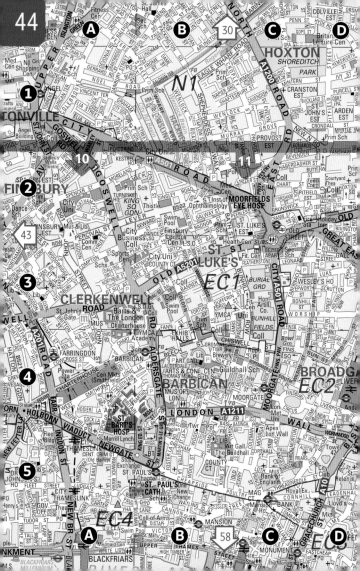

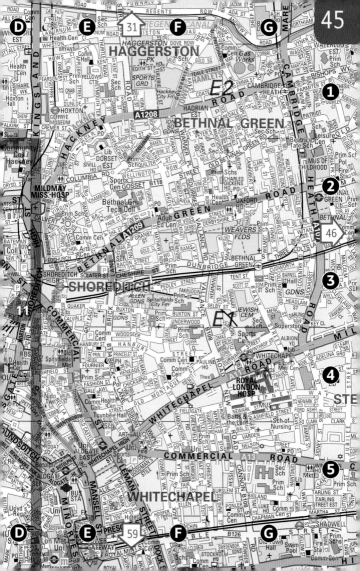

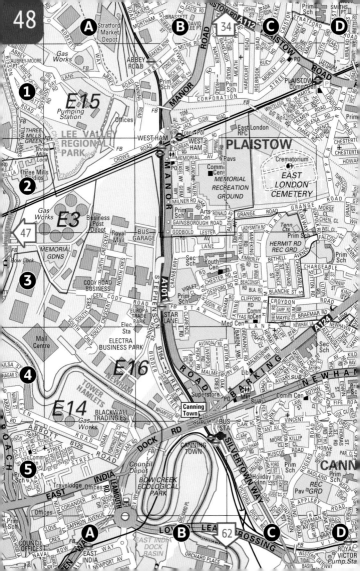

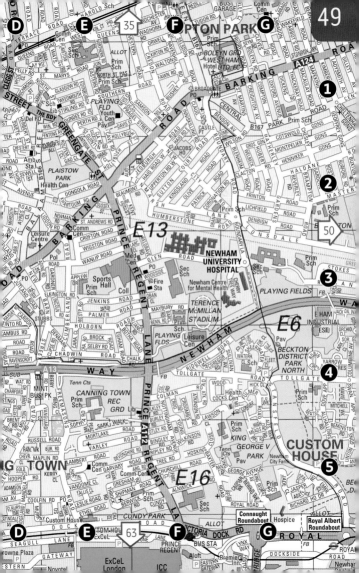

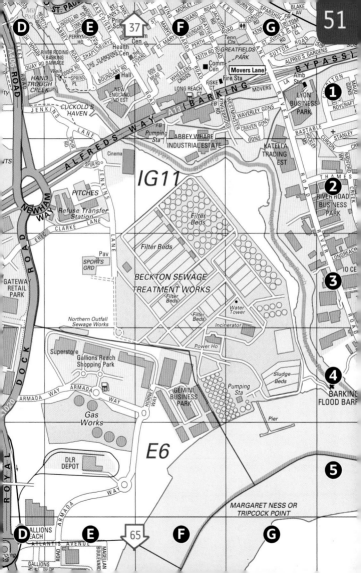

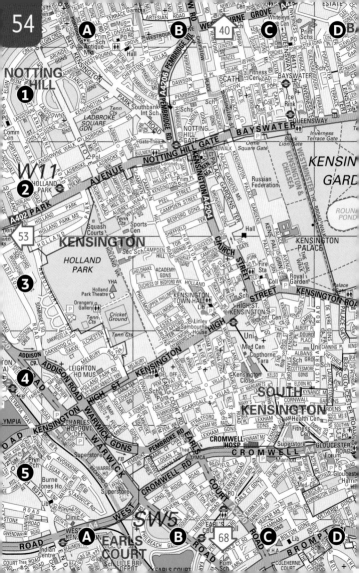

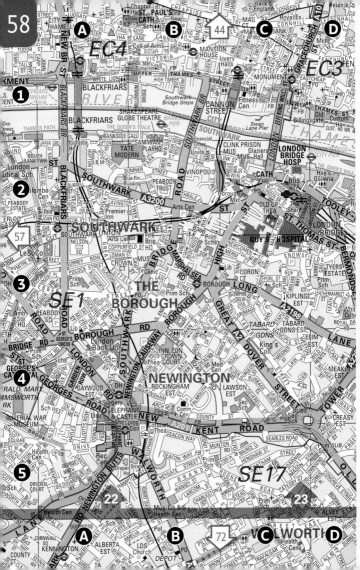

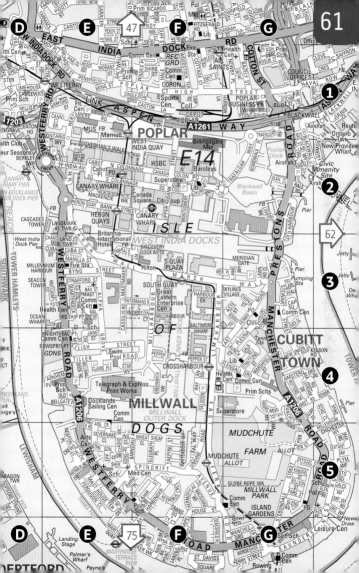

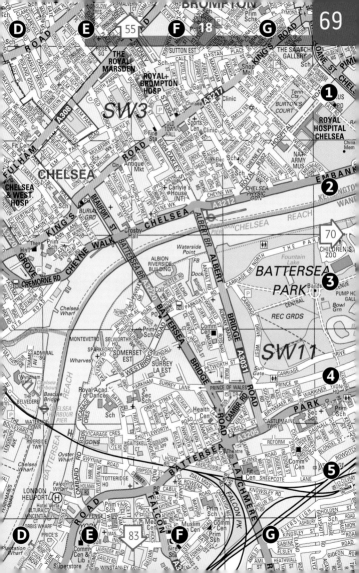

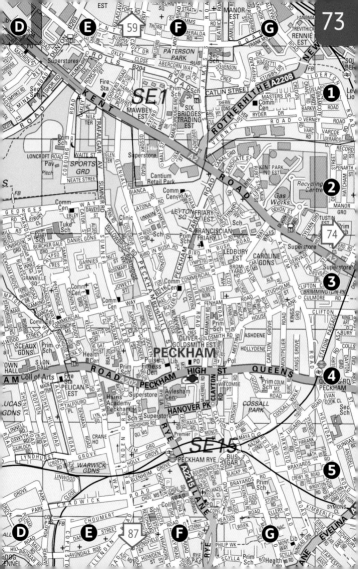

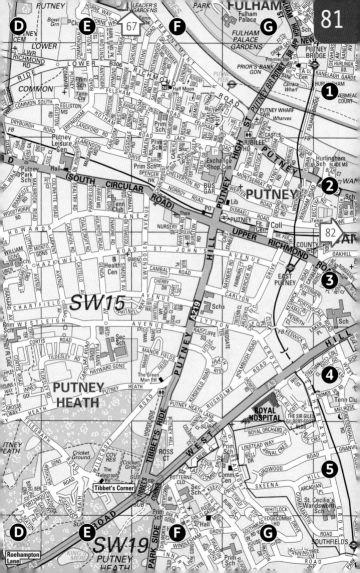

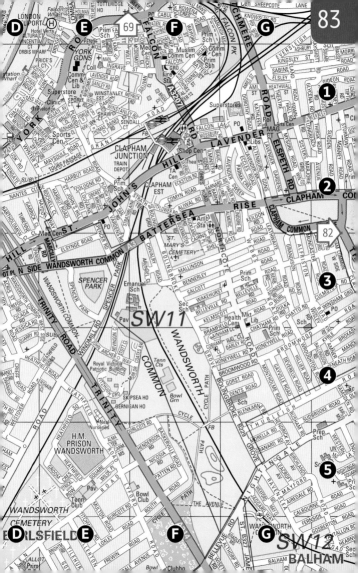

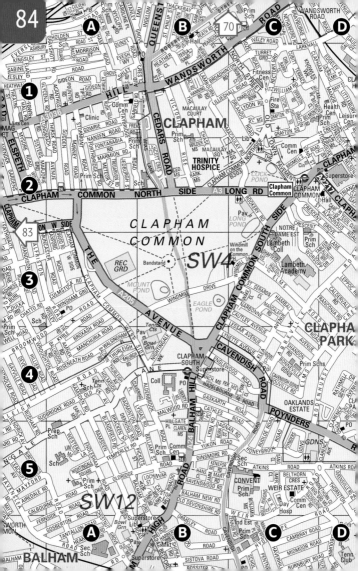

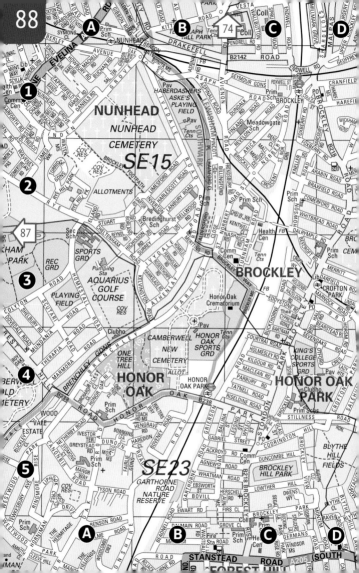

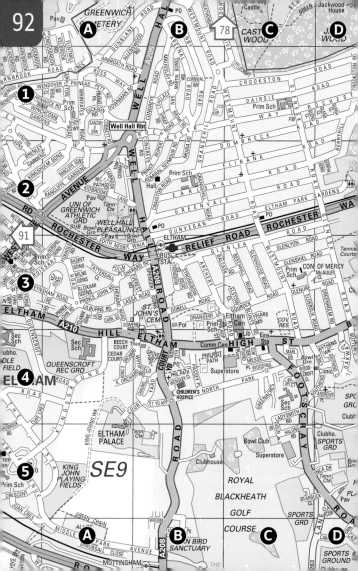

Index to streets
General abbreviations

All	Alley	Dws	Dwellings	Ind	Industrial	S	South
App	Approach	E	East	Junct	Junction	Sch	School
Apts	Apartments	Embk	Embankment	La	Lane	Shop	Shopping
Arc	Arcade	Est	Estate	Lo	Lodge	Sq	Square
Av	Avenue	Ex	Exchange	Mans	Mansions	St	Saint
Bdy	Broadway	Fld	Field	Mkt	Market	St	Street
Bldgs	Buildings	Flds	Fields	Mkts	Markets	Sta	Station
Br	Bridge	Fm	Farm	Ms	Mews	Ter	Terrace
Cen	Central, Centre	Gdn	Garden	Mt	Mount	Trd	Trading
Ch	Church	Gdns	Gardens	N	North	Twr	Tower
Chyd	Churchyard	Gra	Grange	Par	Parade	Vs	Villas
Circ	Circus	Grd	Ground	Pas	Passage	Vw	View
Cl	Close	Grds	Grounds	Pk	Park	W	West
Cor	Corner	Grn	Green	Pl	Place	Wd	Wood
Cotts	Cottages	Gro	Grove	Prec	Precinct	Wf	Wharf
Cres	Crescent	Gt	Great	Pt	Point	Wk	Walk
Ct	Court	Ho	House	Rbt	Roundabout	Yd	Yard
Ctyd	Courtyard	Hos	Houses	Rd	Road		
Dr	Drive	Hts	Heights	Ri	Rise		

Abbreviations of Post Towns

Bark.	Barking	Ilf.	Ilford	Sid.	Sidcup	Well.	Welling

Notes

The figures and letters following a street name indicate the Postal District, page and map square where the name can be found. All street names appear on this index.

1 Canada Sq E14	61 F2
A	
Aaron Hill Rd E6	50 C4
Abbeville Ms SW4	84 D2
Abbeville Rd SW4	84 C4
Abbey Cl E5	31 F1
Abbey Cl SW8	71 D4
Abbeyfield Rd SE16	60 A5
Abbey Gdns NW8	41 D1
Abbey Gdns W6	67 G2
Abbey La E15	47 G1
Abbey Orchard St SW1	20 D3
Abbey Retail Pk, Bark.	36 D5
Abbey Rd E15	48 B1
Abbey Rd NW6	26 C4
Abbey Rd NW8	40 D1
Abbey Rd, Bark.	37 D4
Abbey Rd Est NW8	26 C5
Abbey St E13	49 D3
Abbey St SE1	23 J3
Abbey Wf Ind Est, Bark.	51 F1
Abbotsbury Cl E15	47 G1
Abbotsbury Ms SE15	88 A1
Abbotsbury Rd W14	53 G3
Abbotshade Rd SE16	60 B2
Abbots La SE1	17 J6
Abbots Manor Est SW1	19 H6
Abbot's Pl NW6	26 C5
Abbot's Rd E6	35 G5
Abbotstone Rd SW15	81 E1
Abbot St E8	31 E3
Abbotswell Rd SE4	89 D3
Abbotswood Rd SE22	87 D2
Abbott Rd E14	47 G4
Abchurch La EC4	17 G3
Abchurch Yd EC4	17 F3
Abdale Rd W12	53 D2
Aberavon Rd E3	46 C2
Abercorn Cl NW8	40 D2
Abercorn Pl NW8	40 D2
Abercorn Way SE1	59 H1
Abercrombie St SW11	69 F5
Aberdare Gdns NW6	26 C4
Aberdeen La N5	30 A2
Aberdeen Pk N5	30 A2
Aberdeen Pk Ms N5	30 B1
Aberdeen Pl NW8	41 E3
Aberdeen Rd N5	30 B1
Aberdeen Rd NW10	24 B2
Aberdeen Ter SE3	76 A5
Aberdour St SE1	23 H5
Aberfeldy St E14	47 G5
Aberford Gdns SE18	78 A4
Abergeldie Rd SE12	91 E4
Abernethy Rd SE13	90 B2
Abersham Rd E8	31 E2
Abery St SE18	65 G5
Ability Twrs EC1	10 D1
Abingdon Rd W8	54 B4
Abingdon St SW1	21 D2
Abingdon Vil W8	54 B4
Abinger Gro SE8	74 D2
Abinger Rd W4	52 A4
Ablett St SE16	74 A1
Acacia Cl SE8	60 C5
Acacia Pl NW8	41 E1
Acacademy Gdns W8	54 B3
Academy Pl SE18	78 B4
Academy Rd SE18	78 B4
Acanthus Dr SE1	73 H1
Acanthus Rd SW11	84 A1
Acfold Rd SW6	68 C4
Achilles Cl SE1	73 H1
Achilles Rd NW6	26 B2
Achilles St SE14	74 C3
Achilles Way W1	13 F6
Acklam Rd W10	40 A4
Ackmar Rd SW6	68 B4
Ackroyd Dr E3	47 D4
Ackroyd Rd SE23	88 B5
Acland Cres SE5	86 C2
Acland Rd NW2	25 D3
Acol Rd NW6	26 B4
Acorn Wk SE16	60 C2
Acre Dr SE22	87 F2
Acre La SW2	85 E2
Acris St SW18	83 D3
Acton La NW10	38 A1
Acton Ms E8	31 E5
Acton St WC1	9 G2
Ada Gdns E14	48 A5
Ada Gdns E15	48 C1
Adair Rd W10	39 G3
Adam & Eve Ct W1	14 B1
Adam & Eve Ms W8	54 B4
Adams Ct EC2	17 G1
Adamson Rd E16	49 D5
Adamson Rd NW3	27 E4
Adams Row W1	13 G4
Adam St WC2	15 F4
Adam Wk SW6	67 E3
Ada Pl E2	31 F5
Ada Rd SE5	72 D3
Ada St E8	31 G5
Adderley St E14	47 G5
Addington Rd E3	47 E2
Addington Rd E16	48 B3
Addington Sq SE5	72 B3
Addington St SE1	21 H2
Addison Av W11	53 G2
Addison Br Pl W14	54 A5
Addison Cres W14	53 G4
Addison Gdns W14	53 F4
Addison Gro W4	52 A4
Addison Pl W11	53 G2
Addison Rd W14	53 G3
Addle Hill EC4	16 C3
Addle St EC2	10 E6
Adelaide Av SE4	89 D2
Adelaide Gro W12	52 C2
Adelaide Rd NW3	27 E4
Adelaide St WC2	15 E4
Adelina Gro E1	46 A4
Adeline Pl WC1	8 D6
Adelphi Ter WC2	15 F4
Adeney Cl W6	67 F2
Aden Gro N16	30 C1
Adenmore Rd SE6	89 E5
Aden Ter N16	30 C1
Adie Rd W6	53 E4
Adine Rd E13	49 E3
Adler St E1	45 F5
Adley St E5	32 C2
Admaston Rd SE18	79 E3
Admiral Pl SE16	60 C2
Admiral Seymour Rd SE9	92 B2
Admirals Gate SE10	75 F4
Admiral Sq SW10	69 D4
Admiral St SE8	75 E5
Admirals Way E14	61 E3
Admiral Wk W9	40 B4
Adolphus St SE8	75 D3
Adpar St W2	41 E3
Adrian Ms SW10	68 C2
Adys Rd SE15	87 E1
Afghan Rd SW11	69 F5
Agamemnon Rd NW6	26 A2
Agar Gro NW1	28 C4
Agar Gro Est NW1	28 D4
Agar Pl NW1	28 C4
Agar St WC2	15 E4
Agate Cl E16	49 G5
Agate Rd W6	53 E4
Agave Rd NW2	25 E1
Agdon St EC1	10 B3
Agincourt Rd NW3	27 G1
Agnes Av, Ilf.	36 D1
Agnes Cl E6	64 C1
Agnes Rd W3	52 B2
Agnes St E14	47 D5
Agnew Rd SE23	88 B5
Aileen Wk E15	34 C4
Ainger Rd NW3	27 G4
Ainsdale Dr SE1	73 F1
Ainsley St E2	45 G2
Ainslie Wk SW12	84 B5
Ainsty St SE16	60 B3
Ainsworth Rd E9	32 A4
Ainsworth Way NW8	26 D5
Aintree Av E6	36 A5
Aintree St SW6	67 G3
Airdrie Cl N1	29 F4
Airedale Av W4	52 B5
Airedale Rd SW12	83 G5
Airport Rbt E16	63 G2
Air St W1	14 B4
Aisgill Av W14	68 A1
Aislibie Rd SE12	90 B2
Ajax Rd NW6	26 B2
Akehurst St SW15	80 C4
Akenside Rd NW3	27 E2
Akerman Rd SW9	72 A5
Alabama St SE18	79 F3
Alan Hocken Way E15	48 B1
Alanthus Cl SE12	90 C4
Alaska St SE1	15 J6
Albacore Cres SE13	89 F4
Albany W1	14 A4
Albany Mans SW11	69 F3
Albany Rd E12	35 G1
Albany Rd SE5	72 C2
Albany St NW1	42 B1
Albatross Cl E6	50 B3
Albatross St SE18	79 G3
Albatross Way SE16	60 B3
Albemarle St W1	13 J4
Albemarle Way EC1	10 B4
Alberta Est SE17	72 A1
Alberta St SE17	72 A1

Street	Ref	Street	Ref	Street	Ref	Street	Ref
Albert Av SW8	71 F3	Alexandra Cl SE8	74 D2	Alsace Rd SE17	72 D1	Angel Gate EC1	10 C1
Albert Barnes Ho SE1	22 D4	Alexandra Cotts SE14	75 D4	Alscot Rd SE1	59 E5	Angelica Dr E6	50 C4
Albert Basin E16	65 D1	Alexandra Ct N16	31 D1	Alscot Way SE1	59 E5	Angel La E15	34 A3
Albert Basin Way E16	65 D1	Alexandra Gdns W4	66 A3	Altenburg Gdns SW11	83 G2	Angell Pk Gdns SW9	85 G1
Albert Bigg Pt E15	33 G5	Alexandra Pl NW8	27 D5	Althea St SW6	68 C5	Angell Rd SW9	85 G1
Albert Br SW3	69 F2	Alexandra Rd E6	50 C2	Altior Vw E20	33 G3	Angel Ms N1	43 G1
Albert Br SW11	69 F2	Alexandra Rd E17	27 D4	Altmore Av E6	36 B4	Angel Pas EC4	17 F3
Albert Br Rd SW11	69 F3	Alexandra Rd E18	48 D4	Alton St E14	47 F4	Angel Pl SE1	23 F1
Albert Embk SE1	71 E1	Alexandra Rd SE14	74 C3	Alum Way E16	50 B4	Angel St EC1	16 D1
Albert Gdns E1	46 B5	Alexis St SE16	59 F5	Alvanley Gdns NW6	26 C2	Angel Wk W6	53 E5
Albert Gate SW1	19 E1	Alfearn Rd E5	32 A1	Alverstone Rd E12	36 C1	Angerstein La SE3	76 C3
Albert Pl W8	54 C3	Alfreda St SW11	70 B4	Alverstone Rd NW2	25 E4	Angler's La NW5	28 B3
Albert Rd E16	64 A2	Alfred Ms W1	8 C5	Alverton St SE8	74 D1	Anglesea Av SE18	64 D5
Albert Rd NW6	40 A1	Alfred Pl WC1	8 C5	Alvey Est SE17	72 D1	Anglesea Rd SE18	64 D5
Albert Sq SW8	71 F3	Alfred Prior Ho E12	36 C1	Alvey St SE17	23 H6	Anglia Ho E14	46 C5
Albert St NW1	28 B5	Alfred Rd E15	34 C2	Alvington Cres E8	31 E2	Anglia Wk E6	36 B5
Albert Ter NW1	28 A5	Alfred Rd W2	40 B4	Alwold Cres SE12	91 E4	Anglo Rd E3	46 D1
Albert Way SE15	73 G3	Alfred's Gdns, Bark.	51 G1	Alwyne Pl N1	30 B3	Angrave Ct E8	31 E5
Albion Av SW8	70 D5	Alfred St E3	47 D2	Alwyne Rd N1	30 B4	Angus Rd E13	49 F2
Albion Cl W2	12 C3	Alfreds Way, Bark.	51 E2	Alwyne Sq N1	30 B3	Angus St SE14	74 C3
Albion Dr E8	31 E4	Alfriston Rd SW11	83 G3	Alwyne Vil N1	30 A4	Anhalt Rd SW11	69 F3
Albion Est SE16	60 A3	Algernon Rd NW6	26 B5	Alzette Ho E2	46 B2	Ankerdine Cres SE18	78 C3
Albion Ms N1	30 D1	Algernon Rd SE13	89 F2	Ambassador Gdns E6	50 B4	Anley Rd W14	53 F3
Albion Ms W2	12 C2	Algiers Rd SE13	89 E2	Ambassador's Ct SW1	14 B6	Annabel Cl E14	47 F5
Albion Pl EC1	10 B5	Alice Gilliatt Ct W14	68 A2	Ambergate St SE17	72 A1	Anna Cl E8	31 E5
Albion Pl W6	53 D5	Alice La E3	32 D5	Amberley Rd W9	40 B4	Annandale Rd SE10	76 C2
Albion Riverside Bldg SW11	69 F3	Alice St SE1	23 H4	Ambleside Rd NW10	24 B4	Annandale Rd W4	52 A5
Albion Rd N16	30 C1	Alie St E1	45 E5	Ambrosden Av SW1	20 B5	Annandale Rd, Sid.	93 G5
Albion Sq E8	31 E4	Alison Cl E6	50 C5	Ambrose Ms SW11	69 F5	Anne Compton Ms SE12	90 C5
Albion St SE16	60 A3	Aliwal Rd SW11	83 F2	Ambrose St SE16	59 G5	Annesley Rd SE3	77 E4
Albion St W2	12 C2	Alkerden Rd W4	66 A1	Amelia St SE17	72 A1	Anne St E13	48 D3
Albion Ter E8	31 E4	Allard Gdns SW4	85 D3	Amen Cor EC4	16 C2	Annette Rd N7	29 F1
Albion Way EC1	10 D6	Allardyce St SW4	85 F2	Amen Ct EC4	16 C1	Annis Rd E9	32 C3
Albion Way SE13	89 G2	Allcroft Rd NW5	28 A2	America St SE1	16 D6	Ann La SW10	69 E3
Albrighton Rd SE22	87 D1	Allenby Rd SE28	65 E4	Amerland Rd SW18	82 A4	Ann Moss Way SE16	60 A4
Albury St SE8	74 E4	Allen Edwards Dr SW8	71 E4	Amersham Gro SE14	74 D3	Ann's Cl SW1	19 E2
Albyn Rd SE8	75 E4	Allen Rd E3	46 D1	Amersham Rd SE14	74 D3	Ann St SE18	65 F5
Aldbourne Rd W12	52 B2	Allen Rd N16	30 D1	Amersham Vale SE14	75 D3	Ansdell Rd SE15	74 A5
Aldbridge St SE17	73 D1	Allensbury Pl NW1	29 D4	Amery Gdns NW10	25 D5	Ansdell St W8	54 C4
Aldburgh Ms W1	13 G1	Allen St W8	54 B4	Amethyst Rd E15	34 A1	Anselm Rd SW6	68 B2
Aldebert Ter SW8	71 E3	Allenswood Rd SE9	92 A1	Amhurst Pas E8	31 F1	Ansleigh Pl W11	53 F1
Aldeburgh St SE10	76 D1	Allestree Rd SW6	67 G3	Amhurst Rd E8	31 G2	Anson Pl SE28	65 F3
Alden Av E15	48 C2	Allfarthing La SW18	82 C4	Amhurst Rd N16	31 E1	Anson Rd N7	28 C1
Aldenham St NW1	42 D1	Allhallows La EC4	17 F4	Amhurst Ter E8	31 F1	Anson Rd NW2	25 F2
Aldensley Rd W6	53 D4	Allhallows Rd E6	50 A4	Amiel St E1	46 A3	Anstey Rd SE15	87 F1
Alderbrook Rd SW12	84 B4	Alliance Rd E13	49 F3	Amies St SW11	83 G1	Anstice Cl W4	66 A3
Alderbury Rd SW13	66 C2	Allingham St N1	44 B1	Amity Rd E15	34 C5	Anstridge Path SE9	93 F4
Alder Cl SE15	73 E2	Allington Rd W10	39 G1	Amner Rd SW11	84 A4	Anstridge Rd SE9	93 F4
Aldermanbury EC2	17 E1	Allington St SW1	20 A4	Amor Rd W6	53 E4	Antelope Rd SE18	64 B4
Aldermanbury Sq EC2	11 E6	Allnutt Way SW4	84 D3	Amott Rd SE15	87 F1	Antill Rd E3	46 C2
Alderman's Wk EC2	11 H6	Alloa Rd SE8	74 B1	Amoy Pl E14	47 E5	Antill Ter E1	46 B5
Alderney Ms SE1	23 F3	Alloway Rd E3	46 C2	Ampton Pl WC1	9 G2	Antonine Hts SE1	23 H2
Alderney Rd E1	46 B3	All Saints Dr SE3	76 B5	Ampton St WC1	9 G2	Anton St E8	31 F2
Alderney St SW1	56 B5	All Saints Rd W11	40 A4	Amsterdam Rd E14	61 G4	Antrim Gro NW3	27 G3
Aldersey Gdns, Bark.	37 F3	All Saints Rd N1	43 F1	Amwell St EC1	9 J1	Antrim Mans NW3	27 F3
Aldersford Cl SE4	88 B3	Allsop Pl NW1	7 E4	Amyruth Rd SE4	89 E3	Antrim Rd NW3	27 G3
Aldersgate St EC1	10 D5	All Souls Av NW10	38 D1	Ancaster St SE18	79 G3	Apollo Pl SW10	69 E3
Aldershot Rd NW6	26 A5	All Souls Pl W1	7 J6	Anchorage Pt Ind Est SE7	63 F4	Apothecary St EC4	16 B2
Alderton Rd SE24	86 B1	Almack Rd E5	32 A1	Anchor & Hope La SE7	63 E4	Appach Rd SW2	85 G3
Alderville Rd SW6	68 A5	Alma Gro SE1	59 E5	Anchor Ms SW12	84 A4	Appleby Rd E8	31 F4
Alder, Ilf.	37 E2	Alma Rd SW18	82 D3	Anchor Retail Pk E1	46 A3	Appleby Rd E16	48 C5
Alderwood Rd SE9	93 F4	Alma Sq NW8	41 D2	Anchor St SE16	59 G5	Appleby St E2	45 E1
Aldford St W1	13 F5	Alma St E15	34 A3	Anchor Yd EC1	10 E3	Appleford Rd W10	39 G3
Aldgate EC3	45 D5	Alma St NW5	28 B3	Ancill Cl W6	67 G2	Applegarth Rd W14	53 F4
Aldgate High St EC3	45 E5	Almeida St N1	30 A4	Ancona Rd NW10	38 C1	Appleton Rd SE9	92 A1
Aldine St W12	53 E3	Almeric Rd SW11	83 G2	Ancona Rd SE18	79 F1	Apple Tree Yd SW1	14 B5
Aldington Rd SE18	63 G4	Almond Cl SE15	73 F5	Andalus Rd SW9	85 E1	Applewood Dr E13	49 E3
Aldred Rd NW6	26 B2	Almond Rd SE16	59 G5	Anderson Rd E9	32 B3	Appold St EC2	11 H5
Aldridge Rd Vil W11	40 C4	Almorah Rd N1	30 C4	Anderson St SW3	69 G1	Approach Rd E2	46 A1
Aldsworth Cl W9	40 C3	Alnwick Rd E16	49 F5	Anderton Cl SE5	86 C1	April St E8	31 E1
Aldworth Gro SE13	89 G4	Alnwick Rd SE12	91 E5	Andover Pl NW6	40 C1	Apsley Way W1	19 G1
Aldworth Rd E15	34 B4	Alperton St W10	39 G3	Andre St E8	31 F2	Aquila St NW8	41 E1
Aldwych WC2	15 G3	Alpha Cl NW1	6 C3	Andrew Borde St WC2	14 D1	Aquinas St SE1	16 A5
Alestan Beck Rd E16	49 G4	Alpha Gro E14	61 E3	Andrewes Gdns E6	50 A5	Arabella Dr SW15	80 A2
Alexander Av NW10	24 D4	Alpha Pl NW6	40 B1	Andrewes Ho EC2	11 E6	Arabin Rd SE4	88 C2
Alexander, Cl. Sid.	93 G3	Alpha Pl SW3	69 F2	Andrews Crosse WC2	15 J2	Aragon Ter SE8	61 D5
Alexander Pl SW7	18 B5	Alpha Rd SE14	75 D4	Andrews Pl SE9	92 D4	Arbery Rd E3	46 B5
Alexander Sq SW3	18 B5	Alpha Rd E8	31 G5	Andrew's Rd E8	31 G5	Arbour Sq E1	46 B5
Alexander St W2	40 B5	Alpha St SE15	73 F5	Anerley St SW11	69 G5	Arbroath Rd SE9	92 A1
Alexandra Av SW11	70 A4	Alpine Gro E9	32 A4	Angel Ct EC2	17 G1	Arbuthnot Rd SE14	74 B5
		Alpine Rd SE16	60 A5	Angel Ct SW1	14 B6		
		Alpine Way E6	50 C4				

Name	Ref
Arbutus St E8	31 D5
Arcade, The EC2	11 H6
Arcadian Pl SE16	81 G5
Arcadia St E14	47 E5
Archangel St SE16	60 B3
Archbishops Pl SW2	85 F4
Archdale Rd SE22	87 E3
Archel Rd W14	68 A2
Archer St W1	14 C3
Archery Cl W2	12 C2
Archery Rd SE9	92 B3
Arches, The WC2	15 F5
Archibald Ms W1	13 G4
Archibald Rd N7	28 D1
Archibald St E3	47 E2
Archie St SE1	23 J2
Arch St SE1	22 D4
Archway Cl W10	39 F4
Archway St SW13	80 A1
Arcola St E8	31 E2
Ardberg Rd SE24	86 C4
Arden Cres E14	61 E5
Arden Est N1	44 D1
Ardgowan Rd SE6	90 B5
Ardilaun Rd N5	30 B1
Ardleigh Rd N1	30 C3
Ardmere Rd SE13	90 A4
Ardwick Rd NW2	27 J2
Argon Ms SW6	68 B3
Argyle Pl W6	53 D5
Argyle Rd E1	46 B3
Argyle Rd E15	34 B1
Argyle Rd E16	49 F5
Argyle Sq WC1	9 F1
Argyle St WC1	9 E1
Argyle Wk WC1	9 F2
Argyle Way SE16	73 F1
Argyll Rd SE18	65 E4
Argyll Rd W8	54 B3
Argyll St W1	14 A2
Aria Ho WC2	15 F1
Arica Ho SE16	59 G4
Arica Rd SE4	88 C2
Ariel Rd NW6	26 B3
Ariel Way W12	53 E2
Aristotle Rd SW4	85 D1
Arklow Rd SE14	74 D2
Arkwright Rd NW3	26 D2
Arlesey Cl SW15	81 G3
Arlesford Rd SW9	85 E1
Arlingford Rd SW2	86 G3
Arlington Av N1	44 B1
Arlington Cl SE13	90 A3
Arlington Cl, Sid.	93 G5
Arlington Lo SW2	85 F2
Arlington Rd NW1	28 B5
Arlington Sq N1	30 B5
Arlington St SW1	14 A5
Arlington Way EC1	10 A1
Armadale Rd SW6	68 B3
Armada St SE8	75 E2
Armagh Rd E3	33 D5
Arminger Rd W12	53 D2
Armitage Rd SE10	76 C1
Armoury Rd SE8	75 F5
Armoury Way SW18	83 B4
Armstrong Rd NW10	24 A4
Armstrong Rd SE18	65 E4
Armstrong Rd SW7	55 E4
Armstrong Rd W3	52 B2
Arnal Cres SW18	81 G5
Arne St WC2	15 F2
Arne Wk SE3	90 C2
Arneway St SW1	20 D4
Arngask Rd SE6	90 A5
Arnhem Pl E14	61 E4
Arnold Circ E2	45 E2
Arnold Est SE1	59 E3
Arnold Rd E3	47 E2
Arnould Av SE5	86 C2
Arnside St SE17	72 B2
Arodene Rd SW2	85 F4
Arragon Rd E6	35 G5
Arran Wk N1	30 B4
Arrol Ho SE1	22 E4
Arrow Rd E3	47 F2
Arsenal Rd SE9	78 B5
Arsenal Way SE18	65 E4
Artesian Rd W2	40 B5
Arthingworth St E15	34 B5
Arthurdon Rd SE4	89 E3
Arthur Gro SE18	65 E5
Arthur Henderson Ho SW6	68 A5
Arthur Rd E6	50 B1
Arthur Rd N7	29 F1
Arthur St EC4	17 G4
Artillery La E1	11 J6
Artillery La W12	38 C5
Artillery Pas E1	11 J6
Artillery Pl SW1	20 C4
Artillery Row SW1	20 C4
Artizan St E1	17 J1
Arundel Cl E15	34 B1
Arundel Cl SW11	83 F3
Arundel Gdns W11	54 A1
Arundel Gt Ct WC2	15 H3
Arundel Gro N16	30 D2
Arundel Pl N1	29 G3
Arundel Sq N7	29 G3
Arundel St WC2	15 H3
Arundel Ter SW13	67 D2
Arvon Rd N5	29 G2
Ascalon St SW8	70 C3
Ascham St NW5	28 B2
Ascot Rd E6	50 B2
Ashbourne Gro SE22	87 E3
Ashbourne Gro W4	66 A1
Ashbridge St NW8	6 B4
Ashburn Gdns SW7	54 D5
Ashburnham Gro SE10	75 F3
Ashburnham Pl SE10	75 F3
Ashburnham Retreat SE10	75 F3
Ashburnham Rd NW10	39 E2
Ashburnham Rd SW10	69 D3
Ashburton Av, Ilf.	37 G1
Ashburton Rd E16	48 D5
Ashbury Rd SW11	83 G1
Ashby Gro N1	30 B4
Ashby Ms SE4	74 D5
Ashby Rd SE4	75 D5
Ashby St EC1	10 A1
Ashchurch Gro W12	52 C3
Ashchurch Pk Vil W12	52 C3
Ashchurch Ter W12	52 C4
Ashcombe St SW6	68 C5
Ashcroft Rd E3	47 E2
Ashdene SE15	73 G4
Ashdon Rd NW10	24 A5
Ashdown Wk E14	61 E5
Ashenden SE17	22 D5
Ashenden Rd E5	32 B2
Ashentree Ct EC4	16 A2
Asher Way E1	59 F2
Ashfield Rd W3	52 B2
Ashfield St E1	45 G4
Ashford Rd E6	36 C3
Ashford Rd NW2	27 F1
Ashford St N1	31 G5
Ash Gro E8	31 G5
Ash Gro NW2	25 F1
Ashington Rd SW6	68 A5
Ashland Pl W1	7 F5
Ashleigh Rd SW14	80 A1
Ashley Cres SW11	84 A1
Ashley Gdns SW1	20 B4
Ashley Pl SW1	20 A4
Ashley Rd E7	35 F4
Ashlin Rd E15	34 A1
Ashlone Rd SW15	81 E1
Ashmead Rd SE8	75 E5
Ashmere Gro SW2	85 E2
Ashmill St NW1	6 B5
Ashmole Pl SW8	71 F2
Ashmole St SW8	71 F2
Ashmore Cl SE15	73 E3
Ashmore Gro, Well.	93 F1
Ashmore Rd W9	40 A3
Ashness Rd SW11	83 G3
Ashridge Cres SE18	79 E3
Ash Rd E15	34 B2
Ashton Rd E15	34 A2
Ashton St E14	61 G1
Ashworth Rd W9	40 C2
Aske St N1	11 H1
Askew Cres W12	52 B2
Askew Rd W12	52 B2
Askham Ct W12	52 C2
Askham Rd W12	52 C2
Askill Dr SW15	81 G3
Asland Rd E15	34 B5
Aslett St SW18	82 C5
Asmara Rd NW2	25 G2
Asolando Dr SE17	23 E6
Aspen Gdns W6	67 D1
Aspenlea Rd W6	67 F2
Aspen Way E14	61 E1
Aspern Gro NW3	27 F2
Aspinall Rd SE4	88 B1
Aspinden Rd SE16	59 G5
Aspley Rd SW18	82 C3
Assam St E1	46 A4
Assembly Pas E1	46 A4
Astbury Ho SE11	21 J4
Astbury Rd SE15	74 A4
Astell St SW3	69 F1
Aste St E14	61 G3
Astle St SW11	70 A5
Astley Av NW2	26 C5
Aston St E14	46 C5
Astoria Wk SW9	85 G1
Astrop Ms W6	53 E4
Astrop Ter W6	53 E4
Astwood Ms SW7	54 C5
Asylum Rd SE15	73 G3
Atalanta St SW6	67 F4
Athelstane Gro E3	47 E1
Athelstan Gdns NW6	25 G4
Athenaeum Ct N5	30 B1
Athenlay Rd SE15	88 A3
Atherden Rd E5	32 A1
Atherfold Rd SW9	85 E1
Atherstone Ms SW7	55 D5
Atherton Ms E7	34 C3
Atherton Rd E7	34 C2
Atherton Rd SW13	66 C3
Atherton St SW11	69 F5
Athlone Rd SW2	85 F5
Athlone St NW5	28 A3
Athol Sq E14	47 G5
Atkinson Rd E16	49 G1
Atkins Rd SW12	84 D5
Atlantic Rd SW9	85 G2
Atlas Gdns SE7	63 F5
Atlas Ms N7	29 F3
Atlas Rd E13	48 D1
Atlas Rd NW10	38 A2
Atley Rd E3	33 E5
Atney Rd SW15	81 G2
Atterbury St SW1	20 D6
Attneave St WC1	9 J4
Atwood Rd W6	52 D5
Aubert Ct N5	30 A1
Aubert Pk N5	30 A1
Aubert Rd N5	30 A1
Aubrey Moore Pt E15	47 G1
Aubrey Rd W8	54 A2
Aubrey Wk W8	54 A2
Auburn Cl SE14	74 C3
Aubyn Sq SW15	80 C2
Auckland Rd SW11	83 F2
Auden Pl NW1	28 A5
Audley Cl SW11	84 A1
Audley Sq W1	13 G5
Audrey St E2	45 F1
Augurs La E13	49 E2
Augusta St E14	47 F5
Augustine Rd W14	53 F4
Augustus Ct SE1	23 H5
Augustus Sq NW1	8 B2
Aulton Pl SE11	71 G1
Auriga Ms N1	30 C2
Auriol Rd W14	53 G5
Austen Ho NW6	40 B2
Austin Cl SE23	88 D5
Austin Friars EC2	17 G1
Austin Friars Pas EC2	17 G1
Austin Friars Sq EC2	17 G1
Austin Rd SW11	70 A4
Austin St E2	45 E2
Australia Rd W12	52 D1
Austral St SE11	22 B5
Autumn St E3	33 E5
Avalon Rd SW6	68 C4
Aveline St SE11	71 G1
Ave Maria La EC4	16 C2
Avening Ter SW18	82 B4
Avenons Rd E13	48 D3
Avenue, The SE10	76 A3
Avenue, The SW4	84 B3
Avenue, The SW4	83 F5
Avenue, The SW18	83 F5
Avenue, The W4	52 A4
Avenue Cl NW8	27 F5
Avenue Gdns SW14	80 A1
Avenue Rd E7	35 E2
Avenue Rd NW3	27 E4
Avenue Rd NW8	27 E4
Avenue Rd NW10	38 B1
Averill St W6	67 F2
Avery Fm Row SW1	19 H6
Avery Hill Rd SE9	93 F4
Avery Row W1	13 H3
Aviary Cl E16	48 C4
Avignon Rd SE4	88 B1
Avis Sq E1	46 B5
Avocet Ms SE28	65 F4
Avondale Pk Gdns W11	53 G1
Avondale Pk Rd W11	53 G1
Avondale Ri SE15	87 E1
Avondale Rd E16	48 B4
Avondale Sq SE1	73 F1
Avonley Rd SE14	74 A3
Avonmore Rd W14	54 A5
Avonmouth St SE1	22 D3
Avon Pl SE1	22 E2
Avon Rd SE4	89 E1
Axe St, Bark.	37 E5
Aybrook St W1	7 F6
Aycliffe Rd W12	52 B2
Aylesbury Rd SE17	72 C1
Aylesbury St EC1	10 B4
Aylesford St SW1	70 D1
Aylesham Cen SE15	73 F4
Aylestone Av NW6	25 F5
Aylmer Rd W12	52 A3
Aylward St E1	46 A5
Aylwyn Est SE1	23 J3
Aynhoe Rd W14	53 F5
Ayres Cl E13	49 D2
Ayres St SE1	22 E1
Aysgarth Rd SE21	86 D4
Aytoun Pl SW9	71 F5
Aytoun Rd SW9	71 F5
Azalea Cl, Ilf.	36 D2
Azania Ms NW5	28 B2
Azenby Rd SE15	73 E5
Azof St SE10	62 B5

B

Name	Ref
Baalbec Rd N5	30 A2
Babmaes St SW1	14 C4
Baches St N1	11 G2
Back Ch La E1	59 F1
Back Hill EC1	9 J4
Backhouse Pl SE17	23 J6
Bacon Gro SE1	59 E4
Bacon St E1	45 E3

Street	Ref
Bacon St E2	45 E3
Bacton NW5	28 A2
Baden Pl SE1	23 F1
Baden Rd, Ilf.	36 D2
Badminton Rd SW12	84 A4
Badsworth Rd SE5	72 B3
Bagley's La SW6	68 C4
Bagshot St SE17	73 D1
Baildon St SE8	75 D3
Bailey Cl SE28	65 G2
Bailey Ms SW2	85 G3
Bainbridge St WC1	14 D1
Baird St EC1	11 E3
Baizdon Rd SE3	76 B5
Baker Rd NW10	24 A5
Baker Rd SE18	78 A3
Bakers Fld N7	29 D1
Bakers Hall Ct EC3	17 J4
Baker's Ms W1	13 F1
Bakers Row E15	48 B1
Baker's Row EC1	9 J4
Baker St NW1	6 E4
Baker St W1	7 E5
Baker's Yd EC1	9 J4
Bakery Cl SW9	71 G5
Balaam St E13	49 D2
Balaclava Rd SE1	59 E5
Balcaskie Rd SE9	92 B3
Balchen Rd SE3	77 G5
Balchier Rd SE22	87 G4
Balcombe St NW1	6 D4
Balcorne St E9	32 A4
Balderton St W1	13 G2
Baldock St E3	47 F1
Baldwin Cres SE5	72 B4
Baldwin's Gdns EC1	9 J5
Baldwin St EC1	11 F2
Baldwin Ter N1	44 B1
Bale Rd E1	46 C4
Balfern Gro W4	66 A1
Balfern St SW11	69 F4
Balfe St N1	43 E1
Balfour Ms W1	13 G5
Balfour Pl SW15	80 D2
Balfour Pl W1	13 G4
Balfour Rd N5	30 B1
Balfour St SE17	23 F5
Balham Gro SW12	84 A5
Balham Hill SW12	84 B5
Balham New Rd SW12	84 B5
Balladier Wk E14	47 F4
Ballance Rd E9	32 B3
Ballantine St SW18	82 D2
Ballast Quay SE10	76 A1
Ballater Rd SW2	85 E2
Ballina St SE23	88 B5
Ballingdon Rd SW11	84 A4
Balliol Rd W10	39 E5
Ballogie Av NW10	24 A1
Balls Pond Rd N1	30 C3
Balmer Rd E3	46 D1
Balmes Rd N1	30 C5
Balmoral Cl SW15	81 F4
Balmoral Gro N7	29 F3
Balmoral Ms W12	52 B4
Balmoral Rd E7	35 F1
Balmoral Rd NW2	24 D3
Balmore Cl E14	47 G5
Balmuir Gdns SW15	80 D3
Balnacraig Av NW10	24 A1
Balniel Gate SW1	71 D1
Baltic Ct SE16	60 B3
Baltic St E EC1	10 D4
Baltic St W EC1	10 D4
Balvaird Pl SW1	71 D1
Balvernie Gro SW18	82 A5
Bamborough Gdns W12	53 E3
Bamford Rd, Bark.	37 E3
Banbury Ct WC2	15 E3
Banbury Rd E9	32 B4
Banbury St SW11	69 F5
Banchory Rd SE3	77 E3
Bancroft Rd E1	46 A2
Banfield Rd SE15	87 G1
Bangalore St SW15	81 E1
Banim St W6	53 D4
Banister Ms NW6	26 C4
Banister Rd W10	39 F2
Bank End SE1	17 E5
Bankhurst Rd SE6	89 D5
Bank La SW15	80 A3
Banks Ho SE1	22 D4
Bankside SE1	16 D4
Bankside Av SE13	89 F1
Bankside Lofts SE1	16 C5
Bankside Rd, Ilf.	37 E2
Bank St E14	61 A2
Banks Way E12	36 C1
Bankton Rd SW2	85 G2
Bankwell Rd SE13	90 B2
Bannerman Ho SW8	71 E2
Banner St EC1	10 E4
Banning St SE10	76 B1
Bannockburn Rd SE18	65 G5
Banstead St SE15	88 A1
Bantry St SE5	72 C3
Barandon Wk W11	53 F1
Barbara Castle Cl SW6	54 A6
Barbers All E13	49 E2
Barbers Rd E15	47 F1
Barbican, The EC2	10 D5
Barb Ms W6	53 E4
Barbon Cl WC1	9 F5
Barchard St SW18	82 C3
Barchester St E14	47 F4
Barclay Cl SW6	54 A6
Barclay Rd E11	34 B3
Barclay Rd E13	49 F3
Barclay Rd SW6	68 B4
Barden St SE18	79 G5
Bardolph Rd N7	29 E1
Bard Rd W10	53 F1
Bardsley La SE10	75 G2
Barfett St W10	40 A3
Barfleur La SE8	60 D5
Barford St N1	29 G5
Barforth Rd SE15	87 G1
Barge Ho Rd E16	64 D2
Barge Ho St SE1	16 A5
Barge Wk SE10	62 C4
Baring Rd SE12	90 D5
Baring St N1	30 C5
Barker Dr NW1	28 C4
Barker St SW10	68 D2
Barkham Ter SE1	22 A3
Barking Rd E6	49 G1
Barking Rd E13	49 E3
Barking Rd E16	48 C4
Bark Pl W2	54 C1
Barkston Gdns SW5	54 C5
Barkworth Rd SE16	59 G3
Barlborough St SE14	74 A3
Barlby Gdns W10	39 F3
Barlby Rd W10	39 F4
Barleycorn Way E14	60 D1
Barley Mow Pas EC1	10 C6
Barlow Dr SE18	78 A4
Barlow Pl W1	13 J4
Barlow Rd NW6	26 A3
Barlow St SE17	23 G5
Barmouth Rd SW18	83 D4
Barnabas Rd E9	32 B2
Barnaby Pl SW7	55 E5
Barnard Cl SE18	64 C5
Barnard Ms SW11	83 F2
Barnard Rd SW11	83 F2
Barnard's Inn EC1	16 A1
Barnby St E15	34 B5
Barnby St NW1	42 C1
Barn Elms Pk SW15	67 E5
Barnes Av SW13	66 C3
Barnes Br SW13	66 A5
Barnes Br W4	66 A5
Barnesbury Ho SW4	85 D3
Barnes Cl E12	35 G1
Barnes High St SW13	66 B5
Barnes Rd, Ilf.	37 E2
Barnes St E14	46 C5
Barnes Ter SE8	75 D1
Barnet Gro E2	45 F2
Barney Cl SE7	77 F1
Barnfield Pl E14	61 E5
Barnfield Rd SE18	79 D2
Barnham St SE1	23 J1
Barnsbury Gro N7	29 F4
Barnsbury Pk N1	29 G4
Barnsbury Rd N1	43 G1
Barnsbury Sq N1	29 G4
Barnsbury St N1	29 G4
Barnsbury Ter N1	29 G4
Barnsdale Av E14	61 E5
Barnsdale Rd W9	40 A3
Barnsley St E1	45 G3
Barnwell Rd SW2	85 G3
Barnwood Cl W9	40 C3
Barons Cl E14	47 G1
Barons Keep W14	67 G1
Baronsmead Rd SW13	66 C4
Barons Pl SE1	22 A2
Baron St N1	43 G1
Baron Wk E16	48 C4
Barque Ms SE8	75 E2
Barratt Ind Pk E13	49 G2
Barretts Gro N16	31 D2
Barrett St W1	13 G2
Barriedale SE14	74 C4
Barrier App SE7	63 G4
Barrier Pt Rd E16	63 F2
Barrington Cl NW5	28 A2
Barrington Rd E12	36 C3
Barrington Rd SW9	86 A1
Barrington Vil SE18	78 C4
Barrow Hill Rd NW8	41 F1
Barry Rd E6	50 A5
Barry Rd SE22	87 F4
Barset Rd SE15	88 A1
Barter St WC1	9 F6
Barth Ms SE18	65 G5
Bartholomew Cl EC1	10 D6
Bartholomew Cl SW18	83 D2
Bartholomew La EC2	17 G2
Bartholomew Pl EC1	10 D6
Bartholomew Rd NW5	28 C3
Bartholomew Sq EC1	11 E3
Bartholomew St SE1	23 F4
Bartholomew Vil NW5	28 C3
Barth Rd SE18	65 G5
Bartle Av E6	50 A1
Bartle Rd W11	39 G5
Bartlett Cl E14	47 E5
Bartlett Ct EC4	16 A1
Bartletts Pas EC4	16 A1
Barton Cl E6	50 B5
Barton St SW1	20 E3
Bartram Rd SE4	88 D3
Barwick Rd E7	35 E1
Bascombe St SW2	85 G4
Baseing Cl E6	64 C1
Basevi Way SE8	75 F2
Basil Av E6	50 A1
Basil St SW3	18 D3
Basing Cl SE15	73 E4
Basingdon Way SE5	86 C2
Basinghall Av EC2	11 F6
Basinghall St EC2	17 F1
Basing Ho Yd E2	11 J1
Basing Pl E2	11 J1
Basing St W11	40 A5
Basire St N1	30 B5
Baskerville Rd SW18	83 F5
Basket Gdns SE9	92 A3
Basnett Rd SW11	84 A1
Bassano St SE22	87 E3
Bassein Pk Rd W12	52 B3
Bassett Rd W10	39 F5
Bassett St NW5	28 A3
Bassingham Rd SW18	82 D5
Bastable Av, Bark.	51 G1
Bastion Highwalk EC2	10 D6
Bastwick St EC1	10 D3
Basuto Rd SW6	68 B4
Batavia Rd SE14	74 C3
Batchelor St N1	43 G1
Bateman's Bldgs W1	14 C2
Bateman's Row EC2	11 J3
Bateman St W1	14 C2
Bateson St SE18	65 G5
Bath Ct EC1	9 J4
Bath Pl EC2	11 H2
Bath Rd E7	35 G3
Bath Rd W4	52 A5
Bath St EC1	11 E2
Bath Ter SE1	22 D4
Bathurst Gdns NW10	38 D5
Bathurst St W2	55 E1
Bathway SE18	64 C5
Batman Cl W12	53 D2
Batoum Gdns W6	53 E4
Batson St W12	52 C3
Batten St SW11	83 F1
Battersea Br SW3	69 E3
Battersea Br SW11	69 E3
Battersea Br Rd SW11	69 F3
Battersea Ch Rd SW11	69 E4
Battersea High St SW11	69 E4
Battersea Pk SW11	69 G3
Battersea Pk Rd SW8	70 B4
Battersea Pk Rd SW11	69 F5
Battersea Ri SW11	83 F3
Battery Rd SE28	65 G3
Battle Br La SE1	17 H6
Battledean Rd N5	30 A2
Batty St E1	45 F5
Baulk, The SW18	82 B5
Bavent Rd SE5	72 B5
Bawdale Rd SE22	87 E3
Bawtree Rd SE14	74 C3
Baxendale St E2	45 F2
Baxter Rd E16	49 F5
Baxter Rd N1	30 C3
Baxter Rd N18	38 A3
Baxter Rd, Ilf.	36 D2
Bayfield Rd SE9	91 G2
Bayford Rd NW10	39 F2
Bayford St E8	31 G4
Bayham Pl NW1	28 C5
Bayham Rd W4	52 A4
Bayley St WC1	8 C6
Baylis Rd SE1	21 J2
Baynes St NW1	28 C4
Bayonne Rd W6	67 G2
Bayswater Rd W2	12 A3
Baythorne St E3	47 D4
Baytree Ms SE17	23 F5
Baytree Rd SW2	85 F2
Bazely St E14	61 G1
Beacham Cl SE7	77 G1
Beachy Rd E3	33 E4
Beacon Gate SE14	88 B1
Beacon Hill N7	29 E2
Beacon Rd SE13	90 A4
Beaconsfield Cl SE3	76 D2
Beaconsfield Rd E16	48 C3
Beaconsfield Rd NW10	24 B3
Beaconsfield Rd SE3	76 C3
Beaconsfield Rd SE17	72 C1
Beaconsfield St N1	29 E5
Beaconsfield Ter Rd W14	53 G4
Beaconsfield Wk SW6	68 A4
Beadon Rd W6	53 E5
Beak St W1	14 B3
Beale Pl E3	46 D1
Beale Rd E3	32 D5
Beanacre Cl E9	33 D3
Bear All EC4	16 B1
Bear Gdns SE1	16 D5
Bear La SE1	16 C5
Bearstead Ri SE4	88 D3
Beaton Cl SE15	73 E4
Beatrice Pl W8	54 C4

Beatrice Rd SE1 59 F5
Beatson Wk SE16 60 B2
Beatty Rd N16 31 D1
Beatty St NW1 42 C1
Beauchamp Pl SW3 18 C3
Beauchamp Rd E7 35 E4
Beauchamp Rd SW11 83 F2
Beauchamp St EC1 9 J6
Beauclerc Rd W6 53 D4
Beaufort Cl SW15 81 D5
Beaufort Gdns SW3 18 C3
Beaufort St SW3 69 E2
Beaufoy Wk SE11 21 H6
Beaulieu Av E16 63 E2
Beaulieu Cl SE5 86 C1
Beaumont Av W14 68 A1
Beaumont Cres W14 68 A1
Beaumont Gro E1 46 B3
Beaumont Ms W1 7 G5
Beaumont Pl W1 8 B3
Beaumont Rd E13 49 E2
Beaumont Rd SW19 81 E5
Beaumont Sq E1 46 B3
Beaumont St W1 7 G5
Beaumont Wk NW3 27 G2
Beauval Rd SE22 87 E4
Beavor La W6 52 C5
Bebbington Rd SE18 65 G5
Beccles Dr, Bark. 37 G3
Beccles St E14 61 D1
Beck Cl SE13 75 F4
Beckers, The N16 31 F1
Becket Av E6 50 C2
Becket St SE1 23 F3
Beckett Ho SW9 85 F4
Beckford Cl W14 54 A5
Becklow Rd W12 52 C3
Beck Rd E8 31 G5
Beckton Pk Rbt E16 64 A1
Beckton Retail Pk E6 50 C4
Beckton Rd E16 48 C4
Beckton Triangle Retail Pk E6 50 C3
Beckway St SE17 23 G6
Beckwith Rd SE24 86 C4
Bective Rd E7 35 D1
Bective Rd SW15 82 A2
Bedale St SE1 17 F6
Bedford Av WC1 8 D6
Bedfordbury WC2 15 E3
Bedford Cl W4 66 A2
Bedford Gdns W8 54 B2
Bedford Ho SW4 85 E2
Bedford Pl WC1 9 E5
Bedford Rd SW4 36 C5
Bedford Rd W4 85 E1
Bedford Row WC1 9 H5
Bedford Sq WC1 8 D6
Bedford St WC2 15 E3
Bedford Way WC1 8 D4
Bedgebury Rd SE9 91 G2
Bedlam Ms SE11 21 H5
Beeby Rd E16 49 E4
Beech Av W3 52 A2
Beech Cl SW15 80 B5
Beech Ct SE9 92 A4
Beechdale Rd SW2 85 F4
Beechhill Rd SE9 92 B1
Beechmore Rd SW11 69 G4
Beech St EC2 10 D5
Beech Tree Cl N1 29 G4
Beechwood Gro W3 52 A1
Beechwood Rd E8 31 E3
Beecroft Rd SE4 88 C3
Beehive Cl E8 31 E4
Beehive Pas EC3 12 H2
Beehive Pl SW9 85 G1
Beeston Pl SW1 19 J4
Beethoven St W10 39 G2
Begbie Rd SE3 77 F4
Begonia Cl E6 50 A4
Beira St SW12 84 B5

Belfont Wk N7 29 E1
Belford Gro SE18 64 C5
Belfort Rd SE15 74 A5
Belgrade Rd N16 31 D1
Belgrave Gdns NW8 26 C5
Belgrave Ms N SW1 19 F2
Belgrave Ms S SW1 19 G3
Belgrave Ms W SW1 19 F3
Belgrave Pl SW1 19 G3
Belgrave Rd E13 49 F3
Belgrave Rd E11 20 A6
Belgrave Rd SW1 66 B3
Belgrave Rd SW13 66 B3
Belgrave Sq SW1 19 F3
Belgrave St E1 46 B5
Belgrave Yd SW1 19 H4
Belgravia Ho SW4 85 D4
Belgrove St WC1 9 E1
Belinda Rd SW9 86 A1
Belitha Vil N1 29 F4
Bellamy St SW12 84 B5
Bell Dr SW18 81 G5
Bellefields Rd SW9 85 F1
Belleville Rd SW11 83 F3
Bellenden Rd SE15 73 E5
Bellevue Pl E1 46 A3
Bellevue Rd SW13 66 C5
Bell Inn Yd EC3 17 G2
Bell La E1 45 E4
Bell La E16 62 D2
Bello Cl SE24 86 A5
Bellot St SE10 76 B1
Bells All SW6 68 B5
Bell St NW1 6 B5
Bell St SE18 78 A4
Bell Water Gate SE18 64 C4
Bell Wf La EC4 16 E2
Bellwood Rd SE15 88 B2
Bell Yd WC2 15 J1
Bell Yd Ms SE1 23 J2
Belmont Cl SW4 84 C1
Belmont Gro SE13 90 A1
Belmont Hill SE13 90 A1
Belmont Ms SW19 80 A2
Belmont Pk Cl SE13 90 A2
Belmont Rd SW4 84 C1
Belmont St NW1 28 A4
Belmore La N7 29 D2
Belmore St SW8 70 D4
Beloe Cl SW11 80 C1
Belsham St E9 32 A3
Belsize Av NW3 27 E2
Belsize Cres NW3 27 E2
Belsize Gro NW3 27 F3
Belsize La NW3 27 E3
Belsize Pk NW3 27 E3
Belsize Pk Gdns NW3 27 F3
Belsize Pk Ms NW3 27 E3
Belsize Rd NW6 26 C5
Belsize Sq NW3 27 E3
Belsize Ter NW3 27 E3
Belson Rd SE18 64 B5
Belthorn Cres SW12 84 C5
Belton Rd E7 35 E4
Belton Rd E11 34 B1
Belton Rd NW2 24 C3
Belton Way E3 47 E4
Beltran Rd SW6 68 C5
Belvedere, The SW10 69 D5
Belvedere Bldgs SE1 22 C2
Belvedere Ms SE15 88 A1
Belvedere Pl SE1 22 C2
Belvedere Rd SE1 21 H1
Belvoir Rd SE22 87 F5
Bembridge Cl NW6 25 G4
Bemerton Est N1 29 E4
Bemerton St N1 29 F5
Bemish Rd SW15 81 F1
Benbow Rd W6 53 D4
Benbow St SE8 75 E2
Bendall Ms NW1 6 C5
Bendemeer Rd SW15 81 F1
Bendish Pt SE28 65 E3

Bendish Rd E6 36 A4
Bendon Valley SW18 82 C5
Benedict Rd SW9 85 F1
Bengal Rd, Ilf. 36 D1
Bengeworth Rd SE5 86 B1
Benham St SW11 83 E1
Benhill Rd SE5 72 C3
Benin St SE13 90 A5
Benjamin Cl E8 31 F5
Benjamin Ms SW12 84 C5
Benjamin St EC1 10 B5
Ben Jonson Rd E1 46 C4
Benledi Rd E14 48 A5
Bennelong Cl W12 53 D1
Bennerley Rd SW11 83 F3
Bennet's Hill EC4 16 C3
Bennet St SW1 14 A5
Bennett Gro SE13 75 F4
Bennett Pk SE3 90 C1
Bennett Rd E13 49 F3
Bennett Rd N16 30 D1
Bennett St W4 66 A2
Bennetts Yd SW1 20 D4
Benn St E9 32 C3
Bensbury Cl SW15 81 D5
Benson Av E6 49 F1
Bentham Rd E9 32 B3
Bentinck Ms W1 13 G1
Bentinck St W1 13 G1
Bentworth Rd W12 38 D5
Benwell Rd N7 29 G1
Benworth St E3 47 D2
Berber Rd SW11 83 G3
Berens Rd NW10 39 F2
Beresford Rd N5 30 B2
Beresford Sq SE18 64 D5
Beresford St SE18 64 D4
Beresford Ter N5 30 B2
Berestede Rd W6 66 B1
Berger Rd E9 32 B3
Bering Wk E16 49 G5
Berisford Ms SW18 82 C4
Berkeley Ho E3 47 D3
Berkeley Ms W1 13 E1
Berkeley Rd E12 36 A2
Berkeley Rd SW13 66 C4
Berkeley Sq W1 13 J4
Berkeley St W1 13 J4
Berkley Ms NW1 27 G4
Berkley Rd NW1 27 G4
Berkshire Rd E9 33 D3
Bermans Way NW10 24 A1
Bermondsey Sq SE1 23 J3
Bermondsey St SE1 17 H6
Bermondsey Wall E SE16 59 F3
Bermondsey Wall W SE16 59 F3
Bernard Ashley Dr SE7 77 E1
Bernard Cassidy St E16 48 C4
Bernard St WC1 9 E4
Bernays Gro SW9 85 F2
Bernersmede SE3 90 D1
Berners Ms W1 8 B6
Berners Pl W1 14 B1
Berners Rd N1 43 G1
Berners St W1 8 B6
Bernhardt Cres NW8 6 B3
Berryfield Rd SE17 72 A1
Berryhill SE9 92 D2
Berryhill Gdns SE9 92 D2
Berry Pl EC1 10 C2
Berry St EC1 10 C3
Berthon St SE8 75 E3
Bertie Rd NW10 24 C3
Bertrand St SE13 89 F1
Berwick Cres, Sid. 93 G4
Berwick Rd E16 49 E5
Berwick Rd N22 14 C2
Beryl Av E6 50 A4
Beryl Rd W6 67 F1
Besant Rd NW2 25 G1

Bessborough Gdns SW1 71 D1
Bessborough Pl SW1 70 D1
Bessborough St SW1 70 D1
Bessemer Pl SE10 62 C4
Bessemer Rd SE5 72 B5
Bessie Lansbury Cl E6 50 C5
Besson St SE14 74 A4
Bestwood St SE8 60 B5
Bethell Av E16 48 C3
Bethnal Grn Rd E1 45 E3
Bethnal Grn Rd E2 45 E3
Bethune Rd N16 72 A3
Bethwin Rd SE5 72 A3
Betterton St WC2 15 E2
Bettons Pk E15 34 B5
Bettridge Rd SW6 68 A5
Bevan St N1 30 B5
Bevenden St N1 11 G1
Beveridge Rd NW10 24 A4
Beverley Cl SW13 66 B5
Beverley Ct SE4 89 D1
Beverley Gdns SW13 80 B1
Beverley Path SW13 66 B5
Beverley Rd E6 49 G2
Beverley Rd SW13 80 B1
Beverley Rd W4 66 B1
Beverly NW8 6 B2
Beverstone Rd SW2 85 F3
Beverston Ms W1 6 D6
Bevin Ct WC1 9 H1
Bevington Rd W10 39 G4
Bevington St SE16 59 F3
Bevin Way WC1 9 J1
Bevis Marks EC3 17 J1
Bewdley St N1 29 G4
Bewick Ms SE15 73 G3
Bewick St SW8 70 B5
Bexhill Rd SE4 88 D5
Bexley Rd SE9 92 D3
Bianca Rd SE15 73 E2
Bibury Cl SE15 73 D2
Bickenhall St W1 6 E5
Bicknell Rd SE5 86 B1
Bicycle Ms SW4 84 D1
Bidborough St WC1 8 E2
Bidder St E16 48 B4
Biddestone Rd N7 29 F1
Biddulph Rd W9 40 C2
Bidwell St SE15 73 G4
Biggerstaff Rd E15 33 G5
Bigland St E1 45 G5
Bignell Rd SE18 78 D1
Bignold Rd E7 35 D1
Billingford Cl SE4 88 B2
Billing Pl SW10 68 C3
Billing Rd SW10 68 C3
Billingsgate Mkt E14 61 F2
Billington Rd SE14 74 B3
Billiter Sq EC3 17 J3
Billiter St EC3 17 J2
Billson St E14 61 G5
Bina Gdns SW5 54 D5
Binden Rd W12 52 B4
Binfield Rd SW4 71 E4
Bingfield St N1 29 E5
Bingham Pl W1 7 G5
Bingham St N1 30 C3
Bingley Rd E16 49 F5
Binney St W1 13 G3
Binns Rd W4 66 A1
Birch Cl E16 48 B4
Birchdale Rd E7 35 F2
Birches, The SE7 77 E2
Birchfield St E14 61 E1
Birch Gro SE12 90 C5
Birchington Rd NW6 26 B5
Birchin La EC3 17 G2
Birchlands Av SW12 83 G5
Birchmere Row SE3 76 C5
Birdbrook Rd SE3 91 F1
Birdcage Wk SW1 20 B2
Birdhurst Rd SW18 82 D2

Bird in Bush Rd SE15 73 F3
Birdsfield La E3 32 D5
Bird St W1 13 G2
Birdwood Av SE13 90 A4
Birkbeck Rd E8 31 E2
Birkbeck St E2 45 G2
Birkenhead St WC1 9 F1
Birkwood Cl SW12 85 D5
Birley St SW11 70 A5
Birrell Ho SW9 71 F5
Birse Cres NW10 24 A1
Biscay Rd W6 67 F1
Biscoe Way SE13 90 A1
Bishop Kings Rd W14 53 G5
Bishop's Av E3 33 G5
Bishop's Av SW6 67 F5
Bishop's Br Rd W2 41 D5
Bishops Br Rd W2 40 C5
Bishop's Ct EC4 16 B1
Bishop's Ct WC2 15 J1
Bishopsgate EC2 17 H2
Bishopsgate EC2 11 J6
Bishopsgate Chyd EC2 11 H6
Bishop's Pk SW6 67 F5
Bishop's Pk Rd SW6 67 F5
Bishops Rd SW6 67 F5
Bishops Rd SW11 69 F3
Bishops Sq E1 11 J5
Bishops Ter SE11 22 A5
Bishop St N1 30 B5
Bishops Way E2 45 G1
Bisson Rd E15 47 G1
Bittern St SE1 22 D2
Blackall St EC2 11 H3
Blackburne's Ms W1 13 F3
Blackburn Rd NW6 26 C3
Blackett St SW15 81 F1
Blackfen Rd, Sid. 93 G3
Blackfriars Br EC4 16 B3
Blackfriars Br SE1 16 B3
Blackfriars Ct EC4 16 B3
Blackfriars Pas EC4 16 B3
Blackfriars Rd SE1 22 B2
Blackheath Av SE10 76 A3
Blackheath Gro SE3 76 C5
Blackheath Hill SE10 75 G4
Blackheath Pk SE3 90 C1
Blackheath Ri SE13 75 G5
Blackheath Ri SE10 75 F4
Blackheath Vale SE3 76 B5
Blackheath Village SE3 76 C5
Black Horse Ct SE1 23 H3
Blackhorse Rd SE8 74 C1
Blacklands Ter SW3 18 D6
Black Lion La W6 52 C5
Blackpool Rd SE15 73 G5
Black Prince Rd SE1 21 G6
Black Prince Rd SE11 21 H6
Blackstone Est E8 31 F1
Blackstone Rd NW2 25 E2
Black Swan Yd SE1 23 H2
Blackthorn Rd, Ilf. 37 F2
Blackthorn St E3 47 E3
Blacktree Ms SW9 85 G1
Blackwall La SE10 76 B1
Blackwall Pier E14 62 B1
Blackwall Trd Est E14 48 A4
Blackwall Tunnel E14 62 A2
Blackwall Tunnel App SE10 62 B3
Blackwall Tunnel Northern App E3 47 E1
Blackwall Tunnel Northern App E14 47 E1
Blackwall Way E14 61 G1
Blackwater Cl E7 34 C1
Blackwater St SE22 87 E3
Blackwell Cl E5 32 B5
Blackwood St SE17 72 C1
Blagdon Rd SE13 89 G4
Blagrove Rd W10 39 G4
Blair Cl N1 30 B3
Blair Cl, Sid. 93 G3

Blair St E14 47 G5
Blake Av, Bark. 37 G5
Blake Cl W10 39 E4
Blake Cl, Well. 79 G4
Blake Gdns SW6 68 C3
Blake Rd E16 48 C3
Blaker Rd E15 33 G5
Blakes La SE15 73 D3
Blanchard Way E8 31 F3
Blanchedowne SE5 86 C2
Blanche St E16 48 C3
Blandfield Rd SW12 84 A4
Blandford Rd W4 52 A4
Blandford Sq NW1 6 C4
Blandford St W1 13 E1
Bland St SE9 78 A1
Blaney Cres E6 50 D2
Blann Cl SE9 91 G4
Blantyre St SW10 69 E3
Blashford NW3 27 G4
Blashford St SE13 90 A5
Blasker Wk E14 75 E1
Bledlow Cl NW8 6 A4
Bleeding Heart Yd EC1 10 A6
Blendon Ter SE18 79 E1
Blenheim Cres W11 39 G5
Blenheim Gdns NW2 25 E2
Blenheim Gdns SW2 85 F4
Blenheim Gro SE15 73 F5
Blenheim Rd E6 49 G2
Blenheim Rd E15 34 B1
Blenheim Rd NW8 41 D1
Blenheim Rd SW20 94 C4
Blenheim Rd W4 52 A4
Blenheim St W1 13 H2
Blenheim Ter NW8 40 D1
Blenkarne Rd SW11 83 G4
Blessington Cl SE13 90 A1
Blessington Rd SE13 90 A1
Bletchley Ct N1 44 C1
Bletchley St N1 44 B1
Bliss Cres SE13 75 F5
Blissett St SE10 75 G4
Blithfield St W8 54 C4
Bloemfontein Av W12 52 D1
Bloemfontein Rd W12 52 D1
Blomfield Rd W9 41 D4
Blomfield St EC2 11 G6
Blomfield Vil W2 40 C4
Blondel St SW11 70 A5
Blondin St E3 47 E1
Bloomburg St SW1 20 B6
Bloomfield Pl W1 13 J3
Bloomfield Rd SE18 79 D1
Bloomfield Ter SW1 70 A1
Bloom Pk Rd SW6 68 A3
Bloomsbury Ct WC1 9 F6
Bloomsbury Ms WC4 85 D4
Bloomsbury Pl WC1 9 F5
Bloomsbury Sq WC1 9 F6
Bloomsbury St WC1 8 D6
Bloomsbury Way WC1 15 E1
Blore Ct W1 14 C2
Blossom St E1 11 J5
Blount St E14 46 C5
Bloxam Gdns SE9 92 A3
Blucher Rd SE5 72 B5
Blue Anchor La SE16 59 F5
Blue Anchor Yd E1 59 F1
Blue Ball Yd SW1 14 A6
Bluebell Av E12 35 G2
Bluebell Way, Ilf. 36 D3
Bluebird Way SE28 65 F3
Bluelion Pl SE1 23 H3
Blundell St N7 29 E4
Blunts Rd SE9 92 C3
Blurton Rd E5 32 A1
Blythe Cl SE6 88 D5
Blythe Hill SE6 88 D5
Blythe Hill La SE6 88 D5
Blythe Rd W14 53 F4
Blythe St E2 45 G2
Boardwalk Pl E14 61 G2
Boathouse Wk SE15 73 E3
Bobbin Cl SW4 84 C1

Bocking St E8 31 G5
Bodney Rd E8 31 G2
Bohemia Pl E8 31 G3
Bohn Rd E1 46 C4
Boileau Rd SW13 66 C3
Bolden St SE8 75 F5
Boleyn Rd E6 49 G1
Boleyn Rd E7 35 D4
Boleyn Rd N16 31 D2
Bolina Rd SE16 74 A1
Bolingbroke Gro SW11 83 F2
Bolingbroke Rd W14 53 F4
Bolingbroke Wk SW11 69 E3
Bolney Gate SW7 18 B2
Bolney St SW8 71 F3
Bolsover St W1 7 J4
Bolt Ct EC4 16 A2
Bolton Cres SE5 72 A2
Bolton Gdns NW10 39 F1
Bolton Gdns SW5 68 C1
Bolton Gdns Ms SW5 68 C1
Bolton Rd E15 34 C3
Bolton Rd NW8 26 C5
Bolton Rd NW10 24 A5
Boltons, The SW10 68 D1
Boltons Pl SW5 68 D1
Bolton St W1 13 J5
Bombay St SE16 59 G5
Bomore Rd W11 53 F1
Bonar Rd SE15 73 F3
Bonchurch Rd W10 39 G4
Bond Ct EC4 17 F2
Bond St E15 34 B2
Bond St W4 52 A5
Bondway SW8 71 E2
Boneta Rd SE18 64 B4
Bonfield Rd SE13 89 G2
Bonham Rd SW2 85 F3
Bonhill St EC2 11 G4
Bonita Ms SE4 88 B1
Bonner Rd E2 46 A1
Bonner St E2 46 A1
Bonneville Gdns SW4 84 C4
Bonnington Sq SW8 71 F2
Bonny St NW1 28 C4
Bonsor St SE5 72 D3
Book Ms WC2 14 D2
Boones Rd SE13 90 B2
Boone St SE13 90 B2
Booth La EC4 16 D3
Booth's Pl W1 8 B6
Boot St N1 11 H2
Bordon Wk SW15 80 C5
Boreham Av E16 48 D5
Borgard Rd SE18 64 B5
Borland Rd SE15 88 A2
Borneo St SW15 81 E1
Borough High St SE1 22 D2
Borough Rd SE1 22 B3
Borough Sq SE1 22 D2
Borrodaile Rd SW18 82 C4
Borthwick Rd E15 34 B1
Borthwick St SE8 75 E1
Boscobel Pl SW1 19 G5
Boscobel St NW8 6 A4
Boscombe Cl E5 32 C2
Boscombe Rd W12 52 C2
Boston Gdns W4 66 A2
Boston Rd E6 50 A4
Boston Rd E6 50 A4
Boswell Ct WC1 9 F5
Boswell St WC1 9 F5
Bosworth Rd W10 39 G3
Botha Rd E13 49 E4
Bothwell Cl E16 48 C4
Botolph All EC3 17 H3
Botolph La EC3 17 G4
Boughton Rd SE28 65 G4
Boulcott St E1 46 B5
Boulevard, The SW6 69 D4
Boultwood Rd E6 50 A5
Boundary La E13 49 G2
Boundary La SE17 72 B2

Boundary Rd E13 49 F1
Boundary Rd NW8 26 C5
Boundary Rd, Bark. 51 E1
Boundary Rd, Sid. 93 G3
Boundary Row SE1 22 B1
Boundary St E2 45 E3
Bourchier St W1 14 C3
Bourdon Pl W1 13 J3
Bourdon St W1 13 J3
Bourke Cl NW10 24 A3
Bourke Cl SW4 85 E4
Bourlet Cl W1 8 A6
Bournbrook Rd SE3 91 G1
Bourne Est EC1 9 J5
Bourne St SW1 19 F6
Bourne Ter W2 40 C4
Bournville Rd SE6 89 E5
Bousfield Rd SE14 74 B5
Boutflower Rd SW11 83 F2
Bouverie Pl W2 12 A1
Bouverie Rd EC4 16 A2
Bouverie St EC4 16 A2
Boveney Rd SE23 88 B5
Bovill Rd SE23 88 B5
Bovingdon Rd SW6 68 C4
Bowater Cl SW2 85 E4
Bowater Pl SE3 77 E3
Bowater Rd SE18 63 G4
Bow Back Rivers Wk E15 33 F4
Bow Br Est E3 47 F2
Bow Chyd EC4 16 E2
Bow Common La E3 46 D3
Bowden St SE11 71 G1
Bowditch SE8 74 D1
Bowen St E14 47 F5
Bower Av SE10 76 B4
Bowerdean St SW6 68 C4
Bowerman Av SE14 74 C2
Bower St E1 46 B5
Bowers Wk E6 50 A5
Bowes Rd W3 52 A1
Bowfell Rd W6 67 E2
Bowhill Cl SW9 71 G3
Bowie Cl SW4 85 D5
Bow Ind Est E15 33 E4
Bowland Rd SW4 85 D2
Bowland Yd SW1 19 E2
Bow La EC4 16 E2
Bowl Ct EC2 11 J4
Bowling Grn Cl SW15 81 D5
Bowling Grn La EC1 10 A3
Bowling Grn Pl SE1 23 F1
Bowling Grn St SE11 71 G2
Bowling Grn Wk N1 11 H1
Bowman Av E16 62 C1
Bowmans Lea SE23 88 A5
Bowman's Ms N7 29 E5
Bowood Rd SW11 84 A2
Bow Rd E3 47 D2
Bowsprit Pl E14 61 E4
Bow St E15 34 B2
Bow St WC2 15 F2
Bowyer Cl E6 50 B4
Bowyer Pl SE5 72 C3
Bowyer St SE5 72 B3
Boxall Rd SE21 86 D4
Boxley St E16 63 E2
Boyard Rd SE18 78 D1
Boyce St SE1 15 H6
Boydell Ct NW8 27 E1
Boyd St E1 45 F5
Boyd Way SE3 91 F2
Boyfield St SE1 22 C2
Boyle St W1 14 A3
Boyne Rd SE13 89 G1
Boyne Ter Ms W11 54 A2
Boyson Rd SE17 72 C2
Brabant Ct EC3 17 H3
Brabazon St E14 47 F5
Braburn Gro SE15 74 A5
Bracewell Rd W10 39 E4
Bracken Av SW12 84 A4

Entry	Ref
Brackenbury Gdns W6	53 D4
Brackenbury Rd W6	53 D4
Bracken Cl E6	50 B4
Bracken Gdns SW13	66 C5
Brackley Av SE15	87 G1
Brackley Rd W4	66 A1
Brackley St EC1	10 D5
Brackley Ter W4	66 A1
Bracklyn St N1	7 G1
Bracknell Gdns NW3	26 C1
Bracknell Gate NW3	26 C1
Bracknell Way NW3	26 C1
Bradbourne St SW6	68 B5
Bradbury St N16	31 D2
Braddyll St SE10	76 B1
Bradenham Cl SE17	72 C2
Bradfield Rd E16	63 D3
Bradgate Rd SE6	89 E4
Brading Rd SW2	85 F5
Brading Ter W12	52 D4
Bradiston Rd W9	40 A2
Bradley Stone Rd E6	50 B4
Bradmead SW8	70 B3
Bradmore Pk Rd W6	53 D4
Bradstock Rd E9	32 B3
Brad St SE1	16 A6
Bradwell St E1	46 B2
Bradymead E6	50 C5
Brady St E1	45 G3
Braemar Av E13	48 C3
Braes St N1	30 A4
Braganza St SE17	72 A1
Braham St E1	45 E5
Braid Av W3	38 A5
Braidwood St SE1	17 H6
Brailsford Rd SW2	85 G3
Braintree St E2	46 A2
Braithwaite Ho EC1	11 E3
Braithwaite Twr W2	41 E4
Braman Grn SW9	71 G4
Bramah Rd SW9	71 G4
Bramber Rd W14	68 A2
Bramblebury Rd SE18	79 E1
Bramble Gdns W12	52 B1
Bramcote Gro SE16	74 A1
Bramcote Rd SW15	81 D2
Bramerton St SW3	69 F2
Bramfield Rd SW11	83 F4
Bramford Rd SW18	82 D2
Bramham Gdns SW5	68 C1
Bramhope La SE7	77 E2
Bramlands Cl SW11	83 F1
Bramley Rd W10	53 F1
Brampton Rd E6	49 G2
Bramshaw Rd E9	32 B3
Bramshill Rd NW10	38 B1
Bramshot Av SE7	77 D2
Bramston Rd NW10	38 C1
Bramwell Ms N1	29 F5
Brancaster Rd E12	36 B1
Branch Pl N1	30 C5
Branch Rd E14	60 C1
Branch St SE15	73 D3
Brandlehow Rd SW15	82 A2
Brandon Est SE17	72 A2
Brandon Rd N7	29 E4
Brandon St SE17	22 D6
Brandram Ms SE13	90 B1
Brandram Rd SE13	90 B1
Brandreth Rd E6	50 B5
Brand St SE10	75 G3
Brangton Rd SE11	71 F1
Branksea St SW6	67 E3
Branksome Rd SW2	85 E3
Branscombe St SE13	89 F1
Brantwood Rd SE24	86 B3
Brasenose Dr SW13	67 E2
Brassett Pl E15	34 B5
Brassey Rd NW6	26 A3
Brassey Sq SW11	84 A1
Brassie Av W3	38 A5
Brathway Rd SW18	82 B5
Bravington Rd W9	40 A1
Braxfield Rd SE4	88 C2
Bray NW3	27 F4
Brayards Rd SE15	73 G5
Braybrook St W12	38 B4
Brayburne Av SW4	70 C5
Bray Dr E16	62 C1
Bray Pas E16	62 D1
Bray Pl SW3	18 D6
Braywood Rd SE9	93 F2
Bread St EC4	15 F2
Breakspears Rd SE4	89 D1
Bream Gdns E6	50 C2
Bream's Bldgs EC4	15 J1
Bream St E3	33 E4
Breasley Cl SW15	81 D2
Brecknock Rd N7	28 C1
Brecknock Rd N19	28 C1
Brecknock Rd Est N19	28 C1
Brecon Rd W6	67 G2
Brecon Cl E6	50 C2
Bredgar SE13	89 G3
Bredinghurst SE22	87 F5
Breer St SW6	82 C1
Bremner Rd SW7	55 D3
Brenchley Gdns SE23	88 A4
Brendon Av NW10	24 A1
Brendon St W1	12 C1
Brenley Gdns SE9	91 G2
Brenthouse Rd E9	32 A3
Brenthurst Rd NW10	24 B2
Brenton St E14	46 C5
Brent Rd E16	49 D4
Brent Rd SE18	78 D3
Bressenden Pl SW1	19 J3
Brett Rd E8	31 G2
Brewer's Grn SW1	20 C3
Brewers Hall Gdns EC2	11 E6
Brewer St W1	14 B3
Brewery Rd N7	29 E4
Brewery Rd SE18	79 F1
Brewery Sq EC1	10 B3
Brewhouse La E1	59 G2
Brewhouse La SW15	81 G1
Brewhouse Rd SE18	64 B5
Brewhouse Wk SE16	60 C2
Brewhouse Yd EC1	10 C3
Brewster Gdns W10	39 E4
Brewster Ho E14	61 D1
Briant Est SE1	21 J4
Briant Ho SE1	21 H4
Briant St SE14	74 B4
Briar Rd NW2	25 E1
Briar Wk SW15	81 D2
Briarwood Rd SW4	84 D3
Brick Ct EC4	15 J2
Brick La E1	45 E4
Brick La E2	45 E2
Bricklayer's Arms Distribution Cen SE1	23 J6
Bricklayer's Arms Rbt SE1	23 F5
Brick St W1	13 H5
Bride Ct EC4	16 B2
Bride La EC4	16 B2
Bride St N7	29 F3
Bridewain St SE1	59 E4
Bridewell Pl EC4	16 B2
Bridford Ms W1	7 J5
Bridge App NW1	28 A4
Bridge Av W6	67 E1
Bridgefoot SE1	71 E1
Bridgeland Rd E16	63 D1
Bridgeman Rd N1	29 F4
Bridgeman St NW8	41 F1
Bridge Meadows SE14	74 B2
Bridgend Rd SW18	82 D2
Bridge Pk SW18	82 B3
Bridge Pl SW1	19 J5
Bridge Rd E6	36 B4
Bridge Rd E15	34 A4
Bridge Rd NW10	24 A3
Bridges Ct SW11	83 E1
Bridges Pl SW6	68 A4
Bridges Pl SW6	21 E2
Bridge Vw W6	67 E1
Bridgewater Sq EC2	10 D5
Bridgewater St EC2	10 D5
Bridgeway St NW1	42 C1
Bridge Yd SE1	17 G5
Bridgwater Rd E15	33 G5
Bridle La W1	14 B3
Bridport Pl N1	44 C1
Brief St SE5	72 A4
Brierley Rd E11	34 A1
Brightfield Rd SE12	90 C3
Brightling Rd SE4	89 D4
Brightlingsea Pl E14	60 D1
Brighton Rd E6	50 C2
Brighton Rd N16	31 D1
Brighton Ter SW9	85 F2
Bright St E14	47 F5
Brill Pl NW1	43 D1
Brindley St SE14	74 D4
Brinklow Cres SE18	79 D3
Brinklow Ho W2	40 C4
Brinkworth Way E9	33 D3
Brinton Wk SE1	16 B6
Brion Pl E14	47 G4
Brisbane St SE5	72 C3
Briset Rd SE9	91 G1
Briset St EC1	10 C5
Bristol Gdns W9	40 C3
Bristol Rd E7	35 F3
Britannia Gate E16	63 D2
Britannia Rd E14	61 E5
Britannia Rd SW6	68 C3
Britannia Row N1	30 A5
Britannia St WC1	9 G1
Britannia Wk N1	11 F1
British Gro W4	66 B1
British Gro Pas W4	66 B1
British St E3	47 D2
Brittany Pk SE11	21 J6
Britten St SW3	69 F1
Britton St EC1	10 B4
Brixham Gdns, Ilf.	37 G2
Brixham St E16	64 B2
Brixton Hill SW2	85 E5
Brixton Oval SW2	85 G2
Brixton Rd SW9	71 G5
Brixton Sta Rd SW9	85 F3
Brixton Water La SW2	85 F3
Broadbent St W1	13 H3
Broadbridge Cl SE3	76 D3
Broad Ct WC2	15 F2
Broadfield La NW1	29 E4
Broadfield Rd SE6	90 B5
Broadfields Way NW10	24 B2
Broadgate E13	49 F1
Broadgate EC2	11 H5
Broadgate Circle EC2	11 H5
Broadgate Rd E16	49 G5
Broadhinton Rd SW4	84 B1
Broadhurst Gdns NW6	26 C3
Broad La EC2	11 H5
Broadley St NW8	6 A5
Broadley Ter NW1	6 C4
Broad Sanctuary SW1	20 D2
Broadstone Pl W1	7 F6
Broad St Av EC2	11 H6
Broad St Pl EC2	11 G6
Broad Wk NW1	7 H2
Broad Wk SE3	91 F1
Broad Wk W1	13 F5
Broad Wk, The W8	54 D2
Broadwalk Ct W8	54 B2
Broadwall SE1	16 A5
Broadwater Rd SE28	65 F4
Broadway E15	34 A4
Broadway SW1	20 C3
Broadway, Bark.	37 E5
Broadway, The E13	49 E1
Broadway Mkt E8	31 G5
Broadwick St W1	14 B3
Broad Yd EC1	10 B4
Brockenhurst Gdns, Ilf.	37 F1
Brockham St SE1	22 E3
Brockill Cres SE4	88 C2
Brocklebank Rd SE7	63 E5
Brocklebank Rd SW18	82 D5
Brocklehurst St SE14	74 B3
Brockley Footpath SE15	88 A2
Brockley Gdns SE4	75 D5
Brockley Gro SE4	88 D3
Brockley Hall Rd SE4	88 C4
Brockley Ms SE4	88 C3
Brockley Pk SE23	88 C5
Brockley Ri SE23	88 C4
Brockley Rd SE4	88 D1
Brockley Vw SE23	88 C5
Brockley Way SE4	88 B3
Brock Pl E3	47 F3
Brock Rd E13	49 E4
Brockwell Pk Gdns SE24	85 G5
Brockwell Pk Row SW2	85 G4
Brodlove La E1	60 B1
Broken Wf EC4	16 D3
Brokesley St E3	47 D3
Broke Wk E8	31 F5
Bromar Rd SE5	87 D1
Bromell's Rd SW4	84 C2
Brome Rd SE9	92 B1
Bromfield Rd SW4	85 D1
Bromfelde Vw SW4	71 D5
Bromfield St N1	43 G1
Bromley Hall Rd E14	47 G4
Bromley High St E3	47 F2
Bromley Pl W1	8 A5
Bromley St E1	46 B4
Brompton Arc SW3	18 D2
Brompton Pk Cres SW6	68 C2
Brompton Pl SW3	18 C3
Brompton Rd SW1	18 C3
Brompton Rd SW3	18 B5
Brompton Rd SW7	18 C3
Brompton Sq SW3	18 B3
Bromyard Av W3	52 A2
Bromyard Ho SE15	73 G3
Bromyard Ho W3	52 A2
Brondesbury Ct NW2	25 E3
Brondesbury Pk NW2	25 D4
Brondesbury Pk NW6	25 F4
Brondesbury Rd NW6	40 A1
Brondesbury Vil NW6	40 A1
Bronsart Rd SW6	67 G4
Bronte Ho NW6	40 B2
Bronti Cl SE17	72 B1
Bronze St SE8	75 E3
Brookbank Rd SE13	89 E1
Brookdale Rd SE6	89 F4
Brook Dr SE11	22 A4
Brooke's Ct EC1	9 J5
Brookes Mkt EC1	10 A5
Brooke St EC1	9 J6
Brookfield Rd E9	32 C3
Brook Gdns SW13	80 B1
Brook Gate W1	13 F4
Brook Grn W6	53 F5
Brookhill Cl SE18	78 D1
Brookhill Rd SE18	78 D1
Brooking Rd E7	35 D2
Brooklands Pk SE3	90 D1
Brook La SE3	77 E5
Brookmill Rd SE8	75 E4
Brooks Av E6	50 B3
Brooksbank St E9	32 A3
Brooksby St N1	29 F4
Brooksby's Wk E9	32 B2
Brook's Ms W1	13 H3
Brooks Rd E13	34 D5
Brook St W1	13 G3
Brook St W2	12 A3
Brooksville Av NW6	25 G5
Brookville Rd SW6	68 A3
Brookway SE3	90 D1
Brookwood Av SW13	80 B1
Broome Way SE5	72 C3
Broomfield St E14	47 E4
Broomgrove Rd SW9	71 F5

Broomhill Rd SW18 82 B3
Broomhouse La SW6 68 B5
Broomhouse Rd SW6 68 B5
Broomsleigh St NW6 26 A2
Broomwood Rd SW11 83 G4
Brougham Rd E8 31 F5
Brougham St SW11 69 G5
Broughton Dr SW9 85 G2
Broughton Rd SW6 68 B5
Broughton St SW8 70 A5
Brownfield St E14 47 E5
Brown Hart Gdns W1 13 G3
Brownhill Rd SE6 79 G4
Browning Ms W1 7 H6
Browning Rd E12 36 B3
Browning St SE17 72 B1
Brownlow Ms WC1 9 H4
Brownlow Rd E8 31 E5
Brownlow Rd NW10 24 A4
Brownlow St WC1 9 H6
Brown's Bldgs EC3 17 H3
Browns La NW5 28 B2
Brown St W1 12 D1
Broxash Rd SW11 84 A4
Broxwood Way NW8 27 F5
Bruce Rd E3 33 G1
Bruckner St W10 40 A2
Bruford St E8 75 E2
Brune St E1 45 E4
Brunswick Ct SE1 23 J2
Brunswick Gdns W8 55 G3
Brunswick Ms W1 12 E1
Brunswick Pk SE5 72 C4
Brunswick Pl N1 11 G2
Brunswick Pl NW1 7 G3
Brunswick Quay SE16 60 B4
Brunswick Shop Cen WC1 9 F4
Brunswick Sq WC1 9 F4
Brunswick Vil SE5 72 D4
Brunton Pl E14 46 C5
Brushfield St E1 11 J5
Brussels Rd SW11 83 E2
Bruton La W1 13 J4
Bruton Pl W1 13 J4
Bruton St W1 13 J4
Bryan Av NW10 25 D4
Bryan Rd SE16 60 D3
Bryanston Ms E W1 6 D6
Bryanston Ms W W1 6 D6
Bryanston Pl W1 6 D6
Bryanston Sq W1 6 D6
Bryanston St W1 12 D2
Bryant Ct E2 45 E1
Bryant St E15 34 A4
Bryantwood Rd N7 29 G2
Brydges Pl WC2 14 E4
Brydges Rd E15 34 A2
Brymay Cl E3 47 E1
Brynmaer Rd SW11 69 G4
Bryony Rd W12 52 C1
Buchanan Gdns NW10 38 D1
Buchan Rd SE15 88 A1
Bucharest Rd SW18 82 D5
Buckfast St E2 45 F2
Buck Hill Wk W2 12 A4
Buckhold Rd SW18 82 B4
Buckhurst St E1 45 G3
Buckingham Arc WC2 15 F4
Buckingham Gate SW1 20 A2
Buckingham La SE23 88 C5
Buckingham Ms SW1 20 A3
Buckingham Palace Rd SW1 19 H6
Buckingham Pl SW1 20 A3
Buckingham Rd E15 34 C2
Buckingham Rd N1 30 D3
Buckingham Rd NW10 38 B1

Buckingham St WC2 15 F4
Buckland Cres NW3 27 F4
Buckland St N1 44 C1
Bucklebury NW1 8 A3
Buckler's All SW6 68 A2
Bucklersbury EC4 17 F2
Bucklersbury Pas EC4 17 F2
Buckley Cl SE23 87 G5
Buckley Rd NW6 26 A4
Buckley St SE1 15 J6
Buckmaster Rd SW11 83 F2
Bucknall St WC2 14 D1
Bucknell Cl SW2 85 F2
Buckner Rd SW2 85 F2
Buckstone Cl SE23 87 E4
Buck St NW1 28 B4
Buckters Rents SE16 60 C2
Buckthorne Rd SE4 88 C4
Budge Row EC4 17 F3
Budge's Wk W2 55 D1
Bugsby's Way SE7 63 G5
Bugsby's Way SE10 62 C5
Bulinga St SW1 20 D6
Bullace Row SE5 72 C3
Bullards Pl E2 46 B2
Bullen St SW11 69 F5
Buller Cl SE15 73 F3
Buller Rd, Bark 37 G4
Bullied Way SW1 19 J6
Bull Inn Ct WC2 15 F4
Bullivant St E14 61 G1
Bull Rd E15 48 C1
Bulls Gdns SW3 18 C5
Bull's Head Pas EC3 17 H2
Bulmer Pl W11 54 B2
Bulstrode Pl W1 7 G6
Bulstrode St W1 13 G1
Bulwer St W12 53 E2
Bunhill Row EC1 11 F3
Bunhouse Pl SW1 70 A1
Bunning Way N7 29 E4
Bunton St SE18 64 C4
Burbage Cl SE1 23 F4
Burbage Rd SE21 86 C4
Burcham St E14 47 F5
Burchell Rd SE15 73 D3
Burcher Gale Gro SE15 73 D3
Burder Cl N1 31 D3
Burdett Rd E3 46 D3
Burdett Rd E14 46 D3
Burdett St SE1 21 J3
Burford Rd E6 50 A2
Burford Rd E15 34 A4
Burges Ct E6 36 C4
Burges Gro SW13 67 D3
Burges Rd E6 36 A4
Burgess Business Pk SE5 72 C3
Burgess Hill NW2 26 B1
Burgess Rd E15 34 B1
Burgess St E14 47 E4
Burge St SE1 23 G4
Burghley Hall Cl SW19 81 G5
Burghley Rd NW5 28 B2
Burghley Twr W3 52 B1
Burgh St N1 44 A1
Burgon St EC4 16 C2
Burgos Gro SE10 75 F4
Burgoyne Rd SW9 85 F1
Burke Cl SW15 80 A2
Burke St E16 48 C5
Burland Rd SW11 83 G3
Burleigh Pl SW15 81 F3
Burleigh St WC2 15 G3
Burley Rd E16 49 F5
Burlington Arc W1 14 A4
Burlington Gdns W1 14 A4
Burlington La W4 66 A3
Burlington Ms SW15 82 A3
Burlington Rd SW6 67 G5

Burma Rd N16 30 C1
Burnaby St SW10 68 D3
Burne Jones Ho W14 54 A5
Burnels Av E6 50 C2
Burne St NW1 6 B5
Burnett Cl E9 32 A2
Burney St SE10 75 G3
Burnfoot Av SW6 67 G4
Burnham NW3 27 F4
Burnham St E2 46 A2
Burnley Rd NW10 24 C2
Burnley Rd SW9 71 F5
Burnsall St SW3 69 F1
Burnside Cl SE16 60 B2
Burns Rd NW10 24 B5
Burns Rd SW11 69 G5
Burnt Ash Hill SE12 90 C4
Burnt Ash Rd SE12 90 C3
Burnthwaite Rd SW6 68 B3
Burrage Gro SE18 65 E5
Burrage Pl SE18 79 D1
Burrage Rd SE18 79 E2
Burrard Rd E16 49 E5
Burrard Rd NW6 26 B2
Burr Cl E1 59 F2
Burrell St SE1 16 B5
Burrells Wf Sq E14 75 F1
Burrow Rd SE22 86 B2
Burrows Ms SE1 22 B1
Burrows Rd NW10 39 E2
Burrow Wk SE21 86 B5
Burr Rd SW18 82 B5
Burslem St E1 45 F5
Burstock Rd SW15 81 G2
Burston Rd SW15 81 F3
Burton La SW9 71 G5
Burton Ms SW1 19 G6
Burton Pl WC1 8 D2
Burton Rd NW6 26 A4
Burton Rd SW9 71 G5
Burton St WC1 8 D2
Burwash Ho SE1 23 G2
Burwash Rd SE18 79 F1
Burwell Wk E3 47 E3
Burwood Pl W2 12 C1
Bury Ct EC3 17 J1
Bury Pl WC1 9 E6
Bury St EC3 17 J2
Bury St SW1 14 B5
Bury Wk SW3 18 B6
Busby Pl NW5 28 D1
Bushbaby Cl SE1 23 H4
Bushberry Rd E9 32 C3
Bushey Hill Rd SE5 73 D4
Bushey Rd E13 49 F1
Bush La EC4 17 F3
Bushmoor Cres SE18 79 E3
Bush Rd E8 31 G5
Bush Rd SE8 60 B5
Bushwood Dr SE1 59 E5
Butcher Row E1 60 B1
Butcher Row E14 60 B1
Butchers Rd E16 48 D5
Bute Gdns W6 53 F5
Bute St SW7 55 E5
Butler Pl SW1 20 C3
Butler Rd NW10 24 B4
Butlers Wf SE1 59 E2
Butterfly La SE9 92 D4
Buttermere Cl SE1 34 A1
Buttermere Dr SW15 81 G3
Buttermere Wk E8 31 E3
Butterwick W6 53 E3
Buttesland St N1 11 G1
Buttmarsh Cl SE18 79 D1
Buttsbury Rd, Ilf. 37 E2
Buxhall Cres E9 32 D3
Buxted Rd E8 31 E4
Buxted Rd SE22 87 D2
Buxton Ct N1 10 E1
Buxton Ms SW4 71 D5
Buxton Rd E6 50 A2
Buxton Rd E15 34 B2

Buxton Rd NW2 25 D3
Buxton Rd N19 80 A1
Buxton St E1 45 E3
Byam St SW6 68 D5
Byfeld Gdns SW13 66 C4
Byfield Cl SE16 60 C3
Byford Cl E15 34 B4
Bygrove St E14 47 F5
Byng Pl WC1 8 C4
Byng St E14 61 E3
Byron Av E12 36 A3
Byron Cl E8 31 F5
Byron Ms NW3 27 F2
Bythorn St SW9 85 F1
Byward St EC3 17 J4
Bywater Pl SE16 60 C2
Bywater St SW3 69 G1
Bywell Pl W1 8 A6

C
Cabbell St NW1 6 B6
Cable St E1 59 F1
Cable Trade Pk SE7 63 F5
Cabot Pl E14 61 E2
Cabot Sq E14 61 E2
Cabul Rd SW11 69 F5
Cade Rd SE10 76 A4
Cader Rd SW18 82 D4
Cadet Dr SE1 59 F5
Cadet Pl SE10 76 B1
Cadiz St SE17 72 B1
Cadogan Cl E9 32 D3
Cadogan Gdns SW3 18 E5
Cadogan Gate SW1 18 E5
Cadogan La SW1 19 F4
Cadogan Pl SW1 19 E3
Cadogan Rd SE18 65 E4
Cadogan Sq SW1 18 E4
Cadogan St SW3 18 D6
Cadogan Ter E9 32 D3
Caedmon Rd N7 29 F1
Cahill St EC1 11 E4
Cahir St E14 61 F5
Caird St W10 39 G2
Cairns Rd SW11 83 F3
Caistor Pk Rd E15 34 C5
Caistor Rd SW12 84 B5
Caithness Rd W14 53 F5
Calabria Rd N5 30 A3
Calais St SE5 72 A4
Calbourne Rd SW12 83 G5
Caldecot Rd SE5 72 B5
Calderon Rd E11 33 G1
Caldervale Rd SW4 84 D3
Calderwood St SE18 64 C5
Caldwell St SW9 71 F3
Caleb St SE1 22 D1
Caledonia Rd N1 43 F1
Caledonian Rd N1 29 F2
Caledonian Wf E14 62 A5
Caledonia St N1 43 E1
Caledon Rd E6 36 A5
Cale St SW3 18 B6
Caletock Way SE10 76 C1
Calidore Cl SW2 85 F4
Callaghan Cl SE13 90 B2
Callcott Rd NW6 26 A4
Callendar Rd SW7 55 E4
Callow St SW3 69 E2
Calmington Rd SE5 73 D1
Calshot St N1 43 F1
Calthorpe St WC1 9 H3
Calton Av SE21 87 D3
Calvert Av E2 45 E1
Calverton SE5 72 D2
Calverton Rd E6 36 C5
Calvert Rd SE10 76 C1
Calvert's Bldgs SE1 17 F6
Calvin St E1 45 E3
Calydon Rd SE7 77 E1
Calypso Cres SE15 73 E3
Calypso Way SE16 60 D4
Cambalt Rd SW15 81 F3

Street	Ref
Cambert Way SE3	91 E2
Camberwell Ch St SE5	72 C4
Camberwell Glebe SE5	72 C4
Camberwell Grn SE5	72 C4
Camberwell Gro SE5	72 C4
Camberwell New Rd SE5	71 G3
Camberwell Rd SE5	72 B2
Camberwell Sta Rd SE5	72 B4
Camborne Rd SW18	82 B5
Cambria Rd SE5	86 B1
Cambria St SW6	68 C3
Cambridge Av NW6	40 B1
Cambridge Barracks Rd SE18	79 J4
Cambridge Circ WC2	14 D2
Cambridge Cres E2	45 G1
Cambridge Dr SE12	90 D3
Cambridge Gdns NW6	40 B1
Cambridge Gdns W10	39 G5
Cambridge Gate NW1	7 J2
Cambridge Gate Ms NW1	7 J2
Cambridge Gro W6	53 D5
Cambridge Heath Rd E1	45 G1
Cambridge Heath Rd E2	45 G1
Cambridge Pl W8	54 C3
Cambridge Rd NW6	40 B2
Cambridge Rd SW11	69 G4
Cambridge Rd SW13	66 B5
Cambridge Rd, Bark.	37 E4
Cambridge Row SE18	79 D1
Cambridge Sq W2	12 B1
Cambridge St SW1	19 J6
Cambridge Ter NW1	7 J2
Cambridge Ter Ms NW1	7 J2
Cambus Rd E16	49 D4
Camden High St NW1	28 B5
Camdenhurst St E14	46 C5
Camden Ms NW1	28 D3
Camden Pk Rd NW1	28 D3
Camden Pas N1	44 A1
Camden Rd N7	29 D2
Camden Rd NW1	28 C5
Camden Row SE3	76 B5
Camden Sq NW1	28 D3
Camden St NW1	28 B4
Camden Wk N1	30 A5
Camelot Cl SE28	65 F3
Camera Pl SW10	69 E2
Camilla Rd SE16	59 G5
Camlet St E2	45 E3
Camley St NW1	28 D4
Camomile St EC3	17 H1
Campana Rd SW6	68 B4
Campbell Gordon Way NW2	24 D1
Campbell Rd E3	47 E2
Campbell Rd E6	36 A5
Campden Gro W8	54 B3
Campden Hill W8	54 B3
Campden Hill Gdns W8	54 B2
Campden Hill Rd W8	54 B3
Campden Hill Sq W8	54 A2
Campden St W8	54 B2
Campfield Rd SE9	91 G5
Campion Cl E6	64 B1
Campion Rd SW15	81 E2
Camplin St SE14	74 B3
Campshill Rd SE13	89 G3
Cam Rd E15	34 A5
Canada Est SE16	60 A4
Canada Gdns SE13	89 G3
Canada Sq E14	61 F2
Canada St SE16	60 B3
Canada Way W12	53 D1
Canal App SE8	74 C2
Canal Boul NW1	28 D3
Canal Cl E1	46 C3
Canal Cl W10	39 F3
Canal Gro SE15	73 F2
Canal Path E2	31 E5
Canal Reach N1	29 E5
Canal St SE5	72 C2
Canal Wk N1	30 C5
Canal Way NW1	6 C1
Canal Way NW8	6 B2
Canal Way W10	38 B3
Canal Way W10	39 F2
Canal Way Wk W10	39 F2
Canberra Rd SE7	77 F2
Cancell Rd SW9	71 G4
Candle Gro SE15	87 G1
Candover St W1	8 A6
Candy St E3	33 D5
Canfield Gdns NW6	26 D4
Canford Rd SW11	84 A3
Canham Rd W3	52 A3
Cann Hall Rd E11	34 B1
Canning Cross SE5	72 D5
Canning Pas W8	54 D4
Canning Pl W8	54 D4
Canning Rd E15	48 B1
Canning Town E16	48 B4
Cannon Dr E14	61 E1
Cannon Hill NW6	26 B2
Cannon Pl SE7	78 A1
Cannon St EC4	16 D2
Cannon St Rd E1	45 G5
Cannon Wf Business Cen SE8	60 C5
Canon Beck Rd SE16	60 A3
Canonbie Rd SE23	88 A5
Canonbury Cres N1	30 B4
Canonbury Gro N1	30 B4
Canonbury La N1	30 A4
Canonbury Pk N N1	30 B3
Canonbury Pk S N1	30 B3
Canonbury Pl N1	30 A3
Canonbury Rd N1	30 A3
Canonbury Sq N1	30 A4
Canonbury St N1	30 B4
Canonbury Vil N1	30 A4
Canon Row SW1	21 E2
Canon St N1	30 B5
Canrobert St E2	45 G2
Cantelowes Rd NW1	28 D3
Canterbury Cres SW9	85 H1
Canterbury Ho SE1	21 H3
Canterbury Pl SE17	22 C6
Canterbury Rd NW6	40 B1
Canterbury Ter NW6	40 B1
Cantium Retail Pk SE1	73 F2
Canton St E14	47 E5
Cantrell Rd E3	47 D3
Cantwell Rd SE18	78 D3
Canute Gdns SE16	60 B5
Canvey St SE1	16 C5
Capel Ct EC2	17 G2
Capel Pt E7	35 E1
Capel Rd E7	35 E1
Capel Rd E12	35 F1
Capener's Cl SW1	19 F2
Capland St NW8	6 A3
Caple Rd NW10	38 B1
Capper St WC1	8 B4
Capstan Rd SE8	60 D5
Capstan Sq E14	61 G3
Capstan Way SE16	60 C2
Caradoc Cl W2	40 B5
Caradoc St SE10	76 B1
Caraway Cl E13	49 E4
Carbis Rd E14	46 D5
Carden Rd SE15	87 G1
Cardiff St SE18	79 G3
Cardigan Rd E3	47 D1
Cardigan Rd SW13	66 C5
Cardigan St SE11	71 G1
Cardinal Bourne St SE1	23 G4
Cardinal Hinsley Cl NW10	38 C1
Cardinal Pl SW15	81 F2
Cardine Ms SE15	73 G3
Cardington St NW1	8 A1
Cardozo Rd N7	29 E2
Cardross St W6	52 D4
Cardwell Rd N7	29 E1
Carew St SE5	72 B5
Carey Gdns SW8	70 C4
Carey La EC2	16 D1
Carey Pl SW1	20 C6
Carey St WC2	15 H2
Carker's La NW5	28 B2
Carleton Rd N7	28 D2
Carlile Cl E3	47 D1
Carlingford Rd NW3	27 E1
Carlisle Av EC3	17 J2
Carlisle La SE1	21 H4
Carlisle Ms NW8	6 A5
Carlisle Pl SW1	20 A4
Carlisle Rd NW6	25 G5
Carlos Pl W1	13 G4
Carlton Dr SW15	81 G3
Carlton Gdns SW1	14 C6
Carlton Gro SE15	73 G4
Carlton Hill NW8	40 C1
Carlton Ho Ter SW1	14 C6
Carlton Rd E12	35 G1
Carlton St SW1	14 C4
Carlton Twr Pl SW1	18 E3
Carlton Vale NW6	40 C1
Carlyle Pl SW15	81 F2
Carlyle Rd E12	36 A1
Carlyle Sq SW3	69 E1
Carmalt Gdns SW15	81 E2
Carmarthen Pl SE1	23 H1
Carmelite St EC4	16 A3
Carmen St E14	47 F5
Carmichael Ms SW18	83 E5
Carnaby St W1	14 A2
Carnarvon Rd E15	34 C3
Carnbrook Rd SE3	91 G1
Carnecke Gdns SE9	92 A3
Carnegie St N1	29 F5
Carnoustie Dr N1	29 F4
Carnwath Rd SW6	82 B1
Carolina Cl E15	34 B2
Caroline Gdns SE15	73 G3
Caroline Pl SW11	70 A5
Caroline Pl W2	54 C1
Caroline Pl Ms W2	54 C1
Caroline Ter SW1	19 F6
Caroline Wk W6	67 G2
Carol St NW1	28 C5
Carpenters Business Pk E15	33 E4
Carpenters Pl SW4	84 D2
Carpenters Rd E15	33 E3
Carpenter St W1	13 H4
Carrara Ms E8	31 F3
Carrara Wf SW6	81 G1
Carr Gro SE18	64 A5
Carriage Dr E SW11	70 A3
Carriage Dr N SW11	70 A2
Carriage Dr S SW11	69 G4
Carriage Dr W SW11	69 G3
Carriage St SE18	65 D4
Carrington St W1	13 H6
Carrol Cl NW5	28 B1
Carroll Cl E15	34 C2
Carronade Pl SE28	65 E4
Carron Cl E14	47 F5
Carroun Rd SW8	71 F3
Carr St E14	46 C4
Carslake Rd SW15	81 E4
Carson Rd E16	48 D5
Carston Cl SE12	90 C3
Carswell Rd SE6	89 G5
Carteret St SW1	20 C2
Carteret Way SE8	60 C5
Carter La EC4	16 C2
Carter Pl SE17	72 B1
Carter St SE17	72 B2
Carthew Rd W6	53 D4
Carthew Vil W6	53 D4
Carthusian St EC1	10 D5
Cartier Circle E14	61 F2
Carting La WC2	15 F4
Cartmel NW1	8 A1
Carton St W1	13 E1
Cartridge Pl SE18	65 D4
Cartwright Gdns WC1	8 E3
Cartwright St E1	59 E1
Cartwright Way SW13	67 D3
Carver Rd SE24	86 B4
Cary Rd E11	34 B1
Casby Ho SE16	59 F4
Cascades Twr E14	61 D2
Casella Rd SE14	74 B3
Casey Cl NW8	6 B2
Casino Av SE24	86 B3
Caspian St SE5	72 C3
Caspian Wk E16	49 G5
Cassidy Rd SW6	68 B3
Cassilis Rd E14	61 E3
Cassland Rd E9	32 A4
Casslee Rd SE6	89 D5
Casson St E1	45 F4
Castellain Rd W9	40 C3
Castello Av SW15	81 E3
Castelnau SW13	66 D2
Casterbridge NW6	26 C5
Casterbridge Rd SE3	91 D1
Castillon Rd SE6	90 C4
Castle Baynard St EC4	16 C3
Castlebrook Cl SE11	22 B5
Castlecombe Dr SW19	81 F5
Castle Ct EC3	17 G2
Castle Ct SW15	81 G1
Castlehaven Rd NW1	28 B4
Castle La SW1	20 B3
Castlemaine Twr SW11	69 G4
Castlemain St E1	45 G4
Castlemead SE5	72 B3
Castle Pl NW1	28 B3
Castlereagh St W1	12 C1
Castle Rd NW1	28 B3
Castle St E6	49 F1
Castleton Rd SE9	91 G1
Castletown Rd W14	67 G1
Castlewood Dr SE9	78 B5
Castle Yd SE1	16 C5
Castor La E14	61 F1
Caterham Rd SE13	89 G1
Catesby St SE17	23 G6
Catford Br SE6	89 E5
Catford Bdy SE6	89 F5
Catford Gyratory SE6	89 F5
Cathay St SE16	59 G3
Cathcart Rd SW10	68 D2
Cathcart St NW5	28 B3
Cathedral Piazza SW1	20 A4
Cathedral St SE1	17 F5
Cathedral Wk SW1	20 A3
Catherine Griffiths Ct EC1	10 A3
Catherine Gro SE10	75 F4
Catherine Pl SW1	20 A3
Catherine St WC2	15 G3
Catherine Wheel All E1	11 J6
Catherine Wheel Yd SW1	14 A6
Cathles Rd SW12	84 B4
Cathnor Rd W12	52 D3
Catlin St SE16	73 F1
Cato Rd SW4	85 D1
Cator St SE15	73 E2
Cato St W1	6 C6
Catton St WC1	9 G6
Caulfield Rd E6	36 B4
Caulfield Rd SE15	73 G5
Causeway, The SW18	82 C2
Causton St SW1	20 D6
Cautley Av SW4	84 C3
Cavalry Gdns SW15	81 G3
Cavell St E1	45 G4
Cavendish Av NW8	41 E1

Cavendish Cl NW8 **6** A1
Cavendish Ct EC3 **19** F1
Cavendish Gdns SW4 **84** C4
Cavendish Gdns, Bark. **37** G2
Cavendish Ms N W1 **7** J5
Cavendish Ms S W1 **7** J6
Cavendish Pl W1 **25** F3
Cavendish Pl W2 **13** J1
Cavendish Rd NW6 **25** G4
Cavendish Rd SW12 **84** B4
Cavendish Sq W1 **13** J1
Cavendish St N1 **44** C1
Cave Rd E13 **49** E1
Caversham Rd NW5 **28** C3
Caversham St SW3 **69** G2
Caverswall St W12 **39** E5
Caxton Gro E3 **47** E2
Caxton Rd W12 **53** F3
Caxton St SW1 **20** B3
Cayford Ho NW3 **27** F2
Cayton Pl EC1 **11** F2
Cayton St EC1 **11** F2
Cearns Ho E6 **35** G5
Cecil Av, Bark. **37** F4
Cecil Ct WC2 **14** D4
Cecilia Rd E8 **31** F2
Cecil Rd E13 **35** D5
Cecil Rd NW10 **24** A5
Cecil Rd, Ilf. **36** D1
Cedar Cl E3 **33** G5
Cedar Cl, Ilf. **37** F2
Cedar Ct SE9 **92** A4
Cedarhurst Dr SE9 **91** F3
Cedarne Rd SW6 **68** C3
Cedar Rd NW2 **25** E1
Cedars SE13 **90** A1
Cedars Rd E15 **34** B3
Cedars Rd SW4 **84** B1
Cedars Rd SW13 **66** B5
Cedar Way NW1 **28** D4
Celandine Cl E14 **47** E4
Celandine Dr E8 **31** E4
Celandine Way E15 **48** B2
Celebration Av E220 **33** G2
Celestial Gdns SE13 **90** A2
Celia Rd N19 **28** C1
Celtic Rd E14 **47** F4
Cemetery La SE7 **78** A2
Cemetery Rd E7 **34** C1
Centaur St SE1 **21** H3
Central Av SW11 **69** G3
Central Pk Rd E6 **49** H2
Central St EC1 **10** D2
Centrepoint WC1 **14** D1
Centre St E2 **45** G1
Centurion Cl N7 **29** F4
Centurion Sq SE18 **78** A4
Cephas Av E1 **46** A3
Cephas St E1 **46** A3
Cerise Rd SE15 **73** F4
Ceylon Rd W14 **53** F4
Chabot Dr SE15 **87** G4
Chadbourn St E14 **47** F4
Chadd Grn E13 **35** D5
Chadwell St EC1 **10** A1
Chadwick Cl SW15 **80** B5
Chadwick Rd NW10 **24** B5
Chadwick Rd SE15 **73** E5
Chadwick St SW1 **20** D4
Chadwin Rd E13 **49** E4
Chagford St NW1 **6** D4
Chalbury Ms N1 **43** F1
Chalcot Cres NW1 **27** G3
Chalcot Gdns NW3 **27** G3
Chalcot Rd NW1 **28** A4
Chalcot Sq NW1 **28** A4
Chalcroft Rd SE13 **90** B3
Chaldon Rd SW6 **67** G3
Chale Rd SW2 **85** E4
Chalk Fm Rd NW1 **28** A4
Chalk Rd E13 **49** E4
Challoner St W14 **68** A1
Chaloner Ct SE1 **23** F1

Chalsey Rd SE4 **89** D2
Chalton St NW1 **8** D1
Chamberlayne Rd NW10 **39** F2
Chambers La NW10 **25** D4
Chambers Rd N7 **29** E1
Chambers St SE16 **59** F3
Chamber St E1 **59** E1
Chambord St E2 **45** E2
Champion Gro SE5 **86** C1
Champion Hill SE5 **86** C1
Champion Hill Est SE5 **86** D1
Champion Pk SE5 **72** C5
Chancellors Rd W6 **67** E1
Chancellors St W6 **67** E1
Chancel St SE1 **16** B5
Chancery La WC2 **15** J1
Chance St E1 **45** E3
Chance St E2 **45** E3
Chandler Av E14 **48** D4
Chandlers Av SE10 **62** C4
Chandlers Ms E14 **61** E3
Chandlers Way SE15 **85** G5
Chandler Way SE15 **73** D2
Chandos Pl WC2 **15** E4
Chandos Rd E15 **34** A2
Chandos Rd NW2 **25** E2
Chandos Rd NW10 **38** A3
Chandos St W1 **7** J6
Change All EC3 **17** G2
Channelsea Rd E15 **34** A5
Chantrey Rd SW9 **85** F1
Chantry Cres NW10 **24** B3
Chantry St N1 **30** A5
Chant Sq E15 **34** A4
Chant St E15 **34** A4
Chapel Cl NW10 **24** B2
Chapel Ct SE1 **23** F1
Chapel Ho St E14 **75** F1
Chapel Mkt N1 **43** G1
Chapel Pl EC2 **11** H2
Chapel Pl N1 **43** H2
Chapel Pl W1 **54** C1
Chapel Side W2 **54** C1
Chapel St NW1 **6** B6
Chapel St SW1 **19** G3
Chaplin Cl SE1 **22** A1
Chaplin Rd E15 **48** B1
Chaplin Rd NW2 **24** B3
Chapman Pk Ind Est NW10 **24** B3
Chapman Rd E9 **32** D3
Chapman St E1 **59** G1
Chapone Pl W1 **14** C2
Chapter Ho Ct EC4 **16** D2
Chapter Rd NW2 **24** C2
Chapter Rd SE17 **72** A1
Chapter St SW1 **20** C6
Charcroft Way W12 **53** F3
Charcroft Way W14 **53** F3
Charford Rd E16 **49** D4
Chargeable La E13 **48** C3
Chargeable St E16 **48** C3
Charing Cross SW1 **14** D5
Charing Cross Rd WC2 **14** D2
Charlbert St NW8 **41** F1
Charlemont Rd E6 **50** B2
Charles Barry Cl SW4 **84** C1
Charles Coveney Rd SE15 **73** E4
Charles Dickens Ho E2 **45** J2
Charles Gardner Ct N1 **11** G1
Charles Grinling Wk SE18 **64** C5
Charles Pl NW1 **8** B2
Charles Rowan Ho WC1 **9** J2
Charles II St SW1 **14** C5
Charles Sq N1 **11** G2
Charles Sq Est N1 **11** G2
Charles St SW13 **66** A5
Charles St W1 **13** H5
Charleston St SE17 **22** E6
Charles Townsend Ho EC1 **10** A3

Charles Whincup Rd E16 **63** E2
Charleville Rd W14 **67** G1
Charlotte Despard Av SW11 **70** A4
Charlotte Ms W1 **8** B5
Charlotte Ms W10 **39** F5
Charlotte Pl SW1 **20** A6
Charlotte Pl W1 **8** B6
Charlotte Rd EC2 **11** H3
Charlotte Rd SW13 **66** B4
Charlotte Row SW4 **84** C1
Charlotte St W1 **8** B5
Charlotte Ter N1 **29** F5
Charlton Ch La SE7 **77** F1
Charlton Dene SE7 **77** F3
Charlton Kings Rd NW5 **28** D2
Charlton La SE7 **77** G1
Charlton Pk La SE7 **77** G3
Charlton Pk Rd SE7 **77** G2
Charlton Pl N1 **44** A1
Charlton Rd NW10 **24** A5
Charlton Rd SE3 **77** D3
Charlton Rd SE7 **77** E3
Charlton Way SE3 **76** B4
Charlwood Pl SW1 **20** B6
Charlwood Rd SW15 **81** F1
Charlwood St SW1 **20** B6
Charlwood Gdns E14 **61** E5
Charrington St NW1 **42** D1
Charterhouse, The EC1 **10** C5
Charterhouse Bldgs EC1 **10** C4
Charterhouse Ms EC1 **10** C5
Charterhouse Rd E8 **31** F1
Charterhouse Sq EC1 **10** C5
Charterhouse St EC1 **10** A6
Chartfield Av SW15 **81** D3
Chartfield Sq SW15 **81** F3
Chartham Ct SW9 **85** G1
Chart St N1 **11** G1
Chase, The E12 **35** G1
Chase, The SW4 **84** B1
Chaseley St E14 **46** C5
Chatfield Rd SW11 **83** D1
Chatham Cl SE18 **65** D4
Chatham Pl E9 **32** A3
Chatham Rd SW11 **83** G4
Chatham St SE17 **23** F5
Chatsworth Ct W8 **54** B5
Chatsworth Rd E5 **32** C2
Chatsworth Rd NW2 **25** F3
Chatto Rd SW11 **83** G3
Chaucer Ct N16 **30** D1
Chaucer Dr SE1 **59** E5
Chaucer Rd E7 **35** D3
Chaucer Rd SE24 **85** G3
Chaucer Rd, Well. **79** G4
Chaundrye Cl SE9 **92** B4
Chaundler Cl E16 **49** E5
Cheapside EC2 **16** E2
Cheering La E20 **33** G2
Cheesemans Ter SW14 **68** A1
Chelmer Rd E9 **32** B2
Chelmsford Cl W6 **67** F2
Chelmsford Sq NW10 **25** E5
Chelsea Br SW1 **70** B2
Chelsea Br SW8 **70** B2
Chelsea Br Rd SW1 **70** A1
Chelsea Cloisters SW3 **69** F2
Chelsea Embk SW3 **69** F2
Chelsea Harbour SW10 **69** D4
Chelsea Harbour Dr SW10 **68** D4
Chelsea Manor Gdns SW3 **69** F2
Chelsea Manor St SW3 **69** E2
Chelsea Pk Gdns SW3 **69** E2
Chelsea Sq SW3 **69** E1
Chelsea Wf SW10 **69** E3
Chelsham Rd SW4 **85** D1

Chelsworth Dr SE18 **79** F2
Cheltenham Gdns E6 **50** A1
Cheltenham Rd SE15 **88** A2
Cheltenham Ter SW3 **69** G1
Chelverton Rd SW15 **81** F1
Chelwood Wk SE4 **88** C2
Chenappa Cl E13 **48** D2
Chenies Ms WC1 **8** C4
Chenies Pl NW1 **43** D1
Chenies St WC1 **8** C5
Cheniston Gdns W8 **54** C4
Chepstow Cl SW15 **81** G4
Chepstow Cres W11 **54** B1
Chepstow Pl W2 **40** B5
Chepstow Rd W2 **40** B5
Chepstow Vil W11 **54** A1
Chequer St EC1 **11** E4
Cherbury St N1 **44** C1
Cheriton St SE18 **79** F3
Cherry Gdn St SE16 **59** G3
Cherry Orchard SE7 **77** F3
Cherry Tree Wk EC1 **11** E4
Cherry Tree Way E13 **49** G3
Cherrywood Cl E3 **46** C2
Cherrywood Dr SW15 **81** F3
Chertsey Rd, Ilf. **37** F1
Cheryls Cl SW6 **68** C4
Chesham Cl SW1 **19** F4
Chesham Ms SW1 **19** F3
Chesham Pl SW1 **19** F4
Chesham St SW1 **19** F4
Cheshire Cl SE4 **74** D5
Cheshire Ct EC4 **16** A2
Cheshire St E2 **45** E3
Cheshunt Rd E7 **35** E3
Chesil Ct E2 **46** A1
Chesilton Rd SW6 **68** A4
Chesley Gdns E6 **49** G1
Chesney St SW11 **70** A4
Chesson Rd W14 **68** A2
Chester Cl SW1 **19** G2
Chester Cl SW13 **81** D1
Chester Cl N N W1 **7** J1
Chester Cl S N W1 **7** J2
Chester Cotts SW1 **19** F6
Chesterfield Gdns W1 **13** H5
Chesterfield Gro SE22 **87** E3
Chesterfield Hill W1 **13** H4
Chesterfield St W1 **13** H5
Chesterfield Wk SE10 **76** A4
Chesterfield Way SE15 **74** A3
Chesterford Gdns NW3 **26** C1
Chesterford Rd E12 **36** B2
Chester Gate NW1 **7** H2
Chester Ms SW1 **19** H3
Chester Pl NW1 **7** H1
Chester Rd E7 **35** G4
Chester Rd E16 **48** B3
Chester Rd NW1 **7** G2
Chester Rd, Sid. **93** G3
Chester Row SW1 **19** F6
Chester Sq SW1 **19** H5
Chester Sq Ms SW1 **19** H4
Chester St E2 **45** F3
Chester St SW1 **19** G3
Chester Ter NW1 **7** H1
Chesterton Cl SW18 **82** B3
Chesterton Rd E13 **48** D2
Chesterton Rd W10 **39** F4
Chesterton Ter E13 **48** D2
Chester Way SE11 **22** A6
Chestnut Av E7 **35** E1
Chestnut Cl SE14 **74** D4
Chestnut Gro SW12 **84** A5
Chestnut Ri SE18 **79** F2
Chettle Cl SE1 **23** F3
Chetwood Wk E6 **50** A5
Chetwynd Rd NW5 **28** B1
Cheval Pl SW7 **18** C3
Cheval St E14 **61** E4
Chevening Rd NW6 **39** F1
Chevening Rd SE10 **76** C1
Chevron Cl E16 **49** D5

Cheyne Gdns SW3 69 F2
Cheyne Ms SW3 69 F2
Cheyne Pl SW3 69 G2
Cheyne Row SW3 69 F2
Cheyne Wk SW3 69 F2
Cheyne Wk SW10 69 E3
Chichele Rd NW2 25 F2
Chicheley St SE1 21 H1
Chichester Cl E6 50 A5
Chichester Cl SE3 77 F3
Chichester Rents WC2 15 J1
Chichester Rd NW6 40 B1
Chichester Rd W2 40 C4
Chichester St SW1 70 C1
Chichester Way E14 62 A5
Chicksand St E1 45 E4
Chiddingstone St SW6 68 B5
Childeric Rd SE14 74 C3
Childers St SE8 74 C2
Child La SE10 62 C4
Child's Pl SW5 54 B5
Child's St SW5 54 B5
Chillington Dr SW11 83 D2
Chillingworth Rd N7 29 F2
Chiltern Rd E3 47 E3
Chiltern St W1 7 F5
Chilton Gro SE8 60 B5
Chiltonian Ind Est SE12 90 C4
Chilton St E2 45 E3
Chilver St SE10 76 C1
Chilworth Ms W2 41 D5
Chilworth St W2 41 D5
China Ms SW2 85 F5
Ching Ct WC2 14 E2
Chipka St E14 61 G3
Chipley St SE14 74 C2
Chippenham Gdns NW6 40 B2
Chippenham Ms W9 40 B3
Chippenham Rd W9 40 B3
Chipstead St SW6 68 B4
Chip St SW4 84 D1
Chisenhale Rd E3 46 C1
Chiswell St E1 11 E5
Chiswick La W4 66 A1
Chiswick La S W4 66 B1
Chiswick Mall W4 66 B2
Chiswick Mall W6 66 B2
Chiswick Pier W4 66 B3
Chiswick Wf W4 66 B2
Chitty St W1 8 B5
Chivalry Rd SW11 83 F3
Chobham Rd E15 34 A2
Cholmondeley Av NW10 38 A1
Choumert Gro SE15 73 F5
Choumert Ms SE15 73 F5
Choumert Rd SE15 87 E1
Choumert Sq SE15 73 F5
Chrisp St E14 47 F4
Chris Pullen Way N7 29 E3
Christchurch Av NW6 25 G4
Christchurch Ct NW6 25 G4
Christ Ch Pas EC1 16 C1
Christchurch St SW3 69 G2
Christchurch Way SE10 62 B5
Christian Ct SE16 60 D2
Christian St E1 45 F5
Christie Rd E9 32 C3
Christina St EC2 11 H3
Christopher Cl SE16 60 B3
Christopher Pl NW1 8 D2
Christopher St EC2 11 G4
Chryssell Rd SW9 71 G3
Chubworthy St SE14 74 C2
Chudleigh Cres, Ilf. 37 H1
Chudleigh Rd NW6 25 F4
Chudleigh Rd SE4 89 D3
Chudleigh St E1 46 B5
Chumleigh St SE5 72 D2
Churchbury Rd SE9 91 G5
Church Cres E9 32 B4

Churchcroft Cl SW12 84 A5
Church Entry EC4 16 C2
Church Gate SW6 81 G1
Church Gro SE13 89 F2
Church Hill SE18 64 B4
Churchill Gdns SW1 70 C1
Churchill Gdns Rd SW1 70 B1
Churchill Pl E14 61 F2
Churchill Rd E16 49 F5
Churchill Rd NW2 24 D3
Churchill Rd NW5 28 B1
Churchill Wk E9 32 A2
Churchmead Rd NW10 24 C3
Church Path N5 30 A2
Church Path NW10 24 A4
Church Pl SW1 14 B4
Church Rd E12 36 A2
Church Rd N1 30 B3
Church Rd NW10 24 A3
Church Rd SW13 66 B5
Church Rd, Bark. 37 E3
Church Row NW3 26 D1
Church St E15 34 B5
Church St E16 64 D2
Church St NW8 6 A5
Church St W2 6 A5
Church St W4 66 A2
Church St Est NW8 6 A5
Church Ter SE13 90 B1
Church Wk N16 30 C1
Church Wk SW13 66 C4
Church Wk SW15 81 D3
Churchway NW1 8 D1
Churchwell Path E9 32 A2
Churchyard Row SE11 22 C5
Churston Av E13 35 E5
Churton Pl SW1 20 B6
Churton St SW1 20 B6
Cicada Rd SW18 83 D3
Cicely Rd SE15 73 F4
Cinnabar Wf E1 59 F2
Cinnamon Row SW11 83 D1
Cinnamon St E1 59 G2
Circular Way SE18 78 B2
Circus Ms W1 6 D5
Circus Pl EC2 11 G6
Circus Rd NW8 41 E2
Circus St SE10 75 G3
Cirencester St W2 40 C4
Citius Wk E20 33 G3
Citizen Rd N7 29 G1
City Forum EC1 10 D1
City Gdn Row N1 44 A1
City Mill River Towpath E15 33 F4
City Pt EC2 11 F5
City Rd EC1 44 A1
Cityview Ct SE22 87 F5
City Wk SE1 23 H2
Clabon Ms SW1 18 D4
Clack St SE16 60 A3
Clacton Rd E6 49 G2
Claire Pl E14 61 E4
Clancarty Rd SW6 68 B5
Clandon St SE8 75 E5
Clanricarde Gdns W2 54 B1
Clapham Common SW4 84 C1
Clapham Common N Side SW4 84 B2
Clapham Common S Side SW4 84 A4
Clapham Common W Side SW4 84 A2
Clapham Cres SW4 84 D2
Clapham Est SW11 83 F2
Clapham High St SW4 84 D2
Clapham Junct Sta SW11 83 E2
Clapham Manor St SW4 84 C1

Clapham Pk Est SW4 84 D4
Clapham Pk Rd SW4 84 D2
Clapham Rd SW9 85 E1
Clapham Rd Est SW4 85 D1
Claps Gate La E6 50 C3
Clapton Pas E5 32 A2
Clapton Sq E5 32 A2
Clapton Way E5 31 F5
Clara Pl SE18 64 C5
Clare Cor SE9 92 D5
Claredale St E2 45 F1
Clare Gdns E7 34 D1
Clare Ho E3 32 D5
Clare La N1 30 B4
Clare Mkt WC2 15 G2
Claremont Cl E16 64 C2
Claremont Cl N1 43 G1
Claremont Rd E7 35 E2
Claremont Rd W9 39 G1
Claremont Sq N1 43 G1
Claremont St E16 64 C2
Claremont St SE10 75 F3
Clarence Av SW4 85 D4
Clarence Cres SW4 84 D4
Clarence Gdns NW1 7 J2
Clarence La SW15 80 A4
Clarence Ms E5 31 G2
Clarence Ms SE16 60 B2
Clarence Ms SW12 84 B5
Clarence Pl E5 31 G2
Clarence Rd E5 31 G1
Clarence Rd E12 35 G2
Clarence Rd E16 48 B3
Clarence Rd NW6 26 A4
Clarence St SE8 75 F2
Clarence Ter NW1 6 E3
Clarence Wk SW4 71 E5
Clarence Way NW1 28 B4
Clarence Way Est NW1 28 B4
Clarendon Cl E9 32 A4
Clarendon Cl W2 12 B3
Clarendon Dr SW15 81 E2
Clarendon Gdns W9 41 D3
Clarendon Gro NW1 8 C1
Clarendon Ms W2 12 B2
Clarendon Pl W2 12 B3
Clarendon Ri SE13 89 G1
Clarendon Rd W11 53 G1
Clarendon Rd W11 70 B1
Clarendon Wk W11 39 G5
Clare Rd NW10 24 C4
Clare Rd SE14 74 C4
Clare St E2 45 G1
Clareville Gro SW7 55 D5
Clareville St SW7 55 D5
Clarewood Wk SW9 86 A2
Clarges Ms W1 13 H5
Clarges St W1 13 J5
Claribel Rd SW9 72 A5
Clarissa St E8 31 E5
Clarke's Ms W1 7 G5
Clarkson Rd E16 48 C5
Clarkson Row NW1 42 C1
Clarksons, The, Bark. 51 E1
Clarkson St E2 45 G2
Clarks Pl EC2 17 H1
Clark St E1 45 G4
Claude Rd E13 35 E5
Claude Rd SE15 73 G5
Claude St E14 61 E5
Claudia Jones Way SW2 85 E4
Claughton Rd E13 49 F1
Clavell St SE10 75 F2
Claverdale Rd SW2 85 F5
Clavering Av SW13 67 D2
Claverton St SW1 70 C1
Claxton Gro W6 67 F1
Claybrook Rd W6 67 F2
Claylands Pl SW8 71 G3
Claylands Rd SW8 71 F2
Claymill Ho SE18 79 E1
Claypole Rd E15 47 G1

Clay St W1 7 E6
Clayton Cres N1 29 E5
Clayton Ms SE10 76 A4
Clayton Rd SE15 73 F4
Clayton St SE11 71 G2
Cleanthus Cl SE18 79 D4
Cleanthus Rd SE18 79 D4
Clearwell Dr W9 40 C3
Cleaver Sq SE11 71 G1
Cleaver St SE11 71 G1
Clegg St E13 49 D1
Clematis St W12 52 B1
Clem Attlee Ct SW6 68 A2
Clemence St E14 46 D4
Clement Av SW4 85 D2
Clement Cl NW6 25 E4
Clements Av E16 62 D1
Clement's Inn WC2 15 H2
Clement's Inn Pas WC2 15 H2
Clements La EC4 17 G3
Clements Rd E16 36 B4
Clements Rd SE16 59 F4
Clennam St SE1 22 E1
Clenston Ms W1 12 D1
Clephane Rd N1 30 B3
Clere St EC2 11 G3
Clerkenwell Cl EC1 10 A3
Clerkenwell Grn EC1 10 A4
Clerkenwell Rd EC1 9 J4
Clermont Rd E9 32 A5
Cleveland Av W4 52 B5
Cleveland Gdns SW13 66 B5
Cleveland Gdns W2 40 D5
Cleveland Ms W1 8 A5
Cleveland Pl SW1 14 B5
Cleveland Rd N1 30 C4
Cleveland Rd SW13 66 B5
Cleveland Row SW1 14 A6
Cleveland Sq W2 40 D5
Cleveland St W1 8 A4
Cleveland Ter W2 40 D5
Cleveland Way E1 46 A3
Cleveley Cl SE7 63 G5
Cleverly Est W12 52 C2
Cleve Rd NW6 26 B4
Cleves Rd E6 35 G5
Clichy Est E1 46 A4
Clifden Rd E5 32 A2
Clifford Dr SW9 86 A2
Clifford Gdns NW10 39 E1
Clifford Rd E16 48 C3
Clifford's Inn Pas EC4 15 J2
Clifford St W1 14 A4
Clifford Way NW10 24 B1
Cliff Rd NW1 29 D3
Cliff Ter SE8 75 E5
Cliffview Rd SE13 89 E1
Cliff Vil NW1 29 D3
Cliff Wk E16 48 C4
Clifton Av W12 52 B2
Clifton Cres SE15 73 G3
Clifton Gdns W9 40 D3
Clifton Gro E8 31 F3
Clifton Hill NW8 40 C1
Clifton Pl W2 12 A3
Clifton Ri SE14 74 C3
Clifton Rd E7 35 G3
Clifton Rd E16 48 B4
Clifton Rd N1 30 B3
Clifton Rd NW10 38 C1
Clifton Rd W9 41 D3
Clifton's Rbt SE12 91 E4
Clifton St EC2 11 H5
Clifton Vil W9 40 C4
Clifton Wk E6 50 A5
Clifton Way SE15 73 G3
Clinch Ct E16 49 D4
Clink St SE1 17 E5
Clinton Rd E3 46 C2
Clinton Rd E7 35 D1
Clipper Way SE13 89 G2
Clipstone Ms W1 8 A4
Clipstone St W1 7 J5

Clitheroe Rd SW9	71 E5	Colehill La SW6	67 G4	Comerford Rd SE4	88 C2	Cook's Rd E15	47 F1

Clitheroe Rd SW9 71 E5
Cliveden Pl SW1 19 F5
Cloak La EC4 17 E5
Clockhouse Av, Bark. 37 E5
Clockhouse Pl SW15 81 G3
Clock Twr Pl N7 29 E3
Clonbrook Rd N16 30 D1
Cloncurry St SW6 67 F5
Clonmel Rd SW6 68 A3
Cloth Ct EC1 10 C6
Cloth Fair EC1 10 C6
Clothier St E1 17 J1
Cloth St EC1 10 C5
Clothworkers Rd SE18 79 F3
Cloudesley Pl N1 29 G5
Cloudesley Rd N1 29 G5
Cloudesley Sq N1 29 G5
Cloudesley St N1 29 G5
Clova Rd E7 34 C3
Clove Cres E14 62 A1
Clove Hitch Quay SW11 83 D1
Cloysters Grn E1 59 F2
Club Row E1 45 E3
Club Row E2 45 E3
Cluny Est SE1 23 H3
Cluny Ms SW5 54 B5
Cluny Pl SE1 23 H3
Clutton St E14 46 F2
Clydesdale Rd W11 40 A5
Clyde St SE8 75 D2
Clyston St SW8 70 C5
Coach & Horses Yd W1 13 J3
Coach Ho Ms SE23 88 B4
Coalecroft Rd SW15 81 E2
Coates Av SW18 83 F4
Coate St E2 45 F1
Cobbett Rd SE9 92 A1
Cobbett St SW8 71 F3
Cobbold Est NW10 24 B3
Cobbold Rd NW10 24 B3
Cobbold Rd W12 52 A3
Cobb St E1 45 E4
Cobham Cl SW11 83 F4
Coborn Rd E3 46 D2
Coborn St E3 47 D2
Cobourg Rd SE5 73 E2
Cobourg St NW1 8 B2
Coburg Cl SW1 20 B5
Cochrane St NW8 41 E1
Cockayne Way SE8 74 C1
Cock Hill E1 11 J6
Cock La EC1 10 B6
Cockpit Steps SW1 20 D2
Cockpit Yd WC1 9 H5
Cocksparr Ct SW1 14 D5
Cocksparr St SW1 14 D5
Coda Cen, The SW6 67 G4
Code St E1 45 E3
Codrington Hill SE23 88 C5
Cody Rd E16 48 A3
Cody Rd Business Cen E16 48 A3
Coffey St SE8 75 E3
Coin St SE1 15 J5
Coity Rd NW5 28 A3
Coke St E1 45 F5
Colbeck Ms SW7 54 C5
Coldbath Sq EC1 9 J3
Coldbath St SE13 75 F4
Cold Blow La SE14 74 B3
Cold Harbour E14 61 G3
Coldharbour La SE5 85 G2
Coldharbour La SW9 85 G2
Coldstream Gdns SW18 82 A4
Colebeck Ms N1 30 A3
Colebert Av E1 46 A4
Colebrooke Row N1 44 A1
Coleford Rd SW18 82 D3
Colegrave Rd E15 34 A2
Colegrove Rd SE15 73 E5
Coleherne Ct SW5 68 C1
Coleherne Ms SW10 68 C1
Coleherne Rd SW10 68 C1

Colehill La SW6 67 G4
Coleman Flds N1 30 B5
Coleman Rd SE5 72 D3
Coleman St EC2 17 F1
Colenso Rd E5 32 A1
Colepits Wd Rd SE9 93 E3
Coleraine Rd SE3 76 C2
Coleridge Av E12 36 A3
Coleridge Cl SW8 70 B5
Coleridge Gdns SW10 68 C3
Coleridge Sq SW10 68 C3
Colestown St SW11 69 F5
Cole St SE1 23 E2
Colet Gdns W14 53 F5
Coley St WC1 9 H4
Colinette Rd SW15 81 E2
Colin Rd NW10 24 C3
Coliston Rd SW18 82 B5
College App SE10 75 G2
College Cres NW3 27 E3
College Cross N1 29 G4
College Hill EC4 17 E3
College La NW5 28 B1
College Ms SW1 21 E3
College Pk Cl SE13 90 A2
College Pl NW1 28 C5
College Pl E15 34 C3
College Rd NW10 39 E1
College Rd SE21 86 D5
College Row E9 32 B2
College St EC4 17 E3
College Ter N1 46 D2
Collent St E9 32 A3
Collett Rd SE16 59 F4
Collier St N1 44 A1
Collingbourne Rd W12 52 D2
Collingham Gdns SW5 54 C5
Collingham Pl SW5 54 C5
Collingwood St E1 45 G3
Collinson St SE1 22 D2
Collinson Wk SE1 22 D2
Collins Rd N5 30 B1
Collins St SE3 76 B5
Colls Rd SE15 74 A4
Colman Rd E16 49 F4
Colmore Ms SE15 73 G4
Colnbrook St SE1 22 B4
Colne Ho, Bark. 37 E3
Colne Rd E5 32 C1
Cologne Rd SW11 83 E2
Colombo St SE1 16 B6
Colomb St SE10 76 B1
Colonnade WC1 9 E4
Colonnade Wk SW1 19 H6
Colston Rd E7 35 G3
Coltman St E14 46 C4
Columbia Rd E2 45 E2
Columbia Rd E13 48 C3
Columbine Av E6 50 A4
Columbine Way SE13 75 G5
Colvestone Cres E8 31 E2
Colville Est N1 30 C5
Colville Gdns W11 40 A5
Colville Ho W11 40 A5
Colville Pl W1 8 B6
Colville Rd W11 40 A5
Colville Sq W11 40 A5
Colville Ter W11 40 A5
Colvin Rd E6 35 J5
Colwell Rd SE22 87 E3
Colworth Gro SE17 22 E6
Colyer Cl N1 43 F1
Colyton Rd SE22 87 G3
Combe, The NW1 7 J2
Combe Av SE3 76 C3
Combedale Rd SE10 76 D1
Combemartin Rd SW18 81 J5
Combe Ms SE3 76 C3
Comber Gro SE5 72 C3
Combermere Rd SW9 85 F1
Comeragh Ms W14 67 G1
Comeragh Rd W14 67 G1

Comerford Rd SE4 88 C2
Comet Cl E12 35 G1
Comet Pl SE8 75 E3
Comet St SE8 75 E3
Comfort St SE15 72 D2
Commercial Rd E1 45 F5
Commercial Rd E14 46 A5
Commercial St E1 45 E3
Commercial Way SE15 73 E3
Commerell St SE10 76 B1
Commodore St E1 46 C3
Common, The E15 34 B3
Commondale SW15 81 E1
Common Mile Cl SW4 85 D3
Common Rd SW13 80 C1
Commonwealth Av W12 53 D1
Community La N7 28 D2
Community Rd E15 34 A2
Compayne Gdns NW6 26 C4
Compton Av E6 49 G1
Compton Av N1 30 A3
Compton Cl E3 47 E4
Compton Cl NW1 7 J2
Compton Pas EC1 10 C3
Compton Pl WC1 9 E3
Compton Rd N1 30 A3
Compton St EC1 10 B3
Compton Ter N1 30 A3
Comus Pl SE17 23 H6
Comyn Rd SW11 83 F2
Comyns Cl E16 48 C4
Concanon Rd SW2 85 F2
Concert Hall App SE1 15 H6
Concorde Dr E6 50 B4
Concorde Way SE16 60 B5
Condell Rd SW8 70 C4
Condover Cres SE18 78 D3
Condray Pl SW11 69 F3
Conduit Ct WC2 15 E3
Conduit Ms SE18 79 D1
Conduit Ms W2 41 E5
Conduit Pl W2 41 E5
Conduit Rd SE18 79 D1
Conduit St W1 13 J3
Coney Way SW8 71 F2
Congleton Gro SE18 79 E1
Congo Rd SE18 79 E1
Congreve Rd SE9 92 B1
Congreve St SE17 23 H5
Congreve Wk E16 49 G4
Coniger Rd SW6 68 B5
Coningham Rd W12 52 D3
Conington Rd SE13 75 F5
Coniston Av, Bark. 37 G4
Coniston Av, Well. 93 G1
Conistone Way N7 29 E4
Coniston Ho SE5 72 B3
Conlan St W10 24 A3
Conley Rd NW10 24 A3
Connaught Br E16 63 G2
Connaught Cl W2 12 B2
Connaught Ms SE18 78 C1
Connaught Pl W2 12 D3
Connaught Rd E16 63 G2
Connaught Rd NW10 24 A5
Connaught Rbt E16 63 G1
Connaught Sq W2 12 D2
Connaught St W2 12 B2
Conrad Ho N16 31 D2
Consort Rd SE15 73 G4
Cons St SE1 22 A1
Constance Rd NW3 27 E3
Constance St E16 63 G3
Constitution Hill SW1 19 H1
Constitution Ri SE18 78 C4
Content St SE17 23 E6
Conway Ms W1 8 A5
Conway Rd SE18 65 F5
Conway St E13 48 D3
Conway St W1 8 A4
Conyer St E3 46 C1
Cooke St, Bark. 37 E5

Cook's Rd E15 47 F1
Cooks Rd SE17 72 A2
Coolfin Rd E16 49 D5
Coombe Lo SE7 77 F2
Coombe Rd W4 66 A1
Coombs St N1 44 A1
Coomer Ms SW6 68 A2
Coomer Pl SW6 68 A2
Cooper Cl SE1 22 A2
Cooper Rd NW10 24 B2
Coopersale Rd E9 32 B2
Coopers Cl E1 46 A3
Coopers La NW1 43 D1
Coopers Rd SE1 73 E1
Copeland Dr E14 61 E5
Copeland Ho SE11 21 H4
Copeland Rd SE15 73 F5
Copenhagen Pl E14 46 D5
Copenhagen St N1 29 E5
Cope Pl W8 54 B4
Cope St SE16 60 B5
Copleston Pas SE15 87 E1
Copleston Rd SE15 87 E1
Copley St E1 46 B4
Coppelia Rd SE3 90 C2
Copperas St SE8 75 F2
Copperfield Rd E3 46 C3
Copperfield St SE1 22 C1
Copper Row SE1 59 E2
Coppice Dr SW15 80 D4
Coppock Cl SW11 69 F5
Copse Cl SE7 77 E2
Copsewood Cl, Sid. 93 G4
Copthall Av EC2 17 G1
Copthall Bldgs EC2 17 F1
Copthall Cl EC2 17 F1
Copthall Ct EC2 17 F1
Copthorne Av SW12 84 D5
Coptic St WC1 8 E6
Coral St SE1 22 A2
Coram St WC1 8 E4
Corbden Cl SE15 73 E4
Corbet Ct EC3 17 G2
Corbiere Ho N1 30 D5
Corbridge Cres E2 45 G1
Corbylands Rd, Sid. 93 G5
Cordelia Cl SE24 86 A2
Cordelia St E14 47 F5
Cordwell Rd SE13 90 B3
Corelli Rd SE3 78 A5
Corfield St E2 45 G2
Coriander Av E14 48 A5
Corinne Rd N19 28 C1
Cork St W1 14 A4
Cork St Ms W1 14 A4
Corlett St NW1 6 B5
Cormont Rd SE5 72 A4
Cormorant Rd E7 34 C1
Cornelia St N7 29 F3
Corner Grn SE3 90 D1
Corner Ho St WC2 15 E5
Corney Reach Way W4 66 A3
Corney Rd W4 66 A2
Cornflower Ter SE22 87 G4
Cornhill EC3 17 G2
Cornmill La SE13 89 F1
Cornmow Dr NW10 24 B2
Cornwall Av E2 46 A2
Cornwall Av, Well. 93 G1
Cornwall Cres W11 53 G1
Cornwall Gdns NW10 25 D3
Cornwall Gdns SW7 54 C4
Cornwall Gro W4 66 A1
Cornwallis Rd SE18 65 E5
Cornwallis Wk SE9 92 B1
Cornwall Ms S SW7 54 D4
Cornwall Ms W SW7 54 C4
Cornwall Rd SE1 15 J5
Cornwall Sq SE11 71 G1
Cornwall Ter NW1 7 E4
Cornwall Ter Ms NW1 7 E4
Cornwood Dr E1 46 A5
Corona Rd SE12 91 D5
Coronation Rd E13 49 F2
Coronet St N1 11 H2
Corporation Row EC1 10 A3

Name	Ref		Name	Ref		Name	Ref		Name	Ref
Corporation St E15	48 B1		Cowley St SW1	20 E3		Crefeld Cl W6	67 F2		Croombs Rd E16	49 F4
Corporation St N7	29 E2		Cowper Av E6	36 A4		Creighton Av E6	49 G1		Crooms Hill SE10	76 A3
Corrance Rd SW2	85 E2		Cowper Rd N16	30 D2		Creighton Cl W12	52 C1		Crooms Hill Gro SE10	75 G3
Corry Dr SW9	86 A2		Cowper St EC2	11 G3		Creighton Rd NW6	39 F1		Cropley St N1	44 C1
Corsham St N1	11 G2		Cowthorpe Rd SW8	71 D4		Cremer St E2	45 E1		Cropthorne Ct W9	40 D2
Corsica St N5	30 A3		Coxmount Rd SE7	77 G1		Cremorne Rd SW10	69 D3		Crosby Ct SE1	23 F1
Cortayne Rd SW6	68 A5		Coxwell Rd SE18	79 F1		Crescent, The SW13	66 B5		Crosby Rd E7	34 D3
Cortis Rd SW15	81 D4		Crabtree Cl E2	45 E1		Crescent, The W3	38 A5		Crosby Row SE1	23 F2
Cortis Ter SW15	81 D4		Crabtree La SW6	67 F3		Crescent Gro SW4	84 D3		Crosby Sq EC3	17 H2
Corunna Rd SW8	70 C4		Craigerne Rd SE3	77 E3		Crescent La SW4	84 D3		Crosby Wk SW2	85 G5
Corunna Ter SW8	70 C4		Craigholm SE18	78 C5		Crescent Pl SW3	18 B5		Crosier Cl SE3	78 A4
Cosbycote Av SE24	86 B3		Craignair Rd SW2	85 G5		Crescent Rd E6	35 F5		Cross Av SE10	76 A2
Cosmo Pl WC1	9 F5		Craigs Ct SW1	14 E5		Crescent Rd E13	35 D5		Crossbrook Rd SE3	78 A5
Cosmur Cl W12	52 B4		Craigton Rd SE9	92 B2		Crescent Rd SE18	78 D1		Crossfield Rd NW3	27 E4
Cossall Wk SE15	73 G4		Crail Row SE17	23 G6		Crescent Row EC1	10 D4		Crossfield St SE8	75 E3
Cossar Ms SW2	85 G4		Cramer St W1	7 G6		Crescent Stables SW15	81 G3		Crossford St SW9	71 F5
Cosser St SE1	21 J3		Crammond Cl W6	67 G2		Crescent St N1	29 F4		Cross Keys Cl W1	7 G6
Costa St SE15	73 F5		Crampton St SE17	22 D6		Crescent Way SE4	89 E1		Cross Keys Sq EC1	10 D6
Coswig St NW1	6 C5		Cranberry La E16	48 B3		Cresford Rd SW6	68 C4		Cross La EC3	17 H4
Cotall St E14	47 E5		Cranborne Rd, Bark.	37 F5		Cresset Rd E9	32 A3		Crosslet St SE17	23 G5
Cotham St SE17	23 E6		Cranbourne Rd E15	33 G1		Cresset St SW4	84 D1		Crosslet Vale SE10	75 F4
Cotleigh Rd NW6	26 B4		Cranbourn St WC2	14 D3		Cressfield Cl NW5	28 A2		Crossley St N7	29 G3
Cotman Cl SW15	81 F4		Cranbrook Rd SE8	75 E4		Cressingham Rd SE13	89 G1		Crossmount Ho SE5	72 B3
Cotswold Ct EC1	10 D3		Cranbrook Rd W4	66 A1		Cresswell Gdns SW5	68 D1		Cross Rd SE5	73 D5
Cotswold Gdns SE26	49 G2		Cranbury Rd SW6	68 C5		Cresswell Pk SE3	90 C1		Cross St N1	30 A5
Cottage Grn SE5	72 C3		Crane Ct EC4	16 A2		Cresswell Pl SW10	68 D1		Cross St SW13	66 A5
Cottage Gro SW9	85 E1		Crane Gro N7	29 G3		Cressy Ct W6	52 D4		Crossthwaite Av SE5	86 C2
Cottage Pl SW3	18 B3		Crane St SE10	76 A1		Cressy Pl E1	46 A4		Crosswall EC3	59 E1
Cottage Rd N7	29 F2		Crane St SE15	73 E4		Cressy Rd NW3	27 G2		Crossway N16	31 D2
Cottage St E14	61 F1		Cranfield Rd SE4	88 D1		Crestfield St WC1	9 F1		Croston St E8	31 F5
Cottesloe Ms SE1	22 A3		Cranfield Row SE1	22 A3		Crestway SW15	80 D4		Crowder St E1	59 G1
Cottesmore Gdns W8	54 C4		Cranford St E1	60 B1		Creton St SE18	64 C4		Crowfoot Cl SE28	65 G2
Cottingham Rd SW8	71 F3		Cranhurst Rd NW2	25 E2		Creukhorne Rd NW10	24 A4		Crowhurst Cl SW9	71 G5
Cotton Row SW11	83 D1		Cranleigh Gdns, Bark.	37 F4		Crewdson Rd SW9	71 G3		Crowland Ter N1	30 C4
Cottons Gdns E2	11 J1		Cranleigh Ms SW11	69 F5		Crewe Pl NW10	38 B2		Crown Cl E3	33 E5
Cottons La SE1	17 G5		Cranleigh St NW1	42 C1		Crews St E14	61 E5		Crown Cl NW6	26 C3
Cotton St E14	61 G1		Cranley Gdns SW7	69 D1		Crewys Rd SE15	73 G5		Crown Ct EC2	17 E2
Coulgate St SE4	88 C1		Cranley Ms SW7	69 D1		Cricketers Ct SE11	22 B6		Crown Ct SE12	91 E4
Coulson St SW3	69 G1		Cranley Pl SW7	55 E5		Cricketfield Rd E5	31 G1		Crown Ct WC2	15 F2
Coulter Rd W6	53 D4		Cranley Rd E13	49 E4		Cricklewood La NW2	25 F1		Crowndale Rd NW1	42 C1
Councillor St SE5	72 B3		Cranmer Ct SW3	69 G1		Crieff Rd SW18	82 D4		Crownfield Rd E15	34 A2
Counter St SE1	17 H5		Cranmer Ct SW4	85 D1		Crimscott St SE1	23 J4		Crownhill Rd NW10	24 B5
Countess Rd NW5	28 C2		Cranmer Rd E7	35 E1		Crimsworth Rd SW8	71 D4		Crown Ms W6	52 C5
County Gro SE5	72 B4		Cranmer Rd SW9	71 G3		Crinan St N1	43 E1		Crown Office Row EC4	15 J3
County Rd E6	50 D4		Cranston Est N1	11 G1		Cringle St SW8	70 C3		Crown Pas SW1	14 B6
County St SE1	22 E4		Cranswick Rd SE16	73 G1		Cripplegate St EC2	10 D5		Crown Pl EC2	11 H5
Coupland Pl SE18	79 E1		Cranwell Cl E3	47 F3		Crispian Cl NW10	24 A1		Crownstone Rd SW2	85 G3
Courland Gro SW8	70 D4		Cranwood St EC1	11 F2		Crispin St E1	45 E4		Crown St SE5	72 B3
Courland Gro Hall SW8	70 D5		Cranworth Gdns SW9	71 G4		Crisp Rd W6	67 E1		Crown Wds La SE9	79 D5
Courland St SW8	71 D4		Craster Rd SW2	85 F5		Cristowe Rd SW6	68 A5		Crown Wds La SE18	79 D5
Courtenay St SE11	22 B5		Crathie Rd SE12	91 E4		Croft, The NW10	38 B1		Crown Wds Way SE9	93 F3
Courtfield Gdns SW5	54 C5		Craven Gdns, Bark.	51 G1		Crofters Way NW1	28 D5		Crows Rd E15	48 A2
Courtfield Rd SW7	54 C5		Craven Hill W2	54 D1		Croftongate Way SE4	88 C3		Crows Rd, Bark.	37 D3
Court Gdns N7	29 G3		Craven Hill Gdns W2	54 D1		Crofton Pk Rd SE4	88 D4		Crowthorne Rd W10	39 F5
Courthill Rd SE13	89 G2		Craven Hill Ms W2	55 D1		Crofton Rd E13	49 E3		Croxley Rd W9	40 A2
Courthope Rd NW3	27 G1		Craven Pk NW10	24 A5		Crofton Rd SE5	73 D4		Croxted Cl SE21	86 B5
Courtlands Av SE12	91 E3		Craven Pk Ms NW10	24 A4		Crofts St E1	59 F1		Croxted Rd SE21	86 B5
Court La SE21	87 D4		Craven Pk Rd NW10	24 A5		Croft St SE8	60 C5		Croxted Rd SE24	86 B5
Court La Gdns SE21	87 D5		Craven Pas WC2	15 E5		Croftway NW3	26 B1		Croyde Cl, Sid.	93 F5
Courtmead Cl SE24	86 B4		Craven Rd W2	55 D1		Crogsland Rd NW1	28 A4		Croydon Rd E13	48 C3
Courtnell St W2	40 B5		Craven St WC2	15 E5		Crome Rd NW10	24 A3		Crozier Ter E9	32 B2
Courtrai Rd SE23	88 C4		Craven Ter W2	55 D1		Cromer Vil Rd SW18	82 A4		Crucifix La SE1	23 H1
Court Yd SE9	92 A4		Crawford Est SE5	72 B5		Cromford Rd SW18	82 B3		Cruden St N1	30 A5
Courtyard, The N1	29 F4		Crawford Ms W1	6 D6		Crompton St W2	41 E3		Cruikshank Rd E15	34 B3
Cousin La EC4	17 F4		Crawford Pas EC1	9 J4		Cromwell Av W6	66 D1		Cruikshank St WC1	9 J1
Cousthurst Rd SE3	77 E2		Crawford Pl W1	12 C1		Cromwell Cres SW5	54 B5		Crutched Friars EC3	17 J3
Covelees Wall E6	50 C5		Crawford St SE5	72 B4		Cromwell Gdns SW7	18 A4		Crystal Palace Rd SE22	87 F2
Covent Gdn WC2	15 F3		Crawford St W1	6 D6		Cromwell Gro W6	53 E4		Cuba St E14	61 E3
Covent Gdn Mkt WC2	15 F3		Crawshay Rd SW9	71 G4		Cromwell Ms SW7	18 A5		Cubitt St WC1	9 H2
Coventry Rd E1	45 G3		Crawthew Gro SE22	87 E2		Cromwell Pl SW7	18 A5		Cubitts Yd WC2	15 F3
Coventry Rd E2	45 G3		Crayford Rd N7	29 D1		Cromwell Rd E7	35 F4		Cubitt Ter SW4	84 C1
Coventry St W1	14 C4		Crealock St SW18	82 C4		Cromwell Rd SW5	54 C5		Cuddington SE17	22 D5
Coverdale Rd NW2	25 E4		Creasy Est SE1	23 H4		Cromwell Rd SW7	54 C5		Cudham St SE6	89 G5
Coverdale Rd W12	53 D2		Crebor St SE22	87 F4		Cromwell Rd SW9	72 A4		Cudworth St E1	45 G3
Coverdales, The, Bark.	51 E1		Crediton Hill NW6	26 C2		Cromwell Twr EC2	11 E5		Cuff Cres SE9	91 G4
Coverley Cl E1	45 F4		Crediton Rd NW10	25 F5		Crondace Rd SW6	68 B4		Cuff Pt E2	45 E2
Cowbridge La, Bark.	36 D4		Credon Rd E13	49 F1		Crondall St N1	44 C1		Culford Gdns SW3	18 E6
Cowcross St EC1	10 B5		Credon Rd SE16	73 G1		Cronin St SE15	73 E3		Culford Gro N1	30 D3
Cowdenbeath Path N1	29 F5		Creechurch La EC3	17 J2		Crooked Billet Yd E2	11 J1		Culford Rd N1	30 D4
Cow Leaze E6	50 C5		Creechurch Pl EC3	17 J2		Crooke Rd SE8	74 C1		Cullingworth Rd NW10	24 C2
Cowley Est SW9	71 G4		Creed La EC4	16 C2		Crookham Rd SW6	68 A4		Culloden Cl SE7	77 F2
Cowley Rd E11	34 A1		Creek Rd SE8	75 E2		Crookston Rd SE9	92 C1		Culloden Cl SE16	73 F1
Cowley Rd SW9	71 G4		Creek Rd SE8	75 F3					Culloden St E14	47 G5
Cowley Rd SW14	80 A1		Creekside SE8	75 F3						
Cowley Rd W3	52 B2									

Cullum St EC3 17 H3
Culmore Rd SE15 73 G3
Culmstock Rd SW11 84 A3
Culross St W1 13 F4
Culvert Pl SW11 70 A5
Culvert Rd SW11 69 G5
Cumberland Av, Well. 93 G1
Cumberland Cl E8 31 E3
Cumberland Cres W14 53 G5
Cumberland Gdns WC1 9 H1
Cumberland Gate W1 12 D3
Cumberland Ho SE28 65 E3
Cumberland Mkt NW1 7 J1
Cumberland Mkt Est NW1 7 J1
Cumberland Pk NW10 38 C2
Cumberland Pl NW1 7 H1
Cumberland Rd E13 35 G1
Cumberland Rd E13 49 E4
Cumberland Rd SW13 66 B4
Cumberland St SW1 70 B1
Cumming St N1 43 F1
Cunard Pl EC3 17 J2
Cunard Wk SE16 60 C5
Cundy E16 49 F5
Cundy St SW1 19 G6
Cundy St Est SW1 19 G6
Cunningham Pl NW8 41 E3
Cupar Rd SW11 70 B4
Cureton St SW1 20 D6
Curlew St SE1 59 E3
Curness St SE13 89 G2
Curricle St W3 52 A2
Cursitor St EC4 15 J1
Curtain Pl EC2 11 J3
Curtain Rd EC2 11 H4
Curtis St SE1 59 E5
Curtis Way SE1 59 E5
Curve, The W12 52 C1
Curwen Rd W12 52 C3
Curzon Gate W1 13 G6
Curzon Sq W1 13 G6
Curzon St W1 13 G6
Custom Ho Reach SE16 60 D3
Custom Ho Wk EC3 17 H4
Cut, The SE1 22 A1
Cutcombe Rd SE5 72 B5
Cuthbert St W2 41 E3
Cuthill Wk SE5 72 C4
Cutlers Gdns E1 17 J1
Cutler St E1 17 J1
Cyclops St E14 61 E5
Cygnus Business Cen NW10 24 B3
Cynthia St N1 43 F1
Cyntra Pl E8 31 G4
Cypress Gdns SE4 88 C3
Cypress Pl W1 8 B4
Cyprus Pl E2 46 A1
Cyprus Pl E6 64 C1
Cyprus Rd N9 64 C1
Cyprus St E2 46 A1
Cyrena Rd SE22 87 E4
Cyril Mans SW11 69 G4
Cyrus St EC1 10 C3
Czar St SE8 75 F2

D

Dabin Cres SE10 75 G4
Dacca St SE8 75 D2
Dace Rd E3 33 E4
Dacre Gdns SE13 90 B2
Dacre Pk SE13 90 B1
Dacre Pl SE13 90 B1
Dacre Rd E13 35 E5
Dacre St SW1 20 C3
Daffodil Gdns, Ilf. 36 D2
Daffodil St W12 52 B1
Dagmar Gdns NW10 39 F1
Dagmar Rd SE5 72 D4
Dagmar Ter N1 30 A5

Dagnall St SW11 69 G5
Dagnan Rd SW12 84 B5
Dahlia Gdns, Ilf. 37 D3
Dairsie Rd SE9 92 C1
Dairy Cl NW10 24 C5
Dairy La SE18 64 B5
Dairy Ms SW9 85 J1
Daisy La SW6 82 B1
Dakota Gdns E6 50 A3
Dalberg Rd SW2 85 G2
Dalby Rd SW18 82 D2
Dalby St NW5 28 B3
Dale Rd SE17 90 D1
Daleham Gdns NW3 27 E2
Daleham Ms NW3 27 E3
Dale Rd NW5 42 C1
Dale Rd SE17 72 A2
Dale St W4 66 A1
Daley St E9 32 B3
Daley Thompson Way SW8 70 B5
Dalgarno Gdns W10 39 E4
Dalgarno Way W10 39 E3
Dalgleish St E14 46 C5
Daling Way E3 32 C5
Dallinger Rd SE12 90 C4
Dalling Rd W6 52 D4
Dallington St EC1 10 C3
Dallin Rd SE18 79 E2
Dalmeny Av N7 29 D1
Dalmeny Rd N7 29 D1
Dalmeyer Rd NW10 24 B3
Dalrymple Rd SE4 88 C2
Dalston La E8 31 E3
Dalwood St SE5 72 D4
Dalyell Rd SW9 85 F1
Dame St N1 44 B1
Damien St E1 45 G5
Danbury St N1 44 A1
Danby St SE15 87 E1
Dancer Rd SW6 81 G1
Dando Cres SE3 91 E1
Dandridge Cl SE10 76 C1
Danebury Av SW15 80 A4
Danecroft Rd SE24 86 B3
Danehurst St SW6 67 G4
Danemere St SW15 81 E1
Dane Rd, Ilf. 37 E2
Danesdale Rd E9 32 C3
Danesfield SE5 73 D2
Dane St WC1 14 D1
Daneville Rd SE5 72 C4
Daniel Gdns SE15 73 E3
Daniels Rd SE15 88 A1
Dansey Pl W1 14 C3
Dante Pl SE11 22 C5
Dante Rd SE11 22 B5
Danvers St SW3 69 E2
Daphne St SW18 82 D4
D'Arblay St W1 14 B2
Darfield Rd SE4 88 D3
Darfield Way W10 39 F5
Darfur St SW15 81 E1
Darien Rd SW11 83 E1
Darlan Rd SW6 68 A3
Darley Rd SW11 83 G4
Darling Rd SE4 89 E1
Darling Row E1 45 G3
Darnley Ho E14 46 C5
Darnley Rd E9 31 G3
Darrell Rd SE22 87 F3
Darsley Dr SW8 71 D4
Dartford St SE17 72 B3
Dartmouth Cl W11 40 A5
Dartmouth Gro SE10 75 G4
Dartmouth Hill SE10 75 G4
Dartmouth Pk Rd NW5 28 B1
Dartmouth Pl W4 66 A2
Dartmouth Rd NW2 25 F3
Dartmouth Row SE10 75 G5
Dartmouth St SW1 20 C2
Dartmouth Ter SE10 76 A4
Dart St W10 39 G2
Darwell Cl E6 50 C1

Darwin Ct SE17 23 G6
Darwin St SE17 23 G5
Datchelor Pl SE5 72 C4
Date St SE17 72 B1
Daubeney Rd E5 32 C1
Daubeney Twr SE8 74 D1
Dault Rd SW18 82 C1
Davenant St E1 45 F4
Davenport Rd SE6 89 F4
Daventry St NW1 6 B5
Davern Cl SE10 62 C5
Davey Cl N7 29 F3
Davey Rd E9 33 E4
Davey St SE15 73 E2
Davidge St SE1 22 B2
David Lee Pt E15 34 B5
David Ms W1 6 D5
Davidson Gdns SW8 71 E3
David St E15 34 A3
Davies La E11 34 A3
Davies Ms W1 13 H3
Davies St W1 13 H3
Davis Rd W3 52 B2
Davis St E13 49 E1
Davisville Rd W12 52 C3
Dawes Rd SW6 67 G3
Dawes St SE17 72 C1
Dawlish Dr, Ilf. 37 G4
Dawlish Rd NW2 25 F3
Dawson Av, Bark. 37 G4
Dawson Cl SE18 65 E5
Dawson Hts Est SE22 87 F5
Dawson Pl W2 54 B1
Dawson Rd NW2 25 E2
Dawson St E2 45 E1
Daylesford Av SW15 80 C2
Days La, Sid. 93 G5
Dayton Gro SE15 74 A4
Deacon Ms N1 30 C4
Deacon Rd NW2 24 C2
Deacon Way SE17 22 D5
Deal Porters Way SE16 60 A4
Deals Gateway SE13 75 E4
Deal St E1 45 F4
Dealtry Rd SW15 81 E2
Dean Bradley St SW1 21 E4
Deancross St E1 46 A5
Deanery Ms W1 13 G5
Deanery Rd E15 34 B1
Deanery St W1 13 G5
Dean Farrar St SW1 20 C3
Dean Rd NW2 25 E3
Dean Ryle St SW1 21 E5
Deans Bldgs SE17 23 F6
Deans Ct EC4 16 C2
Deans Ms W1 13 J1
Dean Stanley St SW1 21 E4
Dean St E7 34 D2
Dean St W1 14 C1
Dean's Yd SW1 20 D3
Dean Trench St SW1 21 E4
De Beauvoir Cres N1 30 D5
De Beauvoir Est N1 30 C5
De Beauvoir Rd N1 30 D5
De Beauvoir Sq N1 31 D4
Decima St SE1 23 H3
De Coubertin St E20 33 G2
De Crespigny Pk SE5 72 C5
Deeley Rd SW8 70 D4
Deepdene Gdns SW2 85 F5
Deepdene Rd SE5 86 C2
Deerdale Rd SE24 86 B2
Deerhurst Rd NW2 25 F3
Dee St E14 47 G5
Defence Cl SE28 65 G2
Defiance Wk SE18 64 B4
De Havilland Dr SE18 79 D2
Dekker Rd SE21 86 D4
Delafield Rd SE7 77 E1
Delaford Rd SE16 73 G1
Delaford St SW6 67 G3
Delamere Ter W2 40 C4
Delancey St NW1 28 B5

De Laune St SE17 72 A1
Delaware Rd W9 40 C3
Delawyk Cres SE24 86 B4
Delhi St N1 29 E5
Delia St SW18 82 C5
Delisle Rd SE28 65 G2
Delius Gro E15 48 A1
Dell Cl E15 34 A5
Dellow St E1 59 G1
Dell's Ms SW1 20 B6
Delme Cres SE3 77 E5
Deloraine St SE8 75 E4
Delorme St W6 67 F2
Delverton Rd SE17 72 A1
Delvino Rd SW6 68 B4
De Morgan Rd SW6 82 B3
Dempster Rd SW18 82 D3
Denbigh Cl NW10 24 A1
Denbigh Ms SW1 20 A6
Denbigh Pl SW1 70 C1
Denbigh Rd E6 49 G2
Denbigh Rd W11 54 A1
Denbigh St SW1 20 A6
Denbigh Ter W11 54 A1
Dene Cl SE4 88 C1
Denham St SE10 76 D1
Denham Way, Bark. 37 G5
Denholme Rd W9 40 A2
Denman Rd SE15 73 E4
Denman St W1 14 C4
Denmark Gro N1 43 G1
Denmark Hill SE5 72 C4
Denmark Hill Est SE5 86 C2
Denmark Pl WC2 14 D1
Denmark Rd NW6 40 A1
Denmark Rd SE5 72 B4
Denmark St E13 49 E4
Denmark St WC2 14 D1
Denne Ter E8 31 E5
Dennetts Rd SE14 74 A4
Denning Cl NW8 41 D2
Denning Rd NW3 27 E1
Dennington Pk Rd NW6 26 B3
Dennison Pt E15 33 G4
Denny Cres SE11 22 A6
Denny St SE11 71 G1
Densham Rd E15 34 B5
Denton Rd W8 82 C4
Dents Rd SW11 83 G4
Denyer St SW3 18 C6
Denzil Rd NW10 24 B2
Deodar Rd SW15 81 G2
Depot App NW2 25 F1
Depot Rd W12 53 E1
Deptford Br SE8 75 E4
Deptford Bdy SE8 75 E4
Deptford Ch St SE8 75 E2
Deptford Ferry Rd E14 61 E5
Deptford Grn SE8 75 E2
Deptford Strand SE8 61 D5
Deptford Wf SE8 60 D5
Derby Gate SW1 21 E1
Derby Rd E7 35 F4
Derby Rd E9 32 B5
Derbyshire St E2 45 F2
Derby St W1 13 G6
Dereham Pl EC2 11 J2
Dericote St E8 31 F5
Derifall Cl E6 50 B5
Dering St W1 13 H2
Dermody Gdns SE13 90 A3
Dermody Rd SE13 90 A3
Derry St W8 54 C3
Dersingham Av E12 36 C2
Derwent Gro SE22 87 E2
Derwent St SE10 76 B1
Desborough Cl W2 40 C4
Desenfans Rd SE21 87 D4
Desford Rd E16 48 B3
Desmond St SE14 74 C2
Desvignes Dr SE13 90 A4

Name	Ref
Devalls Cl E6	64 C1
Devas St E3	47 F3
Devenay Rd E15	34 C4
Deventer Cres SE22	86 D3
De Vere Gdns W8	54 D3
Deverell St SE1	23 F4
Devereux Ct WC2	15 J2
Devereux La SW13	66 D3
Devereux Rd SW11	83 G4
Devonia Rd N1	44 A1
Devonport Rd W12	53 D3
Devon Bark.	37 G5
Devons Est E3	47 F2
Devonshire Cl E3	34 B1
Devonshire Cl W1	7 H5
Devonshire Dr SE10	75 F3
Devonshire Gro SE15	73 G2
Devonshire Ms N W1	7 H4
Devonshire Ms S W1	7 H5
Devonshire Ms W W1	7 H4
Devonshire Pas W4	66 A1
Devonshire Pl W1	7 G4
Devonshire Pl Ms W1	7 G4
Devonshire Rd E16	49 E5
Devonshire Rd W4	66 A1
Devonshire Row EC2	11 J3
Devonshire Row Ms W1	7 J4
Devonshire Sq EC2	17 J1
Devonshire St W1	7 G5
Devonshire St W4	66 A1
Devonshire Ter W2	41 D5
Devons Rd E3	47 E4
Devon St SE15	73 G2
De Walden St W1	7 G6
Dewar St SE15	87 F1
Dewberry Gdns E6	50 A4
Dewberry St E14	47 G4
Dewey Rd N1	43 G1
Dewhurst Rd W14	53 F4
Dewsbury Rd NW10	24 C2
D'Eynsford Rd SE5	72 C4
Diadem Ct W1	14 C2
Dial Wk, The W8	54 C3
Diamond St SE15	73 D3
Diamond Ter SE10	75 G4
Diana Ho SW13	66 B4
Dibden St N1	30 A5
Dicey Av NW2	25 E2
Dickens Est SE16	59 E3
Dickens Est SE16	59 E3
Dickens Ho NW6	40 B2
Dickens Ms EC1	10 B5
Dickens Rd E6	49 G1
Dickens Sq SE1	23 E3
Dickens St SW8	70 B5
Dickson Rd SE9	92 A1
Dieppe Cl W14	68 A1
Digby Rd E9	32 B3
Digby St E2	46 A2
Dighton Ct SE5	72 B2
Dighton Rd SW18	80 D3
Dilke St SW3	69 G2
Dimond Cl E7	35 D1
Dimson Cres E3	47 E3
Dingle Gdns E14	61 E1
Dingley Pl EC1	10 E2
Dingley Rd EC1	10 D2
Dingwall Rd SW18	80 D5
Dinsdale Rd SE3	76 C2
Dinsmore Rd SW12	84 B5
Dirleton Rd E15	34 C5
Disbrowe Rd W6	67 G2
Discovery wk E1	59 G2
Disney Pl SE1	22 E1
Disney St SE1	22 E1
Disraeli Rd E7	35 D3
Disraeli Rd SW15	81 G2
Diss St E2	45 E2
Distaff La EC4	16 D3
Distillery Rd W6	67 E1
Distin St SE11	21 J6
Ditch All SE10	75 F4
Ditchburn St E14	61 G1
Divis Way SW15	81 D4
Dixon Ho W10	39 F5
Dixon Rd SE14	74 C4
Dixon's All SE16	59 G3
Dobell Rd SE9	92 B3
Dobree Av NW10	24 D4
Dobson St E14	27 E4
Doby Ct EC4	17 E3
Dockers Tanner Rd E14	61 E4
Dockhead SE1	59 E3
Dock Hill Av SE16	60 B3
Dockland St E16	64 C2
Dockley Rd SE16	59 F4
Dock Rd E16	62 C1
Dockside Rd E16	63 G1
Dock St E1	59 E1
Docwra's Bldgs N1	30 D3
Doddington Gro SE17	72 A2
Doddington Pl SE17	72 A2
Dodson St SE1	22 A2
Dod St E14	47 D5
Doggett Rd SE6	89 E5
Dog Kennel Hill SE22	86 D1
Dog Kennel Hill Est SE22	87 D1
Dog La NW10	24 A1
Doherty Rd E13	49 D3
Dolben St SE1	16 B6
Dolby Rd SW6	68 A5
Dolland St SE11	71 F1
Dolman St SW4	85 F2
Dolphin La E14	61 F1
Dolphin Sq SW1	70 C1
Dolphin Sq W4	66 A3
Dombey St WC1	9 G5
Domett Cl SE5	86 C2
Domingo St EC1	10 D3
Dominica Cl E13	49 F1
Dominion St EC2	11 G5
Donald Rd E13	35 E5
Donaldson Rd NW6	26 A5
Donaldson Rd SE18	78 C4
Donegal St N1	43 F1
Doneraile St SW6	67 F5
Dongola Rd E1	46 C4
Dongola Rd E13	49 E2
Donkey All SE22	87 F5
Donne Ct SE24	86 B4
Donne Pl SW3	18 B5
Donnington Ct NW10	24 D4
Donnington Rd NW10	24 D4
Don Phelan Cl SE5	72 C4
Doon St SE1	15 J6
Dorando Cl W10	53 D1
Doran Gro SE18	79 G3
Doran Wk E15	33 G4
Dora St E14	46 D5
Dora Way SW9	71 G5
Dorchester Ct SE24	86 B3
Dorchester Dr SE24	86 B3
Dorchester Gro W4	66 A1
Dordrecht Rd W3	52 A2
Dore Av E12	36 C2
Doria Rd SW6	68 A5
Doric Way NW1	8 C1
Doris Rd E7	35 D4
Dorking Cl SE8	74 D2
Dorlcote Rd SW18	83 E5
Dorman Way NW8	27 E5
Dormay St SW18	82 C3
Dormer Cl E15	34 C3
Dornberg Cl SE3	77 D3
Dorncliffe Rd SW6	67 G5
Dornfell St NW6	26 A2
Dorothy Rd SW11	83 G1
Dorrington St EC1	9 J5
Dorrit St SE1	22 E1
Dorset Bldgs EC4	16 B2
Dorset Cl NW1	6 D5
Dorset Est E2	45 E2
Dorset Ms SW1	19 H3
Dorset Pl E15	34 A3
Dorset Ri EC4	16 B2
Dorset Rd E7	35 F4
Dorset Rd SW8	71 F3
Dorset Sq NW1	6 D4
Dorset St W1	7 E6
Dorville Cres W6	52 D4
Dorville Rd SE12	90 C3
Dothill Rd SE18	79 F3
Doughty Ms WC1	9 G4
Doughty St WC1	9 G3
Douglas Rd E16	49 D4
Douglas Rd N1	30 B4
Douglas Rd NW6	26 A5
Douglas Rd SE18	20 C6
Douglas Way SE8	75 D3
Douro Pl W8	54 C4
Douro St E3	47 E1
Dove App E6	50 A4
Dove Ct EC2	17 F2
Dovedale Rd SE22	87 G3
Dovehouse Mead, Bark.	51 H1
Dovehouse St SW3	69 F1
Dove Ms SW5	54 D5
Dovercourt Est N1	30 C3
Dovercourt Rd SE22	87 D4
Doverfield Rd SW2	85 E4
Dover Flats SE1	23 J6
Dover Ho Rd SW15	80 C2
Dove Rd N1	30 C3
Dove Row E2	31 F5
Dover Pk Dr SW15	80 D4
Dover St W1	13 J4
Dover Yd W1	14 A5
Doves Yd N1	29 G5
Dowdeswell Cl SW15	80 A2
Dowding Dr SE9	91 F3
Dowdney Cl SE5	72 C2
Dowells St SE10	75 F2
Dowgate Hill EC4	17 F3
Dowland St W10	39 G1
Dowlas St SE5	72 D3
Downfield Cl W9	40 C3
Downham Rd N1	30 C4
Downings E6	50 C5
Downing St SW1	20 E1
Downman Rd SE9	92 A1
Down Pl W6	53 D5
Downsell Rd E15	33 G1
Downshire Hill NW3	27 E1
Downside Cres NW3	27 F2
Downs Pk Rd E5	31 F2
Downs Pk Rd E8	31 F2
Downs Rd E5	31 F1
Downtown Rd SE16	60 C3
Dowson Cl SE5	86 C2
Doyce St SE1	22 D1
Doyle Gdns NW10	24 C5
D'Oyley St SW1	19 F5
Draco St SE17	72 B2
Dragmore St SW4	85 D4
Dragonfly Cl E13	49 E2
Dragon Rd SE15	72 D2
Dragoon Rd SE8	74 B5
Drake Cl W12	53 E3
Drakefell Rd SE4	74 B5
Drakefell Rd SE14	74 B5
Drakeley Ct N5	30 A1
Drake Rd SE4	89 E1
Drakes Ctyd NW6	26 A4
Drake St WC1	9 G6
Drakes Wk E6	36 B5
Draper Ho SE1	22 C5
Drapers Rd E15	34 A1
Drawdock Rd SE10	62 A2
Drawell Cl SE18	79 G1
Draycott Av SW3	18 C5
Draycott Pl SW3	18 D6
Draycott Ter SW3	18 E5
Drayford Cl W9	40 A3
Dray Gdns SW2	85 F3
Drayson Ms W8	54 B3
Drayton Gdns SW10	69 D1
Drayton Pk N5	29 G2
Drayton Rd NW10	24 B5
Dresden Rd N19	28 C3
Dressington Av SE4	89 E4
Drew Rd E16	64 A2
Driffield Rd E3	46 C1
Dromore Rd SW15	81 G4
Droop St W10	39 G3
Drovers Pl SE15	73 G3
Druce Rd SE21	87 D4
Druid St SE1	23 J1
Drummond Cres NW1	8 C1
Drummond Gate SW1	71 D1
Drummond Rd SE16	59 G4
Drummond St NW1	8 A3
Drury La WC2	15 F2
Dryad St SW15	81 F1
Dryburgh Rd SW15	81 D1
Dryden Cl SW4	85 D3
Dryden Ct SE11	22 A6
Dryden Rd, Well.	79 G4
Dryden St WC2	15 F2
Drysdale Pl N1	11 J2
Drysdale St N1	31 F5
Du Cane Cl W12	39 E5
Du Cane Rd W12	38 B5
Duchess Ms W1	7 J6
Duchess of Bedford's Wk W8	54 B3
Duchess St W1	7 J6
Duchy St SE1	16 A5
Ducie St SW4	85 F2
Duckett St E1	46 B3
Duck La W1	14 C2
Dudden Hill La NW10	24 B1
Dudley Rd NW6	39 G1
Dudley Rd, Ilf.	37 D1
Dudley St W2	41 E4
Dufferin Av EC1	11 F4
Dufferin St EC1	11 E4
Duff St E14	47 F5
Dufour's Pl W1	14 B2
Dugard Way SE11	22 B5
Duke Humphrey Rd SE3	76 B4
Duke of Wellington Av SE18	65 D4
Duke of Wellington Pl SW1	19 E6
Duke of York Sq SW3	19 E6
Duke of York St SW1	14 B5
Dukes Ct E6	36 C5
Dukes La W8	54 B3
Dukes Ms W1	13 G1
Dukes Pl EC3	17 J2
Dukes Rd E6	36 C5
Duke's Rd WC1	8 D2
Duke St SW1	14 B5
Duke St W1	13 G1
Duke St Hill SE1	17 G5
Duke's Yd W1	13 G3
Dulford St W11	53 G1
Dulka Rd SW11	83 G3
Dulwich Rd SE24	85 G3
Dulwich Village SE21	86 D4
Dumbarton Rd SW2	85 E4
Dumbreck Rd SE9	92 B2
Dunbar Rd E7	35 D3
Dunblane Rd SE9	92 A1
Dunboyne Rd NW3	27 G2
Dunbridge St E2	45 F3
Duncan Gro W3	38 A5
Duncannon St WC2	15 E4
Duncan Rd E8	31 G5
Duncan Ter N1	44 A1
Duncombe Hill SE23	88 C5
Duncrievie Rd SE13	90 A4
Duncroft SE18	79 G3
Dundalk Rd SE4	88 C1
Dundas Rd SE15	74 A5
Dundas St SE15	74 A5
Dundee Rd E13	49 E1

Dundee St E1 59 G2
Dundonald Rd NW10 25 F5
Dunelm St E1 59 H1
Dunford Rd N7 29 F1
Dungarvan Av SW15 80 C2
Dunlace Rd E5 32 A1
Dunloe St E2 45 E1
Dunmore Rd NW6 25 G5
Dunmow Rd E15 34 A1
Dunnock Rd E6 50 A5
Dunns Pas WC1 15 F1
Dunn St E8 31 E2
Dunollie Rd NW5 27 F2
Dunoon Rd SE23 88 A5
Dunraven Rd W12 52 C2
Dunraven St W1 13 E3
Dunsany Rd W14 53 F4
Dunstable Ms W1 7 G5
Dunstans Gro SE22 87 G4
Dunstans Rd SE22 87 F5
Dunster Ct EC3 17 H3
Dunster Gdns NW6 26 A4
Dunsterville Way SE1 23 G2
Dunston Rd E8 31 E5
Dunston Rd SW11 70 A5
Dunston St E8 31 E5
Dunton Rd SE1 73 E1
Dunvegan Rd SE9 92 B2
Duplex Ride SW1 19 E2
Dupree Rd SE7 77 E1
Durand Gdns SW9 71 F4
Durants Wk SE16 60 D3
Durant St E2 45 F1
Durban Rd E15 48 B2
Durham Ho St WC2 15 F4
Durham Rd E12 35 G1
Durham Rd E16 48 B3
Durham Row E1 46 C4
Durham St SE11 71 F1
Durham Ter W2 40 C5
Durrell Rd SW6 68 A4
Durrington Rd E5 32 C1
Dursley Cl SE3 77 F5
Dursley Gdns SE3 77 G4
Dursley Rd SE3 77 F5
Durward St E1 45 G4
Durweston Ms W1 7 E5
Durweston St W1 6 E5
Dutton St SE10 75 G4
Dye Ho La E3 33 E5
Dyer's Bldgs EC1 9 J6
Dyers La SW15 81 D2
Dylan Rd SE24 86 A2
Dylways SE5 86 C2
Dymock St SW6 82 C1
Dyne Rd NW6 26 A4
Dynham Rd NW6 26 B4
Dyott St WC1 14 E1
Dysart St EC2 11 G4
Dyson St E15 34 C3

E

Eagle Ct EC1 10 B5
Eagle Pl SW1 14 B4
Eaglesfield Rd SE18 79 D3
Eagle St WC1 9 G6
Eagle Wf Rd N1 44 B1
Ealdham Sq SE9 91 F2
Eamont St NW8 41 F1
Eardley Cres SW5 68 B1
Earldom Rd SW15 81 E2
Earlham Gro E7 34 C2
Earlham St WC2 14 D2
Earl Rd SE1 65 F5
Earls Ct Gdns SW5 54 C5
Earls Ct Rd SW5 54 B5
Earls Ct Rd W8 54 B5
Earls Ct Sq SW5 68 C1
Earlsferry Way N1 29 F4
Earlshall Rd SE9 92 B2
Earlsmead Rd NW10 39 E1
Earls Ter W8 54 A4
Earlsthorpe Ms SW12 84 A4

Earlstoke St EC1 10 B1
Earlston Gro E9 31 G5
Earl St EC2 11 H5
Earls Wk W8 54 B4
Earlswood St SE10 76 B1
Earnshaw St WC2 14 D1
Easby St W14 53 G5
Easley's Ms W1 13 G1
East Acton La W3 52 A1
East Arbour St E1 46 B5
East Av E12 36 A4
Eastbourne Ms W1 41 D5
Eastbourne Rd E6 50 C2
Eastbourne Ter W2 41 D5
Eastbrook Rd SE3 77 E3
Eastbury Av, Bark. 37 G5
Eastbury Ct, Bark. 37 G5
Eastbury Gro W4 66 A1
Eastbury Rd E6 50 C3
Eastbury Ter E1 46 B3
Eastcastle St W1 14 A1
Eastcheap EC3 17 G3
Eastcombe Av SE7 77 E2
Eastcote Rd, Well. 79 F5
Eastcote St SW9 71 F5
East Cross Cen E15 33 E3
East Cross Route E3 33 D4
East Cross Route E9 33 D4
Eastdown Pk SE13 90 A2
East Dulwich Gro SE22 86 D4
East Dulwich Rd SE15 87 E2
East Dulwich Rd SE22 87 E2
Eastern Gateway E16 63 F1
Eastern Rd E13 49 E1
Eastern Rd SE4 89 E2
East Ferry Rd E14 61 H4
Eastfields Av SW18 82 B2
Eastfield St E14 46 C4
East Ham Ind Est E6 50 A3
East Ham Manor Way E6 64 B1
East Harding St EC4 16 A1
East Hill SW18 82 C2
East India Dock Rd E14 47 E5
Eastlake Rd SE5 72 A5
Eastlands Cres SE21 87 E4
East La SE16 59 G5
Eastleigh Wk SW15 80 C5
Eastmoor St SE7 63 G4
East Mt St E1 45 G4
Eastney St SE10 76 A1
Easton St WC1 9 J2
East Parkside SE10 62 B3
East Pas EC1 10 C5
East Poultry Av EC1 10 B6
East Rd E15 34 D5
East Rd N1 11 F2
East Rd SW3 70 A1

Eastrow St SW9 71 G4
Eastview Av SE18 79 D3
Eastway E9 32 D3

East Rochester Way SE9 93 G2

East Rochester Way, Sid. 93 G2
East Row W10 39 G3
East Smithfield E1 59 E1
East St SE17 72 B1
East Surrey Gro SE15 73 E3
East Tenter St E1 45 E5
Eastway E9 32 D3

Eastway Commercial Cen E9 33 E2

Eaton Cl SW1 19 F6
Eaton Dr SW9 86 A2
Eaton Gate SW1 19 F5
Eaton La SW1 19 J4
Eaton Ms N SW1 19 G5
Eaton Ms S SW1 19 G5
Eaton Ms W SW1 19 G5
Eaton Pl SW1 19 F4
Eaton Row SW1 19 H3
Eaton Sq SW1 19 H3
Eaton Ter SW1 19 F5

Eaton Ter Ms SW1 19 F5
Ebbisham Dr SW8 71 F2
Ebbsfleet Rd NW2 25 G2
Ebdon Way SE3 91 E1
Ebenezer Ho SE11 22 A6
Ebenezer St N1 11 F1
Ebley Cl SE15 73 E2
Ebner St SW18 82 C3
Ebor St E1 45 E3
Ebsworth St SE23 88 B5
Ebury Br SW1 70 B1
Ebury Br Est SW1 70 B1
Ebury Br Rd SW1 70 A1
Ebury Ms SW1 19 G5
Ebury Ms E SW1 19 H5
Ebury Sq SW1 19 H5
Ebury St SW1 19 H5
Ecclesbourne Rd N1 30 B4
Eccles Rd SW11 83 G2
Eccleston Br SW1 19 J5
Eccleston Ms SW1 19 H4
Eccleston Pl SW1 19 H5
Eccleston Sq SW1 19 J6
Eccleston Sq Ms SW1 20 A6
Eccleston St SW1 19 H4
Eckford St N1 43 G1
Eckstein Rd SW11 83 G2
Eclipse Rd E13 49 E4
Edbrooke Rd W9 40 B3
Eddiscombe Rd SW6 68 A5
Eddystone Rd SE4 88 C3
Eddystone Twr SE8 60 C5
Edenbridge Rd E9 32 B4
Eden Gro N7 29 F2
Edenhurst Av SW6 82 A1
Edensor Gdns W4 66 A3
Edensor Rd W4 66 A3
Edenvale St SW6 82 C1
Edgar Kail Way SE22 86 D2
Edgarley Ter SW6 67 G4
Edgar Rd E3 47 F2
Edgar Wallace Cl SE15 73 D3
Edge Hill SE18 78 D2
Edgeley Rd SW4 84 D1
Edgeworth Rd SE9 91 F2
Edgware Rd W2 12 C1
Edinburgh Gate SW1 18 D1
Edinburgh Ho W9 40 C2
Edinburgh Rd E13 49 E1
Edis St NW1 28 A5
Edith Cavell Way SE18 78 A4
Edith Gro SW10 68 D2
Edithna St SW9 85 E1
Edith Nesbit Wk SE9 92 A3
Edith Rd E6 35 G4
Edith Rd W14 53 G5
Edith Row SW6 68 C4
Edith St E2 45 F1
Edith Ter SW10 68 D3
Edith Vil W14 54 A5
Edmeston Cl E9 32 C3

Edmund Halley Way SE10 62 B3

Edmund Hurst Dr E6 50 D4
Edmund St SE5 72 C3
Edna St SW11 69 F4
Edrich Ho SW4 71 E4
Edric Rd SE14 74 B3
Edward Cl NW2 25 F1
Edwardes Sq W8 54 B4
Edward Pl SE8 75 D2
Edwards Ho N1 29 G4
Edwards Ms W1 13 F2
Edward Sq E16 48 D3
Edward St SE8 75 D2
Edward St SE14 74 C3
Edward Temme Av E15 34 C1
Edwin Av E6 50 C1
Edwin St E1 46 A3
Edwin St E16 48 D4
Effie Pl SW6 68 B3
Effie Rd SW6 68 B3
Effingham Rd SE12 90 B3
Effra Par SW2 85 G3

Effra Rd SW2 85 G2
Egbert St NW1 28 A5
Egeremont Rd SE13 75 F5
Egerton Cres SW3 18 C5
Egerton Dr SE10 75 F4
Egerton Gdns NW10 25 E5
Egerton Gdns SW3 18 C4
Egerton Gdns Ms SW3 18 C4
Egerton Pl SW3 18 C4
Egerton Ter SW3 18 C4
Egham Rd E13 49 E4
Eglantine Rd SW18 82 D3
Eglinton Hill SE18 79 D2
Eglinton Rd SE18 78 C2
Egliston Ms SW15 81 E1
Egliston Rd SW15 81 E1
Egmont St SE14 74 B3
Elder Cl E7 34 C2
Eighth Av E12 36 B1
Eisenhower Dr E6 50 A4
Elaine Gro NW5 28 A2
Elam Cl SE5 72 A5
Elam St SE5 72 A5
Eland Rd SW11 83 G1
Elba Pl SE17 23 E5
Elbe St SW6 68 D5
Elburg Dr E16 49 D5
Elcho St SW11 69 F3
Elcot Av SE15 73 G3
Elderberry Way E6 50 B2
Elderfield Rd E5 32 A1
Elderflower Way E15 34 B4
Eldersie Rd SE9 92 C3
Elder St E1 45 E4
Eldon Gro NW3 27 E2
Eldon Rd W8 54 C4
Eldon St EC2 11 G6
Eldred Rd, Bark. 37 G5
Eleanor Cl SE16 60 B3
Eleanor Gro SW13 80 A1
Eleanor Rd E8 31 G3
Eleanor Rd E15 34 C3
Eleanor Rd SW9 71 G4
Eleanor St E3 47 E2

Electra Business Pk E16 48 A3

Electric Av SW9 85 G2
Electric La SW9 85 G2
Elephant & Castle SE1 22 C4
Elephant La SE16 60 A3
Elephant Rd SE17 22 D5
Elfindale Rd SE24 86 B3
Elford Cl SE3 91 E2
Elfort Rd N5 29 G1
Elf Row E1 60 A1
Elgar St SE16 60 C4
Elgin Av W9 40 C2
Elgin Av W12 52 C3
Elgin Cl W12 52 D3
Elgin Cres W11 40 A5
Elia Ms N1 44 A1
Elias Pl SW8 71 G2
Elia St N1 44 A1
Elibank Rd SE9 92 C2
Elim Est SE1 23 H3
Elim St SE1 23 G3
Elim Way E13 48 C2
Eliot Gdns SW15 80 C2
Eliot Hill SE13 75 G5
Eliot Ms NW8 41 D1
Eliot Pk SE13 89 G5
Eliot Pl SE3 76 B5
Eliot Vale SE3 76 A5
Elis Way E20 33 G2
Elizabeth Av N1 30 B4
Elizabeth Br SW1 19 H6
Elizabeth Cl SW1 20 D4
Elizabeth Est SE17 72 C2
Elizabeth Fry Pl SE18 78 A4
Elizabeth Gdns W3 52 B2
Elizabeth Ms NW3 27 F3
Elizabeth Rd E6 35 G5
Elizabeth Sq SE16 60 C1
Elizabeth Ter SE9 92 B4

Elkington Pt SE11 21 J6
Elkington Rd E13 49 E3
Elkstone Rd W10 40 A4
Ellaline Rd W6 67 F2
Elland Rd SE15 88 A2
Ellenborough Pl SW15 80 C2
Ellen St E1 45 F5
Ellerby St SW6 67 F4
Ellerdale Rd NW3 27 D2
Ellerdale St SE13 89 F2
Ellerslie Gdns NW10 24 C5
Ellerslie Rd W12 52 D2
Ellerslie Sq Ind Est SW2 85 E3
Ellerton Rd SW13 66 C4
Ellery St SE15 73 G5
Ellesmere Rd E3 46 C1
Ellesmere Rd NW10 24 C2
Ellesmere St E14 47 F5
Ellingfort Rd E8 31 G4
Ellingham Rd E15 34 A1
Ellingham Rd W12 52 C3
Ellington Ho SE1 22 E3
Ellington St N7 29 G3
Elliot CI E15 34 B4
Elliott Rd SW9 72 A3
Elliott Rd W4 52 A5
Elliott Sq NW3 27 F4
Elliotts Row SE11 22 B5
Elliscombe Rd SE7 77 F1
Ellisfield Dr SW15 80 B5
Ellison Rd SW13 66 B5
Ellis St SW1 19 E5
Elliston Ho SE18 64 C5
Ellsworth St E2 45 G2
Elm Bk Gdns SW13 66 A5
Elmbrook Gdns SE9 92 A2
Elmc Ct EC4 15 J3
Elmcroft St E5 32 A1
Elmdene Rd SE18 78 D1
Elmer Rd SE6 89 G5
Elmfield Way W9 40 B4
Elm Friars Wk NW1 29 D4
Elm Grn W3 38 A5
Elm Gro NW2 25 F1
Elm Gro SE15 73 E5
Elm Gro Rd SW13 66 C5
Elmhurst Rd E7 35 E4
Elmhurst St SW4 84 D1
Elmington Est SE17 72 C3
Elmington Rd SE5 72 C4
Elmira St SE13 89 F1
Elmley St SE18 65 F5
Elmore St N1 30 B2
Elm Pk SW2 85 F4
Elm Pk Gdns SW10 69 E1
Elm Pk La SW3 69 E1
Elm Pk Rd SW3 69 E2
Elm Pl SW7 69 E1
Elm Quay Ct SW8 70 D2
Elm Rd E7 34 C3
Elms, The SW13 80 B1
Elms Cres SW4 84 C4
Elmshaw Rd SW15 80 C3
Elmslie Pt E3 46 D4
Elms Ms W2 55 E1
Elms Rd SW4 84 C3
Elmstone Rd SW6 68 B4
Elm St WC1 9 H4
Elm Ter CI NW8 92 C4
Elm Tree Ct NW8 41 E2
Elm Tree Rd NW8 41 E2
Elm Way NW10 24 A1
Elmwood Ct SW11 70 B4
Elmwood Rd SE24 86 C3
Elphinstone St N5 30 A1
Elrington Rd E8 31 F3
Elsa St E1 46 C4
Elsdale St E9 32 A3
Elsenham Rd E12 36 B2
Elsham Rd W14 53 G3
Elsham Ter W14 53 G3
Elsiemaud Rd SE4 89 D3
Elsie Rd SE22 87 E2

Elsley Rd SW11 83 G1
Elspeth Rd SW11 83 G2
Elsted St SE17 23 G6
Elstow CI SE9 92 C3
Elstree Gdns, Ilf. 37 E2
Elswick Rd SE13 75 F5
Elswick St SW6 68 D5
Elsworthy Ri NW3 27 F4
Elsworthy Rd NW3 27 F5
Elsworthy Ter NW3 27 F4
Elsynge Rd SW18 83 E3
Eltham Grn SE9 91 F3
Eltham Grn Rd SE9 91 F2
Eltham High St SE9 92 B4
Eltham Hill SE9 91 G3
Eltham Palace Rd SE9 91 F4
Eltham Pk Gdns SE9 92 B2
Eltham Rd SE9 91 F3
Eltham Rd SE12 90 C3
Elthiron Rd SW6 68 B4
Elthruda Rd SE13 90 A4
Eltisley Rd, Ilf. 36 D1
Elton Ho E3 33 D5
Elton Pl N16 30 D2
Eltringham St SW18 82 D2
Elvaston Ms SW7 55 D4
Elvaston PI SW7 54 D4
Elverson Ms SE8 75 F5
Elverson Rd SE8 75 F5
Elverton St SW1 20 C5
Elvis Rd NW2 25 E3
Elwin St E2 45 F2
Elwyn Gdns SE12 90 D5
Ely CI EC1 10 A6
Ely Pl EC1 10 A6
Elystan PI SW3 69 F1
Elystan St SW3 18 B6
Embankment SW15 67 F5
Embankment Gdns SW3 69 G2
Embankment Pier WC2 15 G5
Embankment PI WC2 15 F5
Emba St SE16 59 F3
Emberton SE5 72 D2
Embleton Rd SE13 89 F1
Emden St SW6 68 C4
Emerald CI E16 50 A5
Emerald St WC1 9 G5
Emerson St SE1 16 D5
Emery Hill St SW1 20 B4
Emery St SE1 22 A3
Emlyn Rd W12 52 A3
Emlyn Rd W12 52 A3
Emma CI E8 48 C1
Emma St E2 45 G1
Emmott CI E1 46 C3
Emperor's Gate SW7 54 C4
Empire CI SE7 77 E2
Empire Sq SE1 23 F2
Empire Wf Rd E14 75 E5
Empress Ms SE5 72 B5
Empress Rd E9 32 B1
Empress St SE17 72 B2
Empson St E3 47 F3
Emu Rd SW8 70 B5
Enbrook St W10 39 G2
Endell St WC2 14 E1
Enderby St SE10 76 B1
Endlesham Rd SW12 84 A5
Endsleigh Gdns WC1 8 C3
Endsleigh PI WC1 8 C3
Endsleigh St WC1 8 C3
Endwell Rd SE4 74 C5
Endymion Rd SW2 85 F4
Energen CI NW10 24 A3
Enfield Rd N1 31 D4
Enford St W1 6 D5
Engate St SE13 89 G2
Engineer CI SE18 78 C2
Englands La NW3 27 G3
Englefield Rd N1 30 C3
Engleheart Rd SE6 89 F5
Englewood Rd SW12 84 B4

English Grds SE1 17 H6
English St E3 46 D3
Enid St SE16 59 E4
Enmore Rd SW15 81 E2
Ennerdale Ho E3 46 D3
Ennersdale Rd SE13 90 A3
Ennismore Av W4 52 B5
Ennismore Gdns SW7 18 B3
Ennismore Gdns Ms SW7 18 B3
Ennismore Ms SW7 18 B3
Ennismore St SW7 18 B3
Ennis Rd SE18 79 E2
Ensign St E1 59 F1
Enslin Rd SE9 92 C4
Enterprise Way NW10 38 C2
Enterprise Way SW18 82 B2
Enterprise Way SE8 60 D5
Epirus Ms SW6 68 B3
Epirus Rd SW6 68 A3
Epping CI E14 61 E5
Epping PI N1 29 G3
Epple Rd SW6 68 A4
Epworth St EC2 11 G4
Equinox Ho, Bark. 37 E3
Erasmus St SW1 20 D6
Erconwald St W12 38 B5
Erebus Dr SE28 79 G3
Eresby Pl NW6 26 B4
Erica St W12 52 C1
Eric Clarke La, Bark. 51 D3
Eric CI E7 34 D1
Ericcson CI SW18 82 B3
Eric Rd E7 34 D1
Eric St E3 46 D3
Erin Ct NW2 25 E3
Erindale SE18 79 F2
Erindale Ter SE18 79 F2
Erlanger Rd SE14 74 B4
Ermine Rd SE13 89 F1
Ernald Av E6 50 A1
Ernest St E1 46 B3
Erpingham Rd SW15 81 E1
Errington Rd W9 40 A3
Errol St EC1 11 E4
Erskine Rd NW3 27 G4
Erwood Rd SE7 78 A1
Escreet Gro SE18 64 C5
Esk Rd E13 49 D3
Esme Ho SW15 80 B2
Esmeralda Rd SE1 59 F5
Esmond Rd NW6 26 A5
Esmond St SW15 81 G2
Esparto St SW18 82 C5
Essendine Rd W9 40 B3
Essex Ct EC4 15 J2
Essex Ct SW13 66 B5
Essex Pk Ms W3 52 A2
Essex Rd E12 36 A1
Essex Rd N1 30 A5
Essex Rd NW10 24 A4
Essex Rd, Bark. 37 F4
Essex St E7 34 D2
Essex St WC2 15 J3
Essex Vil W8 54 B3
Essian St E1 46 C4
Estcourt Rd SW6 68 A3
Estelle Rd NW3 27 G1
Esterbrooke St SW1 20 C6
Este Rd SW11 83 F1
Estoria CI SW2 85 G5
Etchingham Rd E15 33 G1
Eternit Wk SW6 67 E4
Ethelburga St SW11 69 F4
Ethelden Rd W12 52 D2
Ethel Rd E16 49 E5
Ethel St SE17 22 D6
Etherow St SE22 87 F4
Ethnard Rd SE15 73 G2
Eton Av NW3 27 E4
Eton CI SW18 82 C5
Eton Coll Rd NW3 27 G3
Eton Gro SE13 90 B1

Eton Rd NW3 27 G4
Eton Rd, Ilf. 37 E2
Eton Vil NW3 27 G3
Etta St SE8 74 C2
Ettrick St E14 47 G5
Eugenia Rd SE16 60 A5
Euro CI NW10 24 C3
Europa Pl EC1 10 D2
Europe Rd SE18 64 B4
Eustace Rd E6 50 A2
Eustace Rd SW6 68 B3
Euston Gro NW1 8 C2
Euston Rd N1 9 E1
Euston Rd NW1 7 J4
Euston Sq NW1 8 C2
Euston Sta NW1 8 B1
Euston Sta Colonnade NW1 8 C2
Euston St NW1 8 B3
Euston Twr NW1 8 A3
Evan Cook CI SE15 74 A4
Evandale Rd SW9 71 G5
Evangelist Rd NW5 28 B1
Evelina Rd SE15 88 A1
Eveline Lowe Est SE1 59 F4
Evelyn Denington Rd E6 50 A3
Evelyn Fox Ct W10 39 E4
Evelyn Gdns SW7 69 E1
Evelyn Rd E16 63 E2
Evelyn St SE8 74 C1
Evelyn Wk N1 44 C1
Evelyn Yd W1 14 C1
Evenwood CI SW15 81 G3
Everdon Rd SW13 66 C2
Everest PI E14 47 G4
Everest Rd SE9 92 B3
Evergreen Sq E8 31 E4
Everilda St N1 29 F5
Everington St W6 67 F2
Eve Rd E11 34 B1
Eve Rd E15 48 B1
Eversholt St NW1 42 C1
Eversleigh Rd E6 35 G5
Eversleigh Rd SW11 83 G1
Eversley Rd SE7 77 E2
Everthorpe Rd SE15 87 E1
Everton Bldgs NW1 8 A2
Evesham CI SE5 34 C5
Evesham Rd E15 53 F1
Evesham Wk SW9 71 G5
Evesham Way SW11 84 A1
Ewald Rd SW6 68 A5
Ewart Rd SE23 88 B5
Ewe CI N7 29 E3
Ewen Cres SW2 85 G5
Ewer St SE1 16 D6
Ewhurst CI E1 46 A4
Ewhurst Rd SE4 89 D4
Exbury Rd SE6 14 D4
Excelsior Gdns SE13 75 G5
Exchange Arc EC2 11 J5
Exchange Ct WC2 15 F4
Exchange PI EC2 11 H5
Exchange Sq EC2 11 H5
Exeter Rd E16 49 D4
Exeter Rd NW2 25 G2
Exeter Rd SE15 73 F3
Exeter St WC2 15 F3
Exeter Way SE14 74 D3
Exhibition CI W12 53 E1
Exhibition Rd SW7 18 A2
Exmoor St W10 39 F3
Exmouth Mkt EC1 9 J3
Exmouth Ms NW1 8 B2
Exmouth PI E8 31 G4
Exning Rd E16 48 C3
Exon St SE17 23 H6
Exton St SE1 15 J6
Eynella Rd SE22 87 E5
Eynham Rd W12 39 E5
Eyot Gdns W6 66 B1
Eyre St Hill EC1 9 J4
Ezra St E2 45 E2

F

Fabian Rd SW6	68 A3
Fabian St E6	50 B3
Factory Rd E16	64 A2
Fairacres SW15	28 A3
Fairbairn Grn SW9	72 A4
Fairbourne Rd SW4	85 C4
Fairburn Ct SW15	81 G3
Fairby Rd SE12	91 E3
Faircharm Trd Est SE8	75 E3
Fairchild Pl EC2	11 J4
Fairchild St EC2	11 J4
Faircross Av, Bark.	45 F5
Faircross Av, Bark.	37 E3
Faircross Par, Bark.	37 G3
Fairdale Gdns SW15	81 D2
Fairfax Gdns SE3	77 G4
Fairfax Pl NW6	81 E2
Fairfax Pl W14	27 D4
Fairfax Pl W14	53 G4
Fairfax Rd NW6	27 D4
Fairfax Rd W4	52 A4
Fairfield Cl N(10)	24 C5
Fairfield Dr SW18	82 C3
Fairfield Gro SE7	77 G1
Fairfield Rd E3	47 E1
Fairfield Rd, Ilf.	37 D3
Fairfield St SW18	82 C3
Fairfoot Rd E3	47 E3
Fairford Ho SE11	58 B2
Fairhazel Gdns NW6	26 C3
Fairholme Rd W14	67 G1
Fairholt St SW7	18 C3
Fairland Rd E15	47 E4
Fairlawn SE7	77 F2
Fairlie Gdns SE23	88 A5
Fairlight Av NW10	38 A1
Fairmont Av E14	62 A2
Fairmount Rd SW2	85 F4
Fairoak Dr SE9	93 F3
Fair St SE1	23 J1
Fairthorn Rd SE7	77 D1
Fairview Pl SW2	85 F5
Fairway, The W3	38 A5
Fairway Gdns, Ilf.	37 F2
Fakruddin St E1	45 F3
Falconberg Ct W1	14 D1
Falconberg Ms W1	14 C1
Falcon Ct EC4	15 J2
Falcon Gro SW11	83 F1
Falcon La SW11	83 F1
Falcon Pk Ind Est NW10	24 B2
Falcon Rd SW11	69 F5
Falcon St E13	48 D3
Falcon Ter SW11	83 F1
Falcon Way E14	61 F5
Falconwood SE9	93 E2
Falconwood Av, Well.	79 F5
Falconwood Par, Well.	93 G2
Falkirk Ho W9	40 C2
Falkirk St N1	45 D1
Falkland Rd NW5	28 C2
Falmouth Cl SE12	90 C3
Falmouth Rd SE1	23 E3
Falmouth St E15	34 A2
Fann St EC1	10 D4
Fann St EC2	10 D4
Fanshawe Av, Bark.	37 E3
Fanshaw St N1	11 H1
Fanthorpe St SW15	81 E1
Faraday Rd E15	34 C3
Faraday Rd W10	39 G4
Faraday Way SE18	63 G4
Fareham St W1	14 C1
Faringford Rd E15	34 B4
Farjeon Rd SE3	77 G4
Farleigh Pl N16	31 F1
Farleigh Rd N16	31 E1
Farley Ms SE6	89 G5
Farley Rd SE6	89 F5
Farlow Rd SW15	81 F1

Farlton Rd SW18	82 C5
Farmdale Rd SE10	77 D1
Farmers Rd SE5	72 A3
Farm La SW6	68 B2
Farm St W1	13 H4
Farnaby Rd SE9	91 F2
Farncombe St SE16	59 F3
Farnham Pl SE1	16 C6
Faroe Rd W14	53 F4
Farrance St E14	47 D5
Farrell Ho E1	46 A5
Farrier St NW1	28 B4
Farrier Wk SW10	68 D2
Farringdon La EC1	10 A4
Farringdon Rd EC1	9 J3
Farringdon St EC4	16 B1
Farrins Rents SE16	60 C2
Farrow La SE14	74 A3
Farthingale Wk E15	34 A4
Fashion St E1	45 E4
Fassett Rd E8	31 F3
Fassett Sq E8	31 F3
Faulkner's All EC1	10 B5
Faulkner St SE14	74 A4
Favart Rd SW6	68 B4
Faversham Rd SE6	89 D5
Fawcett Cl SW11	69 E5
Fawcett Rd NW10	24 B5
Fawcett St SW10	68 D2
Fawe Pk Rd SW15	82 A2
Fawe St E14	47 F4
Fawley Rd NW6	26 C2
Fawnbrake Av SE24	86 A3
Fawn Rd E13	49 F1
Fearon St SE10	76 D1
Feathers Pl SE10	76 A2
Featherstone St EC1	11 F3
Featley Rd SW9	86 A1
Feeny Cl NW10	24 B1
Felday Rd SE13	89 F4
Felden St SW6	68 A4
Felgate Ms W6	52 D5
Felixstowe Rd NW10	39 D2
Fellbrigg Rd SE22	87 E3
Fellmongers Path SE1	23 J2
Fellows Ct E2	45 E1
Fellows Rd NW3	27 E4
Felsberg Rd SW2	85 E4
Felsham Rd SW15	81 F1
Felstead Rd E9	33 D3
Felsted Rd E16	49 G5
Felton St N1	30 C5
Fenchurch Av EC3	17 H2
Fenchurch Bldgs EC3	17 J2
Fenchurch Pl EC3	17 J3
Fenchurch St EC3	17 H3
Fen Ct EC3	17 H2
Fendall St SE1	24 A5
Fenelon Pl W14	54 A5
Fenham Rd SE15	73 F3
Fen La SW13	66 D4
Fennel St SE18	78 C2
Fennings Rd SW4	84 D4
Fenning St SE1	23 H1
Fenn St E9	32 A2
Fentiman Rd SW8	71 E2
Fenton Cl SW9	71 F5
Fentons Av E13	49 E1
Fenwick Cl SE18	78 C2
Fenwick Gro SE15	87 F1
Fenwick Pl SW9	85 E1
Fenwick Rd SE15	87 F1
Ferdinand Dr SE15	73 D3
Ferdinand St NW1	28 A3
Ferguson Cl E14	61 E5
Fermoy Rd W9	40 A3
Fernbank Ms SW12	84 B4
Fernbrook Cres SE13	90 B4
Fernbrook Rd SE13	90 B4
Ferncliff Rd E8	31 F2
Ferndale Ct SE3	76 C3
Ferndale Rd E7	35 E4
Ferndale Rd SW4	85 E2

Ferndale Rd SW9	85 F1
Ferndale St E6	64 D1
Ferndene Rd SE24	86 B2
Ferndown Rd SE9	91 G5
Fernhead Rd W9	40 A3
Fernhill St E16	64 B2
Fernholme Rd SE15	88 B3
Fernhurst Rd SW6	67 G4
Fernleigh Cl W9	40 A2
Fernsbury St WC1	9 J2
Fernshaw Rd SW10	68 D2
Fern St E3	47 E3
Ferntower Rd N5	30 C2
Ferranti Cl SE18	63 G4
Ferrey Ms SW9	71 G5
Ferrier St SW18	82 C2
Ferris Rd SE22	87 F2
Ferrybridge Ho SE11	21 H4
Ferry La SW13	66 B2
Ferryman's Quay SW6	69 D5
Ferry Rd SW13	66 C3
Ferry St E14	75 G1
Festing Rd SW15	81 F1
Festoon Way E16	63 G1
Fetter La EC4	16 A2
Ffinch St SE8	75 E3
Field Ct WC1	9 H6
Fieldgate St E1	45 F4
Fielding Ho NW6	40 B2
Fielding Rd W14	53 F4
Fielding St SE17	72 B2
Field Rd E7	34 C1
Field Rd W6	67 G1
Fields Est E8	31 F4
Field St WC1	9 G1
Fieldway Cres N5	29 G2
Fife Rd E16	48 D4
Fife St N1	43 F1
Fifth Av E12	36 B1
Fifth Av W10	39 G2
Filmer Rd SW6	67 G4
Finborough Rd SW10	68 C1
Finch La EC3	17 G2
Finchley Pl NW8	41 E1
Finchley Rd NW3	27 D3
Finchley Rd NW8	27 E3
Finch Ms SE15	73 E3
Finden Rd E7	35 E2
Findhorn St E14	47 G5
Findon St SW18	82 B4
Fingal St SE10	77 C1
Finland Rd SE4	88 C1
Finland St SE16	60 C4
Finlay St SW6	67 F4
Finnis St E2	45 G2
Finsbury Av EC2	11 G6
Finsbury Av Sq EC2	11 G6
Finsbury Circ EC2	11 G6
Finsbury Est EC1	10 A2
Finsbury Mkt EC2	11 H4
Finsbury Pavement EC2	11 G5
Finsbury Sq EC2	11 G5
Finsbury St EC2	11 F5
Finsbury Twr EC1	11 F4
Finsen Rd SE5	86 B1
Finstock Rd W10	39 F5
Finucane Ri SE13	89 G4
Firbank Cl E16	49 G4
Firbank Rd SE15	73 G5
Firs, The E6	36 A4
Firs Cl SE23	88 B5
First Av E12	36 A1
First Av E13	49 D2
First Av SW14	80 A1
First Av W3	52 A3
First Av W10	40 A4
First St SW3	18 C5
Firth Gdns SW6	67 F4
Fir Trees Cl SE16	60 C2
Fishermans Dr SE16	60 B3

Fisherman's Wk E14	61 E2
Fisher St E16	48 D4
Fisher St WC1	9 F6
Fisherton St NW8	41 E3
Fishguard Way E16	65 D3
Fish St Hill EC3	17 G3
Fitzalan St SE11	21 J5
Fitzgeorge Av W14	53 G5
Fitzgerald Av SW14	80 A1
Fitzgerald Ho E14	47 F5
Fitzhardinge St W1	13 F1
Fitzhugh Gro SW18	83 E4
Fitzjames Av W14	53 G5
Fitzjohn's Av NW3	27 E2
Fitzmaurice Pl W1	13 J5
Fitzneal St W12	38 B5
Fitzpatrick Rd SW9	72 A4
Fitzroy Ct W1	8 B4
Fitzroy Ms W1	8 A4
Fitzroy Rd NW1	28 A5
Fitzroy Sq W1	8 A4
Fitzroy St W1	8 A4
Fitzwilliam Rd SW4	84 C1
Fives Ct SE11	22 B5
Fiveways Rd SW9	71 G5
Flamborough St E14	46 C5
Flamsteed Rd SE7	78 A1
Flanchford Rd W12	52 B4
Flanders Rd E6	50 B1
Flanders Rd W4	52 A5
Flanders Way E9	32 B3
Flask Wk NW3	27 E1
Flavell Ms SE10	76 B1
Flaxman Ct W1	14 C2
Flaxman Rd SE5	72 A5
Flaxman Ter WC1	8 D2
Flaxton Rd SE18	79 F4
Fleet Rd IG11	51 D1
Fleet Rd NW3	27 F2
Fleet Sq WC1	9 H2
Fleet St EC4	15 J2
Fleetwood Cl E16	49 G4
Fleetwood Rd NW10	24 C2
Fleming Rd SE17	72 A2
Fletching St SE7	77 F2
Fleur de Lis St E1	11 J4
Flint Cl E15	34 C4
Flintmill Cres SE3	78 A5
Flinton St SE17	73 D1
Flint St SE17	23 G6
Flitcroft St WC2	14 D1
Flodden Rd SE5	72 B4
Flood St SW3	69 F1
Flood Wk SW3	69 F2
Flora Cl E14	47 F5
Flora Gdns W6	52 D5
Floral St WC2	15 E3
Florence Elson Cl E12	36 C1
Florence Rd E6	35 F5
Florence Rd E13	48 C3
Florence Rd SE14	75 D4
Florence St E16	48 C3
Florence St N1	30 A4
Florence Ter SE14	75 D4
Florian Rd SW15	81 G2
Florida St E2	45 F2
Floss St SW15	67 E5
Flower Wk, The SW7	55 D3
Floyd Rd SE7	77 F1
Fludyer St SE13	90 B2
Foley St W1	8 A6
Folgate St E1	11 J5
Foliot St W12	38 B5
Folkestone Rd E6	50 C1
Follett St E14	47 G5
Folly Wall E14	61 G3
Fontarabia Rd SW11	84 A2
Fontley Way SW15	80 C5
Footpath, The SW15	80 C5
Footscray Rd SE9	92 C4
Fordham St E1	45 F5
Fordingley Rd W9	40 A2
Ford Rd E3	32 C5

Fords Pk Rd E16	48	D5
Ford Sq E1	45	G4
Ford St E3	32	C5
Ford St E16	48	C5
Fordwych Rd NW2	25	G1
Fordyce Rd SE13	89	G4
Foreign St SE5	72	A5
Foreshore SE8	61	D5
Forest Cl NW6	25	G4
Forester Rd SE15	87	G2
Forest Gro E8	31	E3
Forest Hill Rd SE22	87	G3
Forest Hill Rd SE23	87	G3
Forest La E7	34	B2
Forest La E15	34	B2
Fore St EC2	11	E6
Fore St Av EC2	11	F6
Forest Rd E7	35	D1
Forest Rd E8	31	E3
Forest St E7	34	D2
Forest Vw Rd E12	36	A1
Forest Way, Sid.	93	F5
Forfar Rd SW11	70	A4
Formosa St W9	40	C4
Forset St W1	12	C1
Forster Rd SW2	85	E5
Forsyth Gdns SE17	72	A2
Forsythia Cl, Ilf.	36	D2
Fortess Rd NW5	28	B2
Forthbridge Rd SW11	84	A2
Fortis Cl E16	48	B5
Fortius Wk E20	33	G3
Fort Rd SE1	59	E5
Fortrose Cl E14	48	A5
Fort St E1	11	J6
Fort St E16	63	E2
Fortune Gate Rd NW10	24	A5
Fortune Grn Rd NW6	26	B1
Fortune St EC1	10	E4
Fortune Way NW10	38	C2
Forty Acre La E16	48	D4
Forum Magnum Sq SE1	21	G1
Foskett Rd SW6	68	A5
Fossdene Rd SE7	77	E1
Fossil Rd SE13	89	E1
Foster La EC2	16	D1
Foster Rd E13	48	D3
Foster Rd W3	52	A1
Fothergill Cl E13	48	D1
Foubert's Pl W1	14	A2
Foulden Rd N16	31	E1
Foulis Ter SW7	69	E1
Founders Ct EC2	17	F1
Foundry Cl SE16	60	C2
Foundry Ms NW1	8	B3
Fountain Ct SE18	78	D1
Fountain Ct EC4	15	J3
Fountain Ms NW3	27	G3
Fountain Pl SW9	71	G4
Fountain Sq SW1	19	H5
Fount St SW8	71	D3
Fournier St E1	45	E4
Four Seasons Cl E3	47	E1
Fourth Av E12	36	B1
Fourth Av W10	39	G3
Fowler Cl SW11	83	E1
Fowler Rd E7	34	D1
Fownes St SW11	83	F1
Fox & Knot St EC1	10	C5
Foxberry Rd SE4	88	C1
Foxborough Gdns SE4	89	E4
Fox Cl E1	46	A3
Fox Cl E16	48	D4
Foxcote SE5	73	D1
Foxcroft Rd SE18	79	D4
Foxes Dale SE3	90	D1
Foxglove St W12	52	B1
Foxhole Rd SE9	92	A3
Fox Hollow Cl SE18	79	G1
Foxley Rd SW9	71	G3
Foxmore St SW11	69	G4

Fox Rd E16	48	C4
Foxwell St SE4	88	C1
Foxwood Rd SE3	90	C2
Foyle Rd SE3	76	C2
Framfield Rd N5	30	A2
Frampton Pk Est E9	32	A4
Frampton Pk Rd E9	32	A3
Frampton St NW8	41	E3
Francemary Rd SE4	89	E3
Frances St SE18	64	B5
Francis Chichester Way SW11	70	A4
Francis St E15	34	B2
Francis St SW1	20	A5
Franconia Rd SW4	84	C5
Frankfurt Rd SE24	86	B3
Frankham St SE8	75	E3
Frankland Cl SE16	59	G4
Franklin Cl SE13	75	F4
Franklin Pas SE9	92	A1
Franklin Pl SE13	75	F4
Franklin's Row SW3	69	G1
Franklin St E3	47	F2
Franklyn Rd NW10	24	B4
Frank St E13	49	D3
Fraser St W4	66	A1
Frazier St SE1	21	J2
Frean St SE16	59	F4
Frederic Cl W2	12	C3
Frederick Cres SW9	72	A3
Frederick Pl SE18	79	D1
Frederick's Pl EC2	17	F2
Frederick's Row EC1	10	B1
Frederick St WC1	9	G2
Frederic Ms SW1	19	E2
Freedom St SW11	69	G5
Freegrove Rd N7	29	E2
Freemantle St SE17	72	D1
Freeman Wk SE9	91	F3
Freemasons Rd E16	49	E4
Freke Rd SW11	84	A1
Fremont St E9	32	A5
French Ordinary Ct EC3	17	J3
French Pl E1	11	J3
Frendsbury Rd SE4	88	C2
Frensham St SE15	73	F2
Frere St SW11	69	F5
Freshfield Av E8	31	E4
Fresh Wf Rd, Bark.	37	D5
Freston Rd W10	53	F1
Freston Rd W11	53	F1
Friars Cl SE1	16	B6
Friars Mead E14	61	G4
Friars Ms SE9	92	C3
Friars Rd E6	35	G5
Friar St EC4	16	C2
Friary Cl SW1	14	B6
Friary Est SE15	73	F2
Friary Rd SE15	73	F3
Friday St EC4	16	D2
Friendly St SE8	75	E4
Friend St EC1	10	B1
Friern Rd SE22	87	F4
Frimley Way E1	46	B3
Frinstead Ho W10	53	F1
Frinton Rd E6	49	G2
Friston St SW6	68	C5
Frith Rd E11	33	G1
Frith St W1	14	C2
Frithville Gdns W12	53	E2
Frobisher Rd E6	50	B5
Frobisher St SE10	76	B2
Frogley Rd SE22	87	E2
Frogmore SW18	82	B3
Frognal NW3	27	D2
Frognal Cl NW3	26	D2
Frognal Gdns NW3	27	D3
Frognal La NW3	26	C2
Frognal Ri NW3	26	D1
Frognal Way NW3	26	D1
Froissart Rd SE9	91	G3

Frome St N1	44	B1
Frostic Wk E1	45	E4
Froude St SW8	70	B5
Fry Rd E6	35	G4
Fry Rd NW10	24	B5
Fulford St SE16	59	G3
Fulham Bdy SW6	68	B3
Fulham High St SW6	67	G5
Fulham Palace Rd SW6	67	F3
Fulham Palace Rd W6	67	E1
Fulham Pk Gdns SW6	68	A5
Fulham Pk Rd SW6	68	A5
Fulham Rd SW3	69	D2
Fulham Rd SW6	67	G5
Fulham Rd SW10	68	C3
Fullerton Rd SW18	82	D3
Fullwoods Ms N1	11	G1
Fulmead St SW6	68	C4
Fulmer Rd E16	49	G4
Fulthorp Rd SE3	76	C5
Fulwood Pl WC1	9	H6
Furber St W6	52	D4
Furley Rd SE15	73	F3
Furlong Rd N7	29	G3
Furmage St SW18	82	C5
Furness Rd NW10	38	C1
Furness Rd SW6	68	C5
Furnival St EC4	15	J1
Further Grn Rd SE6	90	B5
Furzefield Rd SE3	77	E2
Furze St E3	47	E4
Fyfield Ct E7	34	D3
Fyfield Rd SW9	85	G1
Fynes St SW1	20	C5

G

Gables Cl SE5	72	D4
Gabrielle Cl NW3	27	E3
Gabriel St SE23	88	B2
Gabriel's Wf SE1	15	J5
Gad Cl E13	49	E2
Gadwall Way SE28	65	F3
Gage St WC1	9	F5
Gainsborough Av E12	36	D1
Gainsborough Rd E15	48	B2
Gainsborough Rd W4	52	B5
Gainsford St SE1	59	E3
Gairloch Rd SE5	73	D5
Gaisford St NW5	28	C3
Gaitskell Ct SW11	69	F5
Galata Rd SW13	66	C3
Galbraith St E14	61	G4
Galena Rd W6	53	D5
Galen Pl WC1	9	F6
Galesbury Rd SW18	82	D4
Gales Gdns E2	45	G2
Gale St E3	47	E4
Galleywall Rd SE16	59	G5
Gallia Rd N5	30	A2
Gallions Reach Shop Pk E6	51	E4
Gallions Rd E16	65	E1
Gallions Rd SE7	63	E5
Gallions Rbt E16	64	D1
Gallon Cl SE7	63	F5
Gallosson Rd SE18	65	G5
Galloway Rd W12	52	C2
Gallus Sq SE3	91	E1
Galsworthy Av E14	46	C4
Galsworthy Rd NW2	25	G1
Galton St W10	39	G3
Galveston Rd SW15	81	H3
Galway Ho EC1	11	E2
Galway St EC1	10	E2
Gambetta St SW8	70	B5
Gambia St SE1	16	C6
Gambier Ho EC1	11	E1
Gamlen Rd SW15	81	F2
Ganton St W1	14	A3
Garbutt Pl W1	7	G5
Garden Cl SW15	81	D5

Garden Ct EC4	15	J3
Garden Rd NW8	41	D2
Garden Row SE1	22	B4
Gardens, The SE22	87	F2
Garden St E1	46	B4
Garden Wk EC2	11	H2
Gardiner Av NW2	25	E2
Gardner Rd E13	49	E3
Gardners La EC4	16	D3
Gard St EC1	10	C1
Garfield Rd E13	48	C3
Garfield Rd SW11	84	A1
Garford St E14	61	E1
Garibaldi St SE18	65	G5
Garland Rd SE18	79	F3
Garlick Hill EC4	16	E3
Garlinge Rd NW2	26	A3
Garnault Ms EC1	10	A2
Garnault Pl EC1	10	A2
Garnet Rd NW10	24	A3
Garnet St E1	60	A1
Garnett Cl SE9	92	B1
Garnett Rd NW3	27	G2
Garnies Cl SE15	73	E3
Garratt La SW18	82	C3
Garrett St EC1	10	E3
Garrick Cl SW18	82	D2
Garrick Dr SE28	65	F4
Garrick St WC2	14	E3
Garrison Rd E3	33	G5
Garside Cl SE28	65	F4
Garsington Ms SE4	89	D1
Garthorne Rd SE23	88	B5
Garton Pl SW18	82	D4
Gartons Way SW11	83	D1
Garvary Rd E16	49	E5
Garway Rd W2	40	C5
Gascoigne Pl E2	45	E2
Gascoigne Rd, Bark.	37	E5
Gascony Av NW6	26	B4
Gascoyne Rd E9	32	B4
Gaselee St E14	61	G1
Gaskarth Rd SW12	84	B4
Gaskell St SW4	71	E5
Gaskin St N1	30	A5
Gastein Rd W6	67	F2
Gataker St SE16	59	G4
Gatcombe Rd E16	63	D2
Gateforth St NW8	6	B4
Gate Ho Sq SE1	16	E5
Gateley Rd SW9	85	F1
Gate Ms SW7	18	C2
Gatesborough St EC2	11	H3
Gate St WC2	15	G1
Gateway SE17	72	B2
Gateway Ind Est NW10	38	B2
Gateway Retail Pk E6	51	D3
Gateways, The SW3	18	C6
Gatliff Rd SW1	70	A1
Gatonby St SE15	73	E4
Gatwick Rd SW18	82	A5
Gauden Cl SW4	84	D1
Gauden Rd SW4	70	D5
Gaunt St SE1	22	C3
Gautrey Rd SE15	74	A5
Gautrey Sq E6	50	B5
Gavel St SE17	23	G5
Gavestone Cres SE12	91	E5
Gavestone Rd SE12	91	E5
Gavin St SE18	65	G5
Gawber St E2	46	A2
Gay Cl NW2	25	D2
Gaydon Ho W2	40	C4
Gayfere St SW1	20	E4
Gayford Rd W12	52	B3
Gayhurst Rd E8	31	F4
Gay Rd E15	48	A1
Gay St SW15	81	F1
Gayton Cres NW3	27	E1
Gayton Ho E3	47	E3
Gayton Rd NW3	27	E1
Gayville Rd SW11	83	G4

Gaywood Est SE1 22 B4
Gaywood St SE1 22 C4
Geary Rd NW10 24 C2
Geary St N7 59 E3
Gedling Pl SE1 59 E3
Geere Rd E15 34 C5
Gees Ct W1 13 G2
Gee St EC1 10 D3
Geffrye St E2 45 E1
Geldart Rd SE15 73 G3
Gellatly Rd SE14 74 A5
Gemini Business Pk E6 51 F4
General Gordon Pl
SE18 64 D5
General Wolfe Rd SE10 76 A4
Genesta Rd SE18 79 D2
Geneva Dr SW9 85 G2
Genoa Av SW15 81 E3
Geoffrey Cl SE5 72 B5
Geoffrey Gdns E6 50 A1
Geoffrey Rd SE4 88 D1
George Beard Rd SE8 60 D5
George Ct WC2 15 F4
George Inn Yd SE1 17 F6
George La SE13 89 G4
George Mathers Rd
SE11 22 B5
George Ms NW1 8 A2
George Row SE16 59 F3
George's Rd N7 29 F2
George St E16 48 C5
George St W1 13 E1
George St, Bark. 37 E4
George Yd EC3 17 G2
George Yd W1 13 G3
Georgiana St NW1 28 C5
Geraldine Rd SW18 82 D3
Geraldine St SE11 22 B4
Gerald Ms SW1 19 G5
Gerald Rd E16 48 C3
Gerald Rd SW1 19 G5
Gerard Rd SW13 66 B4
Gerards Cl SE16 74 A1
Germander Way E15 48 B3
Gernon Rd E3 46 C1
Gerrard Pl W1 14 D3
Gerrard Rd N1 44 A1
Gerrard St W1 14 C3
Gerrard Way SE3 91 F2
Gerridge St SE1 22 A2
Gertrude St SW10 69 D2
Gervase St SE15 73 G3
Giant Arches Rd SE24 86 B5
Gibbins Pl E15 33 G4
Gibbon Rd E15 74 A5
Gibbon Rd W3 52 A1
Gibbon Wk SW15 80 C2
Gibbs Grn W14 68 A1
Gibraltar Wk E2 45 F2
Gibson Cl E1 21 H6
Gibson Sq N1 29 G5
Gibson St SE10 76 B1
Gideon Rd SW11 84 A1
Giffin St SE8 75 E3
Gifford St N1 29 E4
Gift La E15 34 B5
Gilbert Cl SE18 78 B4
Gilbert Pl WC1 9 E6
Gilbert Rd SE11 22 A6
Gilbert St E15 34 B1
Gilbert St W1 13 G2
Gilbeys Yd NW1 28 A4
Gildea St W1 7 J6
Gilden Cres NW5 28 A2
Gilkes Cres SE21 86 D4
Gilkes Pl SE21 86 D4
Gill Av E16 49 D5
Gillender St E3 47 G3
Gillender St E14 47 G3
Gillett Av E6 50 A1
Gillett St N16 31 D2
Gillfoot NW1 42 C1
Gillian St SE13 89 F3

Gillies St NW5 28 A2
Gilling Ct NW3 27 F4
Gillingham Row SW1 20 A5
Gillingham St SW1 19 J5
Gillman Dr E15 34 C5
Gill St E14 47 D5
Gilmore Rd SE13 90 A2
Gilpin Av SW14 32 C1
Gilstead Rd SW6 68 C5
Gilston Rd SW10 69 D1
Giltspur St EC1 16 C1
Gipsy La SW15 80 C1
Giraud St E14 47 F5
Girdlers Rd W14 53 F5
Girdwood Rd SW18 82 A5
Gironde Rd SW6 68 A3
Girton Vil W10 39 F5
Given Wilson Wk E13 48 C1
Gladding Rd E12 35 G1
Glade, The SE7 77 F3
Gladiator St SE23 88 C4
Gladstone Av E12 36 A4
Gladstone St SE1 22 B3
Gladwyn Rd SW15 81 F1
Gladys Rd NW6 26 B4
Glaisher St SE8 75 E2
Glamis Pl E1 60 A1
Glamis Rd E1 60 A1
Glanville Rd SW2 85 E3
Glasbrook Rd SE9 91 G5
Glasgow Ho W9 40 C1
Glasgow Rd E13 49 E1
Glasgow Ter SW1 70 C1
Glasshill St SE1 22 C1
Glasshouse Flds E1 60 B1
Glasshouse St W1 14 B4
Glasshouse Wk SE11 71 E1
Glasshouse Yd EC1 10 D4
Glastonbury St NW6 26 A2
Glaucus St E3 47 F4
Glazbury Rd W14 53 G5
Glebe, The SE3 90 B1
Glebe Pl SW3 69 F2
Glebe Rd NW10 24 B3
Glebe Rd SW13 66 C5
Glebe St W4 66 A1
Gledhow Gdns SW5 68 C1
Gledstanes Rd W14 67 G1
Glegg Pl SW15 81 F2
Glenaffric Av E14 62 A5
Glenalvon Way SE18 64 A5
Glenarm Rd E5 32 A2
Glenavon Rd E15 34 B4
Glenbrook Rd NW6 26 B2
Glencairne Cl E16 49 G4
Glendall St SW9 85 F2
Glendarvon St SW15 81 F1
Glendower Pl SW7 55 E5
Glenelg Rd SW2 85 E3
Glenesk Rd SE9 92 C1
Glenfinlas Way SE5 72 A3
Glenforth St SE10 76 C1
Glengall Causeway
E14 61 E4
Glengall Gro E14 61 F4
Glengall Rd NW6 26 A5
Glengall Rd SE15 73 E2
Glengall Ter SE15 73 E2
Glengarnock Av E14 61 G5
Glengarry Rd SE22 87 D3
Glenhouse Rd SE9 92 C3
Glenhurst Av NW5 28 A1
Glenilla Rd NW3 27 F3
Glenister Rd SE10 76 C1
Glenister St E16 64 C2
Glenlea Rd SE9 92 B3
Glenloch Rd NW3 27 F3
Glenluce Rd SE3 76 D3
Glenlyon Rd SE9 92 C3
Glenmore Rd NW12 90 D4
Glenmore Rd NW3 27 F3
Glenny Rd, Bark. 37 E3

Glenparke Rd E7 35 E3
Glen Rd E13 49 F3
Glenrosa St SW6 68 D5
Glenroy St W12 39 E5
Glensdale Rd SE4 89 D1
Glenshiel Rd SE9 92 C3
Glentham Rd SW13 66 C2
Glenthorne Rd W6 53 E5
Glenton Ms SE15 74 A5
Glenton Rd SE13 90 B2
Glentworth St NW1 6 E4
Glenure Rd SE9 92 C3
Glenville Gro SE8 75 D3
Glenville Ms SW18 82 A5
Glenworth Av E14 62 A5
Gliddon Rd E5 31 F1
Gliddon Rd W14 53 G5
Globe Pond Rd SE16 60 C2
Globe Rd E1 46 A2
Globe Rd E2 46 A2
Globe Rd E15 34 C2
Globe Rope Wk E14 61 G5
Globe St SE1 23 E3
Globe Yd W1 13 H2
Gloucester Av NW1 28 A5
Gloucester Circ SE10 75 G3
Gloucester Cres NW1 28 B5
Gloucester Gate NW1 42 B1
Gloucester Ho NW6 40 B1
Gloucester Ms W2 41 D5
Gloucester Ms W1 6 D3
Gloucester Ms W1 6 E5
Gloucester Pl W1 6 E3
Gloucester Pl Ms W1 6 E5
Gloucester Rd SW7 54 D4
Gloucester Sq E2 45 G1
Gloucester Sq W2 12 A2
Gloucester St SW1 70 C1
Gloucester Ter W2 55 E1
Gloucester Wk W8 54 B3
Gloucester Way EC1 10 A2
Glycena Rd SW11 83 G1
Glyndon Ms SW3 18 C4
Glynde St SE4 89 D4
Glyndon Rd SE18 65 E5
Glynfield Rd NW10 24 A4
Goaters All SW6 68 A3
Godalming Rd E14 47 F4
Godbold Rd E15 48 B5
Godfrey Hill SE18 64 A5
Godfrey Rd EC1 11 F2
Godfrey Rd SE18 64 B5
Godfrey St E15 47 G1
Godfrey St SW3 69 F1
Goding St SE11 71 E1
Godliman St EC4 16 D2
Godman Rd SE15 73 G5
Godolphin Rd W12 52 D3
Godson St N1 43 G1
Godwin Rd E7 35 E1
Godwin Rd SE7 76 A4
Golborne Rd W10 39 G4
Golden Jubilee Br SE1 15 G6
Golden Jubilee Br WC2 15 F5
Golden La EC1 10 D4
Golden La Est EC1 10 D4
Golden Sq W1 14 B3
Goldfinch Rd SE28 65 F4
Goldhawk Ms W12 52 B5
Goldhawk Rd W6 52 B5
Goldhawk Rd W12 52 C4
Goldhurst Ter NW6 26 C3
Golding St E1 45 F5
Goldington Cres NW1 42 D1
Goldington St NW1 42 D1
Goldman Cl E2 45 F3
Goldney Rd W9 40 B3
Goldsboro Rd SW8 71 D4
Goldsmith Av E12 36 A3
Goldsmith Rd SE15 73 F4
Goldsmith's Row E2 45 F1
Goldsmith's Sq E2 45 F1
Goldsmith St EC2 16 E1
Goldsworthy Gdns
SE16 60 A5
Goldwin Cl SE14 74 A4

Goldwing Cl E16 49 D5
Gollogly Ter SE7 77 F1
Gomm Rd SE16 60 A4
Gondar Gdns NW6 26 A2
Gonson St SE8 75 F2
Goodge Pl W1 8 B6
Goodge St W1 8 B6
Goodhall St NW10 38 A2
Goodhart Pl E14 60 C1
Goodinge Cl N7 29 E3
Goodman's Stile E1 45 F5
Goodman's Yd E1 59 E1
Goodrich Rd SE22 87 E4
Goodson Rd NW10 24 A4
Goods Way NW1 43 E1
Goodway Gdns E14 48 A5
Goodwin Cl SE16 59 F4
Goodwin Rd W12 52 C3
Goodwins Ct WC2 14 E3
Goodwood Rd SE14 74 C3
Goosander Way SE28 65 F4
Gooseley La E6 50 C2
Gophir La EC4 17 F3
Gopsall St N1 30 C5
Gordon Av SW14 80 A2
Gordonbrock Rd SE4 89 E3
Gordon Gro SE5 72 A5
Gordon Ho Rd NW5 28 A1
Gordon Pl W8 54 B3
Gordon Rd E15 33 G1
Gordon Rd SE15 73 G5
Gordon Rd, Bark. 37 G5
Gordon Rd, Sid. 93 G3
Gordon St WC1 8 D4
Gordon St WC1 8 C3
Gorefield Pl NW6 40 B1
Gore Rd E9 32 A5
Gore St SW7 55 D4
Goring St EC3 17 J1
Gorleston St W14 53 G5
Gorman Rd SE18 64 B5
Gorse Cl E16 48 D5
Gorst Rd SW11 83 G4
Gorsuch St E2 45 E2
Gosfield St W1 8 A5
Goslett Yd WC2 14 C2
Gosling Way SW9 71 G4
Gossage Rd SE18 79 F1
Gosset St E2 45 E2
Gosterwood St SE8 74 C2
Goswell Rd EC1 10 D4
Gough Rd E15 34 C1
Gough Sq EC4 16 A1
Gough St WC1 9 H3
Goulden Ho App SW11 69 F5
Goulston St E1 45 E5
Goulton Rd E5 31 G1
Gourock Rd SE9 92 C3
Govan St E2 45 F1
Gowan Av SW6 67 G4
Gowan Rd NW10 24 D3
Gower Cl SW4 84 C4
Gower Ct WC1 8 C3
Gower Ms WC1 8 C6
Gower Pl WC1 8 B3
Gower Rd E7 35 D3
Gower St WC1 8 B3
Gower's Wk E1 45 F5
Gowlett Rd SE15 87 F1
Gowrie Rd SW11 84 A1
Gracechurch St EC3 17 G3
Grace's All E1 59 F1
Graces Ms SE5 72 D5
Graces Rd SE5 72 D5
Grace St E3 47 F2
Grafton Cres NW1 28 B3
Grafton Ho E3 47 E2
Grafton Ms W1 8 A4
Grafton Pl NW1 8 C2
Grafton Rd NW5 28 A2
Grafton Sq SW4 84 C1
Grafton St W1 13 J4
Grafton Ter NW5 27 G2

Grafton Way W1	8	A4
Grafton Way WC1	8	A4
Graham Rd E8	31	E3
Graham Rd E13	48	D3
Graham St N1	44	A1
Graham Ter SW1	19	F6
Granard Av SW15	81	D3
Granard Rd SW12	83	G5
Granary Mans SE28	65	E3
Granary Rd E1	45	G3
Granary St NW1	28	D5
Granby Pl SE1	21	J2
Granby Rd SE9	78	B5
Granby St E2	45	E3
Grand Av EC1	10	D5
Grand Dep Rd SE18	78	C1
Grandison Rd SW11	83	G3
Grand Junct Wf N1	44	B1
Grand Par Ms SW15	81	G3
Grand Union Cres E8	31	F4
Grand Union Wk NW1	28	B4
Granfield St SW11	69	E4
Grange, The SE1	59	E4
Grange Ct WC2	15	H2
Grange Gro N1	30	A3
Grangehill Rd SE9	92	B2
Grange Pl NW6	26	B4
Grange Rd E13	48	C2
Grange Rd NW10	25	D3
Grange Rd SE1	23	J3
Grange Rd SW13	66	C4
Grange Rd, Ilf.	37	D1
Grange St N1	44	C1
Grange Wk Ms SE1	23	J4
Grangewood St E6	35	F5
Grange Yd SE1	59	E4
Gransden Av E8	31	G4
Grantbridge St N1	44	A1
Grantham Pl W1	13	H6
Grantham Rd E12	36	C1
Grantham Rd SW9	71	F5
Grantham Rd W4	66	A3
Grantley St E1	46	B2
Grant Rd SW11	83	E2
Grant's Quay Wf EC3	17	G4
Grant St E13	48	D2
Grantully Rd W9	40	C2
Granville Ct N1	30	C5
Granville Gro SE13	89	G1
Granville Pk SE13	89	G1
Granville Pl W1	13	F2
Granville Rd NW6	40	B1
Granville Rd SW18	82	B5
Granville Sq SE15	73	D3
Granville Sq WC1	9	H2
Granville St WC1	9	H2
Grape St WC2	15	E1
Grasmere Rd E13	48	D1
Gratton Rd W14	53	G4
Gravel Pit La SE9	93	E3
Gravesend Rd W12	52	C1
Grayling Sq E2	45	F2
Grayshott Rd SW11	70	A5
Gray's Inn WC1	9	H5
Gray's Inn Pl WC1	9	H6
Gray's Inn Rd WC1	9	G2
Gray's Inn Sq WC1	9	J5
Grayson Ho EC1	10	E2
Gray SE1	22	A2
Gray's Yd W1	13	G2
Great Arthur Ho EC1	10	D4
Great Bell All EC2	17	F1
Great Castle St W1	13	J1
Great Cen St NW1	6	D5
Great Cen Way NW10	24	A2
Great Chapel St W1	14	C1
Great Chart St SW11	83	E2
Great Ch La W6	67	F1
Great Coll St SW1	20	E3
Great Cross Av SE10	76	B3
Great Cumberland Ms W1	12	D2
Great Cumberland Pl W1	12	D1
Great Dover St SE1	23	E2
Great Eastern Enterprise Cen E14	61	F3
Great Eastern Rd E15	34	A4
Great Eastern St EC2	11	H2
Great Eastern Wk EC2	11	J6
Greatfield Av E6	50	B3
Greatfield Cl SE4	89	E2
Greatfields Rd, Bark.	37	G2
Great George St SW1	20	D2
Great Guildford St SE1	16	D5
Great James St WC1	9	G4
Great Marlborough St W1	14	A2
Great Maze Pond SE1	17	F6
Great New St EC4	16	A1
Greatorex St E1	45	F4
Great Ormond St WC1	9	F5
Great Percy St WC1	9	H1
Great Peter St SW1	20	C4
Great Portland St W1	7	J5
Great Pulteney St W1	14	B2
Great Queen St WC2	15	F2
Great Russell St WC1	14	D1
Great St. Helens EC3	17	H1
Great St. Thomas Apostle EC4	16	E4
Great Scotland Yd SW1	14	E6
Great Smith St SW1	20	D3
Great Spilmans SE22	86	D3
Great Suffolk St SE1	16	C6
Great Sutton St EC1	10	C4
Great Swan All EC2	17	F1
Great Titchfield St W1	14	A1
Great Twr St EC3	17	H3
Great Trinity La EC4	16	E3
Great Turnstile WC1	9	H6
Great Western Rd W2	40	A4
Great Western Rd W9	40	A4
Great Western Rd W11	40	A4
Great W Rd W6	66	B1
Great Winchester St EC2	17	G1
Great Windmill St W1	14	C3
Great Yd SE1	23	H3
Greaves Cl, Bark.	37	H4
Greek Ct W1	14	D2
Greek St W1	14	D2
Greek Yd WC2	14	E3
Green, The E15	34	B3
Green, The W3	38	A5
Green, The, Well.	93	G2
Greenacres SE9	92	A3
Green Arbour Ct EC1	16	B1
Greenaway Gdns NW3	26	C1
Green Bk E1	59	G2
Greenbay Rd SE7	77	G3
Greenberry St NW8	41	F1
Greencoat Pl SW1	20	A2
Greencoat Row SW1	20	B2
Greencroft Gdns NW6	26	C4
Green Dale SE5	86	C2
Green Dale SE22	86	D3
Green Dragon Ct SE1	17	F5
Greenend Rd W4	52	A3
Greenfield Rd E1	45	F5
Greengate St E13	48	E1
Greenham Cl SE1	21	J2
Green Hill SE18	78	B1
Greenhill Gro E12	36	A1
Greenhill Pk NW10	24	A5
Greenhill Rd NW10	24	A5
Greenhill's Rents EC1	10	C5
Greenhill Ter SE18	78	B1
Greenhithe Cl, Sid.	93	G5
Greenholm Rd SE9	92	D3
Green Hundred Rd SE15	73	F2
Greenland Quay SE16	60	B5
Greenland Rd NW1	28	C5
Greenlaw St SE18	64	C4
Greenman St N1	30	B4
Green Pt E15	34	B3
Greenroof Way SE10	62	C4
Green's Ct W1	14	C3
Green's End SE18	64	D5
Greenside Rd W12	52	C4
Greenstead Gdns SW15	80	C3
Green St E7	35	E3
Green St E13	35	F5
Green St W1	13	E3
Green Ter EC1	10	A2
Greenvale Rd SE9	92	B2
Greenview Cl W3	52	A2
Green Wk SE1	23	H4
Green Way SE9	91	G3
Greenwell St W1	7	J4
Greenwich Ch St SE10	75	G2
Greenwich Foot Tunnel E14	75	G1
Greenwich Foot Tunnel SE10	75	G1
Greenwich Hts SE18	78	A3
Greenwich High Rd SE10	75	F4
Greenwich Ind Est SE7	63	E5
Greenwich Pk SE10	76	A3
Greenwich Pk St SE10	76	A1
Greenwich Quay SE8	75	F2
Greenwich Shop Pk SE7	63	E5
Greenwich S St SE10	75	F4
Greenwich Vw Pl E14	61	F4
Greenwood Ct SW1	20	A3
Greenwood Rd E8	31	F3
Greet St SE1	16	A6
Gregor Ms SE3	77	D3
Gregory Cres SE9	91	G5
Gregory Pl W8	54	C3
Grenada Rd SE7	77	F3
Grenade St E14	61	D1
Grenadier St E16	64	C2
Grenard Cl SE15	73	F3
Grendon St NW8	6	B3
Grenfell Rd W11	53	F1
Grenfell Twr W11	53	F1
Grenfell Wk W11	53	F1
Grenville Pl SW7	54	D4
Grenville St WC1	9	F4
Gresham Rd E6	50	B1
Gresham Rd E16	49	E5
Gresham Rd SW9	85	G1
Gresham St EC2	16	D1
Gressenhall Rd SW18	82	A4
Gresse St W1	8	B6
Greswell St SW6	67	F4
Greville Pl NW6	40	C1
Greville Rd NW6	26	C5
Greville St EC1	10	A6
Greycoat Pl SW1	20	C4
Greycoat St SW1	20	C4
Grey Eagle St E1	45	E4
Greyfriars Pas EC1	16	C1
Greyhound Rd NW10	39	G2
Greyhound Rd W6	67	F2
Greyhound Rd W14	67	G2
Greystead Rd SE23	88	A5
Greystoke Pl EC4	15	J1
Grierson Rd SE23	88	B5
Griffin Cl NW10	24	D2
Griffin Manor Way SE28	65	F4
Griffin Rd SE18	79	F1
Griggs Pl SE1	23	J4
Grimsby Gro E16	65	D2
Grimston Rd SW6	68	A5
Grimthorpe Ho EC1	10	B3
Grimwade Cl SE15	88	A1
Grindal St SE1	21	J2
Grinling Pl SE8	75	E2
Grinstead Rd SE8	74	C1
Grittleton Rd W9	40	B3
Grocer's Hall Ct EC2	17	F2
Groombridge Rd E9	32	B4
Groom Cres SW18	83	E5
Groom Pl SW1	19	G3
Grosse Way SW15	81	D4
Grosvenor Av N5	30	B2
Grosvenor Av SW14	80	A1
Grosvenor Cotts SW1	19	F5
Grosvenor Ct NW6	25	F5
Grosvenor Cres SW1	19	F2
Grosvenor Cres Ms SW1	19	F2
Grosvenor Est SW1	20	D5
Grosvenor Gdns E6	49	G2
Grosvenor Gdns NW2	25	E4
Grosvenor Gdns SW1	19	H3
Grosvenor Gdns SW14	80	A1
Grosvenor Gdns Ms E SW1	19	J3
Grosvenor Gdns Ms N SW1	19	H4
Grosvenor Gdns Ms S SW1	19	J4
Grosvenor Gate W1	13	E4
Grosvenor Hill W1	13	H3
Grosvenor Pk SE5	72	B5
Grosvenor Pl SW1	19	G2
Grosvenor Rd E6	35	G5
Grosvenor Rd E7	35	E3
Grosvenor Rd E11	70	B2
Grosvenor Sq W1	13	G3
Grosvenor St W1	13	H3
Grosvenor Ter SE5	72	A3
Grosvenor Wf Rd E14	62	A5
Grote's Bldgs SE3	76	B5
Grote's Pl SE3	76	B5
Grotto Pas W1	7	G5
Grove, The E15	34	B3
Grove Cotts SW3	69	F2
Grove Cres Rd E15	34	A3
Grove End Rd NW8	41	E2
Grove Gdns NW8	6	C2
Grove Hill Rd SE5	86	D1
Groveland Ct EC4	16	E2
Grovelands Cl SE5	72	D5
Grove La SE5	72	C4
Grove Mkt Pl SE9	92	B4
Grove Pk E11	53	E4
Grove Pk SE5	72	D5
Grove Pas E2	45	G1
Grove Pl SW12	84	B4
Grove Rd E3	32	B5
Grove Rd NW2	25	E3
Grove Rd SW13	66	B5
Grove St SE8	60	D5
Grove Vale SE22	87	D2
Grove Vil E14	61	F1
Groveway SW9	71	F4
Grummant Rd SE15	73	E4
Grundy St E14	47	F5
Gubyon Av SE24	86	A3
Guerin Sq E3	46	D2
Guernsey Gro SE24	86	B5
Guibal Rd SE12	91	E5
Guildford Gro SE10	75	F4
Guildford Rd E6	50	A5
Guildford Rd SW8	71	E4
Guildhall Bldgs EC2	17	F1
Guildhall Yd EC2	17	E1
Guildhouse St SW1	20	A5
Guild Rd SE7	77	G1
Guilford Pl WC1	9	G4
Guilford St WC1	9	F4
Guinness Cl E9	32	C4
Guinness Ct SW3	23	H5
Guinness Trust Bldgs SE11	72	A1
Guinness Trust Bldgs SW3	18	D6
Guinness Trust Bldgs SW9	86	A2

Guion Rd SW6 68 A5
Gulliver St SE16 60 D4
Gulston Wk SW3 18 E6
Gunmakers La E3 32 C5
Gunner La SE18 78 C1
Gunnery Ter SE18 65 E5
Gunning St SE18 66 C5
Gunpowder Sq EC4 16 A1
Gunstor Rd N16 31 D1
Gun St E1 45 E4
Gunter Gro SW10 69 D3
Gunterstone Rd W14 53 G5
Gunthorpe St E1 45 E4
Gunwhale Cl SE16 60 B2
Gurdon Rd SE7 77 D1
Gurney Cl, Bark. 36 D3
Gurney Rd E15 34 B2
Gurney Rd SW6 82 D1
Gutter La EC2 16 E1
Guyscliff Rd SE13 89 G3
Guy St E1 23 G1
Gwendolen Av SW15 81 F3
Gwendolen Cl SW15 81 E3
Gwendoline Av E13 35 E5
Gwendwr Rd W14 67 G1
Gwyn Cl SW6 68 D3
Gwynne Pl WC1 9 H2
Gwynne Rd SW11 69 E5
Gylcote Cl SE5 86 C2

H

Haarlem Rd W14 53 F4
Haberdasher Pl N1 11 G1
Haberdasher St N1 11 G1
Hackford Rd SW9 71 F4
Hackford Wk SW9 71 F4
Hackney Rd E2 45 E2
Hadden Rd SE28 65 G4
Haddonfield SE8 60 B5
Haddo St SE10 75 F2
Hadleigh St E2 46 A3
Hadleigh Wk E6 50 A5
Hadley St NW1 28 B3
Hadrian Est E2 45 F1
Hadrian St SE10 76 B1
Hadyn Pk Rd W12 53 G2
Hafer Rd SW11 83 G2
Haggerston Rd E8 31 E4
Ha-Ha Rd SE18 78 B2
Haig Rd E E13 49 F2
Haig Rd W E13 49 F2
Haimo Rd SE9 91 G3
Haines Cl N1 30 D4
Hainford Cl SE4 88 B2
Hainton Cl E1 45 G5
Halcomb St N1 30 D5
Haldane Rd E6 49 G2
Haldane Rd SW6 68 A3
Haldon Rd SW18 82 A3
Hale Rd E6 50 A3
Hale St E14 61 F1
Halesworth Rd SE13 89 F1
Half Moon Cr N1 10 D6
Half Moon Cres N1 43 F1
Half Moon La SE24 86 B4
Half Moon St W1 13 J5
Halford Rd SW6 68 B2
Halfway St, Sid. 93 F5
Halkin Arc SW1 19 F3
Halkin Ms SW1 19 F3
Halkin Pl SW1 19 F3
Halkin St SW1 19 G2
Hall, The SE3 90 D1
Hallam Ms W1 7 J5
Hallam Rd SW13 81 D1
Hallam St W1 7 J4
Halley Gdns SE13 90 A2
Halley Pl E7 35 F3
Halley Rd E12 35 G3
Halley St E14 46 C4
Hallfield Est W2 40 D5
Halliford St N1 30 B4
Halliwell Rd SW2 85 F4

Hall Pl W2 41 E3
Hall Rd E6 36 B5
Hall Rd E15 34 A1
Hall Rd NW8 41 D2
Hall St EC1 10 C1
Hallsville Rd E16 48 C5
Hall Twr W2 41 E4
Hallywell Cres E6 50 B4
Halons Rd SE9 92 C5
Halpin Pl SE17 23 G6
Halsbrook Rd SE3 91 G1
Halsbury Rd W12 52 D2
Halsey Ms SW3 18 D5
Halsey St SW3 18 D5
Halsmere Rd SE5 72 A4
Halston Cl SW11 83 G4
Halstow Rd NW10 39 F2
Halstow Rd SE10 76 D1
Halton Cross St N1 30 A5
Halton Rd N1 30 A4
Hambalt Rd SW4 84 C3
Hambledon Rd SW18 83 F5
Hambledown Rd, Sid. 93 F5
Hamble St SW6 82 C2
Hambridge Way SW2 85 G5
Hameway E6 50 C3
Hamfrith Rd E15 34 B4
Hamilton Cl NW8 41 E2
Hamilton Gdns NW8 41 D2
Hamilton Ms W1 19 H1
Hamilton Pk N5 30 A1
Hamilton Pk W N5 30 A1
Hamilton Pl W1 19 G1
Hamilton Rd E15 48 B2
Hamilton Rd NW10 24 C2
Hamilton Rd W4 52 A3
Hamilton Rd, Ilf. 36 D1
Hamilton Sq SE1 23 G1
Hamilton Ter NW8 40 C1
Hamlea Cl SE12 90 C3
Hamlet, The SE5 86 C1
Hamlet Cl SE13 90 B2
Hamlets Way E3 46 D3
Hamlet Way SE1 23 G1
Hammersmith Br SW13 67 D2
Hammersmith Br Rd W6 67 D2
Hammersmith Bdy W6 53 E5
Hammersmith Flyover W6 67 E1
Hammersmith Gro W6 53 F5
Hammersmith Rd W6 53 F5
Hammersmith Rd W14 53 F5
Hammersmith Ter W6 66 C1
Hammond St NW5 28 C3
Hamond Sq N1 11 J2
Hampden Gurney St W1 12 D2
Hampson Way SW8 71 F4
Hampstead Grn NW3 27 F2
Hampstead High St NW3 27 D1
Hampstead Hill Gdns NW3 27 D1
Hampstead Rd NW1 42 C1
Hampton Cl NW6 40 B2
Hampton Rd E7 35 E2
Hampton Rd, Ilf. 37 D1
Hampton St SE1 22 C6
Hampton St SE17 22 C6
Ham Yd W1 14 C3
Hanameel St E16 63 D2
Hanbury St E1 45 E4
Hancock Rd E3 47 G2
Hand Ct WC1 9 H6
Handel St WC1 8 E3
Handen Rd SE12 89 G3
Handforth Rd SW9 71 G3

Handley Rd E9 32 A4
Hands Wk E16 49 D5
Handyside St N1 29 E5
Hanging Sword All EC4 16 A2
Hankey Pl SE1 23 G2
Hannah Mary Way SE1 59 F5
Hannell Rd SW6 67 G3
Hannibal Rd E1 46 A4
Hannington Rd SW4 84 B1
Hanover Av E16 62 D2
Hanover Gdns SE11 71 G2
Hanover Gate Mans NW1 6 C2
Hanover Pk SE15 73 F4
Hanover Pl WC2 15 F2
Hanover Rd NW10 25 E4
Hanover Sq W1 13 J2
Hanover St W1 13 J2
Hanover Ter NW1 6 C2
Hanover Ter Ms NW1 6 C2
Hans Cres SW1 18 D3
Hansler Rd SE22 87 E3
Hanson Cl SW12 84 B5
Hanson St W1 8 A5
Hans Pl SW1 18 E3
Hans Rd SW3 18 D3
Hans St SW1 18 E4
Hanway Pl W1 14 C1
Hanway St W1 14 C1
Harben Rd NW6 27 D4
Harberson Rd E15 34 C5
Harbet Rd W2 6 A6
Harbinger Rd E14 75 E5
Harbledown Rd SW6 68 B4
Harbord St SW6 67 F4
Harborough Av, Sid. 93 G5
Harbour Av SW10 68 D4
Harbour Ex Sq E14 61 F3
Harbour Rd SE5 86 B1
Harbridge Av SW15 80 B5
Harbut Rd SW11 83 E2
Harcourt Av E12 36 B1
Harcourt Rd E15 48 C1
Harcourt Rd SE4 88 C2
Harcourt St W1 6 C6
Harcourt Ter SW10 68 C1
Hardens Manorway SE7 63 G4
Harders Rd SE15 73 G5
Hardinge Cres SE18 65 E4
Hardinge Rd NW10 25 D5
Hardinge St E1 46 A5
Hardman Rd SE7 77 E1
Hardwicke Ms WC1 9 H2
Hardwicke St, Bark. 37 E5
Hardwick St EC1 10 A2
Hardwicks Way SW18 82 B3
Hardwidge St SE1 23 H1
Hardy Rd SE3 76 C3
Hare & Billet Rd SE3 76 A4
Harebell Dr E6 50 C4
Hare Ct EC4 15 J2
Harecourt Rd N1 30 B3
Haredale Rd SE24 86 B2
Haredon Cl SE23 88 A5
Harefield Ms SE4 88 D1
Harefield Rd SE4 88 D1
Hare Pl EC4 16 A2
Hare Row E2 45 G1
Hare St SE18 64 C4
Hare Wk N1 45 D1
Harewood Av NW1 6 C4
Harewood Pl W1 13 J2
Harewood Row NW1 6 C5
Harfield Gdns SE5 86 D1
Harford St E1 46 C3
Hargood Rd SE3 77 F4
Hargwyne St SW9 85 F1
Harkett Cl SE18 65 F4
Harlescott Rd SE15 88 A2
Harlesden Gdns NW10 24 B5
Harlesden La NW10 24 C5
Harlesden Rd NW10 24 C5
Harleyford Rd SE11 71 F2

Harleyford St SE11 71 G2
Harley Gdns SW10 69 D1
Harley Gro E3 47 D2
Harley Pl W1 7 H6
Harley Rd NW3 27 E4
Harley Rd NW10 38 A1
Harley St W1 7 H6
Harlinger St SE18 64 A4
Harmood St NW1 28 B4
Harmsworth Ms SE11 22 B4
Harmsworth St SE17 23 J4
Harold Est SE1 23 J2
Harold Gibbons Ct SE7 77 F2
Harold Laski Ho EC1 10 B2
Harold Rd E13 35 E1
Harp All EC4 16 B1
Harper Rd E6 50 B5
Harper Rd SE1 22 D3
Harp La EC3 17 H4
Harpley Sq E1 46 A2
Harpour Rd, Bark. 37 E3
Harpur Ms WC1 9 G5
Harpur St WC1 9 G5
Harraden Rd SE3 77 F4
Harrap St E14 61 G1
Harrier Way E6 50 B3
Harriet Cl E8 31 F5
Harriet St SW1 18 E2
Harriet Tubman Cl SW2 85 G5
Harriet Wk SW1 18 E2
Harrington Gdns SW7 54 C5
Harrington Ho NW1 8 A1
Harrington Rd SW7 55 E5
Harrington Sq NW1 42 C1
Harrington St NW1 8 A1
Harrington Way SE18 63 G4
Harriott Cl SE10 62 C5
Harrison St WC1 9 F2
Harris St SE5 72 C3
Harroway Rd SW11 69 E5
Harrowby St W1 12 C1
Harrowgate Rd E9 32 C3
Harrow La E14 61 G1
Harrow Pl E1 17 J1
Harrow Rd E6 36 A5
Harrow Rd NW10 38 D2
Harrow Rd W2 40 A3
Harrow Rd W9 40 A3
Harrow Rd W10 39 F3
Harrow Rd, Bark. 37 G5
Harrow Rd, Ilf. 37 E1
Hartfield Ter E3 47 E1
Hartham Cl N7 29 E2
Hartham Rd N7 29 E2
Hartington Rd E16 49 F5
Hartington Rd SW8 71 E4
Hartismere Rd SW6 68 A3
Hartland Rd E15 34 C4
Hartland Rd NW1 28 B4
Hartland Rd NW6 40 A1
Hartley Av E6 36 A5
Hartley St E2 46 A2
Hartmann Rd E16 64 A2
Harton St SE8 75 E4
Hartshorn All EC3 17 J2
Hartshorn Gdns E6 50 C3
Harts La SE14 74 C3
Harts La, Bark. 36 D5
Hart St EC3 17 J3
Hartswood Gdns W12 52 B4
Hartswood Rd W12 52 B3
Hartsworth Cl E13 48 C1
Hartville Rd SE18 65 G5
Harvard Rd SE13 89 G3
Harvey Gdns SE7 77 F1
Harvey Rd SE5 72 C4
Harvey Rd, Ilf. 37 D2
Harvey St N1 30 C5
Harvist Est N7 29 F1
Harvist Rd NW6 39 F2

Harwood Rd SW6	68	B3
Harwood Ter SW6	68	C4
Haselrigge Rd SW4	85	D2
Hasker St SW3	18	C5
Haslam Cl N1	29	G4
Haslam St SE15	73	E3
Hassendean Rd SE3	77	E2
Hassett Rd E9	32	B3
Hassop Rd NW2	25	F1
Hasted Rd SE7	77	G1
Hastings Cl SE15	73	F3
Hastings Ho SE18	64	B5
Hastings Rd E16	49	D4
Hastings St SE18	65	E4
Hastings St WC1	8	E2
Hat & Mitre St EC1	10	D5
Hatcham Pk Rd SE14	74	B4
Hatcham Rd SE15	74	A2
Hatchers Ms SE1	23	J2
Hatcliffe Cl SE3	90	C1
Hatcliffe St SE10	76	C1
Hatfield Rd E15	34	B2
Hatfields SE1	16	A5
Hathaway Cres E12	36	B3
Hatherley Gdns E6	49	G1
Hatherley Gro W2	40	C5
Hatherley St SW1	56	B1
Hathorne Cl SE15	73	G5
Hatton Cl SE18	79	F3
Hatton Gdn EC1	10	A5
Hatton Pl EC1	10	A4
Hatton Row NW8	6	A4
Hatton St NW8	6	A4
Hatton Wall EC1	9	J5
Haunch of Venison Yd W1	13	H2
Havannah St E14	61	E3
Havelock St N1	29	E5
Havelock Ter SW8	70	B3
Haven Way SE1	59	E4
Haverfield Rd E3	46	C2
Haverstock Hill NW3	27	F2
Haverstock Rd NW5	28	A2
Haverstock St N1	44	A1
Havil St SE5	72	D3
Hawarden Gro SE24	86	B5
Hawes St N1	30	A4
Hawgood St E3	47	E4
Hawkesbury Rd SW15	80	D3
Hawkins Rd NW10	24	A4
Hawkins Ter SE7	78	A1
Hawkshead NW1	8	A1
Hawkshead Rd NW10	24	B4
Hawkshead Rd W4	52	A3
Hawkslade Rd SE15	88	B3
Hawksmoor Cl SE18	79	G1
Hawksmoor St W6	67	F2
Hawkstone Est SE16	60	A5
Hawkstone Rd SE16	60	A5
Hawley Cres NW1	28	B4
Hawley Rd NW1	28	B4
Hawley St NW1	28	B4
Hawstead Rd SE6	89	F4
Hawthorn Av E3	32	D5
Hawthorn Cl N1	30	D3
Hawthorn Rd NW10	24	C4
Hawtrey Rd NW3	27	F4
Hay Cl E15	34	B4
Haycroft Gdns NW10	24	C5
Haycroft Rd SW2	85	E3
Hay Currie St E14	47	E5
Hayday Rd E16	48	D4
Haydon Way SW11	83	E2
Hayes Gro SE22	87	E2
Hayes Pl NW1	6	C4
Hay Hill W1	13	J4
Hayles St SE11	22	B5
Haymarket SW1	14	C4
Haymarket Arc SW1	14	C4
Haymerle Rd SE15	73	F2
Haynes Cl SE3	90	B1
Hayne St EC1	10	C5
Hay's Galleria SE1	17	H5
Hay's La SE1	17	H6
Hay's Ms W1	13	H4
Hay St E2	31	F5
Hayter Rd SW2	85	E3
Hayward Gdns SW15	80	D4
Hayward's Pl EC1	10	B4
Hazelbourne Rd SW12	84	B4
Hazel Cl SE15	73	F5
Hazeldon Rd SE4	88	C3
Hazelmere Rd NW6	26	B5
Hazel Rd NW10	39	E2
Hazlebury Rd SW6	68	C5
Hazlewell Rd SW15	81	D3
Hazlewood Cres W10	39	G3
Hazlitt Rd W14	53	G4
Headfort Pl SW1	19	G2
Headlam Rd SW4	84	D4
Headlam St E1	45	G3
Head St E1	46	B5
Heald St SE14	75	D4
Healey St NW1	28	B3
Hearn's Bldgs SE17	23	G6
Hearnshaw St E14	46	C4
Hearn St EC2	11	J4
Heathcote St WC1	9	G3
Heath Dr NW3	26	C1
Heatherbank SE9	78	B5
Heather Cl SE13	90	D5
Heather Cl SW8	90	A4
Heather Cl SE13	84	B1
Heather Cl SW8	84	B1
Heatherfield Cl E16	49	G4
Heathfield Gdns SE3	76	B5
Heathfield Gdns SW18	83	E4
Heathfield Pk NW2	25	E3
Heathfield Sq SW18	83	E5
Heath Hurst Rd NW3	27	F1
Heath La SE3	76	A5
Heathlee Rd SE3	90	C2
Heathmans Rd SW6	68	A4
Heath Ri SW15	81	F4
Heath Rd SW8	70	B5
Heath Side NW3	27	E1
Heathstan Rd W12	38	C5
Heathview Gdns SW15	81	E5
Heathwall St SW11	83	G1
Heathway SE3	76	C3
Heathwood Gdns SE7	64	A5
Heaton Rd SE15	87	F1
Heaven Tree Cl N1	30	B2
Heavitree Cl SE18	79	F1
Heavitree Rd SE18	79	F1
Heber Rd NW2	25	F2
Heber Rd SE22	87	E4
Hebron Rd W6	53	D4
Hector St SE18	65	G5
Heddington Gro N7	29	F2
Heddon St W1	14	A3
Hedgers Gro E9	32	C3
Hedger St SE11	22	B5
Hedgley St SE12	90	C3
Heigham Rd E6	35	G4
Heights, The SE7	77	F1
Heiron St SE17	72	A2
Helby Rd SW4	85	D4
Helder Gro SE12	90	C5
Helena Rd E13	48	C1
Helena Rd NW10	24	D2
Helix Rd SW2	85	F4
Helmet Row EC1	11	E3
Helmsley Pl E8	31	G4
Helperby Rd NW10	24	A4
Helsinki Sq SE16	60	C4
Hemans St SW8	71	D3
Hemberton Rd SW9	85	E1
Hemingford Rd N1	29	F5
Hemingway Cl NW5	28	A1
Hemlock Rd W12	52	B1
Hemming St E1	45	F3
Hemp Wk SE17	23	G5
Hemstal Rd NW6	26	B4
Hemsworth St N1	44	D1
Hen & Chicken Ct EC4	15	J2
Henchman St W12	38	B5
Henderson Rd E7	35	F3
Henderson Rd SW18	83	F5
Hendre Rd SE1	23	J6
Hendrick Av SW12	83	G4
Heneage La EC3	17	J2
Heneage St E1	45	E4
Hengist Rd SE12	91	E5
Hengrave Rd SE23	88	B5
Henley Cross SE3	91	E1
Henley Dr SE1	59	E5
Henley Rd E16	64	B3
Henley Rd NW10	25	E5
Henley St SW11	70	A5
Henniker Gdns E6	49	G2
Henniker Pt E15	34	A2
Henniker Rd E15	34	A2
Henning St SW11	69	F4
Henrietta Cl SE8	75	E2
Henrietta Ms WC1	9	F3
Henrietta Pl W1	13	H2
Henrietta St E15	33	G2
Henrietta St WC2	15	F3
Henriques St E1	45	F5
Henry Addington Cl E16	50	D4
Henry Dent Cl SE5	86	C1
Henry Dickens Ct W11	53	F2
Henry Jackson Rd SW15	81	F1
Henry Rd E6	50	A1
Henryson Rd SE4	89	E3
Henshall St N1	30	C3
Henshaw St SE17	23	F5
Henslowe Rd SE22	87	F3
Henson Av NW2	25	E2
Henstridge Pl NW8	41	F1
Henty Cl SW11	69	F3
Henty Wk SW15	80	D3
Henwick Rd SE9	91	G1
Hepplestone Cl SW15	81	D4
Hepscott Rd E9	33	E4
Herald's Pl SE11	22	B5
Herbal Hill EC1	10	A4
Herbert Cres SW1	18	E3
Herbert Gdns NW10	38	D1
Herbert Rd E12	36	A1
Herbert Rd SE18	78	C3
Herbert St E13	49	D1
Herbert St NW5	28	A3
Herbert Ter SE18	78	D3
Herbrand St WC1	8	E3
Hercules Rd SE1	21	H4
Hereford Ho NW6	40	B1
Hereford Rd E3	47	D1
Hereford Rd W2	40	B5
Hereford Sq SW7	55	D5
Hereford St E2	45	F3
Heritage Cl SW9	86	A1
Hermitage, The SW13	66	B4
Hermitage Row E8	31	F2
Hermitage St W2	41	E4
Hermitage Wall E1	59	F2
Hermit Rd E16	48	C4
Hermit St EC1	10	B1
Herndon Rd SW18	82	D3
Herne Hill SE24	86	B4
Herne Hill Rd SE24	86	B1
Herne Pl SE24	86	A3
Heron Cl NW10	24	A3
Heron Pl SE16	60	C2
Heron Quay E14	61	E2
Heron Rd SE24	86	B2
Herrick St SW1	20	D5
Herries St W10	39	G1
Herringham Rd SE7	63	F4
Hersant Cl NW10	24	C5
Herschell Rd SE23	88	B5
Hersham Cl SW15	80	C5
Hertford Pl W1	8	A4
Hertford Rd N1	31	D5
Hertford Rd, Bark.	36	D4
Hertford St W1	13	H5
Hertsmere Rd E14	61	E1
Hervey Rd SE3	77	E4
Hesketh Pl W11	53	G1
Hesper Ms SW5	68	C1
Hesperus Cres E14	61	F5
Hessel St E1	45	G5
Hestercombe Av SW6	67	G5
Hester Rd SW11	69	F3
Heston St SE14	75	D4
Hetherington Rd SW4	85	E2
Hetley Rd W12	52	D2
Hevelius Cl SE10	76	C1
Heversham Rd SE18	65	G5
Hewer St W10	39	F4
Hewetts Quay, Bark.	37	D5
Hewett St EC2	11	J4
Hewison St E3	47	D1
Hewlett Rd E3	46	C1
Heyford Av SW8	71	E3
Heygate St SE17	22	D6
Heyworth Rd E5	31	G1
Heyworth Rd E15	34	C2
Hibbert St SW11	83	D1
Hichisson Rd SE15	88	B3
Hickin Cl SE7	63	G5
Hickling Rd, Ilf.	37	D2
Hickman Cl E16	49	G4
Hickmore Wk SW4	84	C1
Hicks Cl SW11	83	F1
Hicks St SE8	74	C1
Hide Pl SW1	20	C6
Hide Twr SW1	20	C6
High Br SE10	76	A1
Highbridge Rd, Bark.	36	D5
High Br WF SE10	76	A1
Highbrook Rd SE3	91	G1
Highbury Cor N5	29	G3
Highbury Cres N5	29	G2
Highbury Gra N5	30	B2
Highbury Gro N5	30	A1
Highbury Grn N5	30	A3
Highbury New Pk N5	30	B2
Highbury Pl N5	30	A3
Highbury Stadium Sq N5	30	A1
Highbury Sta Rd N1	29	G3
Highbury Ter N5	30	A2
Highbury Ter Ms N5	30	A2
Highcliffe Dr SW15	80	B4
Highcombe SE7	77	E2
Highdown Rd SW15	80	D4
Highfield Cl SE13	90	A4
Highgate Rd NW5	28	B1
High Gro SE18	79	F3
High Holborn WC1	15	F1
Highlands Heath SW15	81	E5
Highlever Rd W10	39	E4
High Meads Rd E16	49	G5
Highmore Rd SE3	76	B3
High Rd (Willesden) NW10	24	D3
High Rd Leytonstone E11	34	B1
High Rd Leytonstone E15	34	B1
Highshore Rd SE15	73	E5
High St E13	48	D1
High St E15	47	G1
High St (Harlesden) NW10	38	B1
High St N E6	36	A5
High St N E12	36	A2
High St S E6	50	B1
High Timber St EC4	16	D3
High Tor Vw SE28	65	G2
Highway, The E1	59	G1
Highway, The E14	59	G1
Hilary Cl SW6	68	C3

Entry	Ref
Hilary Rd W12	38 B5
Hilda Rd E6	35 G4
Hilda Rd E16	48 B3
Hilda Ter SW9	71 G5
Hildyard Rd SW6	68 B2
Hiley Rd NW10	39 E2
Hilgrove Rd NW6	27 D4
Hillbeck Cl SE15	74 A3
Hillcourt Rd SE22	87 G4
Hillcrest SE24	86 C2
Hillcroft Rd E6	50 D4
Hilldrop Cres N7	29 D2
Hilldrop Est N7	28 D2
Hilldrop La N7	29 D2
Hilldrop Rd N7	28 D2
Hillend SE18	78 C4
Hillersdon Av SW13	66 B4
Hillery Cl SE17	23 G6
Hill Fm Rd W10	39 E4
Hillfield Ct NW3	27 F2
Hillfield Rd NW6	26 A2
Hillgate Pl SW12	84 B5
Hillgate Pl W8	54 B2
Hillgate St W8	54 B2
Hillier Rd SW11	83 G4
Hillingdon St SE17	72 A3
Hillman Dr W10	39 E3
Hillman St E8	31 G3
Hillmarton Rd N7	29 E2
Hillmead Dr SW9	86 A2
Hillreach SE18	78 B1
Hill Rd NW8	41 D1
Hillsboro Rd SE22	87 D3
Hillside Cl NW8	40 C1
Hillside Rd W8	54 A2
Hills Pl W1	14 A2
Hill St W1	13 G5
Hilltop Rd NW6	26 B4
Hill Vw Dr SE9	79 G5
Hill Vw Dr, Well.	79 G5
Hillworth Rd SW2	85 G5
Hillyard St SW9	71 G4
Hilly Flds Cres SE14	89 E1
Hilsea St E5	32 A1
Hinckley Rd SE15	87 F2
Hind Ct EC4	16 A2
Hinde St W1	13 G1
Hind Gro E14	47 F3
Hindmans Rd SE22	87 F3
Hindon Ct SW1	20 A5
Hindrey Rd E5	31 G2
Hinstock Rd SE18	79 E2
Hinton Rd SE24	86 B4
Hippodrome Pl W11	53 G1
Hitchcock La E20	33 G3
Hitchin Sq E3	46 C1
Hither Fm Rd SE3	91 J1
Hither Grn La SE13	89 G3
Hobart Pl SW1	19 H3
Hobbes Wk SW15	80 D3
Hobday St E14	47 F4
Hobury St SW10	54 C6
Hockley Av E6	50 A1
Hockley Ms, Bark.	51 G1
Hocroft Rd NW2	26 A1
Hodnet Gro SE16	60 B5
Hofland Rd W14	53 F4
Hogarth Business Pk W4	66 A2
Hogarth Ct E4	49 G4
Hogarth Ct EC3	17 J3
Hogarth La W4	66 A2
Hogarth Rd SW5	54 B2
Hogarth Rd Est SW5	66 B2
Holbeach Gdns, Sid.	93 G4
Holbeach Rd SE6	89 E5
Holbeck Row SE15	73 F3
Holbein Ms SW1	70 A1
Holbein Pl SW1	19 F6
Holberton Gdns NW10	38 D2
Holborn EC1	9 J6
Holborn Circ EC1	10 A6
Holborn Pl WC1	9 G6
Holborn Rd E13	49 E3
Holborn Viaduct EC1	10 A6
Holbrooke Ct N7	29 E1
Holbrook Rd E15	48 C1
Holburne Cl SE3	77 F4
Holburne Gdns SE3	77 G4
Holburne Rd SE3	77 F4
Holcroft Rd E9	32 A4
Holdenby Rd SE4	88 C3
Holden St SW11	70 A5
Holford Pl WC1	9 H1
Holford St WC1	9 J1
Holgate Av SW11	83 E1
Holland Gdns W14	53 G4
Holland Pk W8	54 A3
Holland Pk W11	53 G3
Holland Pk Av W11	53 G3
Holland Pk Gdns W14	53 G2
Holland Pk Ms W11	53 G2
Holland Pk Rd W14	54 A4
Holland Pk Rbt W11	53 F4
Holland Rd E6	36 B5
Holland Rd E15	48 B2
Holland Rd W14	24 C5
Holland Rd W14	53 F3
Holland St SE1	16 C5
Holland St W8	54 B3
Holland Vil Rd W14	53 G3
Holland Wk W8	54 A3
Hollen St W1	14 C1
Holles St W1	13 J1
Holley Rd W3	52 A3
Hollingbourne Rd SE24	86 B3
Hollington Rd E6	50 B2
Holloway Rd E6	50 B2
Holloway Rd N7	29 F1
Hollybush Gdns E2	45 G2
Holly Bush Hill NW3	27 D1
Hollybush St E13	49 E2
Hollydale Rd SE15	74 A4
Hollydene SE15	73 G4
Holly Gro SE15	73 E5
Holly Hedge Ter SE13	90 A3
Holly Hill NW3	27 D1
Hollymount Cl SE10	75 G4
Holly St E8	31 E3
Holly Wk NW3	27 D1
Hollywood Rd SW10	68 C2
Holman Rd SW11	69 E5
Holmbush Rd SW15	81 G4
Holmcote Gdns N5	30 B2
Holmdale Rd NW6	26 B2
Holmdene Av SE24	86 B3
Holmead Rd SW6	68 C3
Holmefield Ct NW3	27 F3
Holme Lacey Rd SE12	90 C4
Holme Rd E6	36 A5
Holmes Cl SE22	87 F2
Holmesley Rd SE23	88 C4
Holmes Rd NW5	28 B2
Holmes Ter SE1	21 J1
Holmewood Gdns SW2	85 F5
Holmewood Rd SW2	85 E5
Holm Oak Cl SW15	82 A4
Holm Oak Ms SW4	85 D3
Holmside Rd SE6	88 A4
Holms St E2	45 F1
Holness Rd E15	34 C3
Holroyd Rd SW15	81 E2
Holsworthy Sq WC1	9 H4
Holt Rd E16	64 A2
Holwood Pl SW4	84 D2
Holybourne Av SW15	80 C5
Holyoak Rd SE11	22 B5
Holyport Rd SW6	67 E3
Holyrood St SE1	17 H6
Holywell Cl SE16	77 D2
Holywell La EC2	11 J3
Holywell Row EC2	11 H4
Homefield Rd W4	52 B5
Homefield St N1	44 D1
Homeleigh Rd SE15	88 B3
Homer Dr E14	61 E5
Home Rd SW11	69 F5
Homer Rd E9	32 C3
Homer Row W1	6 C6
Homer St W1	6 C6
Homerton Gro E9	32 B2
Homerton High St E9	32 A2
Homerton Rd E9	32 C2
Homerton Row E9	32 A2
Homestall Rd SE22	88 A3
Homestead Rd SW6	68 A3
Honduras St EC1	10 D3
Honeybourne Rd NW6	26 C2
Honeybrook Rd SW12	84 C5
Honey La EC2	17 E2
Honeyman Cl NW6	25 F4
Honeywell Rd SW11	83 G4
Honeywood Rd NW10	38 B1
Honiton Rd NW6	40 A1
Honley Rd SE6	89 F5
Honor Oak Pk SE23	88 A4
Honor Oak Ri SE23	88 A4
Hood Ct EC4	16 A2
Hooper Rd E16	49 D5
Hooper's Ct SW3	19 E3
Hooper St E1	45 F5
Hopedale Rd SE7	77 E2
Hopefield Av NW6	39 G1
Hope St SW11	83 E1
Hopewell St SE5	72 C3
Hop Gdns WC2	14 E4
Hopkins St W1	14 B2
Hop St SE10	62 C5
Hopton Rd SE18	65 D4
Hopton's Gdns SE1	16 C5
Hopton St SE1	16 C5
Hopwood Rd SE17	72 C2
Horace Rd E7	35 E1
Horatio St E2	45 E1
Horbury Cres W11	54 B1
Horder Rd SW6	67 G4
Horizon Way SE7	63 E5
Horle Wk SE5	72 A5
Hormead Rd W9	40 A3
Hornbeam Cl SE11	21 J5
Hornbeam Cl, Ilf.	37 F2
Hornby Cl NW3	27 F3
Horncastle Cl SE12	90 D5
Horncastle Rd SE12	91 D5
Horne Way SW15	81 G4
Hornfair Rd SE7	77 F2
Horn La SE10	62 D5
Horn Link Way SE10	63 D5
Horn Pk Cl SE12	91 E3
Horn Pk La SE12	91 E3
Hornsey St N7	29 F2
Hornshay St SE15	74 A2
Horsa Rd SE12	91 D5
Horse & Dolphin Yd W1	14 D3
Horseferry Pl SE10	75 F2
Horseferry Rd E14	60 C1
Horseferry Rd SW1	20 C4
Horse Guards Av SW1	15 E6
Horse Guards Rd SW1	14 D6
Horse Leaze E6	50 C5
Horsell Rd N5	29 G2
Horselydown La SE1	59 E3
Horsemongers Ms SE1	23 E2
Horse Ride SW1	14 B6
Horseshoe Cl E14	75 G1
Horsfeld Gdns SE9	92 A3
Horsfeld Rd SE9	91 G3
Horsford Rd SW2	85 F3
Horsley St SE17	72 C2
Horsmonden Rd SE4	88 D3
Hortensia Rd SW10	68 D3
Horton Av NW2	25 G1
Horton Rd E8	31 G3
Horton St SE13	89 F1
Hosier La EC1	10 B6
Hoskins Cl E16	49 F5
Hoskins St SE10	76 A1
Hospital Way SE13	90 A5
Hotham Rd SW15	81 E1
Hotham St E15	34 B5
Hotspur St SE11	71 G1
Houghton St WC2	15 H2
Houndsditch EC3	17 J1
Hoveden Rd NW2	25 G2
Howard Bldg SW8	70 B2
Howard Cl NW2	25 G1
Howard Rd E6	50 B1
Howard Rd N16	30 C1
Howard Rd NW2	25 F1
Howard Rd, Bark.	37 F5
Howard Rd, Ilf.	36 D1
Howards La SW15	81 D3
Howards Rd E13	48 D2
Howbury Rd SE15	88 A1
Howden St SE15	87 F1
Howell Wk SE1	22 C6
Howerd Way SE18	78 A4
Howick Pl SW1	20 B4
Howie St SW11	69 F3
Howitt Rd NW3	27 F3
Howland Est SE16	60 A4
Howland Ms E W1	8 B5
Howland St W1	8 A5
Howland Way SE16	60 C3
Howletts Rd SE24	86 B4
Howley Pl W2	41 D4
Howsman Rd SW13	66 C2
Howson Rd SE4	88 C2
Hows St E2	45 E1
Hoxton Mkt N1	11 H2
Hoxton Sq N1	11 H2
Hoxton St N1	11 J2
Hoylake Rd W3	38 A5
Hoy St E16	48 C5
Hubbard St E15	34 B5
Hubert Gro SW9	85 E1
Hubert Rd E6	49 G2
Huddart St E3	47 D4
Huddleston Cl E2	46 A1
Huddlestone Rd E7	34 C1
Huddlestone Rd NW2	25 D3
Huddleston Rd N7	28 D1
Hudson Pl SE18	79 E1
Hudson's Pl SW1	19 J5
Huggin Ct EC4	16 E3
Huggin Hill EC4	16 E3
Hughan Rd E15	34 A2
Hugh Dalton Av SW6	68 A2
Hugh Gaitskell Cl SW6	68 A2
Hugh Ms SW1	19 J6
Hugh St SW1	19 J6
Hugon Rd SW6	82 C1
Huguenot Pl E1	45 E4
Huguenot Pl SW18	82 D3
Hull Cl SE16	60 B3
Hull St EC1	10 D2
Hulme Pl SE1	22 E2
Hulse Av, Bark.	37 F3
Humber Dr W10	39 F3
Humber Rd SE3	76 C2
Humberstone Rd E13	49 F2
Humbolt Rd W6	67 G2
Humphrey St SE1	73 E1
Hungerford Br SE1	15 F5
Hungerford Br WC2	15 F5
Hungerford La WC2	15 E5
Hungerford Rd N7	29 D2
Hunsdon Rd SE14	74 B2
Hunt Cl W11	53 F2
Hunter Cl SE1	23 G4
Hunter Cl SW12	84 A1
Hunter Cl, Ilf.	37 D2
Hunter St WC1	9 F3
Hunter Wk E13	48 D1
Huntingdon St E16	48 C5

Huntington St N1 | 29 F4
Huntingfield Rd SW15 | 80 C2
Huntley St WC1 | 8 B4
Hunton St E1 | 45 F3
Hunt's Cl SE3 | 77 D5
Hunt's Ct WC2 | 14 D4
Hunts La E15 | 47 G1
Huntsman St SE17 | 23 G6
Huntsworth Ms NW1 | 6 D4
Hurley Ho SE11 | 22 A6
Hurlingham Business Pk SW6 | 82 B1
Hurlingham Ct SW6 | 82 A1
Hurlingham Gdns SW6 | 82 A1
Hurlingham Rd SW6 | 68 A5
Hurlingham Sq SW6 | 82 B1
Hurren Cl SE3 | 90 B1
Hurry Cl E15 | 34 B4
Hurstbourne Gdns, Bark. | 37 G3
Hurst St SE24 | 86 A4
Hurstway Wk W11 | 53 F1
Huson Cl NW3 | 27 F4
Hutchings St E14 | 61 E3
Hutton St EC4 | 16 A2
Huxbear St SE4 | 89 D3
Huxley St W10 | 39 G2
Hyacinth Cl, Ilf. | 36 D3
Hyde Cl E13 | 49 D1
Hyde Pk SW7 | 12 B5
Hyde Pk W1 | 12 B5
Hyde Pk W2 | 12 B5
Hyde Pk Cor W1 | 19 G1
Hyde Pk Cres W2 | 12 B2
Hyde Pk Gdns W2 | 12 A3
Hyde Pk Gdns Ms W2 | 12 A3
Hyde Pk Gate SW7 | 55 D3
Hyde Pk Pl W2 | 12 C3
Hyde Pk Sq W2 | 12 B2
Hyde Pk Sq Ms W2 | 12 B2
Hyde Pk St W2 | 12 B2
Hyderabad Way E15 | 34 B4
Hyde Rd N1 | 30 C5
Hyde Vale SE10 | 75 G3
Hyndman St SE15 | 73 G2
Hythe Rd NW10 | 38 C3
Hythe Rd Ind Est NW10 | 38 C2

I

Ibbotson Av E16 | 48 C5
Iceland Rd E3 | 33 E5
Ida St E14 | 47 G5
Idmiston Rd E15 | 34 C2
Idol La EC3 | 17 H4
Idonia St SE8 | 75 D3
Iffley Rd W6 | 53 D4
Ifield Rd SW10 | 68 C2
Ilbert St W10 | 39 F2
Ilchester Gdns W2 | 54 C1
Ilchester Pl W14 | 54 A4
Ilderton Rd SE15 | 74 A3
Ilderton Rd SE16 | 73 G1
Ilex Rd NW10 | 24 B3
Iliffe St SE17 | 72 A1
Ilkley Rd E16 | 49 F4
Ilminster Gdns SW11 | 83 F2
Imber St N1 | 30 C5
Imperial Coll London SW7 | 55 E4
Imperial Coll Rd SW7 | 55 E4
Imperial Cres SW6 | 68 D5
Imperial Rd SW6 | 68 C4
Imperial Sq SW6 | 68 C4
Imperial St E3 | 47 G2
Imperial Wf SW6 | 68 D5
Inca Dr SE9 | 92 D5
Indescon Ct E14 | 61 E3
India Pl WC2 | 15 G3
India Way W12 | 52 D1
Indus Rd SE7 | 77 F3
Ingal Rd E13 | 48 D3

Ingate Pl SW8 | 70 B4
Inglebert St EC1 | 9 J1
Ingleborough St SW9 | 71 G5
Ingledew Rd SE18 | 79 F1
Inglesham Wk E9 | 33 D3
Ingleside Gro SE3 | 76 C2
Inglethorpe St SW6 | 67 F4
Ingleton St SW9 | 71 G5
Inglewood Cl E14 | 61 E5
Inglewood Rd NW6 | 26 B2
Inglis St SE5 | 72 A4
Ingram Cl SE11 | 21 H5
Ingrave St SW11 | 83 E1
Inigo Jones Rd SE7 | 78 A3
Inigo Pl WC2 | 15 E3
Inkerman Rd NW5 | 28 B3
Inman Rd NW10 | 24 A5
Inman Rd SW18 | 82 D5
Inner Circle NW1 | 7 F2
Inner Temple La EC4 | 15 J2
Innes Gdns SW15 | 81 D4
Innes St SE15 | 73 D3
Inniskilling Rd E13 | 49 F1
Institute Pl E8 | 31 G2
International Way E20 | 33 G3
Inveresk Gdns W3 | 51 G3
Inverine Rd SE7 | 77 E1
Invermead Cl W6 | 52 C5
Invermore Pl SE18 | 65 E5
Inverness Ms E16 | 65 E2
Inverness Pl W2 | 54 C1
Inverness St NW1 | 28 B5
Inverness Ter W2 | 42 C6
Inverton Rd SE15 | 88 B2
Invicta Plaza SE1 | 16 B5
Invicta Rd SE3 | 77 D3
Inwen Ct SE8 | 74 C1
Inworth St SW11 | 69 F5
Iona Cl SE6 | 89 E5
Ireland Yd EC4 | 16 C2
Irene Rd SW6 | 68 B4
Iris Cl E6 | 50 A4
Iron Br Cl NW10 | 24 A2
Iron Mill Rd SW18 | 82 C4
Ironmonger La EC2 | 17 F2
Ironmonger Pas EC1 | 10 E2
Ironmonger Row EC1 | 10 E2
Iron Wks E3 | 33 E5
Irving Gro SW9 | 71 F5
Irving Rd W14 | 53 F4
Irving St WC2 | 14 D4
Irwin Av SE18 | 79 G3
Irwin Gdns NW10 | 25 D5
Isaac Way SE1 | 22 E1
Isabella Rd E9 | 32 A2
Isabella St SE1 | 16 B6
Isambard Ms E14 | 61 G4
Isis Cl SW15 | 81 E2
Island Rd SE16 | 60 B5
Island Row E14 | 46 D5
Isla Rd SE18 | 79 E2
Islington Grn N1 | 30 A5
Islington High St N1 | 44 A1
Islington Pk St N1 | 29 G4
Islip St NW5 | 28 C2
Ismailia Rd E7 | 35 E4
Ivanhoe Rd SE5 | 87 E1
Ivatt Pl W14 | 68 A1
Iveagh Cl E9 | 32 B5
Iveley Rd SW4 | 70 C5
Iverna Ct W8 | 54 B4
Iverna Gdns W8 | 54 B4
Iverson Rd NW6 | 26 A3
Ives Rd E16 | 48 B4
Ives St SW3 | 18 C5
Ivestor Ter SE23 | 88 A5

Ivimey St E2 | 45 F2
Ivor Pl NW1 | 6 D4
Ivor St NW1 | 28 C4
Ivybridge La WC2 | 15 F4
Ivydale Rd SE15 | 88 B1
Ivy Rd NW2 | 25 E1
Ivy Rd SE4 | 89 D2
Ivy St N1 | 44 D1
Ixworth Pl SW3 | 69 F1

J

Jacaranda Gro E8 | 31 E4
Jack Clow Rd E15 | 48 B1
Jack Cornwell St E12 | 36 C1
Jack Dash Way E6 | 50 A3
Jackman St E8 | 31 G5
Jackson Cl E9 | 32 A4
Jackson Rd N7 | 29 F1
Jackson Rd, Bark. | 37 F5
Jackson St SE18 | 78 C2
Jack Walker Ct N5 | 30 A1
Jacobs Ho E13 | 49 F2
Jacob's Well Ms W1 | 13 G1
Jade Cl E16 | 49 G5
Jaggard Way SW12 | 83 G5
Jago Cl SE18 | 79 E2
Jago Wk SE5 | 72 C3
Jamaica Rd SE1 | 59 E3
Jamaica Rd SE16 | 59 E3
Jamaica St E1 | 46 A5
Jamaica St E1 | 46 A5
James Av NW2 | 25 E2
James Clavell Sq SE18 | 65 D4
Jameson Ct E2 | 46 A1
Jameson St W8 | 54 B2
James Sinclair Pt E13 | 35 F5
James St W1 | 13 G1
James St WC2 | 15 F3
James St, Bark. | 37 E4
Jamestown Rd NW1 | 28 B5
Jamestown Way E14 | 62 A1
Jamuna Cl E14 | 46 C4
Janet St E14 | 61 E4
Janeway St SE16 | 59 F3
Jardine Rd E1 | 60 B1
Jarrow Rd SE16 | 60 A5
Jarrow Way E9 | 32 C1
Jasmine Cl, Ilf. | 37 D2
Jasper Rd E16 | 49 G5
Jasper Wk N1 | 11 F1
Jay Ms SW7 | 55 D3
Jebb Av SW2 | 85 E4
Jebb St E3 | 47 E1
Jedburgh Rd E13 | 49 F2
Jedburgh St SW11 | 84 A2
Jeddo Rd W12 | 52 B3
Jeffreys Rd SW4 | 71 E5
Jeffreys St NW1 | 28 B4
Jeffreys Wk SW4 | 71 E5
Jeger Av E2 | 31 E5
Jeken Rd SE9 | 91 F2
Jelf Rd SW2 | 85 G3
Jenkins La E6 | 50 C1
Jenkins La, Bark. | 50 C1
Jenkins Rd E13 | 49 E3
Jenner Pl SW13 | 66 D2
Jennings Rd SE22 | 87 E4
Jephson Rd E7 | 35 F4
Jephtha Rd SW18 | 82 B4
Jerdan Pl SW6 | 68 B3
Jeremiah St E14 | 47 F5
Jermyn St SW1 | 14 A5
Jerningham Rd SE14 | 74 C5
Jerome Cres NW8 | 6 B3
Jerrard St SE13 | 89 F1
Jersey Rd, Ilf. | 37 D1
Jerusalem Pas EC1 | 10 B4
Jervis Ct W1 | 13 J2
Jessica Rd SW18 | 83 D4
Jessup Cl SE18 | 65 E5
Jewry St EC3 | 45 E5
Jew's Row SW18 | 82 C2

Jeymer Av NW2 | 25 D2
Jeypore Rd SW18 | 83 D5
Joan Cres SE9 | 91 G5
Joan St SE1 | 16 B6
Jocelyn St SE15 | 73 F4
Jockey's Flds WC1 | 9 H5
Jodane St SE8 | 60 D5
Jodrell Rd E3 | 33 D5
Johanna St SE1 | 21 J2
John Adam St WC2 | 15 F5
John Aird Ct W2 | 41 D4
John Archer Way SW18 | 83 E4
John Ashby Cl SW2 | 85 E4
John Barnes Wk E15 | 34 C3
John Burns Dr, Bark. | 37 G4
John Campbell Rd N16 | 31 D2
John Carpenter St EC4 | 16 B3
John Cornwell VC Ho E12 | 36 C1
John Felton Rd SE16 | 59 F1
John Fisher St E1 | 59 F1
John Harrison Way SE10 | 62 C4
John Islip St SW1 | 20 E6
John Maurice Cl SE17 | 23 F5
John Penn St SE13 | 75 F4
John Princes St W1 | 13 J1
John Roll Way SE16 | 59 F4
John Ruskin St SE5 | 72 A3
John Silkin La SE8 | 74 B1
John's Ms WC1 | 9 H4
John Smith Av SW6 | 68 A3
Johnson Cl E8 | 31 F5
Johnson's Pl SW1 | 70 C1
John Spencer Sq N1 | 30 A3
Johnstone Rd E6 | 50 B2
John St E15 | 34 C5
John St WC1 | 9 H4
John Wesley Cl E6 | 50 B2
John Williams Cl SE14 | 74 B2
John Wilson St SE18 | 64 C4
John Woolley Cl SE13 | 90 B2
Joiner St SE1 | 17 G2
Jonathan St SE11 | 71 F1
Jones St W1 | 13 H4
Joseph Hardcastle Cl SE14 | 74 B3
Josephine Av SW2 | 85 F3
Joseph Powell Cl SW12 | 84 C4
Joseph St E3 | 47 D3
Joslings Cl W12 | 52 D1
Joubert St SW11 | 69 G5
Jowett St SE15 | 73 E3
Joyce Page Cl SE7 | 77 G2
Joyce Wk SW2 | 85 G4
Jubilee Cl NW10 | 38 A1
Jubilee Cres E14 | 61 G4
Jubilee Mkt Hall WC2 | 15 F3
Jubilee Pl SW3 | 69 F1
Jubilee St E1 | 46 A5
Judd St WC1 | 9 E2
Jude St E16 | 48 C5
Juer St SW11 | 69 F3
Julian Pl E14 | 75 F1
Juliette Rd E13 | 48 C1
Junction App SE13 | 89 G1
Junction App SW11 | 83 F1
Junction Ms W2 | 12 B1
Junction Pl W2 | 12 A1
Junction Rd E13 | 49 E1
Junction Rd N19 | 28 C1
Juniper Cres NW1 | 28 A4
Juniper Dr SW18 | 82 D2
Juniper La E6 | 50 A4
Juniper Rd, Ilf. | 36 C1
Juno Way SE14 | 74 B2
Jupiter Way N7 | 29 F3
Jupp Rd E15 | 34 A4
Jupp Rd W E15 | 33 G5
Jutland Rd E13 | 49 D3

Jutland Rd SE6	**89**	G5	
Juxon St SE11	**21**	H5	

K

Kambala Rd SW11	**69**	E5
Kara Way NW2	**25**	F1
Kashmir Rd SE7	**77**	G3
Kassala Rd SW11	**69**	G4
Katella Trd Est, Bark.	**51**	G2
Katherine Gdns SE9	**91**	G2
Katherine Rd E6	**35**	G4
Katherine Rd E7	**35**	F2
Kathleen Rd SW11	**83**	G1
Kay Rd SW9	**71**	E5
Kay St E2	**45**	F1
Kean St WC2	**15**	G2
Keats Cl SE7	**77**	F3
Keats Gro NW3	**27**	E1
Keats Pl EC2	**11**	F6
Keats Rd, Well.	**79**	G4
Kebbell Ter E7	**35**	E2
Keel Cl SE16	**60**	B2
Keeley St WC2	**15**	G2
Keeling Rd SE9	**91**	G3
Keemor Cl SE18	**78**	C3
Keep, The SE3	**76**	D5
Keetons Rd SE16	**59**	G4
Keevil Dr SW19	**81**	F5
Keighley Cl N7	**29**	E1
Keildon Rd SW11	**83**	G2
Keith Gro W12	**52**	C3
Keith Rd, Bark.	**51**	F1
Kelbrook Rd SE3	**92**	A1
Kelfield Gdns W10	**39**	E5
Kelfield Rd E13	**49**	D3
Kellaway Rd SE3	**77**	F5
Keller Cres E12	**35**	G1
Kellerton Rd SE13	**90**	B3
Kellett Rd SW2	**85**	G2
Kell St SE1	**22**	C3
Kelly Av SE15	**73**	E3
Kelly St NW1	**28**	B3
Kelman Cl SW4	**71**	D5
Kelmore Gro SE22	**87**	F2
Kelmscott Gdns W12	**52**	C4
Kelmscott Rd SW11	**83**	F3
Kelross Rd N5	**30**	A1
Kelsall Cl SE3	**77**	E5
Kelsey St E2	**45**	G3
Kelson Ho E14	**61**	G4
Kelso Pl W8	**54**	C4
Kelvedon Ho SW8	**71**	E4
Kelvedon Rd SW6	**68**	B3
Kelvington Rd SE15	**88**	B3
Kelvin Rd N5	**30**	A1
Kemble St WC2	**15**	G2
Kemerton Rd SE5	**86**	B1
Kemeys St E9	**32**	C2
Kempe Rd NW6	**39**	F1
Kemplay Rd NW3	**27**	E1
Kemp's Ct W1	**14**	B2
Kempsford Gdns SW5	**68**	B1
Kempsford Rd SE11	**22**	A6
Kempson Rd SW6	**68**	B4
Kempthorne Rd SE8	**60**	C5
Kempton Rd E6	**36**	B5
Kempt St SE18	**78**	C2
Kemsing Rd SE10	**76**	D1
Kemsley SE13	**89**	G3
Kenbury St SE5	**72**	B5
Kenchester Cl SW8	**71**	E3
Kendal Av, Bark.	**37**	G4
Kendal Cl SW9	**72**	A3
Kendall Pl W1	**7**	F6
Kendall Rd SE18	**78**	A4
Kendal Pl SW15	**82**	A3
Kendal Rd NW10	**24**	C1
Kendal St W2	**12**	C2
Kender St SE14	**74**	A3
Kendoa Rd SW4	**85**	D2
Kendrick Pl SW7	**55**	E5
Kenilford Rd SW12	**84**	B5
Kenilworth Gdns SE18	**78**	D5
Kenilworth Rd E3	**46**	C1
Kenilworth Rd NW6	**26**	A5
Kenley Wk W11	**53**	G1
Kenmont Gdns NW10	**38**	D2
Kenmure Rd E8	**31**	G2
Kennard Rd E15	**34**	A4
Kennard St SW11	**70**	A4
Kennedy Cl E13	**49**	D1
Kennedy Rd, Bark.	**37**	G5
Kennet Av, Ilf.	**36**	D1
Kenneth Cres NW2	**25**	D2
Kennet Ho NW8	**6**	A5
Kennet Rd W9	**40**	A3
Kennet St E1	**59**	F2
Kennet Wf La EC4	**16**	E3
Kennings Way SE11	**71**	G1
Kenning Ter N1	**30**	D3
Kennington La SE11	**71**	F1
Kennington Oval SE11	**71**	G3
Kennington Pk Gdns SE11	**71**	G3
Kennington Pk Pl SE11	**71**	H2
Kennington Pk Rd SE11	**21**	J3
Kennington Rd SE1	**21**	J3
Kennington Rd SE11	**21**	J4
Kenrick Pl W1	**7**	F5
Kensal Rd W10	**39**	G3
Kensington Av E12	**36**	A3
Kensington Ch Ct W8	**54**	B3
Kensington Ch St W8	**54**	B2
Kensington Ch Wk W8	**54**	C3
Kensington Ct W8	**54**	C3
Kensington Ct Pl W8	**54**	C4
Kensington Gdns Sq W2	**40**	C5
Kensington Gate W8	**54**	D4
Kensington Gore SW7	**55**	E3
Kensington High St W8	**54**	B4
Kensington High St W14	**53**	G5
Kensington Mall W8	**54**	B2
Kensington Palace W8	**54**	C3
Kensington Palace Gdns W8	**54**	C2
Kensington Pk Gdns W11	**54**	A1
Kensington Pk Rd W11	**54**	A1
Kensington Pl W8	**54**	B2
Kensington Rd SW7	**54**	C3
Kensington Rd W8	**54**	C3
Kensington Sq W8	**54**	C3
Kentish Bldgs SE1	**17**	F6
Kentish Town Rd NW1	**28**	B4
Kentish Town Rd NW5	**28**	B4
Kentlea Rd SE28	**65**	G3
Kentmere Rd SE18	**65**	G5
Kenton Rd E9	**32**	B3
Kenton St WC1	**9**	E3
Kent Pas NW1	**6**	D3
Kent St E2	**45**	E1
Kent St E13	**49**	F2
Kent Ter NW1	**6**	C2
Kentwell Cl SE4	**88**	C2
Kenwood Rd N6	**26**	C3
Kenway SE15	**18**	C2
Kenward Rd SE9	**91**	F3
Kenway Rd SW5	**54**	C5
Kenworthy Rd E9	**32**	C2
Kenwyn Rd SW4	**85**	D2
Kenya Rd SE7	**77**	G3
Kenyon St SW6	**67**	F4
Keogh Rd E15	**34**	B3
Kepler Rd SW4	**85**	E2
Keppel Rd E6	**36**	B4
Keppel Row SE1	**16**	D6
Keppel St WC1	**8**	D2
Kerbey St E14	**47**	F5
Kerfield Cres SE5	**72**	C4
Kerfield Pl SE5	**72**	C4
Kerridge Ct N1	**31**	D3
Kerrison Rd E15	**34**	A5
Kerrison Rd SW11	**83**	F1
Kerry Cl E16	**49**	E5
Kerry Path SE14	**74**	D2
Kerry Rd SE14	**74**	D2
Kersfield Rd SW15	**81**	F4
Kershaw Cl SW18	**83**	D4
Kersley Ms SW11	**69**	G5
Kersley Rd N16	**30**	D4
Kersley St SW11	**69**	G5
Keslake Rd NW6	**39**	F1
Keston Rd SE15	**87**	F1
Kestrel Av SE24	**86**	A3
Kestrel Ho EC1	**10**	D1
Keswick Rd SW15	**81**	G3
Kett Gdns SW2	**85**	F3
Kevan Ho SE5	**72**	B3
Key Cl E1	**45**	G3
Keyes Rd NW2	**25**	F2
Keynsham Gdns SE9	**92**	A3
Keynsham Rd SE9	**91**	G3
Keyworth Cl E5	**32**	C1
Keyworth Pl SE1	**22**	C3
Keyworth St SE1	**22**	C3
Khartoum Rd E13	**49**	E2
Khartoum Rd, Ilf.	**37**	D2
Khyber Rd SW11	**69**	F5
Kibworth St SW8	**71**	F3
Kidbrooke Gdns SE3	**76**	D5
Kidbrooke Interchange SE3	**91**	F1
Kidbrooke La SE9	**92**	A2
Kidbrooke Pk Cl SE3	**77**	E4
Kidbrooke Pk Rd SE3	**77**	E4
Kidbrooke Way SE3	**77**	E5
Kidderpore Av NW3	**26**	B1
Kidderpore Gdns NW3	**26**	B1
Kidd Pl SE7	**78**	A1
Kiffen St EC2	**11**	G3
Kilburn High Rd NW6	**26**	A5
Kilburn La W9	**39**	F2
Kilburn La W10	**39**	F2
Kilburn Pk Rd NW6	**40**	B2
Kilburn Pl NW6	**26**	B5
Kilburn Priory NW6	**26**	B5
Kilburn Sq NW6	**40**	B5
Kildare Gdns W2	**40**	B5
Kildare Rd E16	**48**	D4
Kildare Ter W2	**40**	B5
Kildoran Rd SW2	**85**	E3
Kilgour Rd SE23	**88**	C4
Kilkie St SW6	**68**	D5
Killarney Rd SW18	**83**	D4
Killick St N1	**43**	F1
Killip Cl E16	**48**	C5
Killowen Rd E9	**32**	B3
Killyon Rd SW8	**70**	C5
Killyon Ter SW8	**70**	C5
Kilmaine Rd SW6	**67**	G3
Kilmarsh Rd W6	**53**	E5
Kilmington Rd SW13	**66**	C2
Kilner St E14	**47**	E4
Kiln Pl NW5	**28**	A2
Kilravock St W10	**39**	G2
Kimbell Gdns SW6	**67**	G4
Kimberley Av E6	**50**	A1
Kimberley Av SE15	**73**	G5
Kimberley Rd E16	**48**	C3
Kimberley Rd NW6	**25**	G5
Kimberley Rd SW9	**71**	E5
Kimber Rd SW18	**82**	B5
Kimbolton Cl SE12	**89**	H4
Kimbolton Row SW3	**14**	B6
Kimpton Rd SE5	**72**	C4
Kinburn St SE16	**60**	B3
Kincaid Rd SE15	**73**	G3
Kinder St E1	**45**	G5
King & Queen St SE17	**23**	E6
King Arthur Cl SE15	**73**	G5
King Charles St SW1	**20**	D1
King David La E1	**60**	A1
Kingdon Rd NW6	**26**	B3
King Edward Ms SW13	**66**	C4
King Edwards Rd E9	**31**	G5
King Edwards Rd, Bark.	**37**	F5
King Edward St EC1	**16**	D1
King Edward Wk SE1	**22**	A3
Kingfield St E14	**61**	G5
Kingfisher Ms SE13	**89**	F2
Kingfisher Sq SE8	**75**	D2
Kingfisher St E6	**50**	A4
King Frederik IX Twr SE16	**60**	D4
King George Av E18	**49**	G5
King George V Dock E16	**64**	B2
King George St SE10	**75**	G3
Kingham Cl SW18	**82**	D5
Kingham Cl W11	**53**	G3
King Henry's Reach W6	**67**	E2
King Henry's Rd NW3	**27**	F4
King Henry St N16	**31**	D2
King Henry's Wk N1	**30**	D3
Kinghorn St EC1	**10**	D6
King James Ct SE1	**22**	C2
King James St SE1	**22**	C2
King John Ct EC2	**11**	J3
King John St E1	**46**	B4
Kinglake St SE17	**72**	D1
Kingly Ct W1	**14**	A3
Kingly St W1	**14**	A2
Kings Arms Yd EC2	**17**	F1
King's Av SW4	**85**	D5
Kings Bench St SE1	**22**	C1
Kings Bench Wk EC4	**16**	A2
Kingsbridge Rd W10	**39**	E5
Kingsbridge Rd, Bark.	**51**	F1
Kingsbury Rd N1	**31**	D3
Kingsbury Ter N1	**31**	D3
Kingsclere Cl SW15	**80**	C5
Kings Coll Rd NW3	**27**	F4
Kingscote St EC4	**16**	B3
Kings Ct E13	**35**	E5
Kingscroft Rd NW2	**26**	A3
King's Cross Br N1	**9**	F1
King's Cross Rd WC1	**9**	H1
King's Cross Sta N1	**43**	E1
Kingsdale Gdns W11	**53**	F2
Kingsdown Av W3	**52**	A1
Kingsdown Cl W10	**39**	G5
Kingsford St NW5	**27**	G2
Kingsford Way E6	**50**	B4
Kingsgate Pl NW6	**26**	B4
Kingsgate Rd NW6	**26**	B4
Kingsground SE9	**92**	A5
Kings Gro SE15	**73**	G3
Kings Head Yd SE1	**17**	F6
Kings Highway SE18	**79**	G2
Kingshill SE17	**22**	E6
Kingshold Rd E9	**32**	A4
Kingsholm Gdns SE9	**91**	G2
Kingshurst Rd SE12	**90**	D5
Kingsland Grn E8	**31**	D3
Kingsland High St E8	**31**	E2
Kingsland Rd E2	**11**	J1
Kingsland Rd E8	**45**	D1
Kingsland Rd E13	**49**	F2
Kingsland Shop Cen E8	**31**	E3
Kingslawn Cl SW15	**81**	D3
Kingsley Flats SE1	**23**	H5
Kingsley Rd E7	**35**	D4
Kingsley Rd NW6	**26**	A5
Kingsley Rd SW19	**83**	G1
Kings Mall W6	**53**	E5
Kingsman St SE18	**64**	B4
Kingsmead Est E9	**32**	C2
Kingsmead Way E9	**32**	C1
King's Ms WC1	**9**	H4
Kingsmill Ter NW8	**41**	E1
King's Orchard SE9	**92**	A4
Kings Pl SE1	**22**	D2
King's Reach Twr SE1	**16**	A5
Kings Rd E6	**35**	F5
Kings Rd NW10	**24**	D4
King's Rd SW1	**69**	G1

Name	Ref		Name	Ref
King's Rd SW3	69 G1		Kynance Ms SW7	54 C4
King's Rd SW6	68 C4		Kynance Pl SW7	54 D4
King's Rd SW10	68 C4		Kyrle Rd SW11	84 A3
King's Scholars' Pas SW1	20 A4		**L**	
Kingston Rd, Ilf.	37 D1		Laburnum Ct E2	31 E5
Kingstown St NW1	28 A5		Laburnum St E2	31 E5
King St E13	48 D3		Lacey Ms E3	47 E1
King St EC2	17 E2		Lackington St EC2	11 G5
King St SW1	14 B6		Lacon Rd SE22	87 F2
King St W6	52 C5		Lacy Rd SW15	81 E3
King St WC2	15 E3		Ladbroke Gdns W11	54 A1
Kingsway WC2	15 E3		Ladbroke Gro W10	39 F3
Kingsway Pl EC1	10 A3		Ladbroke Gro W11	39 G5
Kingswood Av NW6	25 G5		Ladbroke Rd W11	54 A2
Kingswood Cl SW8	71 E3		Ladbroke Sq W11	54 A1
Kingswood Pl SE13	90 B2		Ladbroke Ter W11	54 A1
Kingswood Rd SW2	85 E4		Ladbroke Wk W11	54 A2
King William St EC4	17 G4		Ladlands SE22	87 F5
King William Wk SE10	75 G2		Ladycroft Rd SE13	89 F1
Kingwood Rd SW6	67 F4		Lady Margaret Rd N19	28 C1
Kinlet St SE18	79 E4		Lady Margaret Rd NW5	28 C2
Kinnear Rd W12	52 B3		Ladysmith Av E6	50 A1
Kinnerton Pl N SW1	19 E2		Ladysmith Rd E16	48 C2
Kinnerton Pl S SW1	19 E2		Ladysmith Rd SE9	92 C4
Kinnerton St SW1	19 E2		Lady Somerset Rd NW5	28 B1
Kinnerton Yd SW1	19 E2		Ladywell Hts SE4	88 D4
Kinnoul Rd W6	67 G2		Ladywell Rd SE13	89 E3
Kinsale Rd SE15	87 F3		Lafone St SE1	59 E3
Kinveachy Gdns SE7	78 A1		Lagado Ms SE16	60 B2
Kipling Est SE1	23 G2		Lainson St SW18	82 B5
Kipling St SE1	23 G2		Laird Ho SE5	72 B3
Kirby Est SE16	59 G4		Lakedale Rd SE18	79 G2
Kirby Gro SE1	23 H1		Laker Pl SW15	81 G4
Kirby St EC1	10 A5		Lakeside Rd W14	53 F4
Kirkham Rd E6	50 A5		Laleham Rd SE6	89 G4
Kirkham St SE18	79 G2		Lalor St SW6	67 G5
Kirkland Cl, Sid.	93 G4		Lambert Rd E16	49 E5
Kirkland Wk E8	31 E3		Lambert Rd SW2	85 E3
Kirk La SE18	79 E2		Lambert St N1	29 G4
Kirkman Pl W1	8 C6		Lambeth Br SE1	21 F5
Kirkside Rd SE3	76 D2		Lambeth Br SW1	21 F5
Kirk St WC1	9 G4		Lambeth High St SE1	21 G6
Kirkwall Pl E2	46 A2		Lambeth Hill EC4	16 D3
Kirkwood Rd SE15	73 G5		Lambeth Palace Rd SE1	21 G4
Kirtling St SW8	70 C3		Lambeth Pier SE1	21 G4
Kirton Rd E13	49 F1		Lambeth Rd SE1	21 F4
Kitcat Ter E3	47 E2		Lambeth Rd SE11	21 H4
Kitchener Rd E7	35 E3		Lambeth Twrs SE11	21 J4
Kitson Rd SE5	72 B3		Lambeth Wk SE11	21 H5
Kitson Rd SW13	66 C4		Lamb La E8	31 G4
Kitto Rd SE14	74 B5		Lamble St NW5	28 A2
Klea Av SW4	84 C4		Lambolle Pl NW3	27 F3
Knapp Cl NW10	24 A3		Lambolle Rd NW3	27 F3
Knapp Rd E3	47 E3		Lambourne Gro SE16	60 B5
Knaresborough Pl SW5	54 C1		Lambourne Rd, Bark.	37 G4
Knatchbull Rd SE5	72 B4		Lambourn Rd SW4	84 B1
Kneller Rd SE4	88 C2		Lambrook Ter SW6	67 G4
Knighten St E1	59 G2		Lambs Bldgs EC1	11 F4
Knighthead Pt E14	61 E4		Lambs Conduit Pas WC1	9 G5
Knightrider St EC4	16 D3		Lamb's Conduit St WC1	9 G4
Knights Arc SW1	18 D2		Lambs Pas EC1	11 F5
Knightsbridge SW1	19 E2		Lamb St E1	45 E4
Knightsbridge SW7	18 C2		Lamb Wk SE1	23 H2
Knightsbridge Grn SW1	18 D2		Lamerton St SE8	75 D5
Knights Rd E16	63 D3		Lamington St W6	53 D5
Knights Wk SE11	22 B6		Lamlash St SE11	22 B5
Knivet Rd SW6	68 B2		Lammas Rd E9	32 B4
Knobs Hill Rd E15	33 F5		Lammermoor Rd SW12	84 B5
Knockholt Rd SE9	91 G3		Lamont Rd SW10	69 D2
Knoll Rd SW18	82 D3		Lampmead Rd SE12	90 B3
Knottisford St E2	46 A2		Lamp Office Ct WC1	9 G4
Knowle Cl SW9	85 G1		Lamport Cl SE18	64 B5
Knowles Hill Cres SE13	90 A3		Lanark Pl W9	41 D3
Knowles Wk SW4	84 C1		Lanark Rd W9	40 C1
Knowsley Rd SW11	69 G5		Lanark Sq E14	61 F4
Knox Rd E7	34 C3			
Knox St W1	6 D5			
Knoyle St SE14	74 C2			
Kossuth St SE10	76 B1			
Kreedman Wk E8	31 F2			
Kylemore Rd NW6	26 B4			

Name	Ref		Name	Ref
Lanbury Rd SE15	88 B2		Lansdowne Row W1	13 J5
Lancashire Ct W1	13 J3		Lansdowne Ter WC1	9 F4
Lancaster Av, Bark.	37 G4		Lansdowne Wk W1	53 G2
Lancaster Ct SW6	68 A3		Lansdowne Way SW8	71 D4
Lancaster Dr NW3	27 F3		Lansdown Rd E7	35 F4
Lancaster Gate W2	55 D1		Lantern Cl SW15	80 C2
Lancaster Gro NW3	27 E3		Lanterns Ct E14	61 E3
Lancaster Ms W2	55 D1		Lant St SE1	22 D1
Lancaster Pl WC2	15 G3		Lanvanor Rd SE15	74 A5
Lancaster Rd E7	35 D4		Lapford Cl W9	40 A3
Lancaster Rd NW10	24 B2		Lara Cl SE13	89 G4
Lancaster Rd W11	39 G5		Larch Cl E13	49 E3
Lancaster St SE1	22 C2		Larch Av W3	52 A2
Lancaster Ter W2	55 E1		Larch Rd NW2	25 E1
Lancaster Wk W2	55 D2		Larcom St SE17	22 E6
Lancefield St W10	40 A2		Larden Rd W3	52 A2
Lancell Pl SW7	18 B3		Larkhall La SW4	70 D5
Lanchester Way SE14	74 A4		Larkhall Ri SW4	84 C1
Lancing St NW1	8 C2		Lark Row E2	32 A5
Lancresse Ct N1	30 D5		Larks Gro, Bark.	37 G4
Landcroft Rd SE22	87 E4		Larkspur Cl E6	50 A4
Landells Rd SE22	87 E4		Larnach Rd W6	67 F2
Landford Rd SW15	81 E1		Larpent Av SW15	81 E3
Landmann Ho SE16	59 G5		Lassa Rd SE9	92 A3
Landmann Way SE14	74 B2		Lassell St SE10	76 A1
Landmark Hts E5	32 C1		Latchmere Rd SW11	69 G5
Landon Pl SW1	18 D3		Latchmere St SW11	69 G5
Landor Ct E14	61 G2		Latham Ho E1	46 B5
Landor Rd SW9	85 E1		Latham Rd E6	36 B4
Landor Wk W12	52 C3		Latimer Av E6	36 B5
Landridge Rd SW6	68 A5		Latimer Pl W10	39 E5
Landseer Av E12	36 C2		Latimer Rd W10	39 E5
Landstead Rd SE18	79 F3		Latona Rd SE15	73 F2
Lane, The SE3	91 D1		Lattimer Pl W4	66 A2
Lanesborough Pl SW1	19 G1		Latymer Ct W6	53 F5
Laneway SW15	80 D3		Lauderdale Rd W9	40 C2
Lanfranc Rd E3	46 C1		Lauderdale Twr EC2	10 D5
Langbourne Pl E14	75 F1		Launcelot St SE1	21 J2
Langbrook Rd SE3	91 G1		Launceston Pl W8	54 D4
Langdale NW1	8 A1		Launch St E14	61 G4
Langdale Cl SE17	72 B2		Laundry Ms SE23	88 C5
Langdale Rd SE10	75 G3		Laundry Rd W6	67 G2
Langdon Ct NW10	24 A5		Laura Pl E5	32 A1
Langdon Cres E6	50 C1		Laurel Ms SE5	86 B1
Langdon Rd E6	36 C5		Laurel Rd SW13	66 C5
Langford Cl E8	31 F2		Laurel St E8	31 E3
Langford Cl NW8	40 D1		Laurence Pountney Hill EC4	17 F3
Langford Grn SE5	86 D1		Laurence Pountney La EC4	17 F3
Langford Pl NW8	40 D1		Laurie Gro SE14	74 C4
Langford Rd SW6	68 C5		Lauriston Rd E9	32 B5
Langham Pl W1	7 J6		Lausanne Rd SE15	74 A4
Langham Pl W4	66 A1		Lavell St N16	30 C1
Langham St W1	7 J6		Lavender Gdns SW11	83 G2
Langland Gdns NW3	26 C2		Lavender Gro E8	31 E4
Langler Rd NW10	39 E1		Lavender Hill SW11	83 F2
Langley Cl E15	33 E3		Lavender Pl, Ilf.	36 D2
Langley La SW8	71 E2		Lavender Rd SE16	60 C2
Langley St WC2	15 E2		Lavender Rd SW11	83 E1
Langside Av SW15	80 C2		Lavender Sq SW9	71 F4
Langston Rd, Loug.	46 A3		Lavender Sweep SW11	83 G2
Langthorn Ct EC2	17 F1		Lavender Wk SW11	83 G2
Langthorne St SW6	67 E5		Laverstoke Gdns SW15	80 C5
Langton Av E6	50 C2		Laverton Pl SW5	54 C5
Langton Cl WC1	9 H2		Lavington Cl E9	32 D3
Langton Ri SE23	87 G5		Lavington St SE1	16 C6
Langton Rd SW9	72 A3		Lawford Rd N1	30 D4
Langton St SW10	69 D2		Lawford Rd NW5	28 C3
Langton Way SE3	76 C4		Lawless St E14	61 F1
Langtry Rd NW8	26 C5		Lawley St E5	32 A1
Lanhill Rd W9	40 B3		Lawn Ho Cl E14	61 G3
Lanier Rd SE13	89 G4		Lawn La SW8	71 E2
Lanrick Rd E14	48 A5		Lawn Rd NW3	27 G2
Lansbury Est E14	47 G5		Lawnside SE3	90 C2
Lansbury Gdns E14	48 A5		Lawn Ter SE3	90 B1
Lanscombe Wk SW8	71 E4		Lawrence Av E12	36 C1
Lansdowne Cres W11	53 G1		Lawrence Cl E3	47 E1
Lansdowne Dr E8	31 F3		Lawrence La EC2	17 E2
Lansdowne Gdns SW8	71 E4		Lawrence Rd E6	35 G5
Lansdowne Grn SW8	71 E4		Lawrence Rd E13	35 E5
Lansdowne Hill SE27	77 G2		Lawrence St E16	48 C5
Lansdowne La SE7	77 G1			
Lansdowne Ms SE7	77 G1			
Lansdowne Ms W11	53 G2			
Lansdowne Pl SE1	23 G3			
Lansdowne Ri W11	53 G1			
Lansdowne Rd E11	35 G4			
Lansdowne Rd W11	53 G1			

Lawrence St SW3	69	F2
Lawson Cl E16	49	F4
Lawson Cl, Ilf.	37	F2
Lawson Est SE1	23	H4
Law St SE1	23	G3
Lawton Rd E3	46	C2
Laxley Cl SE5	72	A3
Laxton Pl NW1	7	J3
Layard Rd SE16	59	G5
Layard Sq SE16	59	G5
Laycock St N1	29	G3
Laystall St EC1	9	J4
Laytons Bldgs SE1	23	E1
Lazenby Ct WC2	15	E3
Leabank Sq E9	33	E3
Leacroft Av SW12	83	G5
Leadenhall Mkt EC3	17	H2
Leadenhall Pl EC3	17	H2
Leadenhall St EC3	17	H2
Leader Av E12	36	C2
Leahurst Rd SE13	90	A3
Lea Interchange E9	33	E2
Leake St SE1	21	H1
Leamington Cl E12	36	A2
Leamington Rd Vil W11	40	A4
Leamore St W6	53	D5
Leamouth Rd E14	48	A5
Leander Ct SE8	75	E4
Leander Rd SW2	85	F4
Learoyd Gdns E6	64	C1
Leather La EC1	10	A6
Leather Mkt, The SE1	23	H2
Leathermarket Ct SE1	23	H2
Leathermarket St SE1	23	H2
Leather St SE16	60	B5
Leathwaite Rd SW11	83	G2
Leathwell Rd SE8	75	F5
Lea Valley Wk E3	47	G3
Lea Valley Wk E14	47	F4
Lea Valley Wk E15	47	G2
Lebanon Gdns SW18	82	B4
Lebanon Rd SW18	82	B3
Lebrun Sq SE3	91	E1
Lechmere Rd NW2	25	D3
Lecky St SW7	69	E1
Leconfield Av SW13	80	B1
Leconfield Rd N5	30	C1
Leda Rd SE18	64	B4
Ledbury Est SE15	73	G3
Ledbury Rd W11	40	A5
Ledbury St SE15	73	F3
Lee Br SE13	89	G1
Lee Ch St SE13	90	B2
Lee Conservancy Rd E9	32	D2
Leefern Rd W12	52	C3
Leegate SE12	90	C3
Lee High Rd SE12	90	A1
Lee High Rd SE13	90	A1
Leeke St WC1	9	G2
Leeland Way NW10	24	A1
Lee Pk SE3	90	C2
Leerdam Dr E14	61	G4
Lee Rd SE3	90	C1
Leeson Rd SE24	85	G2
Lees Pl W1	13	F3
Lee St E8	31	E5
Lee Ter SE3	90	B1
Lee Ter SE13	90	B1
Leeway SE8	74	D1
Lefroy Rd W12	52	B3
Legard Rd N5	30	A1
Legatt Rd SE9	91	G3
Leggatt Rd E15	47	G1
Legge St SE13	89	G3
Leghorn Rd NW10	38	B1
Leghorn Rd SE18	79	F1
Legion Cl N1	29	G3
Legion Ter E3	33	D5
Leicester Ct WC2	14	D3
Leicester Pl WC2	14	D3
Leicester Sq WC2	14	D4
Leicester St WC2	14	D3
Leigh Gdns NW10	39	E1
Leigh Hunt St SE1	22	D1
Leigh Pl EC1	9	J5
Leigh Rd E6	36	C3
Leigh Rd N5	30	A1
Leigh St WC1	8	E3
Leighton Av E12	36	C2
Leighton Cres NW5	28	C2
Leighton Gdns NW10	39	D1
Leighton Gro NW5	28	C2
Leighton Pl NW5	28	C2
Leighton Rd NW5	28	D2
Leila Parnell Pl SE7	77	F2
Leinster Gdns W2	40	D5
Leinster Ms W2	54	D1
Leinster Pl W2	40	D5
Leinster Sq W2	40	B5
Leinster Ter W2	54	D1
Leirum St N1	29	F5
Leman St E1	45	E5
Lemmon Rd SE10	76	B2
Lemonwell Dr SE9	93	E3
Lemuel St SW18	82	C4
Lena Gdns W6	53	E4
Lendal Ter SW4	85	D1
Lenham Rd SE12	90	C2
Lennon Rd NW2	26	A4
Lennox Gdns NW10	24	B1
Lennox Gdns SW1	18	D4
Lennox Gdns Ms SW1	18	D4
Lensbury Av SW6	69	D5
Lens Rd E7	35	F4
Lenthall Rd E8	31	E4
Lenthorp Rd SE10	62	C5
Lenton Path SE18	79	F2
Lenton St SE18	65	F5
Leonard Rd E7	34	D1
Leonard St E16	64	A2
Leonard St EC2	11	G3
Leontine Cl SE15	73	F3
Leopards Ct EC1	9	J5
Leopold Rd NW10	24	A4
Leopold St E3	47	D4
Leo St SE15	73	G3
Leo Yd EC1	10	C4
Leppoc Rd SW4	84	D3
Leroy St SE1	23	H5
Leslie Rd E11	33	G1
Leslie Rd E16	49	E5
Lessar Av SW4	84	C3
Lessing St SE23	88	C5
Lester Av E15	48	B2
Letchford Gdns NW10	38	C2
Lethbridge Cl SE13	75	G4
Lettice St SW6	68	A4
Lett Rd E15	34	A4
Lett Rd SW9	71	F4
Lettsom St SE5	72	D5
Lettsom Wk E13	48	D1
Levehurst Way SW4	71	F4
Leven Rd E14	47	G4
Leverett St SW3	18	C5
Lever St EC1	10	C2
Leverton St NW5	28	C2
Levett Rd, Bark.	37	G3
Lewey Ho E3	47	D3
Lewis Gro SE13	89	G1
Lewisham Cen SE13	89	G1
Lewisham High St SE13	89	G1
Lewisham Hill SE13	75	G5
Lewisham Pk SE13	89	F4
Lewisham Rd SE13	75	F4
Lewisham St SW1	20	D2
Lewisham Way SE4	74	D4
Lewisham Way SE14	74	D4
Lewis Pl E8	31	F2
Lewis St NW1	28	B3
Lexham Gdns W8	54	C4
Lexham Gdns Ms W8	54	C4
Lexham Ms W8	54	B5
Lexington Apts EC1	11	F3
Lexington St W1	14	B2
Leybourne Rd NW1	28	B4
Leybridge Ct SE12	90	D3
Leyland Rd SE12	90	D3
Leyland Rd N5	74	B3
Leysfield Rd W12	52	C3
Leyton Rd E15	34	A2
Leystonstone Rd E15	34	B2
Leywick St E15	48	B1
Liardet St SE14	74	C2
Liberia Rd N5	30	A3
Liberty Br Rd E20	33	G2
Liberty Ms SW12	84	B4
Liberty St SW9	71	F4
Libra Rd E3	33	D5
Libra Rd E13	48	D4
Library St SE1	22	B2
Lichfield Rd E3	46	C2
Lichfield Rd E6	49	G2
Lichfield Rd NW2	25	G1
Lidcote Gdns SW9	71	G5
Liddell Gdns NW10	39	E1
Liddell Rd NW6	26	B3
Liddington Rd E15	34	C5
Liddon Rd E13	49	E2
Lidfield Rd N16	30	C1
Lidlington Pl NW1	8	B2
Liffler Rd SE18	79	G1
Liffords Pl SW13	66	B5
Lifford St SW15	81	F2
Lighter Cl SE16	60	C5
Lighterman Ms E1	46	B5
Lightermans Rd E14	61	E3
Lilac Pl SE11	21	G6
Lilac St W12	52	C1
Lilburne Gdns SE9	92	A3
Lilburne Rd SE9	92	A3
Lilestone St NW8	6	B4
Lilford Rd SE5	72	A5
Lilian Barker Cl SE12	91	D3
Lillian Rd SW13	66	C2
Lillie Rd SW6	67	G3
Lillieshall Rd SW4	84	B1
Lillie Yd SW6	68	B2
Lillington Gdns Est SW1	20	B6
Lily Cl W14	53	G5
Lily Pl EC1	10	A5
Lilyville Rd SW6	68	A4
Limburg Rd SW11	83	G2
Limeburner La EC4	16	B2
Lime Cl E1	59	F2
Lime Gro W12	53	E3
Limeharbour E14	61	F4
Limehouse Causeway E14	61	D1
Limehouse Link E14	60	C1
Limekiln Dr SE7	77	E2
Limerick Cl SW12	84	C5
Limerston St SW10	68	D1
Limes, The SW18	82	B4
Limes Av NW11	66	B5
Limesford Rd SE15	88	B2
Limes Gdns SW18	82	B4
Limes Gro SE13	89	G2
Lime St EC3	17	H3
Lime St Pas EC3	17	H2
Limes Wk SE15	87	G2
Linacre Cl SE15	87	G1
Linacre Ct W6	67	F1
Linacre Rd NW2	25	D3
Linberg Wk SE8	60	D5
Linchmere Rd SE12	90	C5
Lincoln Rd E7	35	G3
Lincoln Rd E13	49	E3
Lincoln's Inn WC2	15	H1
Lincoln's Inn Flds WC2	15	G1
Lincoln St SW3	18	D6
Lindal Rd SE4	88	D3
Linden Av NW10	39	F1
Linden Ct W12	53	E2
Linden Gdns W2	54	B1
Linden Gro SE15	87	G1
Linden Ms N1	30	C2
Lindfield Gdns NW3	26	C2
Lindfield St E14	47	E5
Lindisfarne Way E9	32	C1
Lindley St E1	46	A4
Lindore Rd SW11	83	G2
Lindrop St SW6	68	D5
Lindsay Sq SW1	71	D1
Lindsell St SE10	75	G4
Lindsey Ms N1	30	B4
Lindsey St EC1	10	C5
Lind St SE8	75	F5
Linford St SW8	70	C4
Lingards Rd SE13	89	G2
Lingfield Cres SE9	93	F2
Lingham St SW9	71	E5
Ling Rd E16	48	D4
Linhope St NW1	6	D3
Link St E9	32	A3
Linnell Rd SE5	73	D5
Linnet Ms SW12	84	A5
Linom Rd SW4	85	E2
Linscott Rd E5	32	A1
Linsdell Rd, Bark.	37	E5
Linsey St SE16	59	F5
Linstead St NW6	26	B4
Linstead Way SW18	81	G3
Linton Cl SE9	93	G4
Linton Gdns E6	50	A5
Linton Rd, Bark.	37	E4
Lintons, The, Bark.	37	E4
Linton St N1	30	B5
Linver Rd SW6	68	B5
Linwood Cl SE5	73	E5
Lion Cl SE4	89	E4
Lionel Gdns SE9	91	G3
Lionel Rd SE9	91	G3
Lion Rd E6	50	B4
Liphook Cres SE23	88	A5
Lisburne Rd NW3	27	G1
Lisford St SE15	73	E4
Lisgar Ter W14	54	A5
Liskeard Gdns SE3	77	D4
Lisle St WC2	14	D3
Lismore Circ NW5	27	G2
Lissenden Gdns NW5	28	A1
Lisson Grn Est NW8	6	B2
Lisson Gro NW1	6	B3
Lisson Gro NW8	6	A2
Lisson St NW1	6	B5
Liston Rd SW4	84	C1
Litchfield Av E15	34	B3
Litchfield Gdns NW10	24	C3
Litchfield St WC2	14	D3
Lithos Rd NW3	26	C3
Little Albany St NW1	7	J3
Little Argyll St W1	14	A2
Little Boltons, The SW5	68	C1
Little Boltons, The SW10	68	C1
Little Britain EC1	16	D1
Littlebury Rd SW4	84	D1
Little Chester St SW1	19	G3
Little Coll St SW1	21	E3
Littlecombe SE7	77	E2
Littlecombe Cl SW15	81	F4
Littlecote Cl SW19	81	F5
Littlecroft SE9	92	C1
Little Dean's Yd SW1	20	E3
Little Dorrit Ct SE1	22	E1
Little Edward St NW1	7	J1
Little Essex St WC2	15	J3
Little George St SW1	20	E2
Little Heath SE7	78	A2
Little Ilford La E12	36	B1
Little Newport St WC2	14	D3
Little New St EC4	16	A1
Little Portland St W1	14	A1
Little Russell St WC1	8	E6
Little St. James's St SW1	14	A6
Little Sanctuary SW1	20	D2

Name	Ref
Little Smith St SW1	20 D3
Little Titchfield St W1	8 A6
Little Trinity La EC4	16 E3
Little Turnstile WC1	15 G1
Littlewood SE13	89 G3
Livermere Rd E8	31 E5
Liverpool Gro SE17	72 C1
Liverpool Rd E16	48 B4
Liverpool Rd N1	43 G1
Liverpool Rd N7	29 G2
Liverpool St EC2	16 H6
Livesey Cl SE28	65 E4
Livingstone Rd E15	33 G5
Livingstone Wk SW11	83 E1
Livonia St W1	14 B2
Lizard St EC1	11 E2
Lizban St SE3	77 E3
Llanover Rd SE18	78 C2
Lloyd Baker St WC1	9 H2
Lloyd Rd E6	36 B5
Lloyd's Av EC3	17 J2
Lloyds Pl SE3	76 B5
Lloyd Sq WC1	9 J1
Lloyd's Row EC1	10 A2
Lloyd St WC1	9 J1
Lloyd Vil SE4	75 E5
Loampit Hill SE13	75 E5
Loampit Vale SE13	89 F1
Loats Rd SW2	85 E4
Lochaber Rd SE13	90 B2
Lochaline St W6	67 E2
Lochinvar St SW12	84 B5
Lochnagar St E14	47 G4
Lock Chase SE3	90 B1
Lockesfield Pl E14	75 F1
Lockhart Cl N7	29 F3
Lockhart St E3	47 D3
Lockhurst St E5	32 B1
Lockington Rd SW8	70 B4
Lockmead Rd SE13	89 G1
Locksley Est E14	46 D5
Locksley St E14	46 D4
Lockton St W10	53 F1
Lockwood Sq SE16	59 G4
Lockyer Est SE1	23 G1
Lockyer St SE1	23 G2
Loddiges Rd E9	32 A4
Loder St SE15	74 A4
Lodge Av SW14	80 A1
Lodge Rd NW8	6 A2
Lodore St E14	47 G5
Loftie St SE16	59 F3
Lofting Rd N1	29 F4
Loftus Rd W12	53 D2
Loftus Rd, Bark.	37 E3
Logan Ms W8	54 B5
Logan Pl W8	54 B5
Lollard St SE11	21 H5
Loman St SE1	22 C1
Lomas Dr E8	31 E4
Lomas St E1	45 F4
Lombard Ct EC3	17 G3
Lombard La EC4	16 A2
Lombard Rd SW11	69 E5
Lombard St EC3	17 G2
Lombard Wall SE7	63 E4
Lomond Gro SE5	72 C3
Loncroft Rd SE5	73 D2
Londesborough Rd N16	30 D1
London Br EC4	17 G5
London Br SE1	17 G5
London Br St SE1	17 F6
London Cen Mkts (Smithfield Mkt) EC1	10 B5
London City Airport E16	64 A2
London Flds E8	31 G4
London Flds E Side E8	31 G4
London Flds W Side E8	31 F4
London Ind Est E6	50 C4
London La E8	31 G4
London Ms W2	12 A2
London Pav, The W1	14 C4
London Rd E13	48 D1
London Rd SE1	22 B3
London Rd, Bark.	36 D4
London Silver Vaults WC2	9 J6
London St EC3	17 J3
London St W2	41 E5
London Trocadero, The W1	14 C4
London Wall EC2	16 E1
London Wall Bldgs EC2	11 G6
Long Acre WC2	14 E3
Longbeach Rd SW11	83 G1
Longbridge Rd, Bark.	37 G1
Longbridge Way SE13	89 G3
Long Dr W3	38 A5
Longfield Est SE1	59 E5
Longfield St SW18	82 B5
Longford St NW1	7 J3
Longhedge St SW11	70 A5
Longhope Cl SE15	73 E2
Longhurst Rd SE13	90 A3
Long La EC1	10 C5
Long La SE1	23 F2
Longley St SE1	59 F5
Longmarsh La SE28	65 G2
Longmoore St SW1	20 A6
Longnor Rd E1	46 B2
Long Pond Rd SE3	76 B4
Long Reach Ct, Bark.	51 F1
Longridge Ho SE1	22 E4
Longridge Rd SW5	54 B5
Long Rd SW4	84 B2
Long's Ct WC2	14 C3
Longshore SE8	60 D5
Longstaff Cres SW18	82 B4
Longstaff Rd SW18	82 B4
Longstone Av NW10	24 B4
Longstone Ct SE1	23 E2
Long St E2	45 E2
Longville Rd SE11	22 B5
Longwall Av SW19	23 J3
Long Wk SE1	23 J3
Long Wk SE18	78 D2
Long Wk SW13	66 A5
Longwood Dr SW15	80 C4
Long Yd WC1	9 G4
Lonsdale Av E6	49 G2
Lonsdale Cl SE9	91 G4
Lonsdale Rd NW6	40 A1
Lonsdale Rd SE25	66 C2
Lonsdale Rd W4	52 B5
Lonsdale Rd W11	40 A6
Lonsdale Sq N1	29 G4
Loraine Rd N7	29 F1
Lord Amory Way E14	61 G3
Lorden Wk E2	45 F2
Lord Hills Rd W2	40 C4
Lord N St SW1	20 E4
Lord Roberts Ter SE18	78 C1
Lordship La SE22	87 E4
Lord St E16	64 A2
Lord Warwick St SE18	64 A6
Lorenzo St WC1	9 G1
Loring Rd SE14	74 C4
Loris Rd W6	53 E4
Lorn Ct SW9	71 G5
Lorne Cl NW8	6 C2
Lorne Gdns W11	53 F3
Lorne Rd E7	35 E1
Lorn Rd SW9	71 F5
Lorrimore Rd SE17	72 A2
Lorrimore Sq SE17	72 A2
Lothair Rd N4	30 A1
Lothbury EC2	16 F1
Lothian Rd SW9	72 A4
Lothrop St W10	39 G2
Lots Rd SW10	69 D3
Loudoun Rd NW8	27 D5
Loughborough Pk SW9	86 A2
Loughborough Rd SW9	71 G5
Loughborough St SE11	71 H1
Lough Rd N7	29 F3
Louisa Ho SW15	80 A2
Louisa St E1	46 B3
Louise Rd E15	34 B3
Louvaine Rd SW11	83 E2
Lovage App E6	50 A4
Lovat La EC3	17 H4
Lovegrove St SE1	73 F1
Lovegrove Wk E14	61 G2
Lovelace Grn SE9	92 B1
Love La EC2	16 E1
Love La SE18	64 D5
Lovelinch Cl SE15	74 A2
Lovell Ho E8	31 F5
Loveridge Rd NW6	26 A3
Lovers Wk SE10	76 B2
Lover's Wk W1	13 F5
Love Wk SE5	72 C5
Lowbrook Rd, Ilf.	37 D2
Lowden Rd SE24	86 A2
Lowell St E14	46 C5
Lower Addison Gdns W14	53 G3
Lower Belgrave St SW1	19 H4
Lower Clapton Rd E5	31 G2
Lower Common S SW15	81 D1
Lower Grosvenor Pl SW1	19 H3
Lower James St W1	14 B3
Lower John St W1	14 B3
Lower Lea Crossing E14	62 B1
Lower Lea Crossing E16	62 B1
Lower Mall W6	66 D4
Lower Marsh SE1	21 J2
Lower Merton Ri NW3	27 F4
Lower Richmond Rd SW15	81 E1
Lower Rd SE1	21 J1
Lower Rd SE8	60 A4
Lower Rd SE16	60 A4
Lower Sloane St SW1	19 F6
Lower Thames St EC3	17 G4
Lowestoft Ms E16	65 D3
Lowfield Rd NW6	26 B4
Lowman Rd N7	29 F1
Lowndes Cl SW1	19 G4
Lowndes Ct W1	14 A2
Lowndes Pl SW1	19 H4
Lowndes Sq SW1	19 E2
Lowndes St SW1	19 E3
Lowther Hill SE23	88 C5
Lowther Rd SW13	66 B4
Lowth Rd SE5	72 B5
Loxford Av E6	49 G1
Loxford Gdns N5	30 A1
Loxford La, Ilf.	37 E2
Loxford Rd, Bark.	37 D3
Loxham St WC1	9 F2
Lubbock St SE14	74 A3
Lucan Pl SW3	18 B6
Lucas Av E13	35 E5
Lucas St SE8	75 E4
Lucerne Rd N5	30 A1
Lucey Rd SE16	59 F4
Lucey Way SE16	59 F4
Lucknow St SE18	79 G3
Lucorn Cl SE12	90 C4
Ludgate Bdy EC4	16 B2
Ludgate Circ EC4	16 B2
Ludgate Hill EC4	16 B2
Ludgate Sq EC4	16 B2
Ludlow St EC1	10 D3
Lumley Ct WC2	15 F4
Lumley St W1	13 G2
Lupino Ct SE11	21 H6
Lupin Pl SE1	59 E4
Lupton St NW5	28 C1
Lupus St SW1	70 B2
Lurgan Av W6	67 F2
Lurline Gdns SW11	70 A4
Luscombe Way SW8	71 E3
Lushington Rd NW10	38 D1
Luton Pl SE10	75 G3
Luton Rd E13	48 D3
Luton St NW8	6 A4
Lutton Ter NW3	27 D1
Luttrell Av SW15	81 D3
Luxborough St W1	7 F5
Luxemburg Gdns W6	53 F5
Luxford St SE16	60 B5
Luxmore St SE4	75 D4
Luxor St SE5	72 A5
Lyall Ms SW1	19 F4
Lyall Ms W SW1	19 F4
Lyall St SW1	19 F4
Lyal Rd E3	46 C1
Lydden Ct SE9	93 G4
Lydden Gro SW18	82 C5
Lydden Rd SW18	82 C5
Lydeard Rd E6	36 B4
Lydford Rd NW2	25 F3
Lydford Rd W9	40 A3
Lydon Rd SW4	84 C5
Lydford Rd SW18	83 C1
Lyford St SE18	64 A5
Lygon Pl SW1	19 H4
Lyham Cl SW2	85 E4
Lyham Rd SW2	85 E3
Lyme Fm Rd SE12	90 D2
Lyme St NW1	28 C4
Lymington Rd NW6	26 C2
Lympstone Gdns SE15	73 F3
Lynbrook Gro SE15	73 D3
Lyncott Cres SW4	84 B2
Lyncroft Gdns NW6	26 B2
Lyndale NW2	26 A1
Lyndale Av NW2	26 A1
Lyndale Cl SE3	76 C2
Lyndhurst Gdns NW3	27 E2
Lyndhurst Gdns, Bark.	37 G3
Lyndhurst Gro SE15	73 D5
Lyndhurst Rd NW3	27 E2
Lyndhurst Sq SE15	73 E4
Lyndhurst Ter NW3	27 E3
Lyndhurst Way SE15	73 E4
Lynette Av SW4	84 B4
Lyn Ms N16	31 D1
Lynn Rd SW12	84 B5
Lynsted Gdns SE9	91 G1
Lynton Cl NW10	24 A2
Lynton Rd NW6	26 A5
Lynton Rd SE1	59 E5
Lynx Way E16	63 G1
Lyon Business Pk, Bark.	51 G1
Lyons Pl NW8	41 E3
Lyons Wk W14	53 G5
Lyric Rd SW13	66 B4
Lysander Gro N19	28 A4
Lysia St SW6	67 F3
Lysons Wk SW15	80 C3
Lytcott Gro SE22	87 E3
Lytham St SE17	72 C1
Lyttelton Cl NW3	27 F4
Lytton Gro SW15	81 F3
Lyveden Rd SE3	77 E3

M

Name	Ref
Mableton Pl WC1	8 D2
Mablethorpe Rd SW6	67 G3
Mabley St E9	32 C3
MacArthur Cl E7	35 D3
MacArthur Ter SE7	77 G2
Macaulay Ct SW4	84 B1
Macaulay Rd E6	49 G1
Macaulay Rd SW4	84 B1

Macaulay Sq SW4 84 B2
McAuley Cl SE1 21 J3
McAuley Cl SE9 92 D3
Macaulay Ms SE13 75 G5
Macbean St SE18 64 C4
Macbeth St W6 67 D1
McCall Cres SE7 78 A1
Macclesfield Br NW1 41 F1
Macclesfield Rd EC1 10 D1
Macclesfield St W1 14 D3
McCoid Way SE1 22 D2
McCullum Rd E3 32 D5
McDermott Cl SW11 83 F1
McDermott Rd SE15 87 F1
Macdonald Rd E7 34 D1
McDowall Cl E16 48 C4
McDowall Rd SE5 72 B4
Macduff Rd SW11 70 A4
Mace St E2 46 B1
McEwen Way E15 34 A5
Macfarland Gro SE15 73 D3
Macfarlane Rd W12 53 E2
Macfarren Pl NW1 7 G4
McGrath Rd E15 34 C2
Macgregor Rd E16 49 F4
McGregor Rd W11 40 A5
Machell Rd SE15 88 A1
Mackay Rd SW4 84 B1
Mackennal St NW8 6 E1
Mackenzie Rd N7 29 F3
Mackenzie Wk E14 61 E2
McKerrell Rd SE15 73 F4
Mackeson Rd NW3 27 G1
Mackie Rd SW2 85 G5
Macklin St WC2 15 F1
Macks Rd SE16 59 F5
Mackworth St NW1 8 A1
Maclean Rd SE23 88 C4
Macleod St SE17 72 B1
Maclise Rd W14 53 H3
McMillan St SE8 75 E2
McNeil Rd SE5 72 D5
Macoma Rd SE18 79 F2
Macoma Ter SE18 79 F2
Maconochies Rd E14 75 F1
Macquarie Way E14 61 F5
Macroom Rd W9 40 A2
Mac's Pl EC4 16 A1
Maddams St E3 47 F3
Maddock Way SE17 72 A2
Madain Rd E16 13 J3
Madeline Gro, Ilf. 37 F2
Madinah Rd E8 31 F3
Madras Pl N7 29 G3
Madras Rd, Ilf. 36 D1
Madrid Rd SW13 66 C4
Madrigal La SE5 72 A3
Madron St SE17 73 D1
Mafeking Av E6 49 G1
Mafeking Rd E16 48 C3
Magdalene Gdns E6 50 C3
Magdalen St SE1 17 H6
Magee St SE11 71 G2
Magnolia Pl SW4 85 D3
Magpie All EC4 16 A2
Magpie Cl E7 34 C2
Maguire St SE1 59 E3
Mahogany Cl SE16 60 C2
Maida Av W2 41 D4
Maida Vale W9 40 C1
Maiden La NW1 29 D4
Maiden La SE1 17 E5
Maiden La WC2 15 F4
Maiden Rd E15 34 B4
Maidenstone Hill SE10 75 G4
Maidstone Bldgs Ms SE1 17 E6
Maitland Cl SE10 75 G4
Maitland Pk Est NW3 27 G3
Maitland Pk Rd NW3 27 G3
Maitland Pk Vil NW3 27 G3
Maitland Rd E15 34 C3

Majendie Rd SE18 79 F1
Major Cl SW9 86 A1
Major Draper St SE18 65 D4
Major Rd E15 33 G2
Makins St SW3 18 C6
Malabar St E14 61 E3
Malbrook Rd SW15 81 D2
Malcolm Pl E2 46 A3
Malcolm Rd E1 46 A3
Malden Cres NW1 28 A3
Malden Rd NW5 28 A2
Maldon Cl N1 30 B5
Maldon Cl SE5 86 D1
Malet Pl WC1 8 C4
Malet St WC1 8 C4
Malfort Rd SE5 87 D1
Mall, The SW1 20 B1
Mallard Cl NW6 40 B1
Mallard Pl SE13 90 A4
Malling SE13 89 G3
Mallinson Rd SW11 83 F3
Mallord St SW3 69 E2
Mallory Cl SE4 88 C2
Mallory St NW8 6 C3
Mallow St EC1 11 F3
Mall Rd W6 67 D1
Malmesbury Rd E3 45 D2
Malmesbury Rd E16 48 C4
Malmesbury Ter E16 48 C4
Malpas Rd E8 31 G3
Malpas Rd SE4 74 D5
Malta St EC1 10 C3
Maltby St SE1 59 E4
Malthouse Dr W4 66 A2
Malting Ho E14 60 D1
Maltings Cl E3 47 G2
Maltings Pl SE1 23 J2
Maltings Pl SW6 68 C4
Malton St SE18 79 G2
Maltravers St WC2 15 H3
Malton Rd W10 40 A4
Malvern Cl W10 40 A4
Malvern Cl SW7 18 A6
Malvern Pl NW6 40 A2
Malvern Rd E6 36 A5
Malvern Rd E8 31 F4
Malvern Rd NW6 40 B2
Malvern Ter N1 29 G5
Malwood Rd SW12 84 B3
Malyons Rd SE13 89 F3
Malyons Ter SE13 89 F3
Manaton Cl SE15 87 G1
Manbey Gro E15 34 B3
Manbey Pk Rd E15 34 B3
Manbey Rd E15 34 B3
Manbey St E15 34 B3
Manbre Rd W6 67 E2
Manbrough Av E6 50 B2
Manchester Ct E16 49 E5
Manchester Dr W10 39 G5
Manchester Gro E14 75 G1
Manchester Ms W1 7 F6
Manchester Rd E14 75 G1
Manchester Sq W1 13 F1
Manchester St W1 7 F6
Manchuria Rd SW11 84 A4
Manciple St SE1 23 F2
Mandalay Rd SW4 84 C3
Mandela Rd E16 49 D5
Mandela St NW1 28 C5
Mandela St SW9 71 G5
Mandela Way SE1 23 J5
Mandeville Pl W1 13 G1
Mandrake Way E15 34 B4
Mandrell Rd SW2 85 E3
Manette St W1 14 D2
Manfred Rd SW15 82 A3
Manger Rd N7 29 E3
Manhattan Wf E16 62 D3
Manilla St E14 61 E3
Manley St NW1 28 A5
Manningford Cl EC1 10 B1
Manor Av SE4 75 D5

Manorbrook SE3 91 D2
Manor Est SE16 59 G5
Manor Flds SW15 81 F4
Manor Gro SE15 74 A2
Manor Ho Dr NW6 26 A4
Manor La SE12 90 B4
Manor La SE13 90 B2
Manor La Ter SE13 90 B2
Manor Ms SE4 75 D5
Manor Pk SE13 90 A2
Manor Pk Rd NW10 24 B5
Manor Pl SE17 72 A1
Manor Rd E15 48 B2
Manor Rd E16 48 B2
Manor Way SE3 90 C2
Manor Way SE23 88 A5
Manresa Rd SW3 69 F1
Mansell St E1 45 E5
Mansergh Cl SE18 78 A3
Mansfield Ms W1 7 H6
Mansfield Rd NW3 27 G2
Mansfield St W1 7 H6
Mansford St E2 45 F1
Mansion Ho EC4 17 F2
Mansion Ho Pl EC4 17 F2
Mansion Ho St EC4 17 F2
Manson Ms SW7 55 D5
Manson Pl SW7 55 E5
Manstone Rd NW2 25 G2
Manthorp Rd SE18 79 E1
Mantle Rd SE4 88 C1
Mantua St SW11 83 E1
Mantus Rd E1 46 A3
Manwood Rd SE4 89 D3
Manwood St E16 64 B2
Mapesbury Rd NW2 25 G4
Mapeshill Pl NW2 25 E3
Maple St E2 45 G3
Maple Av W3 52 A2
Maple Cl SW4 85 D4
Mapledene Rd E8 31 E4
Maple Pl W1 8 B4
Maplestead Rd SW2 85 F1
Maple St E2 45 F1
Maple St W1 8 A5
Mapleton Cres SW18 82 C4
Mapleton Rd SW18 82 C4
Maplin Rd E16 49 D5
Maplin St E3 46 D2
Marabou Cl E12 36 A2
Marathon Ho NW1 6 D5
Marban Rd W9 40 A2
Marble Arch W1 12 E3
Marble Quay E1 59 F2
Marcella Rd SW9 71 G5
Marchant St SE14 74 C2
Marchbank Rd W14 68 A2
Marchmont St WC1 8 E3
Marchwood Cl SE5 72 D3
Marcia Rd SE1 23 J6
Marcilly Rd SW18 83 E3
Marcon Pl E8 31 G3
Marco Rd W6 53 E4
Marcus Ct E15 34 B5
Marcus Garvey Way SE24 85 G2
Marcus St E15 34 C5
Marcus St SW18 82 C4
Marcus Ter SW18 82 C4
Marden Sq SE16 59 G4
Mare St E8 31 G5
Margaret Ct W1 14 A1
Margaret St W1 13 J1
Margaretta Ter SW3 69 F2
Margate Rd SW2 85 E3
Margery Pk Rd E7 34 D3
Margery St WC1 9 J2
Margravine Gdns W6 67 F1
Margravine Rd W6 67 F1
Marian Pl E2 45 G1
Marian Way NW10 24 B4

Maria Ter E1 46 B4
Marigold All SE1 16 B4
Marigold St SE16 59 G3
Marina Dr, Well. 79 G5
Marine Dr SE18 64 B5
Marinefield Rd SW6 68 C5
Mariners Ms E14 62 A5
Marischal Rd SE13 90 A1
Maritime Quay E14 75 E1
Maritime St E3 47 D3
Marjorie Gro SW11 83 G2
Market Ct W1 14 A1
Market Est N7 29 E3
Market Hill SE18 64 C4
Market Ms W1 13 H6
Market Pl W1 14 A1
Market Pl W3 52 A2
Market St E6 50 B1
Market St SE18 64 C5
Market Yd Ms SE1 23 H3
Markham Sq SW3 69 G1
Markham St SW3 69 F1
Markland Ho W10 53 F1
Mark La EC3 17 J4
Mark Sq EC2 11 H3
Mark St E15 34 B4
Mark St EC2 11 H3
Marlborough SW3 18 C5
Marlborough Av E8 31 F5
Marlborough Cl SE17 22 C6
Marlborough Ct W1 14 A2
Marlborough Gro SE1 73 F1
Marlborough Hill NW8 27 D5
Marlborough Pl NW8 41 D1
Marlborough Rd E7 35 F4
Marlborough Rd E15 65 D4
Marlborough Rd SW1 14 B6
Marlborough Rd SW3 18 B6
Marley St SE16 60 B5
Marloes Rd W8 54 C4
Marlow Ct NW6 25 F4
Marlow Gdns SE9 92 C4
Marlowes, The NW8 27 E5
Marlow Rd E6 50 B2
Marlow Way SE16 60 B3
Marmion Rd SW11 84 A2
Marmont Rd SE15 73 F4
Marmora Rd SE22 88 A4
Marne St W10 39 G2
Marney Rd SW11 84 A2
Marnham Av NW2 25 G1
Marnock Rd SE4 88 C3
Maroon St E14 46 C4
Marquess Est N1 30 B3
Marquess Rd N1 30 C3
Marquis Rd NW1 29 D3
Marriott Cl SW15 80 C2
Marriott Rd E15 34 B5
Marryat Sq SW6 67 G4
Marsala Rd SE13 89 F2
Marsden Rd SE15 87 E1
Marsden St NW5 28 A3
Marshall's Gro SE18 64 A5
Marshall St W1 14 B2
Marshalsea Rd SE1 22 E1
Marsham St SW1 20 D4
Marshbrook Cl SE3 91 G1
Marshfield St E14 61 G4
Marshgate La E15 33 F5
Marshgate Sidings E15 33 F5
Marsh Hill E9 32 C2
Marsh Wall E14 61 E2
Marsland Cl SE17 72 A1
Marston Cl NW6 27 D4
Martaban Rd N16 30 E1
Martello St E8 31 G4
Martello Ter E8 31 G4
Martha Ct E2 45 G1
Martha Rd E15 34 B3
Martha's Bldgs EC1 11 F3

Name	Ref
Martha St E1	45 G5
Martin Bowes Rd SE9	92 B1
Martindale Av E16	63 D1
Martindale Rd SW12	84 B5
Martineau St E1	60 A1
Martin Ho SE1	22 E4
Martin La EC4	17 G3
Martin St SE28	65 G2
Martins Wk SE28	65 G2
Martlett Ct WC2	14 E2
Marville Rd SW6	68 A3
Mary Ann Gdns SE8	75 E2
Marybank SE18	64 B5
Mary Datchelor Cl SE5	72 C4
Maryland Pk E15	34 B2
Maryland Rd E15	34 A2
Maryland Sq E15	34 B2
Marylands Rd W9	40 B3
Maryland St E15	34 A2
Mary Lawrenson Pl SE3	76 C3
Marylebone Flyover NW1	6 A6
Marylebone Flyover W2	6 A6
Marylebone High St W1	7 G5
Marylebone La W1	13 H2
Marylebone Ms W1	7 H6
Marylebone Pas W1	14 B1
Marylebone Rd NW1	6 C5
Marylebone St W1	7 G6
Marylee Way SE11	57 F5
Maryon Gro SE7	64 A5
Maryon Rd SE7	64 A5
Maryon Rd SE18	64 A5
Mary Pl W11	53 G1
Mary St N1	30 B5
Mary Ter NW1	28 B5
Masbro Rd W14	53 F4
Mascalls Ct SE7	77 F2
Mascalls Rd SE7	77 F2
Mascotte Rd SW15	81 E2
Masefield Gdns E6	50 C3
Mashie Rd W3	38 A5
Maskelyne Cl SW11	69 F4
Mason Cl E16	62 D1
Masons Arms Ms W1	13 J2
Masons Av EC2	17 F1
Masons Hill SE18	65 D5
Masons Pl EC1	10 C1
Mason St SE17	23 G6
Masons Yd SW1	14 B5
Massey St E6	35 F5
Massinger St SE17	23 H6
Massingham St E1	46 B3
Master Gunner Pl SE18	78 A3
Masterman Ho SE5	72 B3
Masterman Rd E6	50 A2
Masters Dr SE16	73 G1
Masters St E1	46 B4
Mast Ho Ter E14	61 E5
Mast Leisure Pk SE16	60 B4
Mastmaker Rd E14	61 E3
Matchless Dr SE18	78 C3
Matham Gro SE22	87 E2
Matheson Rd W14	54 A5
Mathews Av E6	50 C1
Mathews Pk Av E15	34 C3
Matilda Gdns E3	47 E1
Matilda St N1	29 F5
Matlock Cl SE24	86 B2
Matlock St E14	46 C5
Matrimony Pl SW8	70 C5
Matthew Cl W10	39 F3
Matthew Parker St SW1	20 D2
Matthews St SW11	69 G5
Matthews Yd WC2	15 E2
Matthias Rd N16	30 C2
Maud Cashmore Way SE18	64 B4
Maude Rd SE5	72 D4
Maud Gdns E13	34 C5
Maud Rd E13	48 C1
Maudslay Rd SE9	92 B1
Maud St E16	48 C4
Maud Wilkes Cl NW5	28 C2
Mauleverer Rd SW2	85 E3
Maunsel St SW1	20 C5
Maurice St W12	38 D5
Mauritius Rd SE10	62 B5
Maverton Rd E3	33 E5
Mavis Wk E6	50 A4
Mawbey Est SE1	73 E1
Mawbey Pl SE1	73 E1
Mawbey Rd SE1	71 E3
Mawbey St SW8	65 E5
Maxey Rd SE18	87 E1
Maxted Rd SE15	86 C3
Maxwell Rd SW6	68 C3
Maya Cl SE15	73 G5
Mayall Rd SE24	86 A3
Maybury Gdns NW10	24 D3
Maybury Rd E13	49 F3
Mayday Gdns SE3	78 A5
Maydew Ho SE16	60 A5
Mayerne Rd SE9	91 G3
Mayfair Pl W1	13 J5
Mayfield Av W4	52 A5
Mayfield Cl SW4	85 D3
Mayfield Rd E8	31 E4
Mayfield Rd E13	48 C3
Mayfield Rd W12	52 A3
Mayflower Rd SW9	85 E1
Mayflower St SE16	60 A3
Mayford Cl SW12	83 G5
Mayford Rd SW12	83 G5
Maygood St N1	43 F1
Maygrove Rd NW6	26 A3
Mayhill Rd SE7	77 E2
Mayola Rd E5	32 A1
Mayo Rd NW10	24 A3
Mayplace La SE18	79 D3
May Rd E13	49 D1
Mays Ct WC2	14 E4
Maysoule Rd SW11	83 E2
Mayville Rd, Ilf.	36 D2
May Wk E13	49 E1
Maze Hill SE3	76 B2
Maze Hill SE10	76 B2
Mazenod Av NW6	26 B4
Meadcroft Rd SE11	72 A2
Meadowbank NW3	27 G4
Meadowbank SE3	90 C1
Meadowbank Cl SW6	67 E3
Meadow Cl E9	33 D2
Meadowcourt Rd SE3	90 C1
Meadow Ms SW8	71 F2
Meadow Pl SW8	71 E3
Meadow Rd SW8	71 F2
Meadow Row SE1	22 D4
Meadowside SE9	91 F2
Mead Pl E9	32 A3
Mead Row SE1	21 J3
Meakin Est SE1	23 H3
Meanley Rd E12	36 A1
Meard St W1	14 C2
Meath Cres E2	46 B2
Meath Rd E15	48 C1
Meath St SW11	70 B4
Mecklenburgh Pl WC1	9 G3
Mecklenburgh Sq WC1	9 G3
Mecklenburgh St WC1	9 G3
Medals Way E20	33 G2
Medburn St NW1	42 D1
Medebourne Cl SE3	91 D1
Medfield St SW15	80 D5
Median Rd E5	32 A2
Medlar St SE5	72 B4
Medley Rd NW6	26 B3
Medora Rd SW2	85 F5
Medusa Rd SE6	89 F4
Medway Cl, Ilf.	37 E2
Medway Rd E3	46 C1
Medway Rd SW1	20 D4
Medwin St SW4	85 F2
Meerbrook Rd SE3	91 F1
Meeson Rd E15	34 C5
Meeson St E5	32 C1
Meeting Ho La SE15	73 G4
Mehetabel Rd E9	32 A3
Melba Way SE13	75 F4
Melbourne Gro SE22	87 D2
Melbourne Ms SE6	89 G5
Melbourne Sq SW9	71 G4
Melbourne Pl WC2	15 H3
Melbourne Rd E6	36 B5
Melbury Ct W8	54 A4
Melbury Rd W14	54 A4
Melcombe Pl NW1	6 D5
Melcombe St NW1	6 E4
Melford Av, Bark.	37 G3
Melford Rd E6	50 B3
Melford Rd SE22	87 F5
Melgund Rd N5	29 G2
Melina Pl NW8	41 E2
Melina Rd W12	52 D3
Melior Pl SE1	23 H1
Melior St SE1	23 G1
Melling St SE18	79 G2
Mellish Ind Est SE18	64 A4
Mellish St E14	61 E4
Mellitus St W12	38 D5
Melody La N5	30 A2
Melody Rd SW18	83 D5
Melon Rd SE15	73 F4
Melrose Av NW2	25 D2
Melrose Gdns W6	53 E4
Melrose Rd SW13	66 B5
Melrose Rd SW18	82 A4
Melrose Ter W6	53 E3
Melthorpe Gdns SE3	78 A4
Melton Ct SW7	18 A6
Melton St NW1	8 B3
Melville Rd SW13	66 C4
Memel Ct EC1	10 D4
Memel St EC1	10 D4
Memess Path SE18	78 C2
Memorial Av E15	48 B2
Mendip Rd SW11	83 D1
Mendora Rd SW6	67 G3
Menelik Rd NW2	25 G1
Mentmore Ter E8	31 G4
Mepham St SE1	15 H6
Merbury Cl SE13	89 G3
Merbury Cl SE28	65 F2
Merbury Rd SE28	65 G3
Mercator Rd SE13	90 A2
Merceron St E1	45 G3
Mercers Cl SE10	62 C5
Mercers Pl W6	53 E5
Mercer St WC2	14 E2
Merchant St E3	47 D2
Mercia Gro SE13	89 G2
Mercier Rd SW15	81 G3
Mercury Way SE14	74 B2
Mercy Ter SE13	89 F2
Mere Cl SW15	81 F5
Meredith Av NW2	25 E2
Meredith Ms SE4	88 D2
Meredith St E13	49 D2
Meredith St EC1	10 B2
Meredyth Rd SW13	66 C5
Meretone Cl SE4	88 C2
Mereworth Dr SE18	79 D3
Meridian Gate E14	61 G3
Meridian Pl E14	61 G3
Meridian Rd SE7	77 G3
Meridian Sq E15	34 A4
Meridian Trd Est SE7	63 E5
Merifield Rd SE9	91 F2
Merivale Rd SW15	81 G2
Merlin St WC1	9 J2
Mermaid Ct SE1	23 H1
Mermaid Ct SE16	60 D2
Merredene St SW2	85 F4
Merriam Av E9	33 D3
Merrick Sq SE1	23 E3
Merridale SE12	90 D3
Merriman Rd SE3	77 F4
Merrington Rd SW6	68 B2
Merritt Rd SE4	88 D3
Merrow St SE17	72 B2
Merryfield SE3	76 C5
Merryfields Way SE9	89 F5
Mersea Ho, Bark.	36 D3
Merthyr Ter SW13	67 D2
Merton Av W4	52 B5
Merton Ri NW3	27 F4
Merton Rd SW18	82 B3
Merttins Rd SE15	88 B3
Meru Cl NW5	28 A2
Mervan Rd SW2	85 G2
Messent Rd SE9	91 F3
Messeter Pl SE9	92 C4
Messina Av NW6	26 B4
Meteor St SW11	84 A2
Methley St SE11	71 G1
Methwold Rd W10	39 F4
Metro Cen Hts SE1	22 D4
Mews St E1	59 F2
Mexfield Rd SW15	82 A3
Meymott St SE1	16 B6
Meynell Cres E9	32 B4
Meynell Gdns E9	32 B4
Meynell Rd E9	32 B4
Meyrick Rd NW10	24 C3
Meyrick Rd SW11	83 E1
Micawber St N1	10 E1
Michael Cliffe Ho EC1	10 A2
Michael Rd SW6	68 C4
Michaels Cl SE13	90 B2
Micheldever Rd SE12	90 B4
Michigan Av E12	36 A1
Micklethwaite Rd SW6	68 B2
Middle Fld NW8	27 E5
Middle Pk Av SE9	91 G4
Middle Row W10	39 G3
Middlesex Ct W4	66 B1
Middlesex Pas EC1	10 C6
Middlesex St E1	11 J6
Middle St EC1	10 D5
Middle Temple EC4	15 J3
Middle Temple La EC4	15 J2
Middleton Dr SE16	60 B3
Middleton Gro N7	29 E2
Middleton Pl W1	8 A6
Middleton Rd E8	31 E4
Middleton St E2	45 G2
Middleton Way SE13	90 A2
Middle Yd SE1	17 H5
Midford Pl W1	8 B4
Midhope St WC1	9 F2
Midhurst Way E5	31 F1
Midland Rd NW1	43 D1
Midland Ter NW10	38 A3
Midmoor Rd SW12	84 B1
Midnight Av SE5	72 A3
Midship Pt E14	61 E3
Midstrath Rd NW10	24 A1
Miers Cl E6	36 C5
Milborne Gro SW10	69 D1
Milborne St E9	32 A3
Milborough Cres SE12	90 B4
Milcote St SE1	22 B2
Mildenhall Rd E5	32 A1
Mildmay Av N1	30 C3
Mildmay Gro N N1	30 C2
Mildmay Gro S N1	30 C2
Mildmay Pk N1	30 C2
Mildmay Rd N1	30 D2
Mildmay St N1	30 C3
Mile End Pl E1	46 B3
Mile End Rd E1	46 A4
Mile End Rd E3	46 A4
Miles Cl SE28	65 F2
Miles Dr SE28	65 F2
Miles Pl NW1	6 A5

Miles St SW8 71 E2
Milfoil St SW12 52 C1
Milford La WC2 15 H3
Milk St E16 64 D2
Milk St EC2 16 E2
Milkwell Yd SE5 72 B4
Milkwood Rd SE24 86 A3
Milk Yd E1 60 A1
Millais Av E12 36 C2
Millais Rd E11 33 G1
Millbank SW1 21 E4
Millbank Ct SW1 20 E5
Millbank Twr SW1 20 E6
Millbank Way SE12 90 D3
Millbrook Av, Well. 93 F2
Millbrook Rd SW9 86 A1
Millender Wk SE16 60 A5
Millennium Br EC4 16 D3
Millennium Br SE1 16 D3
Millennium Dr E14 62 A5
Millennium Harbour E14 61 D3
Millennium Pl E2 45 G1
Millennium Way SE10 62 B1
Miller's Av E8 31 E2
Miller's Ter E8 31 E2
Miller St NW1 42 C1
Millers Way W6 53 E3
Miller Wk SE1 16 A6
Millfields Rd E5 32 A1
Millgrove St SW11 70 A5
Millharbour E14 61 F4
Mill Hill Rd SW13 66 C5
Milligan St E14 61 D1
Mill La NW6 26 A2
Mill La SE18 78 C1
Millman Ms WC1 9 G4
Millman St WC1 9 G4
Millmark Gro SE14 74 C5
Mill Rd E16 63 E2
Mill Row N1 31 D5
Mills Ct EC2 11 J2
Millshott Cl SW6 67 E3
Millstream Rd SE1 59 E3
Mill St SE1 59 E3
Mill St W1 13 J4
Millwall Dock Rd E14 61 E4
Milman Rd NW6 39 G1
Milman's St SW10 69 E2
Milne Gdns SE9 92 A3
Milner Pl N1 29 G5
Milner Rd E15 48 B2
Milner Sq N1 30 A4
Milner St SW3 18 D5
Milo Rd SE22 87 E4
Milroy Wk SE1 16 B5
Milson Rd W14 53 G4
Milton Av E6 49 H1
Milton Cl SE1 59 E5
Milton Ct EC2 11 F5
Milton Ct Rd SE14 74 C2
Milton Gro N16 30 C1
Milton Rd SE24 86 A4
Milton St EC2 11 F5
Milverton Rd NW6 25 E4
Milverton St SE11 71 G1
Mimosa St SW6 68 A4
Minard Rd SE6 90 B5
Mina Rd SE17 73 D1
Mincing La EC3 17 H3
Mineral St SE18 65 G5
Minera Ms SW1 19 G5
Minerva Cl SW9 71 G3
Minerva St E2 45 G1
Minet Av NW10 38 A1
Minet Gdns NW10 38 A1
Minet Rd SW9 72 A5
Minford Gdns W14 53 F3
Ming St E14 61 E1
Minnow St SE17 23 J6
Minories EC3 45 E5
Minson Rd E9 32 B5
Minstead Gdns SW15 80 B5

Minster Ct EC3 17 H3
Minster Rd NW2 25 G2
Mint Business Pk E16 49 D4
Mintern St N1 44 C1
Mint St SE1 22 D1
Mirabel Rd SW6 68 A3
Mirabelle Gdns E20 33 G3
Mirfield St SE7 63 G5
Miriam Rd SE18 79 G1
Mission Pl SE15 73 F4
Mitcham Rd E6 50 A2
Mitchell St EC1 10 D3
Mitchell Wk E6 50 A4
Mitchison Rd N1 30 C5
Mitre Ct EC2 16 E1
Mitre Rd E15 48 B1
Mitre Sq EC3 17 J2
Mitre St EC3 17 J2
Mitre Way W10 39 D3
Moat Pl SW9 85 F1
Moberly Rd SW4 85 D5
Modder Pl SW15 81 F2
Modling Ho E2 46 A1
Moira Rd SE9 92 B2
Molesford Rd SW6 68 B4
Molesworth St SE13 89 G1
Molly Huggins Cl SW12 84 C5
Molyneux St W1 6 C6
Monarch Dr E16 49 G4
Mona Rd SE15 74 A5
Mona St E16 48 C4
Monck St SW1 20 D4
Monclar Rd SE5 86 C2
Moncorvo Cl SW7 18 B2
Moncrieff St SE15 73 F5
Monega Rd E7 35 F3
Monega Rd E12 35 G3
Monier Rd E3 33 E4
Monk Dr E16 48 D5
Monkton St SE11 22 A5
Monkwell Sq EC2 10 E6
Monmouth Pl W2 40 B5
Monmouth Rd W2 40 B5
Monmouth St WC2 14 E1
Monnow Rd SE1 59 F5
Monnow Way E5 31 F1
Monson Rd NW10 38 C1
Monson Rd SE14 74 B3
Montacute Rd SE6 88 D5
Montague Av SE4 89 D2
Montague Cl SE1 17 F5
Montague Pl WC1 8 D5
Montague Rd E8 31 D2
Montague Rd E11 34 A3
Montague St EC1 10 D6
Montague St WC1 8 D6
Montagu Mans W1 7 E5
Montagu Ms N W1 6 E6
Montagu Ms S W1 12 E1
Montagu Ms W W1 12 E1
Montagu Pl W1 6 D6
Montagu Row W1 7 E6
Montagu Sq W1 6 E6
Montagu St W1 12 E1
Montaigne Cl SW1 20 D6
Montcalm Rd SE7 77 G3
Monteagle Way SE15 87 G1
Montefiore St SW8 70 B5
Montem Rd SE23 88 D5
Montevetro SW11 69 E4
Montfichet Rd E20 33 G4
Montford Pl SE11 71 G1
Montgomerie Ms SE23 88 A5
Montgomery St E14 61 F2
Montholme Rd SW11 83 G4
Montolieu Gdns SW15 81 D3
Montpelier Gdns E6 49 G2
Montpelier Gro NW5 28 C2
Montpelier Ms SW7 18 C3

Montpelier Pl E1 46 A5
Montpelier Pl SW7 18 C3
Montpelier Rd SE15 73 G4
Montpelier Row SE3 76 C5
Montpelier Sq SW7 18 C2
Montpelier St SW7 18 C2
Montpelier Ter SW7 18 C2
Montpelier Vale SE3 76 C5
Montpelier Wk SW7 18 C3
Montreal Pl WC2 15 G3
Montrose Av NW6 39 G1
Montrose Av, Well. 93 F1
Montrose Ct SW7 18 A2
Montrose Pl SW1 19 G2
Montserrat Rd SW15 82 A2
Monument Gdns SE13 89 G3
Monument St EC3 17 G4
Monza St E1 60 A1
Moodkee St SE16 60 A4
Moody Rd SE15 73 E3
Moody St E1 46 B2
Moon St N1 30 A5
Moordown SE18 78 C4
Moore Pk Rd SW6 68 C3
Moore St SW3 18 D5
Moorfields EC2 11 F6
Moorfields Highwalk EC2 11 F6
Moorgate EC2 17 F1
Moorgate Pl EC2 17 F1
Moorhouse Rd W2 40 B5
Moorland Rd SW9 86 A2
Moorlands Est SW9 85 G2
Moor La EC2 11 F6
Moor Pl EC2 11 F6
Moor St W1 14 D2
Morant St E14 61 E1
Mora Rd NW2 25 E1
Mora St EC1 10 E2
Morat St SW9 71 F4
Moravian St E2 46 A1
Mordaunt St SW9 85 F1
Morden Hill SE13 75 G5
Morden La SE13 75 G4
Morden Rd SE3 76 D5
Morden Rd Ms SE3 76 D5
Morden St SE13 75 F4
Morden Wf Rd SE10 62 B4
Morecambe Cl E1 46 B4
Morecambe St SE17 23 E6
More Cl E16 48 C5
More Cl W14 53 G5
Moreland St EC1 10 C1
Morella Rd SW12 83 G5
More London Pl SE1 17 H6
More London Riverside SE1 17 J6
Morena St SE6 89 F5
Moresby Wk SW8 70 B5
Moreton Cl SW1 70 C1
Moreton St SW1 70 D1
Moreton Ter SW1 70 C1
Morgan Rd N7 29 G2
Morgan Rd W10 40 A4
Morgans La SE1 17 H6
Morgan St E3 46 C2
Morgan St E16 48 C4
Moriatry Cl N7 29 E1
Morie St SW18 82 C2
Morley Rd E15 48 C1
Morley Rd SE13 89 G2
Morley St SE1 22 A3
Morna Rd SE5 72 B5
Morning La E9 32 A3
Mornington Av W14 54 A5
Mornington Cres NW1 42 C1
Mornington Gro E9 47 E2
Mornington Ms SE5 72 B4
Mornington Rd SE8 75 D3
Mornington St NW1 42 B1

Mornington Ter NW1 28 B5
Morocco St SE1 23 H2
Morpeth Gro E9 32 B5
Morpeth Rd E9 32 A5
Morpeth St E2 46 B2
Morpeth Ter SW1 20 A4
Morris Av E12 36 B2
Morris Gdns SW18 82 B5
Morrish Rd SW2 85 E5
Morrison St SW11 84 A1
Morris Rd E14 47 F4
Morris Rd E15 34 B1
Morris St E1 45 G5
Morse Cl E13 48 D2
Morshead Rd W9 40 B2
Morten Cl SW4 85 D4
Mortham St E15 34 A5
Mortimer Cres NW6 26 C5
Mortimer Est NW6 26 C5
Mortimer Mkt WC1 8 B4
Mortimer Pl NW6 26 C5
Mortimer Rd E6 50 B2
Mortimer Rd N1 31 D4
Mortimer Rd NW10 39 E2
Mortimer St W1 14 A1
Mortlake Rd E16 49 E5
Mortlake Rd, Ilf. 37 E1
Morton Pl SE1 21 J4
Morton Rd E15 34 C4
Morton Rd N1 30 B4
Morval Rd SW2 85 G3
Morville St E3 47 E1
Morwell St WC1 8 D6
Moscow Rd W2 54 B1
Moseley Row SE10 62 C5
Mossbury Rd SW11 83 F1
Mossford St E3 47 D2
Mossop St SW3 18 C5
Mostyn Gdns NW10 39 F2
Mostyn Gro E3 47 D1
Mostyn Rd SW9 71 G4
Motcomb St SW1 19 E3
Mothers' Sq E5 31 G1
Motley Av EC2 11 H3
Moulins Rd E9 32 A5
Moulsford Ho N7 29 D2
Mount Adon Pk SE22 87 F5
Mountague Pl E14 61 G1
Mount Angelus Rd SW15 80 B5
Mountbatten Cl SE18 79 G2
Mountfield Cl SE6 90 A5
Mountfield Rd E6 50 C1
Mount Mills EC1 10 C2
Mount Pleasant WC1 9 H4
Mount Pleasant Pl SE18 65 F5
Mount Pleasant Rd NW10 25 E4
Mount Pleasant Rd SE13 89 F4
Mount Rd, Ilf. 36 D2
Mount Row W1 13 H4
Mountsfield Ct SE13 90 A3
Mounts Pond Rd SE3 76 A5
Mount Sq, The NW3 26 E1
Mount St W1 13 H4
Mount St Ms W1 13 H4
Mount Vernon NW3 26 E1
Mowbray Rd NW6 25 G4
Mowlem St E2 45 G1
Mowll St SW9 71 G3
Moxon St W1 7 F6
Moylan Rd W6 67 G2
Mozart St W10 40 A2
Mozart Ter SW1 19 G6
Muir Dr SW18 83 H1
Muirfield W3 38 A5
Mulberry Cl SE7 77 G2
Mulberry Cl SE22 87 F3
Mulberry Ho E8 31 E4

Mulberry Wk SW3 69 E2
Mulgrave Rd NW10 63 E4
Mulgrave Rd SE18 64 B5
Mulgrave Rd SW6 68 A2
Muller Rd SW4 85 D4
Mullins Pl SW4 85 E5
Mulready St NW8 6 B4
Multon Rd SW18 83 E5
Mulvaney Way SE1 23 G2
Muncaster Rd SW11 83 G3
Mundania Rd SE22 87 G4
Munday Rd E16 48 D5
Munden St W14 53 G5
Mund St W14 68 A1
Mundy St N1 11 H1
Munkenbeck Bldg W2 41 E4
Munro Ms W10 39 G4
Munro Ter SW10 69 E4
Munster Rd SW6 68 A4
Munster Sq NW1 7 J2
Munton Rd SE17 23 E5
Murdock St SE15 73 G2
Muriel St N1 43 F1
Murillo Rd SE13 90 A2
Murphy St SE1 21 J2
Murray Cl SE28 65 G2
Murray Gro N1 44 B1
Murray Ms NW1 28 D4
Murray Sq E16 49 D5
Murray St NW1 28 D4
Murrays Yd SE18 64 D5
Mursell Est SW8 71 F4
Musard Rd W6 67 G2
Musard Rd W14 67 G2
Musbury St E1 46 A5
Muscal W6 67 G3
Muschamp Rd SE15 87 E1
Muscovy St EC3 17 J4
Museum La SW7 18 A4
Museum St WC1 8 E6
Musgrave Cres SW6 68 B4
Musgrove Rd SE14 74 B4
Mutrix Rd NW6 26 B5
Myatt Rd SW9 72 A4
Mycenae Rd SE3 76 D3
Myddelton Pas EC1 10 A1
Myddelton Sq EC1 10 A1
Myddelton St EC1 10 A2
Myers La SE14 74 B2
Myrdle St E1 45 F4
Myron Pl SE13 89 G1
Myrtle Rd E6 36 A5
Myrtle Wk N1 44 D1
Mysore Rd SW11 83 G1

N

N1 Shop Cen N1 43 G1
Nadine St SE7 77 F1
Nags Head N7 29 F1
Nags Head Cen N7 29 F1
Nag's Head Ct EC1 11 G5
Nairne Gro SE24 86 C3
Nairn St E14 47 G4
Nankin St E14 47 E5
Nansen Rd SW11 84 A2
Nantes Cl SW18 83 D2
Naoroji St WC1 9 J2
Napier Av E14 75 E1
Napier Av SW6 82 A2
Napier Gro N1 44 B1
Napier Pl W14 54 A4
Napier Rd E6 36 C5
Napier Rd E11 34 B1
Napier Rd E15 35 B2
Napier Rd NW10 38 D2
Napier Rd W14 54 A4
Napier Ter N1 30 A4
Narbonne Av SW4 84 D3
Narborough St SW6 68 C5
Narcissus Rd NW6 26 B2
Narrow St E14 60 C1
Nascot St W12 39 E5

Naseby Cl NW6 27 D4
Nash Rd SE4 88 B2
Nash St NW1 7 J2
Nasmyth St W6 52 D4
Nassau Rd SW13 66 B4
Nassau St W1 8 A6
Nassington Rd NW3 27 F1
Natal Rd, Ilf. 36 D1
Neasden Cl NW10 24 A2
Neasden La NW10 24 A1
Neate St SE5 73 G5
Neathouse Pl SW1 20 A5
Neatscourt Rd E6 49 G4
Nebraska St SE1 23 F2
Neckinger SE16 59 E4
Neckinger Est SE16 59 E3
Neckinger St SE1 59 E3
Nectarine Way SE13 75 F5
Needleman St SE16 60 B3
Nelgarde Rd SE6 89 E5
Nella Rd W6 67 G4
Nelldale Rd SE16 60 A5
Nelson Cl NW6 40 B2
Nelson Gdns E2 45 F2
Nelson Mandela Rd SE3 91 F1
Nelson Pas EC1 10 E2
Nelson Pl N1 44 A1
Nelson Rd SE10 75 G2
Nelson's Row SW4 84 D2
Nelson St E1 45 G5
Nelson St E6 50 A1
Nelson Ter N1 44 A1
Nepaul Rd SW11 69 F5
Nepean St SW15 80 C4
Neptune St SE16 60 A4
Nesbit Rd SE9 91 G2
Nesham St E1 59 F2
Netheravon Rd W4 52 B5
Netheravon Rd S W4 66 B1
Netherby Rd SE23 88 A5

Netherfield Gdns,
Bark. 37 F3
Netherford Rd SW4 70 C5
Netherhall Gdns NW3 27 D3
Netherton Gro SW10 68 D2
Netherwood Rd W14 53 F4
Netherwood St NW6 26 A4
Netley St NW1 8 A2
Nettleton Rd SE14 74 B4
Nevada St SE10 75 G2
Nevern Pl SW5 54 B5
Nevern Rd SW5 54 B5
Nevern Sq SW5 54 B5
Neville Cl NW6 40 A1
Neville Cl SE15 73 F3
Neville Gill Cl SW18 83 B2
Neville Rd E7 35 D4
Neville Rd NW6 40 A1
Neville Ter SW7 69 E1
Nevill Rd N16 31 D1
Nevinson Cl SW18 83 E4
New Acres Rd SE28 65 G3
Newall Ho SE1 23 E5
Newark Knok E6 50 C5
Newark St E1 45 G4

New Barn St E13 49 D3
New Bond St W1 13 H2
New Br St EC4 16 B2
New Broad St EC2 11 H6
Newburgh St W1 14 A2
New Burlington Ms W1 14 A3
New Burlington Pl W1 14 A3
New Burlington St W1 14 A3
Newburn St SE11 71 F1
Newbury St EC1 10 D6
New Butt La SE8 75 E3
Newby Pl E14 61 G1
Newby St SW8 84 B1
New Caledonian Wf SE16 60 D4
Newcastle Cl EC4 16 B1
Newcastle Pl W2 6 A6
Newcastle Row EC1 10 A3
New Cavendish St W1 7 J5
New Change EC4 16 D2
New Charles St EC1 10 C1
New Ch Rd SE5 72 B3
New City Rd E13 49 F2
Newcomen Rd SW11 83 E1
Newcomen St SE1 23 F1
New Compton St WC2 14 D2
Newcourt St NW8 6 C3
New Covent Gdn Flower Mkt SW8 71 D2
New Covent Gdn Mkt SW8 70 D3
New Cross SE14 74 D3
New Cross Rd SE14 74 A3
Newell St E14 47 E5
New End NW3 27 D1
New End Sq NW3 27 E1
Newent Cl SE15 72 D3
New Ferry App SE18 64 C4
New Fetter La EC4 16 A1
Newgate St EC1 16 C1
New Globe Wk SE1 16 D5
Newhams Row SE1 23 J2
Newham Way E6 49 F4
Newham Way E16 48 C4
Newington Butts SE1 22 C6
Newington Butts SE11 22 C6
Newington Causeway SE1 22 C2
Newington Grn N1 30 C2
Newington Grn N16 30 C3
Newington Grn Rd N1 30 C3
New Inn Bdy EC2 11 J3
New Inn Pas WC2 15 H2
New Inn Sq EC2 11 J3
New Inn St EC2 11 J3
New Inn Yd EC2 11 J3
New Kent Rd SE1 22 D4
New Kings Rd SW6 68 A5
New King St SE8 75 E2
Newlands Cl SE9 92 C4
Newlands Quay E1 60 A1
Newland St E16 64 A2
New London St EC3 17 J3
New Lydenburg St SE7 63 F4
Newman Pas W1 8 B6
Newman Rd E13 49 E2
Newman's Ct EC3 17 G2
Newman's Row WC2 9 H6
Newman St W1 8 B6
Newman Yd W1 14 B1
New Mt St E15 34 A4
Newnham Ter SE1 21 J3
New N Pl EC2 11 H4
New N Rd N1 44 C1
New N St WC1 9 G5
New Oxford St WC1 14 D1
New Pk Ct SW2 85 E5
New Pl Sq SE16 59 G4
New Plaistow Rd E15 34 B5
Newport Av E13 49 E3

Newport Av E14 62 A1
Newport Ct WC2 14 D3
Newport Pl WC2 14 D3
Newport Rd SW13 66 C4
Newport St SE11 21 G6
New Providence Wf E14 62 A2
New Quebec St W1 13 E2
New Ride SW7 18 D1
New River Ct N5 30 C1
New River Head EC1 10 A1
New River Wk N1 30 B3
New Rd E1 45 G4
New Row WC2 14 E3
Newstead Rd SE12 90 B5
New St EC2 11 J6
New St Sq EC4 16 A1
Newton Gro W4 52 A5
Newton Pl E14 61 E5
Newton Rd E15 34 A2
Newton Rd W2 40 B5
Newton St WC2 15 F1
New Turnstile WC1 9 G6
New Union Cl E14 61 G4
New Union St EC2 11 F6
New Wf Rd N1 43 E1
New Zealand Way W12 52 D1
Nicholas La EC4 17 G3
Nicholas Pas EC4 17 G3
Nicholas Rd E1 46 A3
Nicholls Pt E15 34 D5
Nicholl St E2 31 F5
Nicholson St SE1 16 B6
Nicoll Rd NW10 24 A5
Nicosia Rd SW18 83 F5
Niger Ho E2 35 F2
Nigel Rd E7 87 F1
Nigel Rd SE15 87 F2
Nigeria Rd SE7 77 F3
Nightingale Gro SE13 90 A3
Nightingale La SW4 83 G5
Nightingale La SW12 83 G5
Nightingale Ms SE11 22 A6
Nightingale Pl SE18 78 B1
Nightingale Pl N1 30 B1
Nightingale Rd NW10 38 B1
Nightingale Sq SW12 84 A5
Nightingale Vale SE18 78 C2
Nightingale Wk SW4 84 B4
Nightingale Way E6 50 A4
Nile Rd E13 49 F1
Nile St N1 11 E1
Nile Ter SE15 73 E1
Nimegen Way SE22 86 D3
Nine Acres Cl E12 36 A2
Nine Elms La SW8 70 C3
Nithdale Rd SE18 78 D3
Niton St SW6 67 F3
No. 1 St SE18 65 D4
Noble St EC2 16 D1
Noel Rd E6 50 A3
Noel Rd N1 44 A1
Noel St W1 14 B2
Noko W10 39 F2
Nolan Way E5 31 F1
Norbiton Rd E14 47 D5
Norbroke St W12 52 B3
Norcroft Gdns SE22 87 F5
Norfolk Cres W2 12 C1
Norfolk Cres, Sid. 93 G5
Norfolk Ho SE3 76 B2
Norfolk Pl W2 12 A1
Norfolk Rd E6 36 B5
Norfolk Rd NW8 27 E5
Norfolk Rd, Bark. 37 G4
Norfolk Row SE1 21 G5
Norfolk Sq W2 12 A2
Norfolk Sq Ms W2 12 A2
Norfolk St E7 34 D1
Norgrove St SW12 84 A5

Norland Ho W11	53 F2	Northumberland Av,		Oaklands Est SW4	84 C4	Old Gloucester St WC1	9 F5
Norland Pl W11	53 G2	Well.	93 F2	Oaklands Gro W12	52 C2	Old Jamaica Rd SE16	59 F4
Norland Rd W11	53 F2	Northumberland Pl W2	40 B5	Oaklands Rd NW2	25 F1	Old James St SE15	87 G1
Norland Sq W11	53 G2	Northumberland Rd E6	50 A5	Oak La E14	60 D1	Old Jewry EC2	17 F2
Normanby Cl SW15	82 A3	Northumberland St		Oak La SE10	90 A4	Old Kent Rd SE1	23 G4
Normanby Rd NW10	24 B1		15 E5	Oakley Dr SE13	90 A4	Old Kent Rd SE15	58 D5
Normand Rd W14	68 A2	Northumbria St E14	47 E5	Oakley Gdns SW3	69 F2	Old Marylebone Rd	
Normandy Rd SW9	71 G4	Northview Cres NW10	24 B1	Oakley Pl SE1	73 E1	NW1	6 C6
Normandy Ter E16	49 E5	North Vil NW1	28 D3	Oakley Rd N1	30 C4	Old Mill Rd SE18	79 F2
Norman Gro E3	46 C1	Northway Rd SE5	86 B1	Oakley Sq NW1	42 C1	Old Mitre Ct EC4	16 A2
Norman Rd E6	50 B3	North Wf Rd W2	41 E4	Oakley St SW3	69 F2	Old Montague St E1	45 F4
Norman Rd SE10	75 F3	Northwick Ter NW8	41 E3	Oak Pk Gdns SW19	81 F5	Old Nichol St E2	45 E3
Norman Rd, Ilf.	37 D2	North Woolwich Rd		Oaks, The SE18	79 E1	Old N St WC1	9 G5
Norris St SW1	14 C4	E16	63 D2	Oakshaw Rd SW18	82 C5	Old Oak Common La	
Norroy Rd SW15	81 F2	North Woolwich Rbt		Oaktree Gro, Ilf.	37 F1	NW10	38 A4
Northampton Gro N1	30 C2	E16	63 F2	Oak Tree Rd NW8	6 A2	Old Oak Common La	
Northampton Pk N1	30 B2	Norton Folgate E1	11 J5	Oak Village NW5	28 A1	W3	38 A4
Northampton Rd EC1	10 A3	Norway Gate SE16	60 C4	Oak Way W3	52 A2	Old Oak La NW10	38 A2
Northampton Row EC1	10 A2	Norway St SE10	75 F2	Oakways SE9	92 D4	Old Oak Rd W3	52 B1
Northampton Sq EC1	10 B2	Norwich Rd E7	34 D2	Oakwood Cl SE13	90 A5	Old Palace Yd SW1	21 E3
Northampton St N1	30 B4	Norwich St EC4	15 J1	Oakwood Ct W14	54 A4	Old Paradise St SE11	21 G5
North Audley St W1	13 F2	Notley Pl SW4	85 E5	Oakwood La W14	54 A4	Old Pk Av SW12	84 A4
North Bk NW8	6 A2	Notley St SE5	72 C3	Oakworth Rd W10	39 E4	Old Pk La W1	13 G6
Northbourne Rd SW4	85 D2	Notre Dame Est SW4	84 C2	Oat La EC2	16 D1	Old Pearson St SE10	75 F3
Northbrook Rd SE13	90 A3	Notting Barn Rd W10	39 F3	Oban Cl E13	49 F3	Old PO La SE3	91 E1
Northburgh St EC1	10 C3	Nottingham Av E16	49 F4	Oban Rd E13	49 F3	Old Pye St SW1	20 C3
North Carriage Dr W2	12 B3	Nottingham Ct WC2	15 E2	Oban St E14	48 A5	Old Quebec St W1	13 E2
Northchurch Rd N1	30 C4	Nottingham Pl W1	7 F4	Oberstein Rd SW11	83 E2	Old Queen St SW1	20 D2
Northchurch Ter N1	30 D4	Nottingham St W1	7 F5	Oborne Cl SE24	85 G4	Oldridge Rd SW12	84 A5
North Circular Rd		Nottingham Ter NW1	7 F4	Observatory Gdns W8	54 B3	Old Rd SE13	90 B2
(A406) E6	51 D1	Notting Hill Gate W11	54 B2	Occupation La SE18	78 D4	Old Royal Free Sq N1	29 G5
North Circular Rd		Novello St SW6	68 B4	Occupation Rd SE17	72 B1	Old Sch Cl SE10	62 B4
(A406) E12	36 D2	Nowell Rd SW13	66 C2	Ocean Est E1	46 B3	Old Sch Cres E7	34 D3
North Circular Rd		Nuding Cl SE13	89 E1	Ocean St E1	46 B4	Old Seacoal La EC4	16 B1
(A406), Bark.	51 D1	Nugent Ter NW8	41 D1	Ocean Wf E14	61 D3	Old S Lambeth Rd SW8	71 E3
North Colonnade, The		Nun Ct EC2	17 F1	Ockendon Rd N1	30 C3	Old Spitalfields Mkt E1	45 E4
E14	61 E2	Nunhead Cres SE15	87 G1	Octagon Arc EC2	11 H1	Old Sq WC2	15 H1
Northcote Rd NW10	24 A4	Nunhead Est SE15	87 G2	Octavia St SW11	69 F4	Old St E13	49 E1
Northcote Rd SW11	83 F2	Nunhead Grn SE15	87 G1	Octavius St SE8	75 E3	Old St EC1	10 D3
North Cres E16	48 A3	Nunhead Gro SE15	87 G1	Odessa Rd NW10	38 C1	Old Town SW4	84 C1
North Cres WC1	8 C5	Nunhead La SE15	87 G1	Odessa St SE16	60 D3	Old Woolwich Rd SE10	76 A2
North Cross Rd SE22	87 E3	Nursery Cl SE4	74 D5	Odger St SW11	69 G5	Old York Rd SW18	82 C3
Northdown St N1	8 C1	Nursery Cl SW15	81 F2	Odhams Wk WC2	15 F2	O'Leary Sq E1	46 A4
North End Cres W14	54 A5	Nursery La E2	31 E5	Offenbach Ho E2	46 B1	Olga St E3	46 A4
North End Ho W14	53 G5	Nursery La E7	35 D3	Offerton Rd SW4	84 C1	Oliphant St W10	39 F2
North End Rd SW6	68 A2	Nursery La W10	39 E4	Offley Rd SW9	71 G3	Oliver Gdns E6	50 A5
North End Rd W14	53 G5	Nursery Rd SW9	85 F1	Offord Rd N1	29 F4	Oliver-Goldsmith Est	
Northern Relief Rd,		Nursery Row SE17	23 F6	Offord St N1	29 F4	SE15	73 F4
Bark.	37 D4	Nutbourne St W10	39 G2	Ogilby St SE18	64 B5	Oliver Ms SE15	73 F5
Northern Rd E13	35 E5	Nutbrook St SE15	87 F1	Oglander Rd SE15	87 E2	Oliver Rd E13	49 F2
North Eyot Gdns W6	66 C1	Nutcroft Rd SE15	73 G3	Ogle St W1	8 A5	Oliver Rd NW2	25 E1
Northey St E14	60 C1	Nutfield Rd E15	33 G1	Ohio Rd E13	48 C3	Olivers Yd EC1	11 G3
Northfield Rd E6	36 B4	Nutfield Rd SE22	87 E3	Oil Mill La W6	66 C1	Olivette St SW15	81 F1
Northfields SW18	82 B2	Nutford Pl W1	12 C1	Okehampton Rd		Ollerton Grn E3	33 D5
North Gower St NW1	8 B2	Nuthatch Gdns SE28	65 F3	NW10	25 E5	Ollgar Cl W12	52 B2
Northiam St E9	31 F4	Nutley Ter NW3	27 D3	Olaf St W11	53 F1	Olliffe St E14	61 G4
Northington St WC1	9 G4	Nutmeg La E14	48 A5	Old Bailey EC4	16 C2	Olmar St SE1	73 F2
Northlands St SE5	72 B5	Nutt St SE15	73 E3	Old Barrack Yd SW1	19 F1	Olney Rd SE17	72 A2
North Lo Cl SW15	81 F3	Nyanza St SE18	79 F2	Old Bellgate Pl E14	61 D4	Olven Rd SE18	79 E3
North Ms WC1	9 H4	Nynehead St SE14	74 C3	Old Bethnal Grn Rd E2	45 F2	Olympia Way W14	53 G4
Northolme Rd N5	30 B1			Old Bond St W1	14 A4	Oman Av NW2	25 E1
North Pk SE9	92 B4	**O**		Old Brewers Yd WC2	15 E2	O'Meara St SE1	16 E6
North Pas SW18	82 B2	Oakbank Gro SE24	86 B2	Old Broad St EC2	17 G2	Omega St SE14	75 E4
Northpoint Sq NW1	28 D3	Oakbury Rd SW6	68 C5	Old Brompton Rd SW5	68 B1	Omega Wks E3	33 E4
North Pole Rd W10	39 E4	Oak Cres E16	48 B4	Old Brompton Rd SW7	68 B1	Ommaney Rd SE14	74 B4
Northport St N1	30 C5	Oakcroft Rd SE13	76 A5	Old Bldgs WC2	15 J1	Ondine Rd SE15	87 E2
North Ride W2	12 B4	Oakdale Rd E7	35 E4	Old Burlington St W1	14 A3	Onega Gate SE16	60 C4
North Rd N7	29 E3	Oakdale Rd SE15	88 A1	Oldbury Pl W1	7 G5	One Hyde Pk SW1	18 D1
North Rd SE18	65 G5	Oakden St SE11	22 A5	Old Castle St E1	45 E4	One Tree Cl SE23	88 A4
North Row W1	13 E3	Oakey La SE1	21 J3	Old Cavendish St W1	13 H1	Ongar Rd SW6	68 B2
North Side Wandsworth		Oakfield Rd E6	36 A5	Old Ch Rd E1	46 B5	Onslow Cres SW7	18 A6
Common SW18	83 D3	Oakfield St SW10	68 D2	Old Ch St SW3	68 D2	Onslow Gdns SW7	69 E1
North St E13	49 D1	Oakford Rd NW5	28 C1	Old Compton St W1	14 C3	Onslow Sq SW7	18 A5
North St SW4	84 C1	Oak Gro NW2	25 G1	Old Ct Pl W8	54 C3	Onslow St EC1	10 A4
North St, Bark.	37 D3	Oakhill Av NW3	26 C1	Old Devonshire Rd		Ontario St SE1	22 C4
North St Pas E13	49 E1	Oak Hill Pk NW3	26 C1	SW12	84 B5	Ontario Twr E14	62 A1
North Tenter St E1	45 E5	Oak Hill Pk Ms NW3	26 D1	Old Dover Rd SE3	77 D3	Ontario Way E14	61 E1
North Ter SW3	18 B4	Oakhill Rd SW15	82 A3	Oldfield Gro SE16	60 B5	Opal Cl E16	49 G5
Northumberland All		Oak Hill Way NW3	26 D1	Oldfield Rd NW10	24 B4	Opal St SE11	22 B6
EC3	17 J2	Oakhurst Gro SE22	87 F2	Old Fish St Hill EC4	16 D3	Ophir Ter SE15	73 F4
Northumberland Av		Oakington Rd W9	40 B3	Old Fleet La EC4	16 B1	Oppenheim Rd SE13	75 G5
WC2	14 E5	Oakland Rd E15	34 A1	Old Ford Rd E2	46 A1	Oppidans Rd NW3	27 G4
				Old Ford Rd E3	46 C1	Orangery La SE9	92 B3

Orange Sq SW1	19 G6
Orange St W2	14 C4
Orange Yd W1	14 D2
Oransay Rd N1	30 B3
Orbain Rd SW6	67 G3
Orbel St SW11	69 F4
Orbis Wf SW11	83 D1
Orb St SE17	23 F6
Orchard, The SE3	76 A5
Orchard Cl N1	30 B4
Orchard Cl W10	39 G4
Orchard Gro E5	31 G2
Orchard Pl E1	62 B1
Orchard Ri W, Sid.	93 G3
Orchard Rd N6	28 B2
Orchard Rd SE18	79 G1
Orchardson St NW8	41 E3
Orchard St W1	13 F2
Orchid Cl E6	50 A4
Orchid Cl SE13	90 A3
Orchid St W12	52 C1
Orde Hall St W1	15 H1
Ordell Rd E3	47 D1
Ordnance Cres SE10	62 A3
Ordnance Hill NW8	27 E5
Ordnance Rd E16	48 C4
Ordnance Rd SE18	78 C2
Oregano Dr E14	48 A5
Oregon Av E12	36 B1
Oriel Dr SW13	67 D2
Oriel Rd E9	32 B3
Oriens Ms E20	33 G3
Oriental Rd E16	63 G2
Orient St SE11	22 B5
Orissa Rd SE18	79 G1
Orkney St SW11	70 A5
Orlando Rd SW4	84 C1
Orleston Ms N7	29 G3
Orleston Rd N7	29 G3
Orlop St SE10	76 B1
Orme Ct W2	54 C1
Orme La W2	54 C1
Ormiston Gro W12	52 D2
Ormiston Rd SE10	76 D1
Ormond Cl WC1	9 F5
Ormonde Gate SW3	69 F6
Ormonde Pl SW1	19 F6
Ormonde Ter NW8	27 G5
Ormond Ms WC1	9 F4
Ormond Yd SW1	14 B5
Ormsby St E2	45 E1
Ormside St SE15	74 A2
Ornan Rd NW3	27 F2
Orpheus St SE5	72 C4
Orsett St SE11	71 F1
Orsett Ter W2	40 D5
Orsman Rd N1	30 D5
Orville Rd SW11	69 E5
Orwell Cl N5	30 B1
Orwell Rd E13	48 E2
Osberton Rd SE12	90 D3
Osbert St SW1	20 C6
Osborn Cl E8	31 F5
Osborne Rd E7	35 E2
Osborne Rd E9	33 D3
Osborne Rd NW2	24 D3
Osborne La SE23	88 C5
Osborn St E1	45 E4
Oscar St SE8	75 E4
Oseney Cres NW5	28 C3
Osier La SE10	62 C4
Osier Ms W4	66 B2
Osiers Rd SW18	82 B2
Osier St E1	46 A3
Oslo Sq SE16	60 C4
Osnaburgh St NW1	7 J4
Osnaburgh St (north section) NW1	7 J2
Osnaburgh Ter NW1	7 J3
Ospringe Ct SE9	93 F4
Ospringe Rd NW5	28 C1
Osric Path N1	44 D1
Ossington Bldgs W1	7 F5
Ossington St W2	54 B1
Ossory Rd SE1	73 F1
Ossulston St NW1	43 D2
Ostade Rd SW2	85 F5
Osterley Rd N16	30 D1
Oswald St E5	59 G2
Oswell Ho E1	59 G1
Oswin St SE11	22 C5
Oswyth Rd SE5	73 D5
Otford Cres SE4	88 D4
Otis St E3	47 G2
Otley Rd E16	49 F5
Otterburn Ho SE5	72 B3
Otter Cl E15	33 G5
Otto St SE17	72 A2
Outer Circle NW1	7 F4
Outgate Rd NW10	24 B4
Outram Pl N1	29 E5
Outram Rd E6	36 A5
Outwich St EC3	17 J1
Oval, The E2	45 G1
Oval Pl SW8	71 F3
Oval Rd NW1	28 B5
Oval Way SE11	71 F1
Overbury St E5	32 B1
Overcliff Rd SE13	89 E1
Overhill Rd SE22	87 F5
Overmead, Sid.	93 F5
Oversley Ho W2	40 B4
Overstone Rd W6	53 E4
Overton Rd SW9	71 G5
Ovex Cl E14	61 G2
Ovington Gdns SW3	18 C4
Ovington Ms SW3	18 C4
Ovington Sq SW3	18 C4
Ovington St SW3	18 C4
Owen's Row EC1	10 B1
Owens Way SE23	88 C5
Oxberry Av SW6	67 G5
Oxendon St SW1	14 C4
Oxenford St SE15	87 E1
Oxenholme NW1	42 C1
Oxestalls Rd SE8	74 C1
Oxford Circ Av W1	14 A2
Oxford Ct EC4	17 F3
Oxford Dr SE1	17 H6
Oxford Gdns W10	39 G5
Oxford Gate W6	53 F5
Oxford Rd E15	34 A3
Oxford Rd NW6	40 B1
Oxford Rd SW15	81 G2
Oxford Rd, Ilf.	37 E1
Oxford Sq W2	12 C2
Oxford St W1	14 B1
Oxleas E6	50 D5
Oxleas Cl, Well.	79 F5
Oxley Cl SE1	73 E1
Oxonian St SE22	87 E2
Oxo Twr Wf SE1	16 A4
Oyster Wf SW11	69 E5
Ozolins Way E16	48 D5

P

Pacific Rd E16	48 D5
Packington Sq N1	30 B5
Packington St N1	30 A5
Packmores Rd SE9	93 F3
Padbury SE17	72 D1
Padbury Ct E2	45 F2
Paddenswick Rd W6	52 C4
Paddington Grn W2	6 A5
Paddington St W2	41 D5
Paddington St W1	7 F5
Paddington Underground Sta W2	41 D5
Paddock Cl SE3	77 D5
Paddock Way SW15	81 E5
Padfield Rd SE5	86 B1
Padfield Rd SW9	86 B1
Pagden St SW8	70 B4
Pageantmaster Ct EC4	16 B2
Page St SW1	20 D5
Pages Wk SE1	23 H5
Paget Ri SE18	78 C3
Paget Rd, Ilf.	36 D1
Paget St EC1	10 B1
Paget Ter SE18	78 C2
Pagnell St SE14	74 D3
Pagoda Gdns SE3	76 A5
Pakenham St WC1	9 H2
Palace Av W8	54 C2
Palace Ct NW3	26 C2
Palace Ct W2	54 B1
Palace Gdns Ms W8	54 B2
Palace Gdns Ter W8	54 B2
Palace Gate W8	54 D3
Palace Grn W8	54 C3
Palace Ms SW1	19 G6
Palace Pl SW1	20 A3
Palace Rd SE19	20 A3
Palace St SW1	31 D1
Palatine Rd N16	31 D1
Palemead Cl SW6	67 E4
Palermo Rd NW10	38 C1
Palfrey Pl SW8	71 F3
Palgrave Gdns NW1	6 C3
Palgrave Ho NW3	27 G2
Palgrave Rd W12	52 B4
Pallet Way SE18	78 A4
Palliser Rd W14	67 G1
Pall Mall SW1	14 B6
Pall Mall E SW1	14 D5
Pall Mall S SW1	14 C5
Palmer Pl N7	29 G2
Palmer Rd E13	49 E3
Palmers Rd E2	46 B1
Palmerston Cres SE18	79 E2
Palmerston Rd E7	35 E2
Palmerston Rd N22	26 B4
Palmer St SW1	20 C2
Pancras La EC4	17 E2
Pancras Rd NW1	42 D1
Pancras Rd NW1	43 E1
Pancras Way E3	47 E1
Pandora Rd NW6	26 B3
Pangbourne Av W10	39 E2
Pangbourne Ho N7	29 E2
Panmure Cl N5	30 A1
Pansy Gdns W12	52 C1
Panton St SW1	14 C4
Panyer All EC4	16 D2
Papillons Wk SE3	76 D5
Papworth Way SW2	85 G5
Parade, The SW11	69 G3
Paradise Pas N7	29 G2
Paradise St SE16	59 G3
Paradise Wk SW3	69 G2
Paragon, The SE3	76 C5
Paragon Cl E16	48 D5
Paragon Ms SE1	23 G5
Paragon Pl SE3	76 C5
Paragon Rd E9	32 A3
Parbury Rd SE23	88 C4
Pardoner St SE1	23 F4
Pardon St EC1	10 C3
Parfett St E1	45 F4
Parfrey St W6	67 E2
Paris Gdn SE1	16 B5
Park Av E6	36 C5
Park Av E15	34 B3
Park Av NW2	25 D3
Park Av NW11	37 E3
Park Av, Bark.	37 D2
Park Av N NW10	25 D2
Park Cl E9	32 A4
Park Cl SW1	18 D2
Park Cl W4	66 A4
Park Cres W1	7 H4
Park Cres Ms E W1	7 J4
Park Cres Ms W W1	7 H5
Parkcroft Rd SE12	90 C5
Parkdale Rd SE18	79 G1
Park Dr SE7	78 A2
Park Dr SW14	81 A1
Parker Cl E16	64 A2
Parker Ms WC2	15 F1
Parke Rd SW13	66 C4
Parker St E16	64 A2
Parker St WC2	15 F1
Parkfield Av SW14	80 A2
Parkfield Rd NW10	24 C4
Parkfield Rd SE14	74 D4
Parkfield Rd SW4	85 D4
Parkfields SW15	81 E2
Parkgate SE3	90 C1
Parkgate Rd SW11	69 F3
Park Gro E15	34 D5
Parkham St SW11	69 F4
Park Hill SW4	85 D3
Parkhill Rd NW3	27 G2
Parkhill Wk NW3	27 G2
Parkholme Rd E8	31 E3
Park La E15	72 C3
Parkhurst Rd E12	36 C1
Parkhurst Rd N7	29 E1
Park La W1	13 G6
Parkmead SW15	80 D4
Park Par NW10	38 B1
Park Pl E14	61 E2
Park Pl N1	30 C5
Park Pl SW1	14 A6
Park Pl Vil W2	41 D4
Park Rd E6	35 F5
Park Rd E15	34 D5
Park Rd NW1	6 B1
Park Rd NW8	6 B1
Park Rd NW10	24 A5
Park Row SE10	76 A2
Parkside SE3	76 C3
Parkside Rd SW11	70 A4
Parkside Wk SE10	76 B1
Park Sq E NW1	7 H3
Park Sq Ms NW1	7 H4
Park Sq W NW1	7 H3
Parkstead Rd SW15	80 C5
Park St SE1	16 D5
Park St W1	13 F3
Parkthorne Rd SW12	84 D5
Park Vw Est E2	46 A1
Park Vw Ms SW9	71 F5
Park Vw Rd NW10	24 B1
Park Village E NW1	42 B1
Park Village W NW1	42 B1
Parkville Rd SW6	68 A3
Park Vista SE10	76 B2
Park Wk SW10	69 D2
Parkway NW1	28 B5
Park W W2	12 C2
Park W Pl W2	12 C1
Parliament Ct E1	11 J6
Parliament Hill NW3	27 F1
Parliament Sq SW1	20 E2
Parliament St SW1	21 E2
Parliament Vw Apts SE1	21 G5
Parma Cres SW11	83 G2
Parmiter St E2	45 G1
Parmoor Ct EC1	10 D3
Parnell Cl W12	52 D4
Parnell Rd E3	33 D5
Parr Rd E6	35 G5
Parr St N1	44 C1
Parry Av E6	50 B5
Parry Pl SE18	65 D5
Parry Rd W10	39 G2
Parry St SW8	71 E2
Parsifal Rd NW6	26 B2
Parsonage St E14	61 G5
Parsons Grn SW6	68 B4
Parsons Grn La SW6	68 B4
Parson's Ho W2	41 E3
Parthenia Rd SW6	68 B4
Parvin St SW8	70 D4
Pascal St SW8	71 D3
Pascoe Rd SE13	90 A3
Passey Pl SE9	92 B4
Passing All EC1	10 C4
Passmore St SW1	19 F6
Paston Cres SE12	91 E5
Pastor St SE11	22 C5

Patcham Ter SW8	70 B4
Paternoster Row EC4	16 D2
Paternoster Sq EC4	16 C2
Pater St W8	54 B4
Patience Rd SW11	69 F5
Patio Cl SW4	84 D4
Patmore Est SW8	70 C4
Patmore St SW8	70 C4
Patmos Rd SW9	72 A3
Paton Cl E3	47 E2
Paton St EC1	10 D2
Patrick Rd E13	49 F2
Patriot Sq E2	45 G1
Patrol Pl SE6	89 F4
Patshull Rd NW5	28 C3
Patten Rd SW18	83 F5
Patterdale Rd SE15	74 A3
Pattina Wk SE15	60 D2
Pattison Wk SE18	79 E1
Paul Cl E15	34 B4
Paulet Rd SE5	72 A5
Paulet Way NW10	24 A4
Pauline Ho E1	45 F4
Paul Julius Cl E14	62 A1
Paul Robeson Cl E6	50 C2
Paul St E15	34 A5
Paul St EC2	11 G4
Paul's Wk EC4	16 C3
Paultons Sq SW3	69 E2
Paultons St SW3	69 E2
Paveley Dr SW11	69 F3
Paveley St NW8	6 C3
Pavement, The SW4	84 C2
Pavilion Rd SW1	18 E4
Pavilion St SW1	18 E4
Paxton Rd W4	66 A2
Paxton Ter SW1	70 B2
Payne Cl, Bark.	37 G4
Payne Rd E3	47 F1
Payne St SE8	75 D2
Paynes Wk W6	67 G2
Peabody Dws WC1	8 E3
Peabody Est (St. Luke's) EC1	10 E4
Peabody Est E2	46 A2
Peabody Est SE17	23 F6
Peabody Est SE24	86 A5
Peabody Est SW1	20 A5
Peabody Est W10	39 E4
Peabody Hill Est SE21	86 A5
Peabody Sq SE1	22 B2
Peabody Trust SE1	16 D6
Peach Rd W10	39 F2
Peachum Rd SE3	76 C2
Peacock St SE17	22 C6
Peacock Wk E16	49 E5
Peacock Yd SE17	22 C6
Peardon St SW8	84 B1
Pearl Cl E6	50 C5
Pearman St SE1	22 A3
Pear Pl SE1	21 J1
Pearscroft Ct SW6	68 C4
Pearscroft Rd SW6	68 C4
Pearson Ms SW4	85 D1
Pearson St E2	45 D1
Pear Tree Cl E2	31 E5
Pear Tree Cl EC1	10 A4
Pear Tree St EC1	10 C3
Peartree Way SE10	62 D5
Peckford Pl SW9	71 G5
Peckham Gro SE15	73 D3
Peckham High St SE15	73 F4
Peckham Hill St SE15	73 F3
Peckham Pk Rd SE15	73 F3
Peckham Rd SE5	72 D4
Peckham Rd SE15	72 D4
Peckham Rye SE15	87 F1
Peckham Rye SE22	87 F3
Peckwater St NW5	28 C2
Pedlars Wk N7	29 E3
Pedley St E1	45 E3
Peel Gro E2	46 A1
Peel Prec NW6	40 B1
Peel Rd NW6	40 A2
Peel St W8	54 A3
Peerless St EC1	11 F2
Pegwell St SE18	79 G3
Pekin St E14	47 E5
Pelham Cl SE5	73 D5
Pelham Cres SW7	18 B6
Pelham Pl SW7	18 B6
Pelham St SW7	18 A5
Pelican Est SE15	73 E4
Pellant Rd SW6	67 G3
Pellatt Rd SE22	87 E3
Pellerin Rd N16	31 D2
Pelling St E14	47 E5
Pellipar Gdns SE18	78 B1
Pelly Rd E13	49 D1
Pelter St E2	45 E2
Pelton Rd SE10	76 B1
Pember Rd NW10	39 F2
Pemberton Row EC4	16 A1
Pembridge Cres W11	54 B1
Pembridge Gdns W2	54 B1
Pembridge Ms W11	54 B1
Pembridge Pl SW15	82 B3
Pembridge Pl W2	54 B1
Pembridge Rd W11	54 B1
Pembridge Sq W2	54 B1
Pembridge Vil W11	54 B1
Pembridge Vil W2	54 B1
Pembroke Av N1	29 E5
Pembroke Cl SW1	19 G2
Pembroke Gdns W8	54 A5
Pembroke Gdns Cl W8	54 B4
Pembroke Pl W8	54 B4
Pembroke Rd E6	50 B4
Pembroke Rd W8	54 B4
Pembroke Sq W8	54 B4
Pembroke St N1	29 E4
Pembroke Studios W8	54 A4
Pembroke Vil W8	54 B5
Pembroke Wk W8	54 B5
Pembry Cl SW9	71 G4
Pembury Pl E5	31 G2
Pembury Rd E5	31 G2
Penang St E1	59 G2
Penarth St SE15	74 A2
Pencraig Way SE15	73 G2
Penderyn Way N7	29 D1
Pendrell Rd SE4	74 C5
Pendrell St SE18	79 F3
Penfold Pl NW1	6 A5
Penfold Rd NW1	6 A4
Penfold St NW8	6 A4
Penford Gdns SE9	91 G1
Penford St SE5	72 A5
Penge Rd E13	35 F4
Penhall Rd SE7	63 G5
Peninsula Hts SE1	71 E1
Peninsular Pk Rd SE7	63 D5
Pennack Rd SE15	73 E2
Pennant Ms W8	54 C5
Pennard Rd W12	53 E3
Pennethorne Rd SE15	73 G3
Pennington St E1	59 F1
Penn Rd N7	29 E2
Penn St N1	30 C5
Penny Brookes St E20	33 G5
Pennyfields E14	61 E1
Penny Ms SW12	84 B5
Pennyroyal Av E6	50 C5
Penpoll Rd E8	31 G3
Penrith Cl SW15	81 G3
Penrose Gro SE17	72 B1
Penrose Ho SE17	72 B1
Penrose St SE17	72 B1
Penryn St NW1	42 D1
Penry St SE1	23 J6
Pensbury Pl SW8	70 D5
Pensbury St SW8	70 C5
Penshurst Rd E9	32 B4
Pentland Rd NW6	40 B2
Pentland St SW18	82 D4
Pentlow St SW15	81 E1
Penton Gro N1	72 A1
Penton Ri WC1	9 H1
Penton St N1	43 G1
Pentonville Rd N1	43 F1
Pentridge St SE15	73 E3
Penywern Rd SW5	68 B1
Penzance Pl W11	53 G2
Penzance St W11	53 G2
Peony Gdns W12	52 C1
Peploe Rd NW6	39 F1
Pepler Ms SE1	50 B4
Peppermead Sq SE13	89 E3
Pepper St E14	61 F4
Pepys Rd SE14	74 B4
Pepys St EC3	17 J3
Perceval Av NW3	27 F2
Perch St E8	31 E1
Percival St EC1	10 B3
Percy Circ WC1	9 H1
Percy Ms W1	8 C6
Percy Pas W1	8 B6
Percy Rd E16	48 B4
Percy Rd W12	52 D3
Percy St W1	8 C6
Percy Yd WC1	9 H1
Peregrine Ho EC1	10 C1
Perham Rd W14	67 G1
Peridot St E6	50 A4
Perkin's Rents SW1	20 C3
Perkins Sq SE1	16 E5
Perpins Rd SE9	93 G4
Perran Rd SE23	88 D2
Perrins La NW3	27 D1
Perrin's Wk NW3	27 D1
Perrott St SE18	65 E5
Perryman Ho, Bark.	37 E5
Perrymead St SW6	68 B4
Perrys Pl W1	14 C1
Perseverance Pl SW9	71 G3
Perth Rd E13	49 E1
Perth Rd, Bark.	51 F1
Peter Av NW10	24 D4
Peterborough Ms SW6	68 B5
Peterborough Rd SW6	68 B5
Peterborough Vil SW6	68 C4
Petergate SW11	83 D2
Peters Cl, Well.	79 G5
Petersham La SW7	54 D4
Petersham Ms SW7	54 D4
Petersham Pl SW7	55 D4
Peters Hill EC4	16 D3
Peter's La EC1	10 C5
Peter St W1	14 B3
Petherton Rd N5	30 B2
Petley Rd W6	67 E4
Peto Pl NW1	7 J3
Petrie Cl NW2	25 G3
Pettacre Cl SE28	65 E4
Petticoat La E1	11 J6
Petticoat Sq E1	45 D5
Pettiward Cl SW15	81 E2
Pettman Cres SE28	65 F4
Pett St SE18	64 A5
Petty France SW1	20 B3
Petty Wales EC3	17 J4
Petworth St SW11	69 F4
Petyward SW3	18 C6
Pevensey Rd E7	34 C1
Peyton Pl SE10	75 G3
Phelp St SE17	72 C2
Phene St SW3	69 F2
Pheonix Cl W12	52 D1
Philbeach Gdns SW5	68 B1
Philimore Cl SE18	79 G1
Philip Path SE9	92 B4
Philip St E13	48 D3
Philip Wk SE15	87 F1
Phillimore Gdns NW10	25 E5
Phillimore Gdns W8	54 B3
Phillimore Pl W8	54 B3
Phillimore Wk W8	54 B3
Phillipp St N1	30 D5
Philpot La EC3	17 H3
Philpot St E1	45 G5
Phineas Pett Rd SE9	92 A1
Phipp's Ms SW1	19 J4
Phipp St EC2	11 H3
Phoebeth Rd SE4	89 E3
Phoenix Pl WC1	9 H3
Phoenix Rd NW1	8 C1
Phoenix St WC2	14 D2
Phoenix Wf SE10	62 C3
Phoenix Yd WC1	9 H3
Piccadilly W1	13 J6
Piccadilly Arc SW1	14 A5
Piccadilly Circ W1	14 C4
Piccadilly Pl W1	14 B4
Pickard St EC1	10 C1
Pickering Av E6	50 C1
Pickering Pl SW1	14 B6
Pickering Rd, Bark.	37 E3
Pickets St SW12	84 B5
Pickfords Wf N1	44 B1
Pickwick Rd SE21	86 C5
Pickwick St SE1	22 D2
Picton Pl W1	13 G2
Picton St SE5	72 C3
Piedmont Rd SE18	79 F1
Piermont Grn SE22	87 G3
Piermont Rd SE22	87 G3
Pier Rd E16	64 C3
Pier St E14	61 G5
Pier Way SE28	65 F4
Pigott St E14	47 E5
Pilgrimage St SE1	23 F3
Pilgrims Cl SE3	77 D4
Pilgrim's La NW3	27 E1
Pilgrim St EC4	16 B2
Pilkington Rd SE15	73 G5
Pilot Busway SE10	62 B3
Pilot Cl SE8	74 D2
Pilton St SE17	72 B1
Pimlico Rd SW1	70 A1
Pimlico Wk N1	11 H1
Pinchin St E1	59 F1
Pincott Rd SE4	88 B2
Pindar St EC2	11 H5
Pineapple Ct SW1	20 A3
Pine Av E15	34 A2
Pinefield Cl E14	61 E1
Pine Rd NW2	25 E1
Pine St EC1	9 J3
Pinnell Rd SE9	91 G2
Pinto Way SE3	91 E2
Pioneer St SE15	73 F4
Piper Cl N7	29 F3
Pirie St E16	64 B2
Pitchford St E15	34 A4
Pitfield Est N1	11 G1
Pitfield St N1	11 H2
Pitlochry Cl SE12	90 D4
Pitman St SE5	72 B3
Pitsea St E1	46 B5
Pittman Gdns, Ilf.	37 E2
Pitt's Head Ms W1	13 G6
Pitt St W8	54 B3
Pixley St E14	47 D5
Plaistow Gro E15	34 C5
Plaistow Pk Rd E13	49 E1
Plaistow Rd E13	34 C5
Plaistow Rd E15	34 C5
Plantain Pl SE1	23 F1
Plantation, The SE3	77 D5
Plantation Wf SW11	83 D1
Plashet Gro E6	35 F5
Plashet Rd E13	35 D5
Plassy Rd SE6	89 F6
Platina St EC2	11 G3
Plato Rd SW2	85 E2
Platt, The SW15	81 F1
Platt's La NW3	26 B1

Platt St NW1 42 D1
Playfield Cres SE22 87 E3
Playhouse Yd EC4 16 B2
Plaza Shop Cen, The W1 14 B1
Pleasance, The SW15 80 D2
Pleasance Rd SW15 80 D3
Pleasant Pl N1 30 A4
Pleasant Row NW1 28 B5
Plender St NW1 28 C5
Pleshey Rd N7 28 D1
Plevna St E14 61 G4
Pleydell Av W6 52 B5
Pleydell Ct EC4 16 A2
Pleydell St EC4 16 A2
Plough Cl NW10 39 D2
Plough Ct EC3 17 G3
Plough La SE22 87 E4
Plough Pl EC4 16 A1
Plough Rd SW11 83 E1
Plough Ter SW11 83 E2
Plough Way SE16 60 B5
Plough Yd EC2 11 J4
Plover Way SE16 60 C4
Plumbers Row E1 45 F4
Plum La SE18 79 D3
Plummer Rd SW4 84 D5
Plumstead Common Rd SE18 78 D2
Plumstead High St SE18 65 G5
Plumstead Rd SE18 65 G5
Plumtree Ct EC4 16 A1
Plymouth Rd E16 48 D4
Plymouth Wf E14 62 A5
Plympton Av NW6 26 A4
Plympton Pl NW8 6 B4
Plympton Rd NW6 26 A4
Plympton St NW8 6 B4
Pocock St SE1 22 B1
Podmore Rd SW18 82 D2
Poets Rd N5 30 C2
Pointers Cl E14 75 F1
Point Hill SE10 75 G3
Point Pleasant SW18 82 B2
Poland Ho E15 34 A5
Poland St W1 14 A2
Polebrook Rd SE3 91 F1
Polesworth Ho W2 40 B4
Pollard Cl E16 62 D1
Pollard Cl N7 29 F2
Pollard Row E2 45 F2
Pollard St E2 45 F2
Pollen St W1 13 J2
Polperro Ms SE11 22 A5
Polsted Rd SE6 89 D5
Polthorne Est SE18 65 E5
Polthorne Gro SE18 65 E5
Polygon Rd NW1 42 D1
Polytechnic St SE18 64 C5
Pomeroy St SE14 74 A4
Pond Cl SE3 76 C5
Ponder St N7 29 F4
Pond Mead SE21 86 C4
Pond Pl SW3 18 B6
Pond Rd E15 48 B1
Pond Rd SE3 76 C5
Pond St NW3 27 F2
Ponler St E1 45 G5
Ponsard Rd NW10 38 D2
Ponsford St E9 32 A3
Ponsonby Pl SW1 71 D1
Ponsonby Rd SW15 80 D5
Ponsonby Ter SW1 71 D1
Ponton Rd SW8 71 D2
Pont St SW1 18 D4
Pont St Ms SW1 18 D4
Pontypool Pl SE1 22 B1
Poole Rd E9 32 B3
Pooles Bldgs EC1 9 J4
Poole St N1 30 C5
Poolmans St SE16 60 B3
Popes Rd SW9 85 G1

Pope St SE1 23 J2
Popham Rd N1 30 B5
Popham St N1 30 A5
Poplar Business Pk E14 61 G1
Poplar Gro W6 53 E3
Poplar High St E14 61 E1
Poplar Pl W2 54 C1
Poplar Rd SE24 86 B2
Poplar Wk SE24 86 B2
Poplars Av NW10 25 E3
Poppins Ct EC4 16 B2
Porchester Cl SE5 86 B2
Porchester Gdns W2 54 C1
Porchester Ms W2 40 C5
Porchester Pl W2 12 C2
Porchester Rd W2 40 C4
Porchester Sq W2 40 C5
Porchester Sq Ms W2 40 C5
Porchester Ter W2 54 D1
Porchester Ter N W2 40 C5
Porden Rd SW2 85 F2
Porlock St SE1 23 F1
Portelet Rd E1 46 B3
Porten Rd W14 53 G4
Porter Rd E6 50 B5
Porter St SE1 16 E5
Porter St W1 7 E5
Porteus Rd W2 41 D4
Portgate Cl W9 40 A3
Portia Way E3 46 D3
Portinscale Rd SW15 81 G3
Portland Gro SW8 71 F4
Portland Ms W1 14 B2
Portland Pl W1 7 H6
Portland Rd W11 53 G1
Portland St SE17 72 C1
Portman Cl W1 13 E1
Portman Gate NW1 6 C4
Portman Ms S W1 13 F2
Portman Pl E2 46 A2
Portman Sq W1 13 E1
Portman St W1 13 F2
Portnall Rd W9 40 A1
Portobello Rd W10 40 A5
Portobello Rd W11 40 A5
Portpool La EC1 9 J5
Portree St E14 48 A5
Portsea Ms W2 12 C2
Portsea Pl W2 12 C2
Portslade Rd SW8 70 C5
Portsmouth Rd SW15 81 D5
Portsmouth St WC2 15 G2
Portsoken St E1 59 E1
Portugal St WC2 15 G2
Portway E15 34 C5
Post Office App E7 35 E2
Post Office Ct EC3 17 G2
Post Office Way SW8 70 D3
Potier St SE1 23 G4
Potterne Cl SW19 81 F5
Potters Flds SE1 17 J6
Potters Rd SW6 68 D5
Pottery St SE16 59 G3
Pott St E2 45 G2
Poulett Rd E6 50 B1
Poultry EC2 17 F2
Pound La NW10 24 C3
Pound Pk Rd SE7 63 G5
Pound Pl SE9 92 C4
Pountney Rd SW11 84 A1
Powell's Wk W4 66 A2
Powerscroft Rd E5 32 A1
Powis Gdns W11 40 A5
Powis Pl WC1 9 F4
Powis Rd E3 47 F2
Powis Sq W11 40 A5
Powis St SE18 64 C4
Powis Ter W11 40 A5
Pownall Rd E8 31 E5
Poynders Gdns SW4 84 C5
Poynders Rd SW4 84 C4
Poynter Ho W11 53 F2

Poyntz Rd SW11 69 G5
Poyser St E2 45 G1
Praed Ms W2 12 A1
Praed St W2 6 B6
Pragel St E13 49 E1
Prague Pl SW2 85 E3
Prairie St SW8 70 A5
Pratt St NW1 28 C5
Pratt Wk SE11 21 H5
Prebend Gdns W4 52 B4
Prebend Gdns W6 52 B4
Prebend St N1 30 B5
Prendergast Rd SE3 90 B1
Prentiss Ct SE7 63 G5
Prescot St E1 59 E1
Prescott Pl SW4 84 D1
President St EC1 10 D1
Prestage Way E14 61 G1
Prestbury Rd E7 35 F4
Preston Cl SE1 23 H5
Preston Pl NW2 24 C3
Prestons Rd E14 61 G3
Pretoria Rd E16 48 C1
Pretoria Rd, Ilf. 36 D2
Price's Cl SW11 83 E1
Prices Ms N1 29 F5
Price's St SE1 16 C6
Prideaux Pl WC1 9 H1
Prideaux Rd SW9 85 E1
Priest Ct EC2 16 D1
Priests Br SW14 80 A2
Priests Br SW15 80 A2
Prima Rd SW9 71 G3
Primrose Cl E3 47 E1
Primrose Gdns NW3 27 F3
Primrose Hill EC4 16 A2
Primrose Hill Ct NW3 27 G4
Primrose Hill Rd NW3 27 F4
Primrose Ms SE3 77 E3
Primrose Sq E9 32 A4
Primrose St EC2 11 H5
Primula St W12 38 C5
Prince Albert Rd NW1 41 F1
Prince Albert Rd NW8 41 F1
Prince Arthur Rd NW3 27 D2
Prince Charles Rd SE3 76 C4
Prince Consort Rd SW7 55 D4
Princedale Rd W11 53 G2
Prince Edward Rd E9 33 D3
Prince George Rd N16 30 D5
Prince Henry Rd SE7 77 G3
Prince Imperial Rd SE18 78 B4
Prince John Rd SE9 92 A3
Princelet St E1 45 E4
Prince of Wales Dr SW8 70 B3
Prince of Wales Rd SW11 69 G4
Prince of Wales Gate SW7 18 B1
Prince of Wales Pas NW1 8 A2
Prince of Wales Rd NW5 28 A3
Prince of Wales Rd SE3 76 C4
Prince of Wales Ter W4 66 A1
Prince Regent La E13 49 F4
Prince Regent La E16 49 F4
Prince Regent Ms NW1 8 A2
Prince Rupert Rd SE9 92 B2
Prince's Arc SW1 14 B5
Princes Cl SE16 60 D4
Princes Ct Business Cen E1 59 G1
Princes Gdns SW7 18 A3
Princes Gate SW7 18 A2
Princes Gate Ms SW7 18 A2
Princes Gate Ms SW7 18 A3
Princes Pl SW1 14 B5
Princes Pl W11 53 G2
Princes Ri SE13 75 G5

Princes Riverside Rd SE16 60 B2
Princess Alice Way SE28 65 F3
Princess Louise Cl W2 6 A5
Princess May Rd N16 31 D1
Princes Sq W2 54 C1
Princess Rd NW1 28 A5
Princess Rd NW6 40 B1
Princess St SE1 22 C4
Princes St EC2 17 F1
Princes St W1 13 J2
Princes Way E13 35 E5
Princes Way SW19 81 F5
Princethorpe Ho W2 40 B4
Princeton St WC1 9 G5
Printers Inn Ct EC4 15 J1
Printers Ms E3 32 C5
Printers Rd SW9 71 F4
Printer St EC4 16 A1
Printing Ho Yd E2 11 J1
Priolo Rd SE7 77 F1
Prior Bolton St N1 30 A3
Prioress St SE1 23 G4
Prior St SE10 75 G3
Priory, The SE3 90 C2
Priory Av W4 52 A5
Priory Ct EC4 16 C2
Priory Ct SW8 71 D4
Priory Gdns SW13 80 B1
Priory Gdns W4 52 A5
Priory Grn Est N1 43 F1
Priory Gro SW8 71 F4
Priory La SW15 80 A4
Priory Ms SW8 71 D4
Priory Pk SE3 90 C1
Priory Pk Rd NW6 26 A5
Priory Rd E6 35 G5
Priory Rd N8 26 C5
Priory Rd, Bark. 37 F4
Priory St E3 47 F2
Priory Ter NW6 26 C5
Priory Wk SW10 69 D1
Pritchard's Rd E2 31 F5
Priter Rd SE16 59 F4
Prize Wk E20 33 G2
Probert Rd SW2 85 G3
Procter St WC1 9 G6
Promenade, The W4 66 A4
Promenade App Rd W4 66 A3
Prospect Pl E1 60 A2
Prospect Quay SW18 82 B2
Prospect Vale SE18 64 A5
Prothero Rd SW6 67 G3
Prout Gro NW10 24 A1
Providence Ct W1 13 G3
Provost Est N1 11 F1
Provost Rd NW3 27 G4
Provost St N1 11 F2
Prudent Pas EC2 17 E1
Prusom St E1 59 G2
Pudding La EC3 17 G4
Pudding Mill La E15 33 F5
Puddle Dock EC4 16 C3
Pulborough Rd SW18 82 A5
Pulleyns Av E6 50 A2
Pullman Gdns SW15 81 E4
Pullman Pl SE9 92 A3
Pulross Rd SW9 85 F1
Pulteney Cl E3 32 D5
Pulteney Ter N1 29 F5
Pulton Pl SW6 68 B3
Pump Ct EC4 15 J2
Pumping Sta Rd W4 66 A3
Pump La SE14 74 A3
Pundersons Gdns E2 45 G2
Purbrook Est SE1 23 J2
Purbrook St SE1 23 J3
Purcell Cres SW6 67 G3
Purcell St N1 44 D1
Purchese St NW1 42 D1
Purdy St E3 47 F3

Purelake Ms SE13 90 A1
Purneys Rd SE9 91 G2
Purser's Cross Rd SW6 68 A4
Purves Rd NW10 39 E1
Puteaux Ho E2 46 B1
Putney Br SW15 81 G1
Putney Br App SW6 81 G1
Putney Br App SW6 81 G1
Putney Br Rd SW15 81 G1
Putney Br Rd SW18 81 G2
Putney Common SW15 81 F2
Putney Ex Shop Cen SW15 81 F2
Putney Heath SW15 81 E4
Putney Heath La SW15 81 F3
Putney High St SW15 81 F2
Putney Hill SW15 81 F3
Putney Pk Av SW15 80 C2
Putney Pk La SW15 80 D2
Putney Wf Twr SW15 81 G1
Pyrland Rd N5 30 C2
Pytchley Rd SE22 87 D1

Q

Quadrangle, The SE24 86 B3
Quadrangle, The W2 12 B1
Quadrangle Cl SE1 23 H5
Quadrant Arc W1 14 B4
Quadrant Gro NW5 27 G2
Quaggy Wk SE3 90 D2
Quaker Ct EC1 11 F3
Quaker St E1 45 E3
Quality Ct WC2 15 J1
Quarrendon St SW6 68 B5
Quarry Rd SW18 83 D4
Quarterdeck, The E14 61 E3
Quay Rd IG11 51 D1
Quebec Ms W1 12 E2
Quebec Way SE16 60 B3
Queen Anne Ms W1 7 J6
Queen Anne Rd E9 32 B3
Queen Anne's Gdns W4 52 A4
Queen Anne's Gate SW1 22 C4
Queen Anne's Gro W4 52 A4
Queen Anne St W1 13 H1
Queen Caroline St W6 67 E1
Queen Caroline St W6 53 E5
Queen Elizabeth St SE1 23 J1
Queen Elizabeth Wk SW13 67 D4
Queenhithe EC4 16 E3
Queen Margaret's Gro N1 30 D2
Queen of Denmark Ct SE16 60 D4
Queensberry Pl SE12 35 G2
Queensberry St SW7 55 E5
Queensborough Ter W2 54 C1
Queensbridge Rd E2 31 E5
Queensbridge Rd E8 31 E4
Queensbury St N1 30 B4
Queens Club Gdns W14 67 G2
Queen's Cres NW5 28 A3
Queenscroft Rd SE9 91 G3
Queensdale Cres W11 53 F2
Queensdale Pl W11 53 G2
Queensdale Rd W11 53 F2
Queensdale Wk W11 53 G2
Queensdown Rd E5 31 G1
Queens Gdns W2 54 D1
Queen's Gate SW7 55 E5
Queen's Gate Gdns SW7 54 D4
Queen's Gate Ms SW7 55 D3

Queensgate Pl NW6 26 B4
Queen's Gate Pl SW7 55 D4
Queen's Gate Pl Ms SW7 55 D4
Queen's Gate Ter SW7 54 D4
Queen's Gro NW8 27 E5
Queen's Gro Ms NW8 27 E5
Queen's Head Pas EC4 16 D1
Queen's Head St N1 30 A5
Queens Head Yd SE1 17 F4
Queensland Rd N7 29 G1
Queensmead NW8 27 E5
Queens Ms W2 54 C1
Queensmill Rd SW6 67 F3
Queens Pk Ct W10 39 F2
Queen Sq WC1 9 F4
Queen Sq Pl WC1 9 F4
Queens Ride SW13 80 C1
Queens Ride SW15 80 C1
Queens Rd E13 35 E5
Queens Rd SE14 73 G4
Queens Rd SE15 73 G4
Queens Rd, Bark. 37 E4
Queens Rd W E13 49 D1
Queen's Row SE17 72 C2
Queens Ter E13 35 E5
Queen's Ter NW8 41 F1
Queensway W2 54 C1
Queenstown Rd SW8 70 B2
Queen St EC4 17 E3
Queen St N17 13 H5
Queen St Pl EC4 17 E4
Queensville Rd SW12 84 D5
Queen's Wk SW1 14 A6
Queen's Wk, The SE1 15 G6
Queensway W2 40 C5
Queens Yd WC1 8 B4
Queen Victoria St EC4 16 C3
Quemerford Rd N7 29 F2
Quentin Pl SE13 90 B1
Quentin Rd SE13 90 B1
Quernn St SW6 68 D5
Quex Rd NW6 26 B5
Quick Rd W4 66 A1
Quick St N1 44 A1
Quill La SW15 81 F2
Quilp St SE1 22 D1
Quilter St E2 45 F2
Quince Rd SE13 75 F5
Quixley St E14 62 A1
Quorn Rd SE22 87 D2

R

Rabbits Rd E12 36 A1
Racton Rd SW6 68 B2
Radbourne Rd SW12 84 C5
Radcliffe Av NW10 38 C1
Radcliffe Rd SE1 23 J3
Radcliffe Sq SW15 81 F4
Radcot St SE11 71 G1
Raddington Rd W10 39 G4
Radfield Way, Sid. 93 F5
Radford Rd SE13 89 G4
Radipole Rd SW6 68 A4
Radland Rd E16 48 C5
Radlett Cl E7 34 C3
Radlett Pl NW8 27 F5
Radley Ms W8 54 B4
Radnor Ms W2 12 A2
Radnor Pl W2 12 B2
Radnor Rd NW6 25 G5
Radnor Rd SE15 73 F3
Radnor St EC1 10 E2
Radnor Ter W14 54 A5
Radnor Wk SW3 69 F3
Radstock St SW11 69 F3
Raeburn Rd, Sid. 93 G4
Raeburn St SW2 85 E2
Raglan Ct SE12 90 D3
Raglan Rd SE18 79 E1
Raglan St NW5 28 B3
Rahere Ho EC1 10 D1
Railey Ms NW5 28 C2
Railton Rd SE24 85 G2

Railway App SE1 17 G5
Railway Av SE16 60 A3
Railway Side SW13 80 A1
Railway St N1 43 E1
Rainbow Av E14 75 F1
Rainbow Quay SE16 60 C4
Rainbow St SE5 72 D3
Raine St E1 59 G2
Rainham Cl SE9 93 F4
Rainham Cl SW11 83 F4
Rainham Rd NW10 39 E2
Rainhill Way E3 47 E2
Rainsborough Av SE8 60 C5
Rainsford St W2 12 B1
Rainton Rd SE7 77 D1
Rainville Rd W6 67 E2
Raleana Rd E14 61 G2
Raleigh St N1 30 A5
Ramac Way SE7 63 E5
Ramillies Cl SW2 85 E4
Ramillies Pl W1 14 A2
Ramillies St W1 14 A2
Rampayne St SW1 70 D1
Ramsay Rd E7 34 B1
Ramsden Rd SW12 84 A4
Ramsey St E2 45 F3
Ramsey Wk N1 30 C3
Ram St SW18 82 C3
Rancliffe Gdns SE9 92 A2
Rancliffe Rd E6 50 A1
Randall Cl SW11 69 F4
Randall Pl SE10 75 G3
Randall Rd SE11 71 E1
Randall Row SE11 21 G6
Randell's Rd N1 29 E5
Randolph App E16 49 G5
Randolph Av W9 41 D3
Randolph Cres W9 40 D3
Randolph Gdns NW6 40 C1
Randolph Ms W9 41 D3
Randolph Rd W9 40 D3
Ranelagh Av SW6 82 A1
Ranelagh Av SW13 66 C5
Ranelagh Gdns SW3 69 G2
Ranelagh Gdns SW6 82 A1
Ranelagh Gdns W6 52 B4
Ranelagh Gro SW1 70 A1
Ranelagh Rd E6 36 C5
Ranelagh Rd E11 34 B1
Ranelagh Rd E15 34 B5
Ranelagh Rd NW10 38 B1
Rangers Sq SE10 76 A4
Rannoch Rd W6 67 E2
Ranston St NW1 6 B5
Ranulf Rd NW2 26 A1
Ranwell St E3 32 D5
Raphael St SW7 18 D2
Ratcliffe Cl SE12 90 D5
Ratcliffe Cross St E1 46 B5
Ratcliffe La E14 46 C5
Ratcliff Rd E7 35 F2
Rathbone Pl W1 14 C1
Rathbone St E16 48 C4
Rathbone St W1 8 B6
Rathmell Dr SW4 84 D4
Rathmore Rd SE7 77 E1
Rattray Rd SW2 85 G2
Raul Rd SE15 73 F5
Raveley St NW5 28 C1
Ravenhill Rd E13 49 F1
Ravenna Rd SW15 81 F3
Raven Row E1 45 G4
Ravensbourne Pk SE6 89 E5
Ravensbourne Pk Cres SE6 89 D5
Ravensbourne Pl SE13 75 F5
Ravensbourne Rd SE6 88 D5
Ravenscourt Av W6 52 C5
Ravenscourt Gdns W6 52 C5
Ravenscourt Pk W6 52 C4
Ravenscourt Pl W6 52 D5
Ravenscourt Rd W6 52 D5

Ravenscourt Sq W6 52 C4
Ravenscroft Cl E16 48 D4
Ravenscroft Rd E16 49 D4
Ravenscroft St E2 45 E1
Ravensdon St SE11 71 G1
Ravenshaw St NW6 26 A2
Ravenslea Rd SW12 83 G5
Ravensmede Way W4 52 B5
Ravenstone SE17 73 D1
Ravens Way SE12 90 D3
Ravenswood Rd SW12 84 B5
Ravensworth Rd NW10 39 D2
Ravey St EC2 11 H3
Ravine Gro SE18 79 G2
Rawlings St SW3 18 D5
Rawstone Wk E13 49 D1
Rawstorne Pl EC1 10 B1
Rawstorne St EC1 10 B1
Rayford Av SE12 90 C5
Rayleas Cl SE18 78 D4
Rayleigh Rd E16 63 E2
Raymere Gdns SE18 79 F3
Raymond Bldgs WC1 9 H5
Raymond Rd E13 35 F4
Raymouth Rd SE16 59 G5
Rayners Rd SW15 81 G3
Raynham W2 12 B2
Raynham Rd W6 52 D5
Ray St EC1 10 A4
Ray St Br EC1 10 A4
Reach, The SE28 65 G3
Reading La E8 31 G3
Reardon Path E1 59 G2
Reardon St E1 59 G2
Reaston St SE14 74 A3
Reckitt Rd W4 66 A1
Record St SE15 74 A2
Rector St N1 30 B5
Rectory Fld Cres SE7 77 F3
Rectory Gro SW4 84 C1
Rectory Pl SE18 64 C5
Rectory Rd E12 36 B2
Rectory Rd SW13 66 C5
Rectory Rd N16 31 E5
Recuver Rd SE16 74 B1
Redan Pl W2 40 C5
Redan St W14 53 F4
Red Barracks Rd SE18 64 B5
Redbridge Gdns SE5 73 D3
Redburn St SW3 69 G2
Redcar St SE5 72 B3
Redcastle Cl E1 60 A1
Redchurch St E2 45 E3
Redcliffe Gdns SW5 68 C1
Redcliffe Gdns SW10 68 C1
Redcliffe Ms SW10 68 C1
Redcliffe Pl SW10 68 D2
Redcliffe Rd SW10 68 D1
Redcliffe Sq SW10 68 C1
Redcliffe St SW10 68 C2
Redclyffe Rd E6 35 F5
Redcross Way SE1 22 E1
Reddins Rd SE15 73 F2
Redesdale St SW3 69 G2
Redfern Rd NW10 24 A4
Redfern Rd SE6 89 G5
Redfield La SW5 54 B5
Redgate Ter SW15 81 G4
Redgrave Rd SW15 81 F1
Redhill St NW1 7 J1
Redington Gdns NW3 26 C1
Redington Rd NW3 26 C1
Redlands Way SW2 85 F5
Red Lion Ct EC4 16 A1
Red Lion La SE18 78 C3
Red Lion Row SE17 72 B2
Red Lion Sq WC1 9 G6
Red Lion St WC1 9 G5
Red Lion Yd W1 13 G5
Redman's Rd E1 46 A4
Redmore Rd W6 52 D5
Red Path E9 32 D3
Red Pl W1 13 F3

Red Post Hill SE21	86	C3
Red Post Hill SE24	86	C2
Redriffe Rd E13	34	C5
Redriff Est SE16	60	D4
Redriff Rd SE16	60	B5
Red Rover SW15	80	B1
Redruth Rd E9	32	B5
Redvers St N1	11	J1
Redwald Rd E5	32	B1
Redwing Path SE28	65	F3
Redwood Cl E3	47	E1
Redwood Cl SE16	60	C2
Reece Ms SW7	55	E5
Reed Cl E16	48	D4
Reed Cl SE12	91	D3
Reedham St SE15	73	F5
Reed Pl SW4	85	D2
Reedworth St SE11	22	A6
Reesland Cl E12	36	C3
Rees St N1	30	B5
Reeves Ms W1	13	F4
Reeves Rd E3	47	F3
Reeves Rd SE18	78	D2
Reform St SW11	69	G5
Regan Way N1	44	D1
Regency Pl SW1	20	D5
Regency St SW10	38	A3
Regency St SW1	20	C5
Regeneration Rd SE16	60	B5
Regent Pl W1	14	B3
Regent Rd SE24	86	A4
Regents Br Gdns SW8	71	E3
Regent's Pk, The NW1	41	G1
Regent's Pk Est NW1	7	J2
Regents Pk Rd NW1	27	G5
Regent's Pl SE3	76	D5
Regent Sq E3	47	G2
Regent Sq WC1	9	F2
Regents Row E8	31	F5
Regent St NW1	14	C4
Regent St W1	13	J1
Reginald Rd E7	34	D4
Reginald Rd SE8	75	E3
Reginald Sq SE8	75	E3
Regis Pl SW2	85	F2
Regis Rd NW5	28	B2
Regnart Bldgs NW1	8	B3
Reidhaven Rd SE18	79	H5
Reinickendorf Av SE9	93	E3
Relay Rd W12	53	E1
Relf Rd SE15	87	F1
Reliance Sq EC2	11	J3
Relton Ms SW7	12	D6
Rembrandt Cl E14	62	A4
Rembrandt Cl SW1	19	F6
Rembrandt Rd SE13	90	B2
Remington Rd E6	50	A5
Remington St N1	44	A1
Remnant St WC2	15	G1
Rendle Av SE10	62	C4
Rendlesham Rd E5	31	F1
Renforth St SE16	60	A3
Renfrew Cl E6	64	C1
Renfrew Rd SE11	22	B5
Rennell St SE13	89	G1
Rennets Cl SE9	93	G3
Rennets Wd Rd SE9	93	F3
Rennie Est SE16	59	G5
Rennie St SE1	16	B5
Rephidim St SE1	23	H4
Reporton Rd SW6	67	G4
Repository Rd SE18	78	B2
Repton St E14	46	C5
Reservoir Rd SE4	74	C5
Resolution Wk SE18	64	B4
Restell Cl SE3	76	B2
Restons Cres SE9	93	F4
Retreat Pl E9	32	A3
Revelon Rd SE4	88	C2
Reverdy Rd SE1	59	F5
Rex Pl W1	13	F3
Reynolds Av E12	36	C2
Reynolds Pl SE3	77	E3
Reynolds Rd SE15	88	A3
Rheidol Ter N1	44	A1
Rhodesia Rd SW9	71	E5
Rhodeswell Rd E14	47	E3
Rhonda Gro E3	46	C2
Rhyl St NW5	28	A3
Ribbons Wk E20	33	G2
Ricardo St E14	47	F5
Richard Cl SE18	64	A5
Richard Ho Dr E16	49	G5
Richardson Rd E15	48	B1
Richardson's Ms W1	8	A4
Richards Pl SW3	18	C5
Richbell Pl WC1	9	G5
Richborne Ter SW8	71	F3
Richborough Rd NW2	25	F1
Richford Rd E15	34	C5
Richford St W6	53	E3
Rich Ind Est SE1	23	J4
Richmond Av N1	29	F5
Richmond Av NW10	25	E3
Richmond Bldgs W1	14	C2
Richmond Cres N1	29	F5
Richmond Gro N1	30	A4
Richmond Ms W1	14	C2
Richmond Rd E7	35	E2
Richmond Rd E8	31	E4
Richmond St E13	49	D1
Richmond Ter W1	21	E1
Richmond Way W12	53	F4
Richmond Way W14	53	F4
Richmondson Gdns SE3	91	D1
Rich St E14	61	D1
Rickett St SW6	68	B2
Rick Roberts Way E15	48	B3
Rickyard Path SE9	92	A5
Ridcout St SE18	64	B5
Rider Cl, Sid.	93	G4
Ridgdale St E3	47	F1
Ridgebrook Rd SE3	91	F2
Ridge Cl SE23	65	F3
Ridgeway Rd SW9	86	A1
Ridgeway W, Sid.	93	G3
Ridgmount Gdns WC1	8	C3
Ridgmount Pl WC1	8	C3
Ridgmount Rd SW18	82	C3
Ridgmount St WC1	8	C3
Ridgwell Rd E16	49	F4
Riding Ho St W1	8	A6
Ridley Rd E7	35	F1
Ridley Rd E8	31	E2
Ridley Rd NW10	38	C1
Riefield Rd SE9	93	E2
Riffel Rd NW2	25	E2
Rifle Ct SE11	71	G2
Rifle St E14	47	F4
Rigault Rd SW6	67	G5
Rigden St E14	47	F5
Rigeley Rd NW10	38	C2
Rigge Pl SW4	85	D2
Riley Rd SE1	23	J3
Riley St SW10	69	E2
Rinaldo Rd SW12	84	B5
Ring, The W2	12	B3
Ringcroft St N7	29	G2
Ringford Rd SW18	82	A3
Ringlet Cl E16	49	E4
Ringmer Av SW6	67	G5
Ringmore Ri SE23	87	G5
Ring Rd W12	53	E1
Ringstead Rd SE6	89	F5
Ripley Rd E16	49	F5
Riplington Cl SW15	80	C5
Ripon Rd SE18	78	D2
Ripple Rd, Bark.	37	E4
Ripplevale Gro N1	29	F4
Risborough St SE1	22	C1
Risdon St SE16	60	A3
Riseldine Rd SE23	88	B3
Risinghill St N1	43	F1
Rising Sun Ct EC1	10	C6
Rita Rd SW8	71	F3
Ritchie St N1	43	G1
Ritson Rd E8	31	F3
Ritter St SE18	78	C2
Rivaz Pl E9	32	A3
River Ct SE1	16	B4
Rivercourt Rd W6	52	D5
Rivermead Ct SW6	82	A1
River Pl N1	30	B4
River Rd, Bark.	51	G1
Riverside SE7	63	E4
Riverside Dr W4	66	A3
Riverside Gdns W6	66	D1
Riverside Rd E15	69	D5
River St EC1	9	J1
Riverton Cl W9	40	A2
Riverview Gdns SW13	67	D2
River Way SE10	62	C4
Rivington Ct NW10	24	C5
Rivington Pl EC2	11	J2
Rivington St EC2	11	H2
Rixon Ho SE18	79	D2
Rixsen Rd E12	36	A2
Roach Rd E3	33	E4
Roan St SE10	75	G2
Robert Adam St W1	13	F1
Roberta St E2	45	F2
Robert Dashwood Way SE17	22	D6
Robert Lowe Cl SE14	74	B3
Robert Owen Ho SE8	67	F4
Roberts Cl SE16	60	B3
Roberts Ms SW1	19	F4
Robertson Rd E15	33	G5
Robertson Rd E16	49	D4
Robertson St SW8	84	B1
Robert's Pl EC1	10	A3
Robert Sq SE13	89	G2
Robert St E16	64	D2
Robert St NW1	7	J2
Robert St SE18	65	F5
Robert St WC2	15	F4
Robin Ct SE16	59	F5
Robin Cres E6	49	G4
Robin Hood La E14	61	G1
Robinson Rd E2	46	A1
Robsart St SW9	71	F5
Robson Av NW10	24	C5
Rocastle Rd SE4	88	C3
Rochelle Cl SW11	83	E2
Rochester Av E13	35	F5
Rochester Ms NW1	28	C4
Rochester Pl NW1	28	C3
Rochester Rd NW1	28	C3
Rochester Row SW1	20	B5
Rochester Sq NW1	28	C3
Rochester St SW1	20	C4
Rochester Ter NW1	28	C3
Rochester Wk SE1	17	F5
Rochester Way SE3	77	E4
Rochester Way SE9	92	B1
Rochester Way Relief Rd SE3	77	E4
Rochester Way Relief Rd SE9	92	A2
Rochford St NW5	27	G2
Rockells Pl SE22	87	G4
Rockhall Rd NW2	25	F1
Rockingham Cl SW15	80	B2
Rockingham Est SE1	22	D4
Rockingham St SE1	22	D4
Rockland Rd SW15	81	G2
Rockley Rd W14	53	F3
Rocks La SW13	66	C4
Rockwood Pl W12	53	E3
Rocombe Cres SE23	88	A5
Rocque La SE3	90	C1
Rodenhurst Rd SW4	84	D4
Roderick Rd NW3	27	G1
Roding Rd E5	32	B1
Roding Rd E6	50	D4
Roding Trd Est, Bark.	36	D4
Rodmarton St W1	7	E6
Rodmill La SW2	85	E5
Rodney Pl SE17	23	E5
Rodney Rd SE17	23	E5
Rodney St N1	43	F1
Rodway Rd SW15	80	C5
Rodwell Rd SE22	87	E4
Roebourne Way E16	64	C3
Roedean Cres SW15	80	A4
Roehampton Cl SW15	80	C2
Roehampton Gate SW15	80	A4
Roehampton High St SW15	80	D5
Roehampton La SW15	80	C2
Roffey St E14	61	G3
Roger Dowley Ct E2	46	A1
Rogers Rd E16	48	C5
Roger St WC1	9	H4
Rokeby Rd SE4	74	D5
Rokeby St E15	34	B5
Rokesby Cl, Well.	79	F5
Roland Gdns SW7	69	D1
Roland Way SE17	72	C1
Rollins St SE15	74	A2
Rolls Bldgs EC4	15	J1
Rollscourt Av SE24	86	B3
Rolls Pas EC4	15	J1
Rolls Rd SE1	73	E1
Rolt St SE8	74	C2
Romanfield Rd SW2	85	F5
Roman Rd E2	46	A2
Roman Rd E3	46	C1
Roman Rd E6	50	A3
Roman Rd W4	52	A5
Roman Rd, Ilf.	37	D3
Roman Way N7	29	F3
Roma Read Cl SW15	80	D5
Romborough Gdns SE13	89	G3
Romborough Way SE13	89	G3
Romero Sq SE3	91	F2
Romford Rd E7	35	E2
Romford Rd E12	36	A1
Romford Rd E15	34	B4
Romford St E1	45	F4
Romilly St W1	14	C3
Romney Ms W1	7	F5
Romney Rd SE10	75	G2
Romney St SW1	20	D4
Ronald Av E15	48	B2
Ronalds Rd N5	29	G2
Ronaldstone Rd, Sid.	93	G4
Rona Rd NW3	28	A1
Rondu Rd NW2	25	G2
Ron Leighton Way E6	36	A5
Ronnie La E12	36	C1
Ronver Rd SE12	90	C5
Rood La EC3	17	H3
Rookery Rd SW4	84	C2
Rooke Way SE10	76	C1
Rootes Dr W10	39	F3
Ropemaker Rd SE16	60	C4
Ropemaker St EC2	11	F5
Roper La SE1	23	J1
Roper St SE9	92	B4
Ropery St E3	46	D3
Ropers Cl SE16	60	C5
Rope Yd Rails SE18	64	D4
Ropley St E2	45	F1
Rosaline Rd SW6	67	G3
Rosary Gdns SW7	54	D5
Rosaville Rd SW6	68	A3
Roscoe St EC1	10	E4
Rose All SE1	16	E5
Rose & Crown Ct EC2	16	D1
Rose & Crown Yd SW1	14	B5
Rosebank Gdns E3	46	D1
Roseberry Pl E8	31	E3
Roseberry St SE16	59	G5
Rosebery Av E12	36	B3

Name	Map	Grid
Roseberry Av EC1	9	J4
Roseberry Av, Sid.	93	G5
Roseberry Rd SW2	85	E4
Roseberry Sq EC1	9	J4
Rosebury Rd SW6	68	C5
Rosedale Ct N5	30	A1
Rosedale Rd E7	35	F2
Rosedene NW6	22	B5
Rosedew Rd W6	67	F2
Rosefield Gdns E14	61	E1
Roseford Ct W12	53	F3
Rosehill Rd SW18	82	D4
Rose Joan Ms NW6	26	B1
Roseleigh Av N5	30	A1
Rosemary Rd E4	48	A5
Rosemary Rd SE15	73	E3
Rosemont Rd NW3	26	D3
Rosemoor St SW3	18	D6
Rosenau Cres SW11	69	F4
Rosenau Rd SW11	69	F4
Rosendale Rd SE21	86	B5
Rosendale Rd SE24	86	B5
Roseneath Rd SW11	84	A4
Rosenthal Rd SE6	89	F4
Rosenthorpe Rd SE15	88	B3
Roserton St E14	61	G3
Rose Sq SW3	69	E1
Rose St EC4	16	C1
Rose St WC2	15	E3
Rosethorn Cl SW12	84	C5
Rosetta Cl SW8	71	E3
Rose Way SE12	90	D3
Roseway SE21	86	C4
Rosher Cl E15	34	A4
Rosina St E9	32	B2
Roskell Rd SW15	81	F1
Rosmead Rd W11	53	G1
Rosoman Pl EC1	10	A3
Rosoman St EC1	10	A2
Ross Ct SW15	81	F5
Rossdale Rd SW15	81	E2
Rosse Ms SE3	77	E4
Rossendale Way NW1	28	C4
Rossetti Rd SE16	73	G1
Rosslyn Av SW13	80	A1
Rosslyn Hill NW3	27	E1
Rosslyn Rd, Bark.	37	F4
Rossmore Ct NW1	6	D3
Rossmore Rd NW1	6	C4
Ross Way SE9	92	A1
Rostrevor Ms SW6	68	A4
Rostrevor Rd SW6	68	A4
Rotary St SE1	22	B3
Rothbury Rd E9	33	D4
Rotherfield St N1	30	B4
Rotherham Rd E16	18	B6
Rotherhithe New Rd SE16	73	F1
Rotherhithe Old Rd SE16	60	B5
Rotherhithe St SE16	60	B3
Rotherhithe Tunnel E1	60	A2
Rotherhithe Tunnel App E14	60	C1
Rotherhithe Tunnel App SE16	60	A3
Rotherwood Rd SW15	81	F1
Rothery Ter SW9	72	A3
Rothsay Rd E7	35	F4
Rothsay St SE1	23	H3
Rothwell St NW1	27	G5
Rotten Row SW1	19	F1
Rotten Row SW7	18	B1
Rotterdam Dr E14	61	G4
Rouel Rd SE16	59	F4
Roundwood Pk NW10	24	B3
Roundwood Rd NW10	24	B3
Rounton Rd E3	47	E3
Roupell St SE1	16	A6
Rousden St NW1	28	C5
Routemaster Cl E13	49	E2
Routh Rd SW18	83	F5
Routh St E6	50	B4
Rowallan Rd SW6	67	G3
Rowan Cl, Ilf.	37	F2
Rowan Rd W6	53	F5
Rowberry Cl SW6	67	E3
Rowcross St SE1	73	E1
Rowditch La SW11	70	A5
Rowdon Av NW10	25	D4
Rowe La E9	32	A2
Rowena Cres SW11	69	F5
Rowhill Rd E5	31	G1
Rowington Cl W2	40	C4
Rowland Ct E16	48	C3
Rowland Hill St NW3	27	F2
Rowley Way NW8	26	C5
Rowse Cl E15	33	G5
Rowstock Gdns N7	29	D2
Rowton Rd SE18	79	E3
Roxby Pl SW6	68	B2
Roxley Rd SE13	89	F4
Roxwell Rd W12	52	C3
Royal Albert Dock E16	64	A1
Royal Albert Rbt E16	63	G1
Royal Albert Way E16	63	G1
Royal Arc W1	14	A4
Royal Av SW3	69	G1
Royal Cl SE8	74	D2
Royal Coll St NW1	28	C4
Royal Ct SE16	60	D4
Royal Cres W11	53	F2
Royal Docks Rd E6	51	D5
Royal Ex EC3	17	G2
Royal Ex Av EC3	17	G2
Royal Ex Bldgs EC3	17	G2
Royal Herbert Pavilions SE18	78	B4
Royal Hill SE10	75	G3
Royal Hosp Rd SW3	69	G2
Royal Ms, The SW1	19	J3
Royal Mint Ct EC3	59	E1
Royal Mint St E1	59	E1
Royal Naval Pl SE14	74	D3
Royal Oak Ct N1	11	F2
Royal Oak Pl SE22	87	G4
Royal Oak Rd E8	31	G3
Royal Oak Yd SE1	23	H2
Royal Opera Arc SW1	14	C5
Royal Orchard Cl SW18	81	G5
Royal Par SE3	76	B5
Royal Pl SE10	75	G3
Royal Rd E16	49	G5
Royal Rd SE17	72	A2
Royals Business Pk, The E16	64	A1
Royal St SE1	21	H3
Royalty Ms W1	14	C2
Royal Victoria Dock E16	63	D1
Royal Victoria Patriotic Bldg SW18	83	E4
Royal Victor Pl E3	46	B1
Roydene Rd SE18	79	G2
Royston St E2	46	A1
Rozel Ct N1	30	D5
Rozel Rd SW4	70	C5
Ruby St SE15	73	G2
Ruckholt Rd E10	33	E1
Rucklidge Av NW10	38	B1
Ruddington Cl E5	32	C1
Ruddstreet Cl SE18	65	D5
Rudloe Rd SW12	84	C5
Rudolph Rd E13	48	C1
Rudolph Rd NW6	40	B1
Rufford St N1	29	E5
Rufus St N1	11	H2
Rugby Rd W4	52	A3
Rugby St WC1	9	G4
Rugg St E14	61	E1
Rumbold Rd SW6	68	C3
Rum Cl E1	60	A1
Rumsey Rd SW9	85	F1
Runcorn Pl W11	53	G1
Rupert Ct W1	14	C3
Rupert Gdns SW9	72	A5
Rupert Rd NW6	40	A1
Rupert Rd W4	52	A4
Rupert St W1	14	C3
Ruscoe Rd E16	48	C5
Rusham Rd SW12	83	G4
Rush Common Ms SW2	85	F5
Rushcroft Rd SW2	85	G2
Rushey Grn SE6	89	F5
Rushey Mead SE4	89	E3
Rushford Rd SE4	89	D4
Rushgrove St SE18	64	B5
Rush Hill Rd SW11	84	A1
Rushmore Rd E5	32	A1
Rusholme Rd SW15	81	F4
Rushton St N1	44	C1
Rushworth St SE1	22	C1
Ruskin Av E12	36	A3
Ruskin Pk Ho SE5	86	C1
Ruskin Wk SE24	86	B3
Russell Cl SE7	77	F3
Russell Cl W4	66	B2
Russell Gdns W14	53	G4
Russell Gdns Ms W14	53	G4
Russell Gro SW9	71	G3
Russell Rd E16	49	D5
Russell Rd W14	53	G4
Russell Sq WC1	15	F3
Russia Ct EC2	17	F6
Russia Dock Rd SE16	60	C2
Russia La E2	46	A1
Russia Row EC2	16	E2
Ruston Rd SE18	64	A4
Ruston St E3	33	D5
Rust Sq SE5	72	C3
Rutherford St SW1	20	C5
Ruthin Rd SE3	76	D2
Rutland Gdns SW7	18	C2
Rutland Gdns Ms SW7	18	C2
Rutland Gate SW7	18	C2
Rutland Gate Ms SW7	18	B2
Rutland Gro W6	67	D1
Rutland Ms E SW7	18	B3
Rutland Ms S SW7	18	B3
Rutland Pk NW2	25	E3
Rutland Pl EC1	10	D4
Rutland Rd E7	35	G4
Rutland Rd E9	32	A5
Rutland Rd, Ilf.	37	D1
Rutland St SW7	18	C3
Rutts Ter SE14	74	B4
Ruvigny Gdns SW15	81	F1
Ryan Cl SE3	91	F2
Rycullff Sq SE3	76	C5
Ryder Cl SW1	14	B5
Ryder Dr SE16	73	G1
Ryder St SW1	14	B5
Ryder Yd SW1	14	B5
Rydons Cl SE9	92	A1
Ryecroft Rd SE13	89	G3
Ryecroft St SW6	68	C4
Ryedale SE22	87	G4
Rye Hill Pk SE15	88	A2
Ryelands Cres SE12	91	F4
Rye La SE15	73	F4
Rye Pas SE15	87	F1
Rye Rd SE15	88	B2
Rye Wk SW15	81	F3
Ryland Rd NW5	28	B3
Rylett Cres W12	52	B4
Rylett Rd W12	52	B3
Rylston Rd SW6	68	A2
Rymer St SE24	86	A4
Rymill St E16	64	C2
Rysbrack St SW3	18	D3

S

Name	Map	Grid
Sabine Rd SW11	83	G1
Sable St N1	30	A4
Sackville St W1	14	B4
Saddle Yd W1	13	H5
Saffron Av E14	62	A1
Saffron Hill EC1	10	A4
Saffron St EC1	10	A5
Sage Way WC1	9	G2
Sail St SE11	21	H5
St. Agnes Pl SE11	71	G2
St. Aidan's Rd SE22	87	G4
St. Albans Av E6	50	B3
St. Albans Ct EC2	16	E1
St. Albans Gro W8	54	C4
St. Alban's Pl N1	30	A5
St. Albans Rd NW10	24	A5
St. Albans St SW1	14	C4
St. Alfege Pas SE10	75	G2
St. Alfege Rd SE7	77	G2
St. Alphage Gdns EC2	11	E6
St. Alphage Highwalk EC2	11	F6
St. Alphonsus Rd SW4	84	C2
St. Andrew's Hill EC4	16	C3
St. Andrews Pl NW1	7	J3
St. Andrews Rd E13	49	E2
St. Andrews Rd NW10	25	D3
St. Andrews Rd W3	52	A1
St. Andrews Rd W14	67	G2
St. Andrew St EC4	10	A6
St. Andrews Way E3	47	F3
St. Anne's Ct W1	14	C2
St. Ann's, Bark.	37	D5
St. Ann's Cres SW18	82	D4
St. Ann's Hill SW18	82	C3
St. Ann's La SW1	20	D3
St. Ann's Pk Rd SW18	82	D4
St. Ann's Pas SW13	80	A1
St. Ann's Rd N15	66	B5
St. Ann's Rd W11	53	F1
St. Ann's St SW1	20	D3
St. Ann's Ter NW8	41	E1
St. Anns Vil W11	53	F2
St. Anselm's Pl W1	13	H2
St. Anthonys Cl E1	59	F2
St. Antony's Rd E7	35	E4
St. Asaph Rd SE4	88	B1
St. Augustines Rd NW1	28	D4
St. Austell Rd SE13	75	G5
St. Awdry's Rd, Bark.	37	F4
St. Barnabas St SW1	70	A1
St. Barnabas Ter E9	32	B2
St. Barnabas Vil SW8	71	E4
St. Bartholomew's Rd E6	36	A5
St. Benet's Pl EC3	17	G3
St. Bernard's Rd E6	35	G5
St. Botolph St EC3	45	E5
St. Brides Av EC4	16	B2
St. Bride St EC4	16	B1
St. Catherine's Ms SW3	18	D5
St. Chad's Pl WC1	9	F1
St. Chad's St WC1	9	F1
St. Charles Sq W10	39	G4
St. Christopher's Pl W1	13	G1
St. Clair Rd E13	49	E1
St. Clement's La WC2	15	H2
St. Clements St N7	29	G3
St. Crispins Cl NW3	27	F1
St. Cross St EC1	10	A5
St. Cuthberts Rd NW2	26	A3
St. Davids Sq E14	75	F1
St. Dionis Rd SW6	68	A5
St. Donatts Rd SE14	74	D4
St. Dunstan's All EC3	17	H3
St. Dunstan's Hill EC3	17	H4
St. Dunstan's La EC3	17	H4
St. Dunstan's Rd E7	35	F3
St. Dunstans Rd W6	67	F1
St. Edmunds Sq SW13	67	E2
St. Edmunds Ter NW8	27	F5
St. Elmo Rd W12	52	B2
St. Elmos Rd SE16	60	B3
St. Erkenwald Rd, Bark.	37	F5
St. Ermin's Hill SW1	20	C3

Name	Ref
St. Ervans Rd W10	39 G4
St. Francis Rd SE22	87 D2
St. Francis Way, Ilf.	37 G1
St. Gabriels Rd NW2	35 F2
St. Georges Av E7	35 E4
St. Georges Av N7	21 J3
St. Georges Circ SE1	22 B3
St. Georges Ct E6	50 B3
St. Georges Ct EC4	16 B1
St. Georges Dr SW1	19 J6
St. Georges Flds W2	12 C2
St. Georges Ms SE1	22 A3
St. Georges Rd E7	35 E3
St. Georges Rd SE1	22 A3
St. Georges Rd W4	52 A3
St. Georges Sq E7	35 E4
St. Georges Sq SE8	60 D5
St. George's Sq SW1	70 D1
St. George's Sq Ms SW1	70 D1
St. Georges Way SE15	72 D2
St. George Wf SW8	71 E1
St. Gerards Cl SW4	84 C3
St. German's Pl SE3	76 D4
St. Giles High St WC2	14 D1
St. Giles Pas WC2	14 D2
St. Giles Rd SE5	72 D3
St. Gilles Ho E2	46 A2
St. Helena Rd SE16	60 B5
St. Helena St WC1	9 J2
St. Helens Gdns W10	39 F5
St. Helens Pl EC3	17 H1
St. Hildas Cl NW6	25 F4
St. Hilda's Rd SW13	66 D2
St. James Ms E14	61 G4
St. James Rd E15	34 C2
St. James's SE14	74 C4
St. James's Av E2	46 A1
St. James's Ct SW1	20 B3
St. James's Cres SW9	85 G1
St. James's Gdns W11	53 G2
St. James's Mkt SW1	14 C4
St. James's Palace SW1	20 B1
St. James's Pk SW1	20 C1
St. James's Pas EC3	17 J2
St. James's Pl SW1	14 A6
St. James's Rd SE1	73 F1
St. James's Rd SE16	59 F4
St. James's Sq SW1	14 B5
St. James's St SW1	14 A5
St. James's Ter Ms NW8	27 G5
St. James St W6	67 E1
St. James's Wk EC1	10 B3
St. John's Av N10	24 B5
St. John's Av SW15	81 F3
St. John's Ch Rd E9	32 A2
St. John's Cres SW9	85 G1
St. John's Est N1	44 C1
St. John's Gdns W11	54 A1
St. John's Hill SW11	83 E2
St. John's Hill Gro SW11	83 E2
St. John's La EC1	10 B4
St. John's Pk SE3	76 C3
St. John's Path EC1	10 B4
St. John's Pl EC1	10 B4
St. Johns Rd E16	48 D5
St. John's Rd SW11	83 F2
St. John's Rd, Bark.	37 G5
St. John's Sq EC1	10 B4
St. Johns Ter E7	35 E3
St. Johns Ter SE18	79 E2
St. John St EC1	10 C4
St. Johns Vale SE8	75 E5
St. John's Wd Ct NW8	6 A2
St. John's Wd High St NW8	41 E1
St. John's Wd Pk NW8	27 E5
St. John's Wd Rd NW8	41 E3
St. John's Wd Ter NW8	41 E1
St. Joseph's Ct SE7	77 E2
St. Joseph's Vale SE3	76 A5
St. Jude's Rd E2	45 G1
St. Jude St N16	31 D2
St. Julian's Rd NW6	26 A4
St. Katharine's Way E1	59 E2
St. Laurence Cl NW6	25 F5
St. Lawrence Ter E14	61 G2
St. Lawrence Ter W10	40 A2
St. Lawrence Way SW9	71 G4
St. Leonards Cl N1	11 G1
St. Leonards Gdns, Ilf.	37 E2
St. Leonards Rd E14	47 F4
St. Leonards Sq NW5	28 A3
St. Leonards St E3	47 F2
St. Leonard's Ter SW3	69 G1
St. Loo Av SW3	69 F2
St. Lucia Dr E15	34 C5
St. Luke's Av SW4	85 D2
St. Luke's Av, Ilf.	37 D2
St. Luke's Cl EC1	10 E3
St. Luke's Est EC1	11 F2
St. Lukes Rd W11	40 A4
St. Lukes Sq E16	48 C5
St. Luke's St SW3	69 F1
St. Luke's Yd W9	40 A1
St. Margarets, Bark.	37 F5
St. Margaret's Ct SE1	17 F6
St. Margaret's Cres SW15	81 D3
St. Margarets Gro SE18	79 E2
St. Margaret's La W8	54 C4
St. Margarets Path SE18	79 E1
St. Margaret's Rd NW10	39 E2
St. Margarets Rd SE4	89 D2
St. Margaret's St SW1	21 E2
St. Margaret's Ter SE18	79 E1
St. Marks Cres NW1	28 A5
St. Mark's Gro SW10	68 C2
St. Marks Pl W11	39 G5
St. Marks Ri E8	31 E2
St. Marks Rd W10	39 F5
St. Marks Rd W11	39 G5
St. Marks Sq NW1	28 A5
St. Mark St E1	45 E5
St. Martins Av E6	49 G1
St. Martins Cl NW1	28 C5
St. Martin's La WC2	14 E3
St. Martin's-le-Grand EC1	16 D1
St. Martin's Ms WC2	14 E4
St. Martin's Pl WC2	14 E4
St. Martin's Rd SW9	71 F5
St. Martin's St WC2	14 D4
St. Mary Abbots Pl W8	54 A4
St. Mary Abbots Ter W14	54 A4
St. Mary at Hill EC3	17 H4
St. Mary Axe EC3	17 H2
St. Marychurch St SE16	60 A3
St. Marys, Bark.	37 F5
St. Marys App E12	36 B2
St. Marys Ct E6	50 B3
St. Mary's Ct SE7	77 G3
St. Mary's Gdns SE11	22 A5
St. Mary's Gate W8	54 C4
St. Mary's Gro N1	30 A3
St. Mary's Gro SW13	80 D1
St. Marys Mans W2	41 D4
St. Marys Path N1	30 A5
St. Mary's Pl W8	54 C4
St. Marys Rd E13	49 E1
St. Mary's Rd NW10	24 A5
St. Marys Rd SE15	74 A4
St. Mary's Rd W2	41 E4
St. Mary's Ter W2	41 E4
St. Mary St SE18	64 B5
St. Mary's Wk SE11	22 A5
St. Matthew's Rd SW2	85 F2
St. Matthew's Row E2	45 F2
St. Matthew St SW1	20 C4
St. Maur Rd SW6	68 A4
St. Merryn Cl SE18	79 F3
St. Michael's All EC3	17 G2
St. Michael's Ms SW1	19 F6
St. Michaels Rd NW2	35 F1
St. Michael's Rd SW9	71 F5
St. Mildreds Rd SE12	90 B5
St. Nirbert Grn SE4	88 C2
St. Norbert Rd SE4	88 C2
St. Olaf's Rd SW6	67 G3
St. Olaves Ct EC2	17 F2
St. Olave's Est SE1	23 J1
St. Olaves Gdns SE11	21 J5
St. Olaves Rd E6	36 C5
St. Olav's Sq SE16	60 A3
St. Oswald's Pl SE11	71 F1
St. Oswulf St SW1	20 D6
St. Pancras Way NW1	28 C4
St. Paul's Av NW2	25 D3
St. Paul's Av SE16	60 B2
St. Paul's Chyd EC4	16 C2
St. Paul's Cl SE7	77 G1
St. Paul's Cres NW1	29 D4
St. Pauls Dr E15	34 A2
St. Paul's Ms NW1	29 D4
St. Paul's Pl N1	30 C3
St. Paul's Rd N1	30 A3
St. Paul's Rd, Bark.	37 E5
St. Paul's Shrubbery N1	30 C3
St. Paul St N1	30 B5
St. Pauls Way E3	46 D4
St. Pauls Way E14	46 D4
St. Peter's All EC3	17 G2
St. Petersburgh Ms W2	54 C1
St. Petersburgh Pl W2	54 C1
St. Peter's Cl E2	45 F1
St. Peter's Gro W6	66 C1
St. Peter's Rd W6	66 C1
St. Peter's Sq W6	66 C1
St. Peters St N1	30 A5
St. Peter's Ter SW6	67 G3
St. Peter's Vil W6	52 B5
St. Peter's Way N1	31 D4
St. Philip Sq SW8	70 B5
St. Philip's Rd E8	31 F3
St. Philip St SW8	70 B5
St. Quintin Av W10	39 E4
St. Quintin Gdns W10	39 E4
St. Quintin Rd E13	49 E1
St. Rule St SW8	70 C5
St. Saviour's Est SE1	59 E4
St. Saviour's Rd SW2	85 F3
Saints Dr E7	35 G2
St. Silas Pl NW5	28 A3
St. Silas St NW5	28 A3
St. Simon's Av SW15	81 E3
St. Stephens Av W12	53 D3
St. Stephens Cres W2	40 B5
St. Stephens Gdns W2	40 B5
St. Stephens Gro SE13	89 G1
St. Stephen's Rd E3	46 D1
St. Stephen's Rd E6	35 F4
St. Stephens Row EC4	17 F2
St. Stephen's Ter SW8	71 F3
St. Stephen's Wk SW7	54 D5
St. Swithin's La EC4	17 F3
St. Swithun's Rd SE13	89 H3
St. Thomas Gdns, Ilf.	37 E3
St. Thomas Rd E16	48 D5
St. Thomas' Pl E9	32 A4
St. Thomas's Rd NW10	24 A5
St. Thomas Sq E9	31 G4
St. Thomas St SE1	17 F6
St. Thomas's Way SW6	68 A3
St. Vincent St W1	7 G6
St. Winefride's Av E12	36 B2
Salamanca Pl SE1	21 G6
Salamanca St SE1	21 F6
Salcombe Rd N16	31 D2
Salcott Rd SW11	83 F3
Salehurst Rd SE4	88 D4
Salem Rd W2	54 C1
Sale Pl W2	6 B6
Salisbury Av, Bark.	37 F4
Salisbury Cl SE17	23 F5
Salisbury Ct EC4	16 B2
Salisbury Pl SW9	72 A3
Salisbury Pl W1	6 D5
Salisbury Rd E7	34 D3
Salisbury Rd E12	35 G2
Salisbury Sq EC4	16 A2
Salisbury St NW8	6 A4
Salisbury Ter SE15	88 A1
Sally Murray Cl E12	36 C1
Salmen Rd E13	48 C1
Salmon La E14	46 C5
Saltcoats Rd W4	52 A3
Salter Rd SE16	60 B2
Salters Hall Ct EC4	17 F3
Salters Rd W10	39 F3
Salter St E14	61 E1
Salter St NW10	38 C2
Saltoun Rd SW2	85 G2
Saltram Cres W9	40 A2
Saltwell St E14	61 E1
Salusbury Rd NW6	25 G5
Salutation Rd SE10	62 B5
Salvin Rd SW15	81 F1
Sam Bartram Cl SE7	77 F1
Samford St NW8	6 A4
Sampson St E1	59 F2
Samson St E13	49 F1
Samuel Cl SE14	74 B2
Samuel Cl SE18	64 A5
Samuel Lewis Trust Dws SW3	18 B6
Samuel Lewis Trust Dws SW6	68 B3
Samuel St SE15	73 E3
Samuel St SE18	64 B5
Sancroft St SE11	71 F1
Sanctuary, The SW1	20 D2
Sanctuary St SE1	22 E2
Sandall Rd NW5	28 C3
Sandal St E15	34 B5
Sandbach Pl SE18	65 E5
Sandbourne Rd SE4	74 C5
Sandby Grn SE9	92 A1
Sandell St SE1	21 J1
Sanderson Cl NW5	28 B1
Sandersted Cl SW12	84 C5
Sandford Cl E6	50 B3
Sandford Rd E6	50 A3
Sandgate St SE15	73 G2
Sandilands Rd SW6	68 C4
Sandison St SE15	87 E1
Sandland St WC1	9 H6
Sandmere Rd SW4	85 E2
Sandpiper Cl SE16	60 D3
Sandpit Pl SE7	78 A1
Sandringham Dr, Well.	79 G5
Sandringham Rd E7	35 F2
Sandringham Rd E8	31 E2
Sandringham Rd Nw2	24 D3
Sandrock Rd SE13	89 E1
Sand's End La SW6	68 C4
Sandstone La E16	63 E1
Sandtoft Rd SE7	77 E2
Sandwell Cres NW6	26 B3
Sandwich St WC1	8 E4
Sandy Hill Av SE18	78 D1
Sandy Hill Rd SE18	78 D1
Sandyhill Rd, Ilf.	36 D1
Sandy's Row E1	11 J6
Sanford St SE14	74 C2
Sangley Rd SE6	89 F5
Sangora Rd SW11	83 E2

Name	Grid		Name	Grid
Sansom St SE5	72 C3		Scrubs La W10	38 C2
Sans Wk EC1	10 A3		Scrutton Cl SW12	84 D5
Santley St SW4	85 F2		Scrutton St EC2	11 H4
Santos Rd SW18	82 B3		Scutari Rd SE22	88 A3
Sapcote Trd Cen NW10	24 B2		Scylla Rd SE15	87 G1
Saperton Wk SE11	21 H5		Seacon Twr E14	61 D3
Sapperton Ct EC1	10 C5		Seaford St WC1	9 F2
Sapphire Cl E6	50 C5		Seaforth Cres N5	30 B2
Sapphire Rd SE8	60 C5		Seagrave Rd SW6	68 B2
Saracen's Head Yd EC3	17 J2		Seagull La E16	63 D1
Saracen St E14	47 E5		Seal St E8	31 E1
Sarah Ho SW15	80 B2		Searles Cl SW11	69 F3
Saratoga Rd E5	32 A1		Searles Dr E6	50 D4
Sardinia St WC2	15 G2		Searles Rd SE1	23 G5
Sark Twr SE28	65 E3		Sears St SE5	72 C3
Sark Wk E16	49 E5		Seaton Av, Ilf.	37 G2
Sarre Rd NW2	26 A2		Seaton Pt E5	31 F1
Sartor Rd SE15	88 B2		Sebastian St EC1	10 C4
Satchwell Rd E2	45 F2		Sebbon St N1	30 A4
Saunders Ness Rd E14	75 G1		Sebert Rd E7	35 E2
Saunders St SE11	21 J6		Secker St SE1	15 J6
Savage Gdns E6	50 B5		Second Av E13	36 A1
Savage Gdns EC3	17 J3		Second Av E13	49 D2
Savernake Rd NW3	27 G1		Second Av SW14	80 A1
Savile Row W1	14 A3		Second Av W3	52 B2
Saville Rd E16	64 A2		Second Av W10	39 G3
Savona Est SW8	70 C3		Sedding St SW1	19 F5
Savona St SW8	70 C3		Seddon St WC1	9 H2
Savoy Bldgs WC2	15 G4		Sedgebrook Rd SE3	77 G5
Savoy Ct WC2	15 F4		Sedgeford Rd W12	52 B2
Savoy Hill WC2	15 G4		Sedgmoor Pl SE5	73 D3
Savoy Ms SW9	85 E1		Sedgwick St E9	32 B2
Savoy Pl WC2	15 F4		Sedleigh Rd SW18	82 A4
Savoy Row WC2	15 G3		Sedlescombe Rd SW6	68 A2
Savoy St WC2	15 G3		Sedley Pl W1	13 H2
Savoy Way WC2	15 G4		Seething La EC3	17 J4
Sawmill Yd E3	33 H5		Sefton St SW15	67 E5
Sawyer St SE1	22 D1		Sekforde St EC1	10 B4
Saxby Rd SW2	85 E5		Selbie Av NW10	24 D3
Saxham Rd, Bark.	51 G1		Selby Rd E13	49 E4
Saxonfield Cl SW2	85 F5		Selby Sq W10	39 G2
Saxon Rd E3	46 D1		Selby St E1	45 F3
Saxon Rd E6	50 B3		Selden Rd SE15	74 A5
Saxon Rd, Ilf.	37 D3		Sellons Av NW10	24 B5
Saxton Cl SE13	90 A1		Selsdon Rd E13	49 E2
Sayes Ct St SE8	75 D2		Selsdon Way E14	61 F4
Scala St W1	8 B5		Selsey St E14	47 E4
Scampston Ms W10	39 F5		Selwood Pl SW7	69 E1
Scandrett St E1	59 G2		Selworthy Ho SW11	69 E4
Scarsbrook Rd SE17	91 G1		Selwyn Ct SE3	76 B3
Scarsdale Vil W8	54 B4		Selwyn Rd E3	46 D1
Scarth Rd SW13	80 B1		Selwyn Rd E13	35 E5
Scawen Rd SE8	74 C1		Semley Pl SW1	19 G6
Scawfell St E2	45 E1		Senate St SE15	74 A5
Sceaux Gdns SE5	73 D4		Sendall Cl SW11	83 E1
Sceptre Rd E2	46 A2		Senior St W2	40 C4
Schoolbank Rd SE10	62 C5		Senrab St E1	46 B5
Schoolhouse La E1	60 B1		Serenaders Rd SW9	71 G5
Schooner Cl E14	62 A4		Serjeants Inn EC4	16 A2
Schubert Rd SW15	82 A3		Serle St WC2	15 H1
Sclater St E1	45 E3		Sermon La EC4	16 C2
Scoresby St SE1	16 B6		Serpentine Rd W2	12 D6
Scotia Rd SW2	85 G5		Setchell Rd SE1	45 E4
Scotland Pl SW1	15 E5		Settles St E1	45 F4
Scotsdale Rd SE12	91 E3		Settrington Rd SW6	68 C5
Scotswood St EC1	10 A3		Sevenoaks Rd SE4	88 C4
Scott Av SW15	81 G4		Seven Sea Gdns E3	47 F4
Scott Ellis Gdns NW8	41 G2		Seventh Av E12	36 B1
Scott Lidgett Cres SE16	59 F3		Severnake Cl E14	61 E5
Scotts Rd W12	52 D3		Severn Way NW10	24 B2
Scott St E1	45 G3		Severus Rd SW11	83 F2
Scoulding Rd E16	48 C5		Seville Ms N1	30 D4
Scout App NW10	24 A1		Seville St SW1	18 E2
Scovell Cres SE1	22 D2		Sevington St W9	40 C3
Scovell Rd SE1	22 D2		Sewardstone Rd E2	46 A1
Scriven St E8	31 E5		Seward St EC1	10 C3
Scrooby St SE6	89 F4		Sewell St E13	49 D2
Scrubs La NW10	38 C2		Sextant Av E14	62 A5
			Seymour Gdns SE4	88 C1
			Seymour Ms W1	13 F1
			Seymour Pl W1	6 D6
			Seymour Rd E6	49 G1
			Seymour Rd SW18	82 A5

Name	Grid		Name	Grid
Seymour St SE18	65 E4		Shepherds Bush Mkt W12	53 E3
Seymour St W1	12 D2		Shepherds Bush Pl W12	53 F3
Seymour St W2	12 D2		Shepherds Bush Rd W6	53 E5
Seymour Wk SW10	68 D3		Shepherds La E8	32 B2
Seussel St E14	61 G5		Shepherds La SE28	65 G2
Shackleton Cl W12	53 D3		Shepherd's Pl W1	13 F3
Shacklewell Grn E8	31 E1		Shepherd St W1	13 H6
Shacklewell La E8	31 E2		Shepherds Wk NW3	27 E2
Shacklewell Rd N16	31 E1		Sheppard Dr SE16	73 G1
Shacklewell Row E8	31 E1		Sheppard St E16	48 C3
Shad Thames SE1	59 E2		Shepperton Rd N1	30 B5
Shaftesbury Av W1	14 C3		Sherard Rd SE9	92 A3
Shaftesbury Av WC2	14 C3		Sheraton St W1	14 C2
Shaftesbury Gdns NW10	38 A3		Sherborne La EC4	17 F3
Shaftesbury Rd E7	35 F4		Sherborne St N1	30 C5
Shaftesbury, The, Bark.	37 E5		Sherbrooke Rd SW6	68 A3
Shaftesbury St N1	44 B1		Sherfield Gdns SW15	80 B4
Shafto Ms SW1	18 D4		Sheridan Rd E12	36 A2
Shafton Rd E9	32 B5		Sheringham Av E12	36 B1
Shakespeare Cres E12	36 B3		Sheringham Rd N7	29 F3
Shakespeare Rd SE24	86 A3		Sherington Rd SE7	77 E2
Shakespeare Twr EC2	10 E5		Sherlock Ms W1	7 F5
Shakspeare Ms E9	30 D1		Sherrard Rd E7	35 F3
Shalcomb St SW10	69 D2		Sherrard Rd E12	35 G3
Shalfleet Dr W10	39 G5		Sherrick Grn Rd NW10	24 D2
Shamrock St SW4	84 D1		Sherriff Rd NW6	26 B3
Shandon Rd SW4	84 C4		Sherrin Rd E10	33 E1
Shand St SE1	23 H1		Sherry Ms, Bark.	37 F4
Shandy St E1	46 B4		Sherwin Rd SE14	74 B4
Shannon Gro SW9	85 F2		Sherwood Gdns E14	61 E5
Shardcroft Av SE24	86 A3		Sherwood Gdns SE16	73 F1
Shardeloes Rd SE4	88 D1		Sherwood Gdns, Bark.	37 F4
Shardeloes Rd SE14	88 D1		Sherwood St W1	14 B3
Sharon Gdns E9	32 A5		Shetland Rd E3	47 D1
Sharpleshall St NW1	27 G4		Shillibeer Pl W1	6 C5
Sharratt St SE15	74 C2		Shinfield St W12	39 E5
Sharsted St SE17	72 A1		Ship & Mermaid Row SE1	23 G1
Shavers Pl SW1	14 C4		Shipman Rd E16	49 E5
Shawbrooke Rd SE9	91 F3		Ship St SE8	75 E4
Shawbury Rd SE22	87 E3		Ship Tavern Pas EC3	17 H3
Shaw Cl SW11	83 E1		Shipton St E2	45 E2
Shaw Cres E14	46 C4		Shipwright Rd SE16	60 C3
Shawfield St SW3	69 F1		Shipwright Yd SE1	17 H6
Shawford Ct SW15	80 C5		Shirbutt St E14	61 F1
Shaw Rd SE22	87 D2		Shirebrook Rd SE3	77 G5
Shearling Way N7	29 E3		Shirland Ms W9	40 A2
Shearman Rd SE3	90 C2		Shirland Rd W9	40 B2
Sheepcote La SW11	69 G5		Shirley Gdns, Bark.	37 G3
Sheep La E8	31 G5		Shirley Gro SW11	84 A1
Sheerness Ms E16	65 D3		Shirley Ho Dr SE7	77 F3
Sheerwater Rd E16	49 G4		Shirley Rd E15	34 B4
Sheffield St WC2	15 G2		Shirley St E16	48 C5
Sheffield Ter W8	54 B2		Shirlock Rd NW3	27 G1
Shelburne Rd N7	29 F1		Shoebury Rd E6	36 B4
Shelbury Rd SE22	87 G3		Shoe La EC4	16 A1
Sheldon Cl SE12	91 E3		Shooters Hill SE18	78 C4
Sheldon Pl E2	45 F1		Shooters Hill, Well.	78 C4
Sheldon Rd NW2	25 F1		Shooters Hill Rd SE3	76 C4
Sheldon Sq W2	12 C6		Shooters Hill Rd SE10	76 C4
Sheldrake Cl E16	64 B2		Shooters Hill Rd SE18	77 E3
Sheldrake Pl W8	54 A3		Shoot Up Hill NW2	25 G2
Shelduck Cl E15	34 C2		Shoreditch High St E1	11 J4
Shelgate Rd SW11	83 F3		Shoreditch Ho N1	11 G2
Shelley Av E12	36 A3		Shore Pl E9	32 A4
Shelley Cl SE15	73 G5		Shore Rd E9	32 A4
Shelley Dr, Well.	79 G4		Shore Way SW9	71 G5
Shellgrove Est N16	31 D2		Shorncliffe Rd SE1	73 E1
Shellness Rd E5	31 G2		Shorrolds Rd SW6	68 A3
Shell Rd SE13	75 F5		Shorter St E1	59 E1
Shellwood Rd SW11	69 G5		Shortlands W6	53 F5
Shelmerdine Cl E3	47 E4		Short Rd W4	66 A2
Shelton St WC2	14 E2		Shorts Gdns WC2	14 E2
Shenfield St N1	45 D1		Short St SE1	22 A1
Shenley Rd SE5	73 D4		Short Wall E15	47 G2
Shepherdess Pl N1	11 E1		Short Way SE9	92 A1
Shepherdess Wk N1	44 B1		Shottendane Rd SW6	68 B4
Shepherd Mkt W1	13 H5		Shottfield Av SW14	80 A2
Shepherds Bush Grn W12	53 E3		Shouldham St W1	6 C6

Shrapnel Cl SE18 78 A3
Shrapnel Rd SE9 92 B1
Shrewsbury La SE18 78 D4
Shrewsbury Rd E7 35 G2
Shrewsbury Rd W2 40 B5
Shrewsbury St W10 39 E3
Shropshire Pl WC1 5 B5
Shroton St NW1 6 B5
Shrubland Rd E8 50 D5
Shuttleworth Rd SW11 69 F5
Sibella Rd SW4 70 D5
Sibley Gro E12 36 A4
Sibthorpe Rd SE12 91 E4
Sicilian Av WC1 9 F6
Sidbury St SW6 67 G4
Sidcup Pl SE9 91 G5
Sidcup Rd SE12 91 E3
Siddons La NW1 6 E4
Sidford Pl SE1 21 H4
Sidmouth Rd NW2 24 E4
Sidmouth St WC1 9 F2
Sidney Rd SW9 71 F5
Sidney Sq E1 46 A5
Sidney St E1 45 G4
Sidney Webb Ho SE1 23 G3
Sidworth St E8 31 G4
Siebert Rd SE3 77 D2
Siemens Brothers Way E16 62 D1
Siemens Rd SE18 63 G4
Sigdon Rd E8 31 F2
Silbury St N1 11 F1
Silchester Rd W10 39 F5
Silex St SE1 22 C2
Silk Cl SE12 90 D3
Silk Mills Sq E9 33 D3
Silk St EC2 11 E5
Silk Weaver Way E2 45 G1
Silver Birch Gdns E6 50 B3
Silverdale NW1
Silverland St E16 64 B2
Silvermere Rd SE6 89 F4
Silver Pl W1 14 B3
Silver Rd SE13 89 F1
Silver Rd W12 53 F1
Silverthorne Rd SW8 70 B5
Silverton Rd W6 67 F2
Silvertown Way E16 48 C5
Silver Wk SE16 60 D2
Silvester Rd SE22 87 E3
Silvester St SE1 23 E2
Silvocea Way E14 48 A5
Silwood St SE16 60 A5
Simla Ho SE1 23 G2
Simmons Rd SE18 78 D1
Simms Rd SE1 59 F5
Simnel Rd SE12 91 E5
Simpsons Rd E14 61 F1
Simpson St SW11 69 F5
Sims Wk SE3 90 C2
Sinclair Gdns W14 53 F3
Sinclair Pl SE4 89 E4
Sinclair Rd W14 53 F3
Singer St EC2 11 G2
Sir Alexander Cl W3 52 B2
Sir Alexander Rd W3 52 B2
Sirdar Rd W11 53 F1
Sir Giles Gilbert Scott Bldg, The SW15 81 G4
Sinnham Pt SW8 71 F2
Sise La EC4 17 F2
Sisley Rd, Bark. 37 G5
Sispara Gdns SW18 82 A4
Sissulu Ct E6 35 F5
Sisters Av SW11 83 G2
Sisulu Pl SW9 85 G1
Sivill Ho E2 45 E2
Six Bridges Trd Est SE1 73 F1
Sixth Av E12 36 B1
Sixth Av W10 39 G2
Skardu Rd NW2 25 G2
Skeena Hill SW18 81 G5

Skeffington Rd E6 36 A5
Skeffington St SE18 65 E4
Skelgill Rd SW15 82 A2
Skelley Rd E15 34 C4
Skelton Rd E7 35 D3
Skelwith Rd W6 67 E2
Sketchley Gdns SE16 74 B1
Skiers St E15 34 B5
Skinner Pl SW1 19 F6
Skinners La EC4 17 E3
Skinner St EC1 10 A2
Skipsea Av E6 50 B2
Skipworth Rd E9 32 A5
Skylines Village E14 61 G3
Slade, The SE18 79 G2
Sladebrook Rd SE3 91 G1
Sladedale Rd SE18 79 G1
Slagrove Pl SE13 89 D2
Slaidburn St SW10 69 D2
Slaithwaite Rd SE13 89 G2
Sleaford Ho E3 47 E3
Sleaford St SW8 70 C3
Slingsby Pl WC2 14 E3
Slippers Pl SE16 59 G4
Sloane Av SW3 18 C6
Sloane Ct W SW3 70 A1
Sloane Gdns SW1 19 F6
Sloane Sq SW1 19 F6
Sloane St SW1 18 E3
Sloane Ter SW1 19 E5
Smart's Pl WC2 15 F1
Smart St E2 46 B2
Smead Way SE13 89 F1
Smeaton Ct SE1 22 D4
Smeaton Rd SW18 82 B5
Smeaton St E1 59 G2
Smedley St SW4 71 D5
Smedley St SW8 71 D5
Smeed Rd E3 33 E4
Smiles Pl SE13 75 G5
Smith Cl SE16 60 B2
Smithfield St EC1 10 B6
Smith's Ct W1 14 B3
Smiths Pt E13 34 D5
Smith Sq SW1 20 E4
Smith St SW3 69 G1
Smith Ter SW3 69 G1
Smithy St E1 46 A4
Smokehouse Yd EC1 10 C5
Smugglers Way SW18 82 C2
Smyrks Rd SE17 73 D1
Smyrna Rd NW6 26 B4
Smythe St E14 61 F1
Snarsgate St W10 39 E4
Sneyd Rd NW2 25 E1
Snowberry Cl E15 34 A1
Snowbury Rd SW6 68 C5
Snowden St EC2 11 H4
Snow Hill EC1 10 B6
Snow Hill Ct EC1 16 C1
Snowman Ho NW6 26 C2
Snowsfields SE1 23 G1
Snowshill Rd E12 36 A2
Soames St SE15 87 E1
Soho Sq W1 14 C1
Soho St W1 14 C1
Solebay St E1 46 C3
Solent Ri E13 48 D2
Solent Rd NW6 26 B2
Soley Ms WC1 9 J1
Solna Av SW15 81 E3
Solomon's Pas SE15 87 G2
Solon New Rd SW4 85 E2
Solon Rd SW2 85 E2
Solway Rd SE22 87 F2
Somali Rd NW2 26 A1
Somerby Rd, Bark. 37 F4
Somerfield St SE16 74 B1
Somerford Gro N16 31 E1
Somerford St E1 45 G3
Somerford Way SE16 60 C3
Somerleyton Pas SW9 86 A2

Somerleyton Rd SW9 85 G2
Somers Cres W2 12 B2
Somerset Est SW11 69 E4
Somerset Gdns SE13 75 F5
Somerset Sq W14 53 G3
Somers Ms W2 12 B2
Somers Rd SW2 85 F5
Somerton Rd SE15 87 G2
Somerville Av SW13 67 D2
Sondes St SE17 72 C2
Sonia Gdns NW10 24 B1
Sophia Rd E16 49 E5
Sopwith Way SW8 70 B3
Sorrel Gdns E6 50 A4
Sorrel La E14 48 A5
Sotheran Cl E8 31 F5
Sotheron Rd SW6 68 C3
Soudan Rd SW11 69 G4
Souldern Rd W14 53 F4
South Africa Rd W12 52 D2
Southall Pl SE1 23 F2
Southampton Bldgs WC2 15 J1
Southampton Pl WC1 9 F6
Southampton Rd NW5 27 G2
Southampton Row WC1 9 F5
Southampton Way SE5 73 F3
Southam St W10 39 G3
South Audley St W1 13 G4
Southbank Business Cen SW8 71 D2
South Black Lion La W6 66 C1
South Bolton Gdns SW5 68 C1
Southborough Rd E9 32 A5
Southbourne Gdns, Ilf. 37 E2
Southbourne Ms SE12 90 C4
Southbrook Rd SE12 90 C4
South Carriage Dr SW1 18 D1
South Carriage Dr SW7 18 A2
Southchurch Rd E6 50 B1
South Circular Rd (A205) SE6 90 A5
South Circular Rd (A205) SE9 92 B1
South Circular Rd (A205) SE12 91 E4
South Circular Rd (A205) SE18 78 C2
South Circular Rd (A205) SW4 84 A3
South Circular Rd (A3) SW11 83 F3
South Circular Rd (A205) SW14 80 A2
South Circular Rd (A205) SW15 81 E2
South Circular Rd (A3) SW18 83 F3
South Colonnade, The E14 61 G2
Southcombe St W14 53 G5
Southcote Rd N19 28 C1
South Cres E16 48 A3
South Cres WC1 8 C6
Southcroft Av, Well. 93 G1
South Eaton Pl SW1 19 G5
South Edwardes Sq W8 54 A4
South End Cl NW3 27 F1
Southend Cres SE9 92 D4
Southend Rd E6 36 B4
South End Rd NW3 27 F1
South End Row W8 54 C4
Southerngate Way SE14 74 C3
Southern Gro E3 46 D2

Southern Rd E13 49 E1
Southern Row W10 39 G3
Southern St N1 43 F1
Southern Way SE10 62 C5
Southerton Rd W6 53 E4
South Esk Rd E7 35 F3
Southey Rd SW9 71 G4
Southfield Rd W4 52 A4
Southfields Pas SW18 82 B4
Southfields Rd SW18 82 B4
Southgate Gro N1 30 C4
Southgate Rd N1 30 C5
South Hill Pk NW3 27 F1
South Hill Pk Gdns NW3 27 F1
South Island Pl SW9 71 F3
South Kensington Underground Sta SW7 18 A5
South Lambeth Pl SW8 71 E2
South Lambeth Rd SW8 71 E2
South Molton La W1 13 H2
South Molton Rd E16 49 D5
South Molton St W1 13 H2
Southmoor Way E9 33 D3
Southolm St SW11 70 B4
South Par SW3 69 E1
South Pk SW6 68 B5
South Pk Dr, Bark. 37 G1
South Pk Dr, Ilf. 37 G1
South Pk Ms SW6 82 C1
South Pl EC2 11 G5
South Pl Ms EC2 11 G6
Southport Rd SE18 65 F5
South Ri Way SE18 79 F1
South Row SE3 76 C5
South Sea St SE16 60 D4
South Side W6 52 B4
Southside Shop Cen SW18 82 C4
Southspring, Sid. 93 F5
South Sq WC1 9 J6
South St W1 13 G5
South Tenter St E1 59 E1
South Ter SW7 18 B5
Southvale Rd SE3 76 B5
Southview Av NW10 24 B2
South Vil NW1 29 D3
Southville SW8 71 D4
Southwark Br EC4 16 E5
Southwark Br SE1 16 E5
Southwark Br Rd SE1 22 C3
Southwark Pk SE16 60 A5
Southwark Pk Est SE16 59 G5
Southwark Pk Rd SE16 59 E5
Southwark St SE1 16 C5
Southwater Cl E14 46 D5
Southway Cl W12 53 D3
Southwell Gdns SW7 54 D5
Southwell Rd SE5 86 B5
South Wf Rd W2 41 E5
Southwick Ms W2 12 A1
Southwick Pl W2 12 B2
Southwick St W2 12 B1
South Worple Av SW14 80 A1
Sovereign Cl E1 59 G1
Sowerby Cl SE9 92 A3
Spafield St EC1 9 J3
Spa Grn Est EC1 10 A1
Spanby Rd E3 47 E3
Spanish Pl W1 13 G1
Spanish Rd SW18 83 D3
Sparkford Ho SW11 69 E4
Spa Rd SE16 59 E4
Sparrows La SE9 93 E5
Sparsholt Rd, Bark. 37 G5
Sparta St SE10 75 F4
Spearman St SE18 78 C2
Spear Ms SW5 54 B5

Street	Pg	Grid
Speed Ho EC2	11	F5
Speedy Pl WC1	9	E2
Speldhurst Rd E9	32	B4
Spelman St E1	45	F4
Spencer Gdns SE9	92	B3
Spencer Pk SW18	83	E3
Spencer Ri NW5	28	B1
Spencer Rd E6	35	G5
Spencer Rd SW18	83	E2
Spencer St EC1	10	B2
Spencer Wk NW3	27	E4
Spencer Wk SW15	81	F2
Spenser Gro N16	30	D1
Spenser Rd SE24	85	G3
Spenser St SW1	20	B3
Spert St E14	60	C1
Spey St E14	47	G4
Spezia Rd NW10	38	C1
Spicer Cl SW9	72	A5
Spindle Cl SE7	64	A4
Spindrift Av E14	61	F5
Spital Sq E1	11	J5
Spital St E1	45	F3
Spital Yd E1	11	J5
Sporle Ct SW11	83	E1
Sportsbank St SE6	89	G5
Spray St SE18	65	D5
Sprimont Pl SW3	69	G1
Springall St SE15	73	G3
Springbank Rd SE13	90	A4
Springdale Rd N16	30	C1
Springfield Gro SE7	77	F2
Springfield Gro Est SE7	77	F2
Springfield La NW6	26	C5
Springfield Rd E6	36	B4
Springfield Rd E15	48	B2
Springfield Wk NW6	26	C5
Spring Gdns SW1	14	D5
Springhill Cl SE5	86	C1
Spring Ms W1	7	E5
Spring Path NW3	27	E2
Spring Pl NW5	28	B2
Springrice Rd SE13	89	G4
Spring St W2	41	E5
Springvale Ter W14	53	F4
Springwater Cl SE18	78	C4
Spring Way SE5	72	C4
Springwell Av NW10	38	A1
Springwood Cl E3	47	E1
Sprowston Ms E7	34	D3
Sprowston Rd E7	35	D2
Sprules Rd SE4	74	C5
Spurgeon St SE1	23	F4
Spurling Rd SE22	87	E2
Spur Rd SE1	21	J1
Spur Rd SW1	20	A2
Spur Rd, Bark.	51	E1
Spurstowe Ter E8	31	G2
Square, The W6	67	A2
Squirrels, The SE13	90	A1
Squirries St E2	45	F2
Stable N1	29	E5
Stables Way SE11	71	G1
Stable Yd SW1	20	A1
Stable Yd Rd SW1	14	A6
Stacey St WC2	14	D2
Stackhouse St SW3	18	D3
Stadium Rd SE18	78	A3
Stadium St SW10	68	C4
Stafford Cl NW6	40	B2
Stafford Ct W8	54	B4
Stafford Pl SW1	20	A3
Stafford Rd E3	46	D1
Stafford Rd E7	35	F4
Stafford Rd NW6	40	B2
Staffordshire St SE15	73	F4
Stafford St W1	14	A5
Stafford Ter W8	54	B4
Staff St EC1	11	G2
Stainer St SE1	17	G6
Staines Rd, Ilf.	37	E1
Staining La EC2	16	E1
Stainsby Rd E14	47	E5
Stainton Rd SE6	90	A4
Stalbridge St NW1	6	C5
Stalham St SE16	59	G2
Stamford Brook Av W6	52	B4
Stamford Brook Rd W6	52	B4
Stamford Cl W6	52	B5
Stamford Rd E6	36	A5
Stamford Rd N1	31	D4
Stamford Rd SE1	15	J6
Stamp Pl E2	45	F1
Stanborough Rd SW15	81	E1
Stanbury Rd SE15	73	G4
Standard Ind Est E16	64	B3
Standard Pl EC2	11	J2
Standen Rd SW18	82	A5
Standish Rd W6	52	C5
Stane Way SE18	77	G3
Stanfield Rd E3	46	C1
Stanford Rd W8	54	C4
Stanford St SW1	20	C6
Stangate SE1	21	G2
Stanhope Gdns SW7	55	D5
Stanhope Gate W1	13	G5
Stanhope Ms E SW7	55	D5
Stanhope Ms S SW7	55	D5
Stanhope Ms W SW7	55	D5
Stanhope Pl W2	12	D2
Stanhope Row W1	13	H6
Stanhope St NW1	8	A2
Stanhope Ter W2	12	A3
Stanlake Ms W12	53	E2
Stanlake Rd W12	53	D2
Stanlake Vil W12	53	D2
Stanley Cl SW8	71	F2
Stanley Cres W11	54	A1
Stanley Gdns NW2	25	E2
Stanley Gdns W3	51	J1
Stanley Gdns W11	54	A1
Stanley Gro SW8	70	A5
Stanley Rd E12	36	A2
Stanley Rd E15	34	A5
Stanley St SE8	75	D3
Stanmer St SW11	69	F4
Stannard Ms E8	31	F3
Stannard Rd E8	31	F3
Stannary St SE11	71	G2
Stansfeld Rd E6	49	G4
Stansfield Rd SW9	85	F1
Stanswood Gdns SE5	73	D3
Stanton Rd SW13	66	B5
Stanway St N1	45	D1
Stanwick Rd W14	54	A5
Stanworth St SE1	59	E3
Stapleford Cl SW19	80	B3
Staplehurst Rd SE13	90	B3
Staple Inn WC1	9	J6
Staple Inn Bldgs WC1	9	J6
Staples Cl SE16	60	C2
Staple St SE1	23	G2
Star All EC3	17	J3
Starboard Way E14	61	E4
Starbuck Cl SE9	92	C5
Starcross St NW1	8	B2
Starfield Rd W12	52	C3
Star La E16	48	B3
Star Rd W14	68	A2
Star St E16	48	C4
Star St W2	12	A1
Star Yd WC2	15	J1
Station App SE1	15	H6
Station App SW6	81	G1
Station Cres SE3	76	D1
Station Par NW2	25	E3
Station Par, Bark.	37	E4
Station Pas SE15	74	A4
Station Rd E7	34	D1
Station Rd E12	36	A2
Station Rd NW10	38	B1
Station Rd SE13	89	G1
Station Rd SW13	80	C1
Station St E15	34	A4
Station St E16	64	D2
Station Ter NW10	39	F1
Station Ter SE5	72	B4
Staunton St SE8	75	D2
Staveley Cl N7	29	E3
Staverton Rd NW2	25	E4
Stave Yd Rd SE16	60	C2
Stavordale Rd N5	30	A1
Stayner's Rd E1	46	B3
Stead St SE17	23	F6
Stean St E8	31	E5
Stebbing Ho W11	53	F2
Stebondale St E14	75	G1
Stedham Pl WC1	14	E1
Steedman St SE17	22	D6
Steele Rd E11	33	G3
Steeles Rd NW3	27	G3
Steelyard Pas EC4	17	F4
Steeple Cl SW6	67	G5
Steers Way SE16	60	C3
Stephan Cl E8	31	F5
Stephendale Rd SW6	68	C6
Stephen Ms W1	8	C6
Stephenson Rd E17	48	B3
Stephenson St NW10	38	A2
Stephenson Way NW1	8	B3
Stephen's Rd E15	34	B5
Stephen St W1	8	C6
Stepney Causeway E1	46	A4
Stepney Grn E1	46	A4
Stepney High St E1	46	B4
Stepney Way E1	45	G4
Sterling Cl NW10	24	C3
Sterling Gdns SE14	74	C2
Sterling St SW7	18	C3
Sterndale Rd W14	53	F4
Sterne St W12	53	F3
Sternhall La SE15	73	F5
Sterry St SE1	23	F2
Steucers La SE23	88	C5
Stevenage Rd E6	36	C3
Stevenage Rd SW6	67	F3
Stevens Av E9	32	A3
Stevenson Cres SE16	73	F1
Stevens St SE1	23	J3
Steventon Rd W12	52	B1
Steward St E1	11	J6
Stewart Rainbird Ho E12	36	C2
Stewart Rd E15	33	G1
Stewart's Gro SW3	55	E5
Stewart's Rd SW8	70	C3
Stewart St E14	61	G3
Stew La EC4	16	D3
Stillingfleet Rd SW13	66	C2
Stillington St SW1	20	B5
Stillness Rd SE23	88	C4
Stirling Rd E13	49	E1
Stirling Rd SW9	71	E5
Stockholm Ho E1	59	F2
Stockholm Rd SE16	74	A1
Stockholm Way E1	59	F2
Stockhurst Cl SW15	67	E5
Stock Orchard Cres N7	29	F2
Stock Orchard St N7	29	F2
Stock St E13	48	D1
Stockwell Av SW9	85	F1
Stockwell Gdns SW9	71	F5
Stockwell Gdns Est SW9	71	E5
Stockwell Grn SW9	71	F5
Stockwell La SW9	71	F5
Stockwell Pk Cres SW9	71	F5
Stockwell Pk Est SW9	71	F5
Stockwell Pk Rd SW9	71	F4
Stockwell Pk Wk SW9	85	F1
Stockwell Rd SW9	71	F5
Stockwell St SE10	75	G2
Stockwell Ter SW9	71	F4
Stoford Cl SW19	81	G5
Stokenchurch St SW6	68	C4
Stoke Newington Rd N16	31	E2
Stoke Pl NW10	38	B2
Stokesley St W12	38	B5
Stokes Rd E6	50	A3
Stondon Pk SE23	88	C5
Stondon Wk E6	49	G1
Stone Bldgs WC2	9	H6
Stonecutter St EC4	16	B2
Stonefield St N1	29	G5
Stone Ho Ct EC3	17	H1
Stone Lake Retail Pk SE7	63	E5
Stone Lake Rbt SE7	63	F5
Stoneleigh Pl W11	53	F1
Stoneleigh St W11	53	F1
Stones End St SE1	22	D2
Stonewall E6	50	C4
Stoney All SE18	78	C5
Stoneycroft Cl SE12	90	C5
Stoney La E1	17	J1
Stoney St SE1	17	F5
Stonhouse St SW4	84	D1
Stonor Rd W14	54	A5
Stopes St SE15	73	E3
Stopford Rd E13	35	D5
Stopford Rd SE17	72	A1
Store Rd E16	64	C3
Storers Quay E14	62	A5
Store St E15	34	A2
Store St WC1	8	C6
Storey's Gate SW1	20	D2
Storey St E16	64	C2
Stories Ms SE5	72	D5
Stories Rd SE5	86	D1
Stork Rd E7	34	C3
Storks Rd SE16	59	F4
Stormont Rd SW11	84	A1
Stott Cl SW18	83	E4
Stoughton Cl SE11	21	H6
Stourcliffe St W1	12	D2
Stour Rd E3	33	E4
Stowage SE8	75	E2
Stowe Rd W12	52	D3
Stracey Rd E7	35	D1
Stradbroke Rd N5	30	B1
Stradella Rd SE24	86	B4
Strafford St E14	61	E3
Strahan Rd E3	46	C2
Straightsmouth SE10	75	G3
Strait Rd E6	64	A1
Straker's Rd SE15	87	G2
Strand WC2	15	E4
Strandfield Cl SE18	79	G1
Strand La WC2	15	H3
Stranraer Way N1	29	E4
Strasburg Rd SW11	70	B4
Stratford Cen, The E15	34	A4
Stratford Gro SW15	81	F2
Stratford Pl W1	13	H2
Stratford Rd E13	34	C5
Stratford Rd W8	54	B4
Stratford Vil NW1	28	C4
Strathan Cl SW18	81	G4
Strathaven Rd SE12	91	E4
Strathblaine Rd SW11	83	E2
Strathearn Pl W2	12	A3
Strathearn Rd SE3	76	D4
Strathleven Rd SW2	85	E3
Strathnairn St SE1	59	F5
Strathray Gdns NW3	27	F3
Strath Ter SW11	83	F2
Strattondale St E14	61	G4
Stratton St W1	13	J5
Streatfeild Av E6	36	B5
Streatham Pl SW2	85	E5
Streatham St WC1	14	D1
Streatley Rd NW6	26	A4
Streetfield Ms SE3	91	D1
Streimer Rd E15	47	G1
Strelley Way W3	52	A1
Strickland Row SW18	83	E5

Name	Ref
Strickland St SE8	75 E5
Stride Rd E7	48 C1
Strode Rd E7	34 D1
Strode Rd NW10	24 C3
Strode Rd SW6	67 F3
Strone Rd E7	35 G3
Strone Rd E12	35 G3
Strongbow Cres SE9	92 B3
Strongbow Rd SE9	92 B3
Stronsa Rd W12	52 B3
Stroudley Wk E3	47 F2
Strutton Grd SW1	20 C3
Stuart Rd NW6	40 B2
Stuart Rd SE15	88 A2
Stuart Twr W9	40 D3
Stubbs Dr SE16	73 G1
Stubbs Pt E13	49 E3
Studdridge St SW6	68 B5
Studd St N1	30 A5
Studholme Ct NW3	26 B1
Studholme St SE15	73 G3
Studio Pl SW1	19 E2
Studland W6	52 D5
Studley Cl E5	32 C2
Studley Est SW4	71 E4
Studley Rd E7	35 E3
Studley Rd SW4	71 E4
Stukeley Rd E7	35 E4
Stukeley St WC1	15 F1
Stukeley St W2	15 F1
Sturdy Rd SE15	72 B1
Sturge St SE1	22 D1
Sturmer Way N7	29 F2
Sturry St E14	47 F5
Sturt St N1	44 B1
Stutfield St E1	45 F5
Styles Gdns SW9	86 A1
Sudbourne Rd SW2	85 E3
Sudbrooke Rd SW12	83 G4
Sudeley St N1	44 A1
Sudlow Rd SW18	78 B3
Sudrey St SE1	22 D2
Suffolk La EC4	17 F3
Suffolk Pl SW1	14 D5
Suffolk Rd E13	48 C2
Suffolk Rd NW10	24 A4
Suffolk Rd SW13	66 B3
Suffolk Rd, Bark.	37 F4
Suffolk St E7	34 D2
Suffolk St SW1	14 D5
Sugar Ho La E15	47 G1
Sugar Quay Wk EC3	17 J4
Sugden Rd SW11	84 A1
Sulgrave Rd W6	53 E3
Sulina Rd SW2	85 E5
Sulivan Ct SW6	82 B1
Sulivan Rd SW6	82 B1
Sullivan Av E16	49 G4
Sullivan Cl SW11	83 F1
Sullivan Rd SE11	22 A5
Sultan St SE5	72 B3
Sumatra Rd NW6	26 B2
Sumburgh Rd SW12	84 A4
Summercourt Rd E1	46 A5
Summerfield Av NW6	39 G1
Summerfield St SE12	90 C5
Summers St EC1	9 J4
Summit Ct NW2	25 G2
Sumner Pl SW7	18 A6
Sumner Pl Ms SW7	18 A6
Sumner Rd SE15	73 E3
Sumner St SE1	16 C5
Sumpter Cl NW3	27 D3
Sunbeam Cres W10	39 E3
Sunbury La SW11	69 E4
Sunbury St SE18	64 B4
Sun Ct EC3	17 G2
Sunderland Ct SE22	87 F5
Sunderland Ter W2	40 C5
Sundew Av W12	52 C1
Sundew Cl W12	52 C1
Sundorne Rd SE7	77 E1
Sundridge Av, Well.	79 F5
Sunfields Pl SE3	77 E3
Sun-In-The-Sands SE3	77 E3
Sun La SE3	77 E3
Sunlight Sq E2	45 G2
Sunningdale Av, Bark.	37 F5
Sunningdale Cl E6	50 B2
Sunninghill Rd SE13	75 F5
Sunningdale Rd SE12	91 E3
Sunnyhill Ct E5	32 C1
Sunnymead Rd SW15	80 D3
Sunray Av SE24	86 C2
Sun Rd W14	68 A1
Sunset Rd SE5	86 B2
Sun St EC2	11 H6
Surma Ct E13	45 G3
Surrendale Pl W9	40 B3
Surrey Canal Rd SE14	74 A2
Surrey Canal Rd SE15	74 A2
Surrey La SW11	69 F4
Surrey La Est SW11	69 F4
Surrey Quays Rd SE16	60 A4
Surrey Quays Shop Cen SE16	60 B4
Surrey Rd SE15	88 B3
Surrey Rd, Bark.	37 G5
Surrey Row SE1	22 B1
Surrey Sq SE17	72 D1
Surrey St E13	49 E2
Surrey St WC2	15 H3
Surrey Ter SE17	23 J6
Surrey Water Rd SE16	60 B2
Surr St N7	29 E2
Susannah St E14	47 F5
Susan Rd SE3	77 E5
Sussex Gdns W2	41 E5
Sussex Ms E W2	12 A2
Sussex Ms W W2	12 A3
Sussex Pl NW1	6 D2
Sussex Pl W2	12 A2
Sussex Pl W6	67 E1
Sussex Rd E6	36 C5
Sussex Sq W2	12 A3
Sussex St E13	49 E2
Sussex St SW1	70 B1
Sutcliffe Rd SE18	79 G2
Sutherland Av W9	40 D2
Sutherland Av, Well.	93 G2
Sutherland Gro SW18	81 G4
Sutherland Pl W2	40 B5
Sutherland Rd W4	66 A1
Sutherland Row SW1	70 B1
Sutherland Sq SE17	72 B1
Sutherland St SW1	70 B1
Sutherland Wk SE17	72 B1
Sutterton St N7	29 F3
Sutton Ct Rd E13	49 F2
Sutton Est SW3	69 F1
Sutton Est W10	39 E4
Sutton Est, The N1	30 A4
Sutton La EC1	10 C6
Sutton Pl E9	32 A2
Sutton Rd E13	48 C3
Sutton Rd, Bark.	51 G1
Sutton Row W1	14 D1
Sutton St E1	46 A5
Sutton's Way EC1	11 E4
Sutton Wk SE1	15 H6
Sutton Way W10	39 E4
Swaffield Rd SW18	82 C5
Swainson Rd W3	52 B3
Swain St NW8	5 E3
Swallow Cl SE14	74 A4
Swallowfield Rd SE7	77 E1
Swallow Pl W1	13 J2
Swallow St E6	50 A4
Swallow St W1	14 B4
Swanage Rd SW18	83 D4
Swan App E6	50 A4
Swanbourne SE17	22 D6
Swandon Way SW18	82 C3
Swanfield St E2	45 E2
Swan La EC4	17 F4
Swan Mead SE1	23 H4
Swan Pl SW13	66 B5
Swan Rd SE16	60 A3
Swan Rd SE18	63 G4
Swanscombe Rd W4	66 B1
Swanscombe Rd W11	53 F2
Swan St SE1	22 E3
Swan Wk SW3	69 G2
Swanwick Cl SW15	80 B5
Swaton Rd E3	47 E3
Swedenborg Gdns E1	59 F1
Sweden Gate SE16	60 C4
Sweeney Cres SE1	59 E3
Swete St E13	49 D1
Sweyn Pl SE3	77 D5
Swift St SW6	68 A4
Swinbrook Rd W10	39 G4
Swinburne Rd SW15	80 C2
Swindon St W12	53 D2
Swinford Gdns SW9	86 A1
Swingate La SE18	79 G2
Swinnerton St E9	32 C2
Swinton Pl WC1	9 G1
Swinton St WC1	9 G1
Swiss Ct W1	14 D4
Swiss Ter NW6	27 E4
Sybil Phoenix Cl SE8	74 B1
Sycamore Av E3	32 D5
Sycamore Gdns W6	53 D3
Sycamore Gdns SE6	89 G4
Sycamore Ms SW4	84 C1
Sycamore St EC1	10 D4
Sydenham Rd SE26	88 A5
Sydner Rd N16	31 E1
Sydney Cl SW3	18 A6
Sydney Ms SW3	18 A6
Sydney Pl SW7	18 A6
Sydney Rd SW3	55 F5
Sylgan Gro NW2	25 G5
Sylvan Gro SE15	73 G3
Sylvan Rd E7	35 D3
Sylvester Rd E8	31 G3
Symington Ho SE1	23 F4
Symister Ms N1	11 H2
Symons Cl SE15	74 A5
Symons St SW3	18 E6

T

Name	Ref
Tabard Gdns Est SE1	23 G2
Tabard St SE1	23 F2
Tabernacle St EC2	11 G4
Tableer Av SW4	84 C3
Tabley Rd N7	29 E1
Tabor Rd W6	53 D4
Tachbrook Est SW1	70 D1
Tachbrook Ms SW1	20 A5
Tachbrook St SW1	20 B6
Tack Ms SE4	89 E1
Tadema Ho NW8	6 A4
Tadema Rd SW10	69 D3
Tadmor St W12	53 E1
Taeping St E14	61 F5
Tait St E1	45 G5
Talacre Rd NW5	28 A3
Talbot Ct EC3	17 G3
Talbot Pl SE3	76 B5
Talbot Rd E6	50 C1
Talbot Rd E7	34 D1
Talbot Rd SE22	87 D2
Talbot Rd W2	40 B5
Talbot Rd W11	40 A5
Talbot Sq W2	12 A2
Talbot Wk W11	39 G5
Talbot Yd SE1	17 F6
Talfourd Pl SE15	73 E4
Talfourd Rd SE15	73 E4
Talgarth Rd W6	67 G1
Talgarth Rd W14	67 G1
Tallis Cl E16	49 E5
Tallis Gro SE7	77 E2
Tallis St EC4	16 A3
Talma Rd SW2	85 G2
Talwin St E3	47 F2
Tamarisk Sq W12	52 B1
Tamworth St SW6	68 B2
Tanfield Av NW2	24 B1
Tangley Gro SW15	80 B5
Tankerton St WC1	9 F2
Tanner St E13	34 D5
Tanners Hill SE8	75 D4
Tanner St SE1	23 J2
Tanner St, Bark.	37 E3
Tanswell Est SE1	21 J2
Tanswell St SE1	21 J2
Tansy Cl E6	50 C5
Tant Av E16	48 C5
Tanza Rd NW3	27 G1
Taplow NW3	27 E4
Taplow St N1	44 B1
Tapper Wk N1	29 E5
Tappesfield Rd SE15	88 A1
Tapp St E1	45 G3
Tarbert Rd SE22	87 D3
Tariff Cres SE8	60 D5
Tarling Rd E16	48 C5
Tarling St E1	45 G5
Tarling St Est E1	46 A5
Tarn St SE1	22 D4
Tarragon Cl SE14	74 C3
Tarrant Pl W1	6 D6
Tarver Rd SE17	72 A1
Tasker Way SE10	75 F3
Tasker Rd NW3	27 G2
Tasman Rd SW9	85 E1
Tasso Rd W6	67 G2
Tate & Lyle Jetty E16	64 A3
Tatham Pl NW8	41 E1
Tatnell Rd SE23	88 C4
Tattersall Cl SE9	92 A3
Tatum St SE17	23 G6
Taunton Ms NW1	6 D3
Taunton Pl NW1	6 D3
Taunton Rd SE12	90 B3
Tavern La SW9	71 G5
Tavistock Cres W11	40 A4
Tavistock Gdns, Ilf.	37 G1
Tavistock Pl WC1	8 D3
Tavistock Rd E7	34 C1
Tavistock Rd E15	34 C3
Tavistock Rd NW10	38 B1
Tavistock Rd W11	40 A5
Tavistock Sq WC1	8 D3
Tavistock St WC2	15 F3
Taviton St WC1	8 C3
Tavy Cl SE11	71 G1
Tawny Way SE16	60 B5
Taybridge Rd SW11	84 A1
Tayburn Cl E14	47 G5
Taylor Cl SE8	74 D2
Taylors Grn W3	38 A5
Tayport Cl N1	29 E4
Teak Cl SE16	60 C2
Teale St E2	45 F1
Teal St SE10	62 C4
Teasel Cres SE28	65 G2
Teasel Way E15	48 B2
Tedworth Sq SW3	69 G1
Tee, The W3	38 A5
Teesdale Cl E2	45 G1
Teesdale St E2	45 G1
Teignmouth Cl SW4	84 D2
Teignmouth Rd NW2	25 F2
Telegraph Pl E14	61 F5
Telegraph Rd SW15	81 D5
Telegraph St EC2	17 F1
Telemann Sq SE3	91 E1
Telford Ho SE1	22 D4
Telford Rd W10	39 G4
Telford Ter SW1	70 C2
Telford Way W3	38 A4
Telham Rd E6	50 C1
Tell Gro SE22	87 E2
Tellson Av SE18	78 A4

Entry	Ref
Temperley Rd SW12	84 A5
Templar St SE5	72 A5
Temple, The EC4	57 G1
Temple Av EC4	16 A3
Temple CI SE28	65 E4
Templecombe Rd E9	32 A5
Temple La EC4	16 A2
Templemead CI W3	38 A5
Temple Mills La E15	33 G2
Temple PI WC2	15 H3
Temple Rd E6	36 A5
Temple Rd NW2	25 E1
Temple St E2	62 A1
Templeton PI SW5	54 B5
Temple W Ms SE11	22 B4
Tench St E1	59 G2
Tenison Ct W1	14 A3
Tenison Way SE1	15 J6
Tennis St SE1	23 F1
Tennyson Av E12	36 A4
Tennyson CI, Well.	79 G4
Tennyson Rd E15	34 B4
Tennyson Rd NW6	26 A5
Tennyson St SW8	70 B5
Tenterden St W1	13 J2
Tent St E1	45 G3
Teredo St SE16	60 B4
Terminus St SW1	19 J4
Terrace, The NW6	26 B5
Terrace, The SW13	66 A5
Terrace Gdns SW13	66 A5
Terrace Rd E9	32 A4
Terrace Rd E13	35 D5
Terrick St W12	39 D5
Tessa Sanderson PI SW8	84 B1
Testerton Wk W11	53 F1
Tetcott Rd SW10	68 D3
Teversham La SW8	71 E2
Teviot St E14	47 G4
Tewson Rd SE18	79 G1
Thackeray Rd E6	49 G1
Thackeray Rd SW8	70 B5
Thackeray St W8	54 C3
Thalia CI SE10	76 A2
Thame Rd SE16	60 B3
Thames Av SW10	69 D4
Thameside Ind Est E16	
Thames PI SW15	81 F1
Thames Rd E16	63 G2
Thames Rd SE10	75 F2
Thames Wf E16	62 D2
Thanet St WC1	8 E2
Thanington Ct SE9	93 G4
Thavies Inn EC1	16 A1
Thaxton Rd W14	68 A2
Thayer St W1	7 G6
Theatre St SW11	83 G1
Theberton St N1	29 G5
Theed St SE1	15 J6
Thelma Gdns SE3	77 G4
Theobald's Rd WC1	9 G5
Theobald St SE1	23 F4
Theodore Rd SE13	89 G4
Therapia Rd SE22	88 A4
Theresa Rd W6	52 C5
Thermopylae Gate E14	61 F5
Thessaly Rd SW8	70 C3
Third Av E12	36 A1
Third Av E13	49 D2
Third Av W3	52 B2
Third Av W10	39 G2
Thirleby Rd SW1	20 B4
Thirsk Rd SW11	84 A1
Thistle Gro SW10	69 D1
Thomas Baines Rd SW11	83 E2
Thomas Cribb Ms E6	50 B5
Thomas Darby Ct W11	39 E5
Thomas Doyle St SE1	22 B3
Thomas La SE6	89 E5
Thomas More St E1	59 F1
Thomas Rd E14	47 D5
Thomas St SE18	64 C5
Thompson Rd SE22	87 E4
Thompsons Av SE5	72 B3
Thorburn Sq SE1	59 F5
Thoresby St N1	12 E1
Thornbury Rd SW2	85 E4
Thorncliffe Rd SW2	85 E4
Thorncombe Rd SE22	87 D3
Thorncroft St SW8	71 E3
Thorndike CI SW10	68 D3
Thorndike Rd N1	30 B3
Thorndike St SW1	20 C6
Thorne CI E11	34 B1
Thorne CI E16	48 D5
Thorne Pas SW13	66 A5
Thorne Rd SW8	71 E3
Thorne St E16	48 C5
Thorne St SW13	80 A1
Thorney Cres SW11	69 E3
Thorney St SW1	21 E5
Thornfield Rd W12	52 D3
Thornford Rd SE13	89 G3
Thorngate Rd W9	40 B3
Thorngrove Rd E13	35 E4
Thornham Gro E15	34 A2
Thornham St SE10	75 F2
Thornhaugh Ms WC1	8 D4
Thornhaugh St WC1	8 D5
Thornhill Av SE18	79 G3
Thornhill Cres N1	29 F4
Thornhill Gdns, Bark.	37 G4
Thornhill Rd N1	29 F4
Thornhill Sq N1	29 F4
Thornton Av W4	52 A5
Thornton Ho SE17	23 G6
Thornton PI W1	6 E5
Thornton Rd SW8	71 G5
Thornton Rd, Ilf.	36 D1
Thornton St SW9	71 G5
Thorntree Rd SE7	77 G1
Thornville St SE8	75 E4
Thornwood Rd SE13	90 B2
Thorogood Gdns E15	34 B2
Thorparch Rd SW8	70 D4
Thorpebank Rd W12	52 C2
Thorpe Rd E6	36 B5
Thorpe Rd E7	34 C1
Thorpe Rd, Bark.	37 F4
Thoydon Rd E3	46 C1
Thrale St SE1	16 D6
Thrawl St E1	45 E4
Threadneedle St EC2	17 G2
Three Barrels Wk EC4	16 E4
Three Colts La E2	45 G3
Three Colt St E14	61 D1
Three Cups Yd WC1	9 H1
Three Kings Yd W1	13 H3
Three Mill La E3	47 G2
Three Quays Wk EC3	17 H4
Threshers PI W11	53 G1
Throckmorton Rd E16	49 E5
Throgmorton Av EC2	17 G1
Throgmorton St EC2	17 G1
Thurland Rd SE16	59 F4
Thurleigh Av SW12	84 A4
Thurleigh Rd SW12	84 A4
Thurloe CI SW7	18 B5
Thurloe PI SW7	18 A5
Thurloe PI Ms SW7	18 A5
Thurloe Sq SW7	18 B5
Thurloe St SW7	18 A5
Thurlow Rd NW3	27 E2
Thurlow St SE17	72 C1
Thurlow Ter NW5	28 A2
Thurston Rd SE13	75 F5
Thurtle Rd E2	31 E5
Thyme CI SE3	91 F1
Tibbatts Rd E3	47 F3
Tibbenham Wk E13	48 C1
Tibbet's Cor SW15	81 F5
Tibbet's Ride SW15	81 F5
Tidal Basin Rd E16	62 C1
Tideslea Path SE28	65 F3
Tideslea Twr SE28	65 F3
Tideswell Rd SW15	81 E3
Tideway Ind Est SW8	70 C2
Tidey St E3	47 E4
Tidlock Ho SE28	65 F3
Tidworth Rd E3	47 E3
Tiger Way E5	31 G1
Tilbrook Rd SE3	91 F1
Tilbury Rd E6	50 B1
Tildesley Rd SW15	81 E4
Tileyard Rd N7	29 E4
Tilia Wk SW9	86 A2
Tiller Rd E14	61 E4
Tillings CI SE5	72 B4
Tilney Ct EC1	11 E3
Tilney Gdns N1	30 C3
Tilney St W1	13 G5
Tilson Gdns SW2	85 E5
Tilson Ho SW2	85 E5
Tilton St SW6	67 G2
Tilt Yd App SE9	92 B4
Timbercroft La SE18	79 F2
Timberland Rd E1	45 G5
Timber Mill Way SW4	84 D1
Timber Pond Rd SE16	60 B3
Timber St EC1	10 D3
Time Sq E8	31 E2
Timothy CI SW4	84 C3
Tindal St SW9	72 A4
Tinsley Rd E1	46 A4
Tintagel Cres SE22	87 E2
Tintern CI SW15	81 G3
Tintern St SW4	85 E2
Tinto Rd E16	49 D3
Tinworth St SE11	71 F1
Tipthorpe Rd SW11	84 A1
Tisdall PI SE17	23 G6
Titchborne Row W2	12 C2
Titchfield Rd NW8	42 B1
Titchwell Rd SW18	83 E5
Tite St SW3	69 G1
Tiverton Rd NW10	25 F5
Tiverton St SE1	22 D4
Tivoli Ct SE16	60 D3
Tivoli Gdns SE18	64 A5
Tobacco Dock E1	59 G1
Tobin CI NW3	27 F4
Toby La E1	46 C3
Tokenhouse Yd EC2	17 F1
Toland Sq SW15	80 C3
Tollet St E1	46 B3
Tollgate Gdns NW6	40 C1
Tollgate Rd E6	49 G4
Tollgate Rd E16	49 F4
Tollington Rd N7	29 F1
Tolmers Sq NW1	8 B3
Tolpuddle St N1	43 G1
Tolsford Rd E5	31 G2
Tom Coombs CI SE9	92 A2
Tom Cribb Rd SE28	65 E4
Tom Jenkinson Rd E16	63 D2
Tomlins Gro E3	47 E2
Tomlinson CI E2	45 E2
Tomlins Orchard, Bark.	37 E5
Tom Mann CI, Bark.	37 G5
Tom Nolan CI E15	48 B1
Tompion St EC1	10 B2
Tonbridge St WC1	9 E1
Tonsley Hill SW18	82 C3
Tonsley PI SW18	82 C3
Tonsley Rd SW18	82 C3
Tonsley St SW18	82 C3
Took's Ct EC4	15 J1
Tooley St SE1	17 G5
Topham St EC1	9 J3
Topley St SE9	91 G2
Topmast Pt E14	61 E3
Torbay Rd NW6	26 A4
Tor Gdns W8	54 B3
Tor Gro SE28	65 G2
Tormount Rd SE18	79 G2
Toronto Av E12	36 B1
Torrance CI SE7	77 G2
Torrens Rd E15	34 C3
Torrens Rd SW2	85 F3
Torrens Sq E15	34 B3
Torrens St EC1	43 G1
Torriano Av NW5	28 D2
Torriano Ms NW5	28 C2
Torridge Gdns SE15	88 A2
Torridon Rd SE13	90 A5
Torrington PI E1	59 F2
Torrington PI WC1	8 B5
Torrington Sq WC1	8 D4
Torwood Rd SW15	80 C3
Tothill St SW1	20 C2
Tottan Ter E1	46 B5
Tottenham Ct Rd W1	8 B4
Tottenham Ms W1	8 B5
Tottenham Rd N1	30 D3
Tottenham St W1	8 B6
Totteridge Ho SW11	69 E5
Toulmin St SE1	22 D2
Toulon St SE5	72 B3
Tournay Rd SW6	68 A3
Tours Pas SW11	83 E2
Towcester Rd E3	47 F3
Tower 42 EC2	17 H1
Tower Br E1	59 E2
Tower Br E1	59 E2
Tower Br App E1	59 E2
Tower Br Rd SE1	23 H4
Tower Br Wf E1	59 F2
Tower CI NW3	27 F2
Tower CI WC2	14 E2
Tower Hamlets Rd E7	34 C1
Tower Millennium Pier EC3	17 J5
Tower Mill Rd SE15	72 D3
Tower PI EC3	17 J4
Tower PI W EC3	17 J4
Tower Rd NW10	24 C4
Tower Royal EC4	17 F3
Tower St WC2	14 D2
Town Hall Rd SW11	83 G1
Townley Ct E15	34 C3
Townley Rd SE22	87 D3
Townmead Rd SE6	68 D5
Town Quay, Bark.	37 D5
Townsend St SE17	23 G6
Townshend Est NW8	41 F1
Townshend Rd NW8	27 F5
Towpath Wk E9	32 D2
Toynbee St E1	45 E4
Tracey Av NW2	25 E2
Trader Rd E6	50 D5
Tradescant Rd SW8	71 E3
Trafalgar Av SE15	73 E1
Trafalgar Gdns E1	46 B4
Trafalgar Gro SE10	76 A2
Trafalgar Ms E9	32 D3
Trafalgar Rd SE10	76 A2
Trafalgar Sq SW1	14 D5
Trafalgar Sq WC2	14 D5
Trafalgar St SE17	72 C1
Trafalgar Way E14	61 G2
Trahorn CI E1	45 F3
Tramway Av E15	34 B4
Tranquil Vale SE3	76 B5
Transept St NW1	6 B6
Transom Sq E14	61 F5
Tranton Rd SE16	59 F4
Treadgold St W11	53 F1
Treadway St E2	45 G1
Treaty St N1	29 F5
Trebeck St W1	13 H5
Trebovir Rd SW5	68 B1
Treby St E3	46 D3
Tredegar Rd E3	46 D1
Tredegar Sq E3	46 D2
Tredegar Ter E3	46 D2
Trederwen Rd E8	31 F5
Treen Av SW13	80 B1
Tree Rd E16	49 F5
Trefil Wk N7	29 E1

Name	Ref
Trefoil Rd SW18	83 D3
Tregarvon Rd SW11	84 A2
Trego Rd E9	33 E4
Tregothnan Rd SW8	85 E1
Tregunter Rd SW10	68 D2
Trehurst St E5	32 C2
Trelawney Est E9	32 A3
Trelawn Rd SW2	85 G3
Trellick Twr W10	40 A3
Tremadoc Rd SW4	84 D2
Tremaine Cl SE4	75 E5
Trenchard St SE10	76 A1
Trenchold St SW8	71 E2
Trenmar Gdns NW10	38 D2
Trent Rd SW2	85 F3
Treport St SW18	82 C5
Tresco Rd SE15	87 G2
Tresham Cres NW8	6 B3
Tressillian Cres SE4	89 E1
Tressillian Rd SE4	89 D2
Trevanion Rd W14	67 G1
Trevelyan Av E12	36 B1
Trevelyan Gdns NW10	25 E5
Trevelyan Rd E15	34 B1
Treveris St SE1	16 B6
Treverton St W10	39 F3
Treville St SW15	80 D5
Trevithick Ho SE16	59 G5
Trevithick St SE8	75 E1
Trevithick Way E3	47 E2
Trevor Pl SW7	18 C2
Trevor Sq SW7	18 D2
Trevor St SW7	18 C2
Triangle, The E1	10 C3
Triangle Pl SW4	84 D2
Triangle Rd E8	31 G5
Trident St SE16	60 B5
Trig La EC4	16 D3
Trigon Rd SW8	71 F3
Trim St SE14	74 D2
Trinidad St E14	61 D1
Trinity Buoy Wf E14	62 C1
Trinity Ch Pas SW13	67 D2
Trinity Ch Rd SW13	67 D2
Trinity Ch Sq SE1	22 E3
Trinity Cl E8	31 E3
Trinity Cl SE13	90 A2
Trinity Gdns SW9	85 F2
Trinity Gro SE10	75 G4
Trinity Rd SW18	83 E3
Trinity Sq EC3	17 J4
Trinity Wk NW3	22 E2
Trinity Way W3	52 A1
Trio Pl SE1	22 E2
Tristan Sq SE3	90 B1
Triton Sq NW1	8 A3
Triumph Rd E6	50 B5
Trossachs Rd SE22	87 D3
Trott St SW11	69 F4
Troughton Rd SE7	77 E1
Troutbeck Rd SE14	74 C4
Trouville Rd SW4	84 C4
Trowbridge Rd E9	33 D3
Troy Town SE15	87 F1
Truesdale Rd E6	50 B5
Truman's Rd N16	30 C1
Trumpington Rd E7	34 C1
Trump St EC2	17 E2
Trundle St SE1	22 D1
Trundleys Rd SE8	74 B1
Trundleys Ter SE8	60 B5
Truro St NW5	28 A3
Trussley Rd W6	53 E4
Tryon Cres E9	32 A5
Tryon St SW3	69 G1
Tuam Rd SE18	79 F2
Tubbs Rd NW10	38 B1
Tudor Cl N3	27 F2
Tudor Cl SW2	85 F4
Tudor Gro E9	32 A4
Tudor Rd E6	35 F5
Tudor Rd E9	31 G5
Tudor St EC4	16 A3
Tudway Rd SE3	91 E1
Tufnell Pk Rd N7	28 C1
Tufnell Pk Rd N19	28 C1
Tufton St SW1	20 D3
Tugboat St SE28	65 G3
Tuilerie St E2	45 F1
Tulip Gdns, Ilf.	36 D3
Tulse Hill SW2	85 G4
Tulse Hill Est SW2	85 G4
Tump Ho SE28	65 G2
Tunis Rd W12	53 D2
Tunley Rd NW10	24 A5
Tunmarsh La E13	49 F2
Tunnan Leys E6	50 C5
Tunnel Av SE10	62 A3
Tunstall Rd SW9	85 F2
Tunworth Cres SW15	80 B4
Turenne Cl SW18	83 D2
Turin St E2	45 F2
Turk's Head Yd EC1	10 B5
Turks Row SW3	69 G1
Turley Cl E15	34 B5
Turnagain La EC4	16 B1
Turner Cl SW9	72 A4
Turners Rd E3	46 D4
Turner St E1	45 G4
Turner St E16	48 C5
Turneville Rd W14	68 A2
Turney Rd SE21	86 C5
Turnham Grn Ter W4	52 A5
Turnham Rd SE4	88 C3
Turnmill St EC1	10 A4
Turnpike Ho EC1	10 C2
Turpin La SE10	75 G2
Turnstone Cl E13	48 D2
Turquand St SE17	23 E6
Turret Gro SW4	84 C1
Tuscan Ho E2	46 A2
Tuscan Rd SE18	79 F1
Tuskar St SE10	76 B1
Tustin Est SE15	74 A2
Tweedmouth Rd E13	49 E1
Tweezer's All WC2	15 J3
Twelvetrees Cres E3	47 G3
Twilley St SW18	82 C5
Twine Ct E1	60 A1
Twisden Rd NW5	28 B1
Twyford Pl WC2	15 G1
Twyford Rd, Ilf.	37 E2
Twyford St N1	29 F2
Tyas Rd E16	48 C3
Tyburn Way W1	12 E3
Tyers Est SE1	23 H1
Tyers Gate SE1	23 H1
Tyers St SE11	71 F1
Tyers Ter SE11	71 F1
Tylehurst Gdns, Ilf.	37 E2
Tyler Cl E2	45 E1
Tyler's Ct W1	14 C2
Tyler St SE10	76 B1
Tylney Rd E7	35 F1
Tyndale La EC1	15 F1
Tyneham Rd SW11	70 A5
Tynemouth St SW6	68 D5
Tynsdale Rd NW10	24 A4
Type St E2	46 B1
Tyrawley Rd SW6	68 C4
Tyrone Rd E6	50 B1
Tyrrell Rd SE22	87 F2
Tyrwhitt Rd SE4	89 E1
Tysoe St EC1	9 J2
Tyson Rd SE23	88 A5
Tyssen Pas E8	31 E3
Tyssen St E8	31 E3

U

Name	Ref
Uamvar St E14	47 F4
Udall St SW1	20 B6
Uffington Rd NW10	24 C5
Ufford St SE1	22 A1
Ufton Gro N1	30 C4
Ufton Rd N1	30 C4
Ullswater Rd SW13	66 C3
Ulster Pl NW1	7 H4
Ulster Ter NW1	7 H4
Ulundi Rd SE3	76 B2
Ulva Rd SW15	81 F3
Ulverscroft Rd SE22	87 E3
Ulysses Pl E20	33 G2
Ulysses Rd NW6	26 A2
Umbria St SW15	80 C4
Undercliff Rd SE13	89 E1
Underhill Rd SE22	87 G4
Undershaft EC3	17 H2
Underwood Rd E1	45 F3
Underwood Row N1	11 E1
Underwood St N1	11 E1
Undine Rd E14	61 F5
Union Cl E11	34 A1
Union Ct EC2	17 H1
Union Gro SW8	70 D5
Union Jack Club SE1	21 J1
Union Pk SE10	76 C1
Union Rd SW4	70 D5
Union Rd SW8	70 D5
Union Sq N1	30 B5
Union St E15	33 G5
Union St SE1	16 C6
Union Wk E2	11 J1
Unity Cl NW10	24 C3
University St WC1	8 B4
University Way E16	64 C1
Unwin Cl SE15	73 F2
Unwin Rd SW7	18 A3
Upcerne Rd SW10	69 D3
Uphall Rd, Ilf.	37 D2
Upham Pk Rd W4	52 A5
Upland Rd SE22	87 F3
Upney La, Bark.	37 G3
Upper Addison Gdns W14	53 G3
Upper Bk St E14	61 F2
Upper Belgrave St SW1	19 G3
Upper Berkeley St W1	12 D2
Upper Brockley Rd SE4	75 D5
Upper Brook St W1	13 F4
Upper Cheyne Row SW3	69 F2
Upper Grosvenor St W1	13 F4
Upper Grd SE1	15 J5
Upper James St W1	14 B3
Upper John St W1	14 B3
Upper Mall W6	66 C1
Upper Marsh SE1	21 H3
Upper Montagu St W1	6 D5
Upper N St E14	47 E4
Upper Pk Rd NW3	27 G2
Upper Phillimore Gdns W8	54 B3
Upper Richmond Rd SW15	81 G2
Upper Rd E13	48 D2
Upper St. Martin's La WC2	14 E3
Upper St N1	43 G1
Upper Tachbrook St SW1	20 A5
Upper Thames St EC4	16 C3
Upperton Rd E13	49 F2
Upper Tulse Hill SW2	85 F5
Upper Wimpole St W1	7 H5
Upper Woburn Pl WC1	8 C2
Upstall St SE5	72 A4
Upton Av E7	35 D4
Upton La E7	35 D4
Upton Pk Rd E7	35 E4
Upton Rd SE18	79 E2
Upwood Rd SE12	90 C4
Urlwin St SE5	72 B2
Urlwin Wk SW9	71 G5
Ursula St SW11	69 F4
Urswick Rd E9	32 A2
Usborne Ms SW8	71 F3
Usher Rd E3	47 D1
Usk Rd SW11	83 D2
Usk St E2	46 B2
Uverdale Rd SW10	69 D3
Uxbridge Rd W12	53 C2
Uxbridge St W8	54 B2

V

Name	Ref
Vale, The SW3	69 E2
Vale Ct W9	40 D2
Valentine Pl SE1	22 B1
Valentine Rd E9	32 B3
Valentine Row SE1	22 B2
Valerian Way E15	48 B2
Vale Rd E7	35 E3
Vale Royal N7	29 E4
Valetta Gro E13	48 D1
Valetta Rd W3	52 A3
Valette St E9	31 G3
Valiant Ho SE7	77 F1
Valiant Way E6	50 B4
Vallance Rd E1	45 F3
Vallance Rd E2	45 F2
Valley Gro SE7	77 F1
Valliere Rd NW10	38 D2
Valmar Rd SE5	72 B4
Valonia Gdns SW18	82 A4
Vambery Rd SE18	79 E2
Vanbrugh Flds SE3	76 C5
Vanbrugh Hill SE3	76 C1
Vanbrugh Hill SE10	76 C1
Vanbrugh Pk SE3	76 C3
Vanbrugh Pk Rd SE3	76 C3
Vanbrugh Pk Rd W SE3	76 C3
Vanbrugh Ter SE3	76 C4
Vandome Cl E16	49 E5
Vandon Pas SW1	20 B3
Vandon St SW1	20 B3
Vandyke Cl SW15	81 F5
Vandyke Cross SE9	92 A5
Vandy St EC2	11 H4
Vane Cl NW3	27 E1
Vane St SW1	20 B5
Van Gogh Wk SW9	71 F4
Vanguard Cl E16	49 D4
Vanguard St SE8	75 E4
Vanneck Sq SW15	80 C3
Vansittart Rd E7	34 C1
Vansittart St SE14	74 C3
Vanston Pl SW6	68 B3
Varcoe Rd SE16	73 G1
Vardens Rd SW11	83 E2
Varden St E1	45 G5
Varley Rd E16	49 E5
Varna Rd SW6	67 G3
Varndell St NW1	8 A1
Vassall Rd SW9	71 F3
Vauban St SE16	59 E4
Vauban St SE16	59 E4
Vaughan Av W6	52 B5
Vaughan Rd E15	34 C3
Vaughan Rd SE5	72 B5
Vaughan St SE16	60 D3
Vaughan Way E1	59 F1
Vauxhall Br SE1	71 E1
Vauxhall Br SW1	71 E1
Vauxhall Br SW1	20 B5
Vauxhall Gdns Est SE11	71 F1
Vauxhall Gro SW8	71 E2
Vauxhall St SE11	71 F1
Vauxhall St SE11	71 F1
Vauxhall Wk SE11	71 F1
Vawdrey Cl E1	46 A3
Veda Rd SE13	89 E2
Velletri Ho E2	46 B1
Venables St NW8	6 A4
Vencourt Pl W6	66 C1
Venetian Rd SE5	72 B5
Venn St SW4	84 C2

Name	Ref
Ventnor Gdns, Bark.	37 G3
Ventnor Rd SE14	74 B3
Venue St E14	47 G4
Venus Rd SE18	64 B4
Vera Rd SW6	67 G4
Verbena Gdns W6	66 C1
Verdun Rd SW13	66 C2
Vereker Rd W14	67 G1
Vere St W1	13 H2
Verity Cl W11	39 G5
Vermont Rd SW18	82 C4
Verney Rd SE16	73 F2
Verney Way SE16	73 G1
Vernham Rd SE18	79 E2
Vernon Av E12	36 B1
Vernon Pl WC1	9 F6
Vernon Ri WC1	9 H1
Vernon Rd E3	47 D1
Vernon Rd E15	34 B4
Vernon Sq WC1	9 H1
Vernon St W14	53 G5
Verran Rd SW12	84 B5
Verulam Bldgs WC1	9 H5
Verulam St WC1	9 J5
Vesage Ct EC1	10 A6
Vespan Rd W12	52 C3
Vesta Rd SE4	74 C5
Vestry Ms SE5	72 D4
Vestry Rd SE5	72 D4
Vestry St N1	11 F1
Viaduct St E2	45 G2
Vian St SE13	89 F1
Vibart Gdns SW2	85 F5
Vicarage Av SE3	77 E4
Vicarage Cres SW11	69 E4
Vicarage Dr, Bark.	37 E4
Vicarage Fld Shop Cen, Bark.	37 E4
Vicarage Gdns W8	54 B2
Vicarage Gate W8	54 C3
Vicarage Gro SE5	72 C4
Vicarage La E6	50 B2
Vicarage La E15	34 B4
Vicarage Pk SE18	79 E1
Vicarage Rd E15	34 C4
Vicarage Rd SE18	79 E1
Vicars Cl E15	34 D5
Vicars Hill SE13	89 F2
Vicars Rd NW5	28 A2
Viceroy Rd SW8	71 E4
Victoria Av E6	35 G5
Victoria Av EC2	11 J6
Victoria Dock Rd E16	48 C5
Victoria Dr SW19	81 F5
Victoria Embk EC4	15 G4
Victoria Embk SW1	15 G1
Victoria Embk WC2	15 G4
Victoria Gdns W11	54 B2
Victoria Gro W8	54 D4
Victoria Ind Est NW10	38 A2
Victoria Ms NW6	26 B5
Victoria Par SE10	75 F2
Victoria Pk E9	32 C4
Victoria Pk Rd E9	32 A5
Victoria Pk Sq E2	46 A2
Victoria Pl SW1	7 D3
Victoria Ri SW4	84 B1
Victoria Rd E11	34 B1
Victoria Rd E13	48 D1
Victoria Rd NW6	26 A5
Victoria Rd W8	54 D4
Victoria Rd, Bark.	37 D3
Victoria Sq SW1	19 J3
Victoria Sta SW1	19 J5
Victoria St E15	34 B4
Victoria St SW1	20 A4
Victoria Way SE7	77 E1
Victoria Wf E14	60 C1
Victor Rd NW10	38 D2
Victory Pl SE17	20 D5
Victory Way SE16	60 C3
Viewfield Rd SW18	82 A4
Vigo St W1	14 A4
Viking Ct SW6	68 B2
Village, The SE7	77 F2
Village Way SE21	86 C4
Villa Rd SW9	85 G1
Villas Rd SE18	65 E5
Villa St SE17	72 C1
Villiers Rd NW2	24 C3
Villiers St WC2	15 E4
Vincent Cl SE16	60 C3
Vincentia Ct SW11	69 D5
Vincent Rd SE18	65 D5
Vincent Sq SW1	20 B5
Vincent St E16	48 C4
Vincent St SW1	20 C5
Vincent Ter N1	44 A1
Vince St EC1	11 G2
Vinegar Yd SE1	23 H1
Vine Hill EC1	9 J4
Vine La SE1	17 J6
Vine Rd E15	34 C4
Vine Rd SW13	80 B1
Vine St W14	68 A1
Vine St W1	14 B4
Vine St Br EC1	10 A4
Vine Yd SE1	22 E1
Vineyard Wk EC1	9 J3
Viney Rd SE13	89 F1
Vining St SW9	85 G2
Vintners Ct EC4	16 E3
Viola Sq W12	52 B1
Violet Cl E16	48 B3
Violet Hill NW8	40 D1
Violet Rd E3	47 F3
Virgil Pl W1	6 D6
Virgil St SE1	21 H3
Virginia Rd E2	45 E2
Virginia St E1	59 F1
Virginia Wk SW2	85 F4
Viscount Dr E6	50 B4
Viscount St EC1	10 D4
Vista, The SE9	91 G4
Vivian Rd E3	46 C1
Voce Rd SE18	79 F3
Voltaire Rd SW4	84 D1
Voss St E2	45 F2
Voysey Sq E3	47 F4
Vulcan Cl E6	50 C5
Vulcan Rd SE4	74 D5
Vulcan Ter SE4	74 D5
Vulcan Way N7	29 F3
Vyner St E2	31 G5

W

Name	Ref
Wadding St SE17	23 F6
Waddington Rd E15	34 A2
Waddington St E15	34 A3
Wadeson St E2	45 G1
Wades Pl E14	61 F1
Wadham Gdns NW3	27 F5
Wadham Rd SW15	81 G2
Wadhurst Rd SW8	70 C4
Wager St E3	46 D3
Waghorn Rd E13	35 F5
Waghorn St SE15	87 F1
Wagner St SE15	73 G3
Waite Davies Rd SE12	90 D5
Waite St SE15	73 E2
Waithman St EC4	16 B2
Wakefield Ms WC1	9 F2
Wakefield St E6	35 G5
Wakefield St WC1	9 F3
Wakeford Cl SW4	84 C3
Wakeham St N1	30 C3
Wakehurst Rd SW11	83 F3
Wakeling St E14	46 C5
Wakelin Rd E15	48 B1
Wakeman Rd NW10	39 E2
Wakering Rd, Bark.	37 E4
Wakley St EC1	10 B1
Walberswick St SW8	71 E3
Walbrook EC4	17 F3
Walcorde Av SE17	22 E6
Walcot Sq SE11	22 A5
Walcott St SW1	20 B5
Waldair Wf E16	64 D3
Waldemar Av SW6	67 G4
Walden St E1	45 G5
Waldo Cl SW4	84 C3
Waldo Rd NW10	38 C2
Walerand Rd SE13	75 G5
Waleran Flats SE1	23 H5
Wales Cl SE15	73 G3
Waley St E1	46 B4
Walford Rd N16	31 D1
Walham Gro SW6	68 B3
Walker Cl SE18	65 E5
Walkers Ct W1	14 C3
Wallace Rd N1	30 B3
Wallbutton Rd SE4	74 C5
Wall End Rd E6	36 B4
Waller Rd SE14	74 B4
Wallflower St W12	52 B1
Wallgrave Rd SW5	54 C5
Wallingford Av W10	39 F4
Wallis All SE1	22 E1
Wallis Rd E9	33 D3
Wallis's Cotts SW2	85 E5
Wallside EC2	10 E6
Wall St N1	30 C3
Wallwood St E14	47 D4
Walmer Pl W1	6 D5
Walmer Rd W11	53 G1
Walmer St W1	6 D5
Walmer Ter SE18	65 E5
Walm La NW2	25 F2
Walnut Tree Cl SW13	66 B4
Walnut Tree Rd SE10	76 B1
Walnut Tree Wk SE11	21 J5
Walpole Rd E6	35 F4
Walpole St SW3	69 G1
Walsham Rd SE14	74 B5
Walsingham Pl SW11	84 A4
Walters Cl SE17	23 E6
Walter St E2	46 B2
Walters Way SE23	88 B4
Walter Ter E1	46 B5
Walterton Rd W9	40 A3
Walton Cl SW8	71 E3
Walton Pl SW3	18 D3
Walton Rd E12	36 C1
Walton Rd E13	49 F1
Walton St SW3	18 C5
Walworth Pl SE17	72 B1
Walworth Rd SE1	22 D5
Walworth Rd SE17	22 D5
Wandon Rd SW6	68 C3
Wandsworth Br SW6	82 C1
Wandsworth Br SW18	82 C1
Wandsworth Br Rd SW6	68 C4
Wandsworth Common SW12	83 H4
Wandsworth Common W Side SW18	83 D3
Wandsworth High St SW18	82 B3
Wandsworth Plain SW18	82 B3
Wandsworth Rd SW8	71 D3
Wandsworth Town SW18	82 B3
Wanless Rd SE24	86 B1
Wanley Rd SE5	86 C2
Wanlip Rd E13	49 E3
Wansbeck Rd E3	33 D4
Wansbeck Rd E9	33 D4
Wansey St SE17	22 E6
Wantage Rd SE12	90 A3
Wapping High St E1	59 F2
Wapping La E1	59 G1
Wapping Wall E1	60 A2
Warbeck Rd W12	53 D2
Warburton Rd E8	31 G5
Wardalls Gro SE14	74 A3
Warden Rd NW5	28 A3
Wardens Gro SE1	16 D6
Wardle St E9	32 B2
Wardo Av SW6	67 G4
Wardour Ms W1	14 B2
Wardour St W1	14 C3
Ward Pt SE11	21 J6
Ward Rd E15	34 A5
Wardrobe Ter EC4	16 C2
Wards Wf App E16	63 G3
Ware Pt Dr SE28	65 F3
Warfield Rd NW10	39 F2
Warham St SE5	72 A3
Warland Rd SE18	79 F3
Warley St E2	46 B2
Warlock Rd W9	40 B3
Warlters Rd N7	29 E1
Warmington Rd SE24	86 B4
Warndon St SE16	60 B5
Warneford St E9	31 G5
Warner Cl E15	34 B2
Warner Pl E2	45 F1
Warner Rd SE5	72 B4
Warner St EC1	9 J4
Warner Yd EC1	9 J4
Warple Way W3	52 A2
Warren, The E12	36 A1
Warren Cl SE21	86 B5
Warren Ct SE7	77 F1
Warren La SE18	64 D4
Warren La Gate SE18	64 D4
Warren Rd E11	8 A4
Warren St W1	7 J4
Warren Wk SE7	77 F2
Warriner Gdns SW11	69 G4
Warrington Cres W9	40 D3
Warrior Cl SE28	65 F2
Warrior Sq E12	36 C1
Warspite Rd SE18	64 A4
Warton Rd E15	33 G4
Warwall E6	50 D5
Warwick Av W2	40 D3
Warwick Av W9	40 D3
Warwick Bldg SW8	70 B2
Warwick Cl SE15	73 F5
Warwick Ct WC1	9 H6
Warwick Cres W2	40 D4
Warwick Dr SW15	80 D1
Warwick Est W2	40 C4
Warwick Gdns W14	54 A4
Warwick Ho St SW1	14 D5
Warwick La EC4	16 C2
Warwick Pas EC4	16 C1
Warwick Pl N9	40 D4
Warwick Pl N SW1	20 A6
Warwick Rd E12	36 A2
Warwick Rd E15	34 C3
Warwick Rd SW5	54 A5
Warwick Rd W14	54 A5
Warwick Row SW1	19 J3
Warwickshire Path SE8	75 D3
Warwick Sq EC4	16 C1
Warwick Sq SW1	70 C1
Warwick Sq Ms SW1	20 A6
Warwick St W1	14 B3
Warwick Ter SE18	79 F2
Warwick Way SW1	20 A6
Warwick Yd EC1	10 E4
Washington Av E12	36 A1
Washington Cl E3	47 F2
Washington Rd SW13	66 C3
Waterden Cres E15	33 E2
Waterden Rd E20	33 E2
Waterford Rd SW6	68 C4
Waterford Way NW10	24 C2
Water Gdns, The W2	12 C1
Watergate EC4	16 B3
Watergate St SE8	75 E2
Watergate Wk WC2	15 F5
Waterhouse Cl E16	49 G4
Waterhouse Sq EC1	9 J6

Name	Ref
Water La E15	34 B3
Water La EC3	17 H4
Water La SE14	74 A3
Waterloo Br SE1	15 G4
Waterloo Br WC2	15 G4
Waterloo Est E2	46 A1
Waterloo Gdns E2	46 A1
Waterloo Pas NW6	26 A4
Waterloo Pl SW1	14 C5
Waterloo Rd E6	35 F4
Waterloo Rd SE1	21 J1
Waterloo Ter N1	30 A4
Waterman St SW15	81 F1
Watermans Wk SE16	60 C4
Waterman Way E1	59 G2
Watermeadow La SW6	68 D5
Waterside Cl E3	32 D5
Waterside Pt SW11	69 F3
Waterside Twr SW6	69 D4
Waterson St E2	11 J1
Water St WC2	15 H3
Waterview Ho E14	46 C4
Waterway Av SE13	89 F1
Waterworks Rd SW2	85 E4
Watford Rd E16	49 D4
Watkinson Rd N7	29 F3
Watling Ct EC4	16 E2
Watling Gdns NW2	25 G3
Watling St EC4	16 D2
Watney St E1	45 G5
Watson Av E6	36 C4
Watsons Ms W1	6 C6
Watson's St SE8	75 E3
Watson St E13	49 E1
Wattsdown Cl E13	34 D5
Watts Gro E3	47 F4
Watts St E1	59 G2
Watts St SE15	73 E4
Watts Way SW7	18 A3
Wat Tyler Rd SE3	75 G5
Wat Tyler Rd SE10	75 G5
Wavell Dr, Sid.	93 G4
Waveney Av SE15	87 G2
Waverley Cres SE18	79 F1
Waverley Gdns, Bark.	51 G1
Waverley Pl NW8	41 E1
Waverley Rd SE18	79 E1
Waverley Wk W2	40 B4
Waverton Ho E3	33 D5
Waverton St W1	13 G5
Waxham NW3	27 G2
Wayfield Link SE9	93 F1
Wayford St SW11	69 F5
Wayland Av E8	31 F2
Wayland Ho SW9	71 G5
Wayman Ct E8	31 G3
Waynflete Sq W10	53 F1
Weardale Rd SE13	90 A2
Wear Pl E2	45 G2
Wearside Rd SE13	89 F2
Weatherley Cl E3	47 D4
Weavers Ter SW6	68 B2
Weaver St E1	45 F5
Weavers Way NW1	28 D5
Webb Cl W10	39 E3
Webber Row SE1	22 A3
Webber St SE1	22 A1
Webb Pl NW10	38 B2
Webb Rd SE3	76 C2
Webbs Rd SW11	83 G3
Webb St SE1	23 H4
Webheath Est NW6	26 A4
Wedderburn Rd NW3	27 F2
Wedderburn Rd, Bark.	37 F5
Wedgwood Ho SE11	21 J4
Wedgwood Ms W1	14 D2
Weech Rd NW6	26 B1
Weedington Rd NW5	28 A2
Weigall Rd SE12	91 D2
Weighhouse St W1	13 G2
Weimar St SW15	81 G1
Weir Est SW12	84 C5
Weir Rd SW12	84 C5
Weir's Pas NW1	8 D1
Weiss Rd SW15	81 F1
Welbeck Rd E6	49 G2
Welbeck St W1	13 H1
Welbeck Way W1	13 H1
Welby St SE5	72 A4
Welfare Rd E15	34 B3
Welland St SE10	75 G2
Wellclose Sq E1	59 F1
Well Ct EC4	17 E2
Weller St SE1	22 D1
Wellesley Av W6	52 D4
Wellesley Ct W9	40 D2
Wellesley Pl NW1	8 C2
Wellesley Rd NW5	28 A2
Wellesley St E1	46 B4
Wellesley Ter N1	10 E1
Well Hall Rd SE9	92 B1
Well Hall Rbt SE9	92 A1
Wellington Gdns SE7	77 F2
Wellington Ms SE7	77 F2
Wellington Pl NW8	6 A1
Wellington Rd E6	50 B1
Wellington Rd E7	34 C1
Wellington Rd NW8	41 E1
Wellington Rd NW10	39 F2
Wellington Row E2	45 E2
Wellington Sq SW3	69 G1
Wellington Sq SW3	
Wellington St SE18	65 F3
Wellington St WC2	15 F3
Wellington Ter E1	59 G2
Wellington Way E3	47 E2
Welling Way SE9	93 F1
Welling Way, Well.	93 F1
Wellmeadow Rd SE6	90 B5
Wellmeadow Rd SE13	90 B4
Wells Ho Rd NW10	38 A4
Wells Ms W1	8 B6
Wells Pl SW18	82 D5
Wells Ri NW8	27 G5
Wells Rd W12	53 E3
Wells Sq WC1	9 G2
Wells St W1	8 A6
Wellstead Rd E6	50 C1
Well St E9	31 G4
Well St E15	34 B3
Wells Way SE5	73 C2
Wells Way SW7	55 E4
Well Wk NW3	27 E1
Welmar Ms SW4	85 D2
Welsford St SE1	73 F3
Welsh Cl E13	48 D2
Welstead Way W4	52 B5
Weltje Rd W6	66 C1
Welton Rd SE18	79 G3
Wemyss Rd SE3	76 C5
Wendell Rd W12	52 B3
Wendle Ct SW8	71 E2
Wendling NW5	27 G2
Wendon St E3	33 D5
Wendover SE17	72 D1
Wendover Rd NW10	38 B2
Wendover Rd SE9	91 G1
Wenlock Rd N1	44 B1
Wenlock St N1	44 B1
Wennington Rd E3	46 B1
Wensley Cl SE9	92 B4
Wentworth Cres SE15	73 F3
Wentworth Ms W3	38 A5
Wentworth Rd E12	35 G1
Wentworth St E1	45 E5
Wernbrook St SE18	79 E2
Werrington St NW1	42 C1
Werter Rd SW15	81 G2
Wesley Av E16	63 D2
Wesley Cl SE17	22 C6
Wesley St W1	7 G6
Wessex St E2	46 A2
West 12 Shop Cen W12	53 F3
West Arbour St E1	46 B5
Westbere Rd NW2	25 G1
Westbourne Br W2	40 D4
Westbourne Cres W2	55 E1
Westbourne Gdns W2	40 C5
Westbourne Gro W2	40 B5
Westbourne Gro W11	40 B5
Westbourne Gro Ter W2	40 C5
Westbourne Pk Rd W2	40 B4
Westbourne Pk Rd W11	39 G5
Westbourne Pk Vil W2	40 B4
Westbourne Rd N7	29 G3
Westbourne St W2	55 E1
Westbourne Ter E7	41 F5
Westbourne Ter Ms W2	40 D5
Westbourne Ter Rd W2	40 D4
Westbridge Rd SW11	69 E4
Westbrook Rd SE3	77 E4
Westbury Rd E7	34 D3
Westbury Rd, Bark.	37 F5
Westbury St SW8	70 C5
Westbury Ter E7	35 E3
West Carriage Dr W2	12 A6
West Cen St WC1	15 E1
Westcliffe Apts W2	6 A6
Westcombe Hill SE3	76 D1
Westcombe Hill SE10	76 D1
Westcombe Pk Rd SE3	76 B2
West Cotts NW6	26 B2
Westcott Rd SE17	72 A2
Westcroft Cl NW2	25 G1
Westcroft Sq W6	52 C5
Westcroft Way NW2	25 G1
West Cromwell Rd SW5	54 A5
West Cromwell Rd W14	54 A5
West Cross Route W10	53 F1
West Cross Route W11	53 F1
Westdale Pas SE18	78 D2
Westdale Rd SE18	79 D2
Westdean Cl SW18	82 C3
Westdown Rd E15	33 G1
Westdown Rd SE6	89 E5
West Eaton Pl SW1	19 F5
West Eaton Pl Ms SW1	19 F5
West Ella Rd NW10	24 A4
West End La NW6	26 B4
Westerdale Rd SE10	76 C1
Western Gateway E16	62 D1
Western La SW12	84 A5
Western Rd E13	35 F5
Western Rd SW9	85 G1
Western Way SE28	65 F4
Westferry Circ E14	61 D2
Westferry Rd E14	61 E2
Westfield Av E20	33 G3
Westfield Cl SW10	68 D3
Westfield London W12	53 E2
Westfields SW13	80 B1
Westfields Av SW13	80 A1
Westfield St SE18	64 B5
Westfield Way E1	46 C2
West Gdns E1	59 G1
Westgate St E8	31 G5
Westgate Ter SW10	68 C1
West Gro SE10	75 G4
Westgrove La SE10	75 G4
West Halkin St SW1	19 F3
West Ham La E15	34 B4
West Ham Pk E7	34 C4
West Hampstead Ms NW6	26 C3
West Harding St EC4	16 A1
West Hill SW15	81 F5
West Hill SW18	82 B3
West Hill Rd SW18	82 B4
Westhorne Av SE9	91 F4
Westhorne Av SE12	90 D5
Westhorpe Rd SW15	81 E1
West India Av E14	61 E2
West India Dock Rd E14	47 D5
Westland Pl N1	11 F1
West La SE16	59 G3
Westleigh Av SW15	81 D3
Westmead SW15	80 D4
West Ms SW1	19 J6
Westminster Br SE1	21 F2
Westminster Br SW1	21 F2
Westminster Gdns SW1	20 E5
Westminster Gdns, Bark.	51 G1
Westmoor St SE7	63 F4
Westmoreland Av, Well.	93 G1
Westmoreland Pl SW1	70 B1
Westmoreland Rd SE17	72 B2
Westmoreland Rd SW13	66 B4
Westmoreland St W1	7 G6
Westmoreland Ter SW1	70 B1
Westmoreland Wk SE17	72 C2
Westmount Rd SE9	78 B5
West One Shop Cen W1	13 G2
Weston Ri WC1	43 F1
Weston St SE1	23 G2
Westover Rd SW18	83 D4
West Parkside SE10	62 B3
Westport Rd E13	49 E3
Westport St E1	46 B5
West Poultry Av EC1	10 B6
West Quarters W12	38 C5
West Rd E15	69 G2
West Rd SW4	85 D3
Westrow SW15	81 E3
West Row W10	39 G3
West Smithfield EC1	10 B6
West Sq SE11	22 B4
West St E2	45 G1
West St WC2	14 D2
West Tenter St E1	45 E5
Westvale Ms W3	52 A2
Westview Cl NW10	24 A2
Westview Cl W10	39 E5
Westville Rd W12	52 C3
West Warwick Pl SW1	20 B6
Westway W2	40 B4
Westway W9	40 B4
Westway W10	39 G5
Westway W12	52 C1
Westwick Gdns W14	53 F3
Westwood Gdns SW13	80 B1
Westwood Pk SE23	87 G5
Westwood Rd E16	63 E2
Westwood Rd SW13	80 B1
Wetherby Gdns SW5	54 D5
Wetherby Pl SW7	54 D5
Wetherell Rd E9	32 B5
Wexford Rd SW12	83 G5
Weybridge Pt SW11	70 A5
Weyman Rd SE3	77 F4
Weymouth Ms W1	7 H5
Weymouth St W1	7 G6
Weymouth Ter E2	45 E1
Whalebone Ct EC2	17 G1
Whardale Rd N1	43 E1
Wharfedale St SW10	68 C1
Wharf Pl E2	31 F5
Wharf Rd N1	43 E1
Wharf Rd (King's Cross) N1	43 E1
Wharfside Rd E16	48 B4
Wharf St E16	48 B4
Wharf St SE8	75 E1

Name	Ref
rton Cl NW10	24 A3
rton St WC1	9 H2
ateley Rd SE2	87 E3
ateley Rd SE23	88 B5
eatley St W1	7 G6
eat Sheaf La E14	61 E5
eatsheaf La SW6	97 E3
eatsheaf La SW8	71 L2
eatsheaf Ter SW8	68 A3
eatstone Rd W10	39 G4
eatstone Ter SW8	51 F1
eelwright St N7	45 E3
eeler St E1	23 G4
ellock Rd W4	15 G1
etstone Pk WC2	77 F5
etstone Rd SE8	15 J6
ichcote St SE1	9 F2
idborne St WC1	65 F4
inchat Rd SE28	92 A1
inyates Rd SE9	10 B2
iskin St EC1	69 E3
istlers Av SW11	30 A1
istler St N5	45 E1
iston Rd E2	88 F2
itbread Rd SE4	89 F2
itburn Rd SE13	64 B5
itby Rd SE18	74 C2
itcher Cl SE14	14 D4
itchurch Rd W11	61 F5
itcomb St WC2	34 A3
hitear Wk E15	E1
hitechapel Rd E1	45 E5
White Ch La E1	45 F5
White City Cl W12	53 E1
White City Est W12	52 D1
White City Rd W12	53 E1
Whitecross Pl EC2	11 G5
Whitecross St EC1	10 E3
Whitefield Cl SW15	16 A2
Whitefriars St EC4	14 E5
Whitehall SW1	15 E6
Whitehall Gdns SW1	15 E6
Whitehall Pl SW1	11 H6
White Hart La EC2	80 A1
White Hart La SW13	65 G5
White Hart Rd SE18	16 F6
White Hart St EC4	71 G1
White Hart St SE11	17 F1
White Hart Yd SE1	6 B4
Whitehaven St NW8	82 D5
Whitehead Cl SW18	69 F1
Whitehead's Gro SW3	10 B5
White Horse Av Al EC1	46 B3
White Horse La E1	22 A3
White Horse Ms SE1	46 C5
White Horse Rd E1	50 B2
White Horse Rd E6	13 H6
White Horse St W1	17 F1
White Horse Yd EC2	17 J1
White Kennett St E1	81 G5
Whitelands Cres SW18	48 C1
Whitelegg Rd E13	40 C5
Whiteleys Shop Cen W2	17 H2
White Lion Ct EC3	16 C3
White Lion Hill EC4	43 G1
White Lion St N1	10 D5
White Lyon Ct EC2	33 J3
White Post La E15	89 E1
White Post St SE15	74 A3
White Rd E15	34 B4
Whites Gdns SE1	23 J2
White's Row E1	47 E4
Whitethorn St E3	8 A4
Whitfield Pl W1	35 F4
Whitfield Rd E6	76 A4
Whitfield Rd SE3	8 C6
Whitfield St W1	
Whitgift St SE11	21 G5
Whiting Av, Bark.	37 D4
Whitings Way E6	50 C4
Whitlock Dr SW19	81 G5
Whitmore Est E2	7 G6
Whitmore Gdns NW10	39 J1
Whitmore Rd N1	30 D5
Whitnell Way SW15	78 B3
Whitstable Ho W10	39 F5
Whittaker Rd E6	55 F4
Whittaker St SW1	19 F6
Whitta Rd E12	35 G1
Whittingstall Rd SW6	68 A4
Whittington Av EC3	17 H2
Whittlesey St SE1	15 J6
Whitton Wk E3	47 E1
Whitwell Rd E13	48 D2
Whitworth Ho SE1	22 E4
Whitworth Rd SE18	78 C3
Whitworth St SE10	76 B1
Whorlton Rd SE15	87 G1
Whyteville Rd E7	35 E3
Wickersley Rd SW11	70 A5
Wickford St E1	46 A3
Wickham Cl E1	46 A4
Wickham Gdns SE4	88 D1
Wickham Ms SE4	88 D1
Wickham Rd SE4	88 D2
Wickham St SE11	71 F1
Wickham St, Well.	79 G5
Wick La E3	47 E1
Wicklow St WC1	9 G1
Wick Rd E9	32 B3
Wicksteed Ho SE1	22 E4
Wickwood St SE5	72 A5
Widdenham Rd N7	29 F1
Widdin St E15	34 A4
Widegate St E1	11 J6
Widley Rd W9	40 B2
Wigeon Path SE28	65 F4
Wigham Ho, Bark.	37 E4
Wigmore Pl W1	13 H1
Wigmore St W1	13 F2
Wigston Rd E13	49 E3
Wigton Pl SE11	19 E5
Wilberforce Rd N4	45 E1
Wilby Ms W11	54 A2
Wilcox Cl SW8	71 E3
Wilcox Pl SW1	20 B4
Wilcox Rd SW8	71 E3
Wild Ct WC2	15 G1
Wildcroft Rd SW15	81 E5
Wilde Cl E8	31 F5
Wilde Pl SW18	83 E5
Wildfell Rd SE6	75 F6
Wild Goose Dr SE14	74 A4
Wild's Rents SE1	23 H3
Wild St WC2	15 F2
Wildwood Cl SE12	90 C5
Wilfred St SW1	20 A3
Wilkes St E1	45 E4
Wilkinson Rd E16	49 F5
Wilkinson St SW8	71 F3
Wilkin St NW5	28 B3
Willard St SW8	84 B1
Will Crooks Gdns SE9	91 E1
Willenhall Rd SE18	78 D1
Willesden La NW2	25 F3
Willesden La NW6	25 F3
Willes Rd NW5	28 B3
William Bonney Est SW4	85 D2
William Cl SE13	75 G5
William Dunbar Ho NW6	40 A1
William IV St WC2	14 E4
William Gdns SW15	81 D3
William Ms SW1	19 E2
William Morley Cl E6	35 G5
William Morris Way SW6	82 D1
William Rd NW1	8 A2
William Saville Ho NW6	40 A1
Williams Bldgs E2	46 A3
Williamson St N7	29 E1
William St N7	19 E2
William St, Bark.	37 E4
Willingham Cl NW5	28 C2
Willingham Ter NW5	28 C2
Willington Rd SW9	85 E1
Willis Rd E15	34 C5
Willis St E14	47 F5
Willoughby Pas E14	61 E2
Willoughby Rd NW3	27 E1
Willoughby St WC1	8 E6
Willoughby Way SE7	63 E5
Willow Av SW13	66 B5
Willow Bk SW6	81 G1
Willow Br Rd N1	30 B3
Willow Business Pk SE13	73 E2
Willow Ct EC2	11 H3
Willowfields Cl SE18	79 G1
Willow La SE18	64 B5
Willow Pl SW1	20 B5
Willow Rd NW3	27 E1
Willow St EC2	11 H3
Willow Vale W12	52 C2
Willow Wk SE1	23 J5
Wilman Gro E8	31 F4
Wilmcote Ho W2	40 B4
Wilmer Gdns N1	30 D5
Wilmer La E15	33 G4
Wilmington Gdns, Bark.	37 F3
Wilmington Sq WC1	9 J2
Wilmington St WC1	9 J2
Wilmot Cl SE15	73 F3
Wilmot Pl NW1	28 C4
Wilmot St E2	45 G3
Wilmount St SE18	64 D5
Wilna Rd SW18	82 C5
Wilsham St W11	53 F2
Wilshaw St SE14	75 E4
Wilson Gro SE16	59 G3
Wilson Rd E6	49 G2
Wilson Rd SE5	72 D4
Wilsons Rd W6	67 F1
Wilson St EC2	11 G5
Wilton Av W4	66 A1
Wilton Cres SW1	19 F2
Wilton Ms SW1	19 G3
Wilton Pl SW1	19 F2
Wilton Rd SW1	19 J4
Wilton Rd, Ilf.	36 D1
Wilton Row SW1	19 F2
Wilton Sq N1	30 C5
Wilton Ter SW1	19 H3
Wilton Vil N1	30 C5
Wilton Way E8	31 F3
Wiltshire Cl SW3	18 D5
Wiltshire Rd SW9	85 G1
Wiltshire Row N1	30 C5
Wimbart Rd SW2	85 F5
Wimbledon Pk Rd SW18	82 A5
Wimbolt St E2	45 F2
Wimborne Cl SE12	90 C3
Wimbourne St N1	44 C1
Wimpole Ms W1	7 H5
Wimpole St W1	13 H1
Winans Wk SW9	71 G5
Wincanton Rd SW18	82 A5
Winchcomb Gdns SE9	77 J5
Winchelsea Cl SW15	81 F3
Winchendon Rd SW6	68 A3
Winchester Av NW6	25 G5
Winchester Av NW9	23 J6
Winchester Cl SE17	22 C6
Winchester Rd NW3	27 E4
Winchester Sq SE1	17 F5
Winchester St SW1	70 B1
Winchester Wk SE1	17 F5
Wincott St SE11	22 A5
Wincrofts Dr SE9	93 F2
Windermere Av NW6	25 G5
Windermere Rd SW15	66 B2
Winders Rd SW11	69 F5
Windlass Pl SE8	60 C5
Windmill Cl SE13	75 G5
Windmill Ct NW2	25 G3
Windmill Dr SW4	84 C3
Windmill La E15	34 A3
Windmill Pas W4	52 A5
Windmill Rd SW18	83 E4
Windmill Rd W4	52 A5
Windmill Row SE11	71 G1
Windmill St W1	8 C6
Windmill Wk SE1	16 A6
Windrose Cl SE16	60 B3
Windsock Cl SE16	60 D5
Windsor Gdns W9	40 B4
Windsor Pl SW1	20 B4
Windsor Rd E7	35 E2
Windsor Rd N7	29 E1
Windsor Rd NW2	24 D3
Windsor Rd, Ilf.	37 D1
Windsor Rd N1	30 A5
Windsor Ter N1	10 E1
Windsor Wk SE5	72 C5
Windsor Way W14	53 F5
Windsor Wf E9	33 D2
Wine Cl E1	60 A1
Wine Office Ct EC4	16 A1
Winford Ho E3	33 D4
Winforton St SE10	75 G4
Winfrith Rd SW18	82 D5
Wingate Rd W6	52 A4
Wingate Rd, Ilf.	37 D2
Wingfield Rd E15	34 B2
Wingfield St SE15	87 F1
Wingford Rd SW2	85 E4
Wingmore Rd SE24	86 B1
Wingrave Rd W6	67 E2
Winifred Gro SW11	83 G2
Winifred St E16	64 B2
Winkfield Rd E13	49 E1
Winkley St E2	45 G1
Winn Common Rd SE18	79 G2
Winnett St W1	14 C3
Winsham Gro SW11	84 A3
Winslade Rd SW2	85 E3
Winsland St W2	41 E5
Winsley St W1	14 A1
Winslow SE17	72 D1
Winslow Rd W6	67 E2
Winsor Ter E6	50 C4
Winstanley Est SW11	83 E1
Winstanley Rd SW11	83 E1
Winston Rd N16	30 C1
Winter Av E6	36 A5
Winterbrook Rd SE24	86 B4
Winterslow Rd SW9	72 A4
Winterton Ho E1	46 A5
Winterwell Rd SW2	85 E3
Winthorpe Rd SW15	81 G2
Winthrop St E1	45 G4
Wise Rd E15	34 A5
Wishart Rd SE3	77 G4
Wisley Rd SW11	84 A3
Wisteria Cl, Ilf.	36 D2
Wisteria Rd SE13	90 A2
Witan St E2	45 G2
Witcombe Pt SE15	73 F4
Witherington Rd N5	29 G2
Withycombe Rd SW19	81 F5
Wivenhoe Cl SE15	87 G1
Wixs La SW4	84 B2
Woburn Pl WC1	8 D3
Woburn Sq WC1	8 D4
Woburn Wk WC1	8 D2
Wodeham Gdns E1	45 F4
Wodehouse Av SE5	73 E4
Woking Cl SW15	80 B2
Wolfe Cres SE7	77 G1
Wolfe Cres SE16	60 B3
Wolferton Rd E12	36 B1
Wolffe Gdns E15	34 C3
Wolffram Cl SE13	90 B3
Wolftencroft Cl SW11	83 E1

Wollaston Cl SE1	22 D5
Wolseley Rd E7	35 E4
Wolseley St SE1	59 E3
Wolsey Av E6	50 C2
Wolsey Ms NW5	28 C3
Wolsey Rd N1	30 C2
Wolverton Gdns W6	53 F5
Woodborough Rd SW15	80 D2
Woodbridge St EC1	10 B3
Woodchester Sq W2	40 C4
Woodchurch Rd NW6	26 B4
Wood Cl E2	45 F3
Woodcocks E16	49 F4
Woodcroft Cl SE9	92 C4
Wooder Gdns E7	34 C1
Woodfall St SW3	69 G1
Woodfarrs SE5	86 C2
Woodfield Pl W9	40 A3
Woodfield Rd W9	40 A4
Woodford Rd E7	35 E1
Woodgrange Rd E7	35 E1
Woodhall NW1	8 A2
Woodhill SE18	64 A5
Woodhouse Cl SE22	87 F2
Woodhouse Gro E12	36 A3
Woodington Cl SE9	92 C4
Woodland Ct N7	29 E3
Woodland Cres SE10	76 B2
Woodland Cres SE16	60 B3
Woodland Gro SE10	76 B1
Woodlands Pk Rd SE10	76 B2
Woodlands Rd SW13	80 B1
Woodlands St SE13	90 A5
Woodlands Way SW15	82 A3
Woodland Ter SE7	64 A5
Woodland Wk NW3	27 F2
Wood La W12	39 E5
Woodlawn Cl SW15	82 A3
Woodlawn Rd SW6	67 F3
Woodmans Gro NW10	24 B2
Woodmans Ms W12	39 D4
Woodman St E16	64 C2
Woodpecker Rd SE14	74 C2
Woodquest Av SE24	86 B3
Wood Retreat SE18	79 F3
Woodrow SE18	64 B5
Woodseer St E1	45 E4
Woodsford Sq W14	53 G3
Woodside Rd E13	49 F3
Woods Ms W1	13 E3
Woods Pl SE1	23 J4
Woods Rd SE15	73 G4
Woodstock Ct SE12	90 D4
Woodstock Gro W12	53 F3
Woodstock Ms W1	7 G6
Woodstock Rd E7	35 F4
Woodstock Rd W4	52 A4
Woodstock St W1	13 H2
Woodstock Ter E14	61 F1
Wood St EC2	16 E2
Wood St W4	66 A1
Woodthorpe Rd SW15	81 D2
Wood Vale SE23	88 A4
Woodville SE3	77 E4
Woodville Cl SE12	90 D3
Woodville Rd N16	30 D2
Woodville Rd NW6	40 A1
Woodville St SE18	64 A5
Woodwarde Rd SE22	87 D4
Wood Wf SE10	75 F2
Woodyard La SE21	86 D5
Woodyates Rd SE12	90 D5
Woolacombe Rd SE3	77 F4
Wooler St SE17	72 C1
Woolf Ms WC1	8 D3
Woolmore St E14	61 G1
Woolneigh St SW6	82 C1

Woolstaplers Way SE16	59 F5
Woolwich Ch St SE18	64 A4
Woolwich Common SE18	78 C2
Woolwich Ferry Pier E16	64 C3
Woolwich Foot Tunnel E16	64 C3
Woolwich Foot Tunnel SE18	64 C3
Woolwich Garrison SE18	78 A2
Woolwich High St SE18	64 C4
Woolwich Manor Way E6	50 B3
Woolwich Manor Way E16	65 D1
Woolwich Mkt SE18	64 C5
Woolwich New Rd SE18	78 C1
Woolwich Rd SE7	77 D1
Woolwich Rd SE10	76 C1
Woolwich Trade Pk SE28	65 F4
Wooster St SE1	48 A5
Wooster Pl SE1	23 G5
Wootton St SE1	22 A1
Worcester Dr W4	52 A3
Worcester Rd E12	36 B1
Wordsworth Av E12	36 A4
Wordsworth Rd N16	31 D1
Wordsworth Rd, Well.	79 G4
Worfield St SW11	69 F3
Worgan St SE11	71 F1
Worgan St SE16	60 B4
Worland Rd E15	34 B4
Worlidge St W6	67 E1
Worlingham Rd SE22	87 E2
Wormholt Rd W12	52 C1
Wormwood St EC2	17 H1
Wornington Rd W10	39 G4
Wornington Rd W10	27 E5
Wornum Path SW	
Worship St EC2	11 G4
Worsley Gro E5	31 F1
Worsley Rd E11	34 B1
Worsopp Dr SW4	84 C3
Wortley Rd E6	35 G4
Wotton Rd NW2	25 E1
Wotton Rd SE8	75 D2
Wouldham Rd E16	48 C5
Wrekin Rd SE18	79 E3
Wren Av NW2	25 E2
Wren Path SE28	65 F4
Wren Rd SE5	72 C4
Wren St WC1	9 H3
Wrentham Av NW10	39 F1
Wrexham Rd E3	47 E1
Wricklemarsh Rd SE3	77 E4
Wrigglesworth St SE14	74 B3
Wrights Cl SE13	90 A2
Wrights La W8	54 C3
Wrights Rd E3	46 D1
Wrottesley Rd NW10	38 C1
Wrottesley Rd SE18	79 E2
Wroughton Rd SW11	83 G4
Wroxton St SE15	73 G5
Wulfstan St W12	38 B5
Wyatt Cl SE16	60 D3
Wyatt Dr SW13	67 E3
Wyatt Rd E7	35 D3
Wybert St NW1	7 J3
Wycherley Cl SE3	76 C3
Wycliffe Rd SW11	70 A5
Wyclif St EC1	10 B2
Wycombe Pl SW18	82 D4
Wycombe Sq W8	54 A2
Wye St SW11	69 E5
Wyfold Rd SW6	67 G3
Wyke Rd E3	33 E4
Wyleu St SE23	88 C5
Wyllen Cl E1	46 A3

Wymering Rd W9	40 B2
Wymond St SW15	81 E1
Wynan Rd E14	75 F1
Wyncliff Rd SE7	77 E2
Wyndham Est SE5	72 B3
Wyndham Ms W1	6 D6
Wyndham Pl W1	6 D6
Wyndham Rd E6	35 G4
Wyndham Rd SE5	72 A3
Wyndham St W1	6 D5
Wyndham Yd W1	6 D6
Wyneham Rd SE24	86 C3
Wynford Rd N1	43 F1
Wynne Rd SW9	71 G5
Wynnstay Gdns W8	54 B4
Wynter St SW11	83 D2
Wynyard Ter SE11	71 F1
Wynyatt St EC1	10 B2
Wythburn Pl W1	12 D2
Wythens Wk SE9	92 D4
Wythes Rd E16	64 A2
Wythfield Rd SE9	92 B4
Wyvil Rd SW8	71 E2
Wyvis St E14	47 F4

Y

Yabsley St E14	61 G2
Yalding Rd SE16	59 F4
Yardley St WC1	9 J2
Yarmouth Pl W1	13 H6
Yarrow Cres E6	50 A4
Yateley St SE18	63 G4
Yates Ct NW2	25 F3
Yeate St N1	30 C4
Yeats Cl NW10	24 A3
Yeldham Rd W6	67 F1
Yelverton Rd SW11	69 E5
Yeoman's Row SW3	18 C4
Yeoman St SE8	60 C5
Yeo St E3	47 F4
Yewfield Rd NW10	24 B4
Yew Gro NW2	25 F1
Yew Tree Rd W12	52 B1
Yolande Gdns SE9	92 A3
York Br NW1	7 F4
York Bldgs WC2	15 F4
York Gate NW1	7 F4
York Gro SE15	74 A4
York Ho Pl W8	54 C3
York Pl SW11	83 E1
York Pl WC2	15 F4
York Rd E7	34 D3
York Rd SE1	21 H1
York Rd SW11	83 D2
York Rd SW18	83 D2
Yorkshire Grey SE9	91 G3
Yorkshire Grey Yd WC1	9 G6
Yorkshire Rd E14	46 C5
York Sq E14	46 C5
York St W1	6 E5
York Ter E NW1	7 G4
York Ter W NW1	7 F4
Yorkton St E2	45 F1
York Way N1	29 E5
York Way N7	29 D3
York Way Ct N1	29 E5
Young Rd E16	49 F5
Young's Bldgs EC1	10 E3
Young St W8	54 C3
Yukon Rd SW12	84 B5

Z

Zampa Rd SE16	74 A1
Zangwill Rd SE3	77 G4
Zealand Rd E3	46 C1
Zenoria St SE22	87 E2
Zetland St E14	47 F4
Zoar St SE1	16 D5